ROBERT BOND

A POLITICAL BIOGRAPHY

Sir Robert Bond in full Privy Council regalia, 1902. (ASC, RBP 12.01.010)

Robert Bond

A POLITICAL BIOGRAPHY

James K. Hiller

ISER Books

LIBRARY AND ARCHIVES CANADA
CATALOGUING IN PUBLICATION
Title: Robert Bond : a political biography / James K. Hiller.
Names: Hiller, James, 1942- author.
Series: Social and economic studies (St. John's, N.L.) ; no. 84.
Description: Series statement: Social and economic studies ; 84 | Includes bibliographical references and index.
Identifiers: Canadiana 20190164565 | ISBN 9781894725477 (softcover)
Subjects: LCSH: Bond, Robert, 1857-1927. | LCSH: Prime ministers—Newfoundland and Labrador—Biography. | LCSH: Legislators—Newfoundland and Labrador—Biography. | LCSH: Politicians—Newfoundland and Labrador—Biography. | LCSH: Newfoundland and Labrador—Biography. | CSH: Newfoundland and Labrador—Politics and government—1855-1934. | LCGFT: Biographies.
Classification: LCC FC2173.1.B66 H55 2019 | DDC 971.8/02092—dc23

Cover image: Robert Bond. Courtesy of Memorial University of Newfoundland Libraries. Archives and Special Collections.

Cover design: Alison Carr
Page design and typesetting: Alison Carr
Copy editing: Sandy Newton

Published by ISER Books
Institute of Social and Economic Research
Memorial University of Newfoundland
PO Box 4200
St. John's, NL A1C 5S7
www.hss.mun.ca/iserbooks/

Printed in Canada
24 23 22 21 20 19 1 2 3 4 5 6 7 8

Contents

Acknowledgements

First and foremost, I must acknowledge the role of Stanley Marshall. He steered me toward this political biography and provided the initial funding for the project. He has been extraordinarily patient with my delays and postponements over a very long period, and he has never interfered in any way. The opinions and judgments in this text are mine alone, although I have profited from his advice and commentary.

I am also grateful to the graduate students who assisted with the initial research and to those at Memorial University of Newfoundland who facilitated the project, including a former President, Dr. Axel Meisen. I have learned a great deal from my students and academic colleagues over the years, many of whom are named in the bibliography. My sincere thanks to them all.

I am also very much indebted to Sandy Newton, who edited the text of this book and made many important suggestions. Robert Hong provided images of Opposition political cartoons published in 1908 and 1913, and went to a great deal of trouble. I am very appreciative of Linda White's assistance in the Archives and Special Collections division of the Queen Elizabeth II Library at Memorial University of Newfoundland.

—J.K.H.

Illustrations

Abbreviations

ASC	Archives and Special Collections Division, QEII Library, MUN
CO	Colonial Office; the "CO" records are housed in the National Archives, London
DCB	*Dictionary of Canadian Biography*
ENL	*Encyclopedia of Newfoundland and Labrador*
FO	Foreign Office; the FO records are housed in the National Archives, London
FPU	Fishermen's Protective Union
FRUS	*Foreign Relations of the United States*
GJBP	Rev. George John Bond Collection (ASC, MUN)
JHA	*Journal of the House of Assembly*
JLC	*Journal of the Legislative Council*
LAC	Library and Archives Canada (Ottawa)
MHA	Member of the House of Assembly
MLC	Member of the Legislative Council
MUN	Memorial University of Newfoundland
PANL	Provincial Archives of Newfoundland and Labrador, The Rooms
PHA	*Proceedings of the House of Assembly*
RBP	Sir Robert Bond Collection (ASC, MUN)
RCA	Roman Catholic Church Archives, St. John's
RNCP	Reid Newfoundland Company Papers (PANL)

About This Book

Readers should note that the research upon which this study is based began in the late 1960s and has continued—off and on—ever since. As a result, it has proved difficult to ensure that all archival references are contemporarily accurate. The references provided are, for the most part, those that existed at the time the relevant papers were consulted, although some have been updated.

In March 2019, the University of Regina Press published *Where Once They Stood: Newfoundland's Rocky Road Towards Confederation* by Raymond B. Blake and Melvin Baker. This manuscript was in the final stages of production at the time, and the book—most unfortunately—could not be used.

Concerning measurement: Newfoundland, British North America, and Britain itself used imperial measures during the period studied here, so they are therefore largely retained. Metric measures are reserved for contemporary information.

Dispatches (or "despatches," in the style of the time) and telegrams to and from the Colonial Office (CO) were of various classifications. Telegrams were usually urgent and encoded; they are identified here as "tgm." or "tgms." Written dispatches were either mundane—routine matters—or "confidential" (here "conf.") and sometimes "secret," depending on which officials would see them.

The original spelling and punctuation in quoted material are retained throughout; they reflect the author, source, or era, but sometimes differ from usages in the rest of the book.

Where the word "populism" appears in this text, it does not have contemporary (2019) political right- or left-wing connotations. Rather, it means politicians or parties that claimed to support the interests of ordinary people.

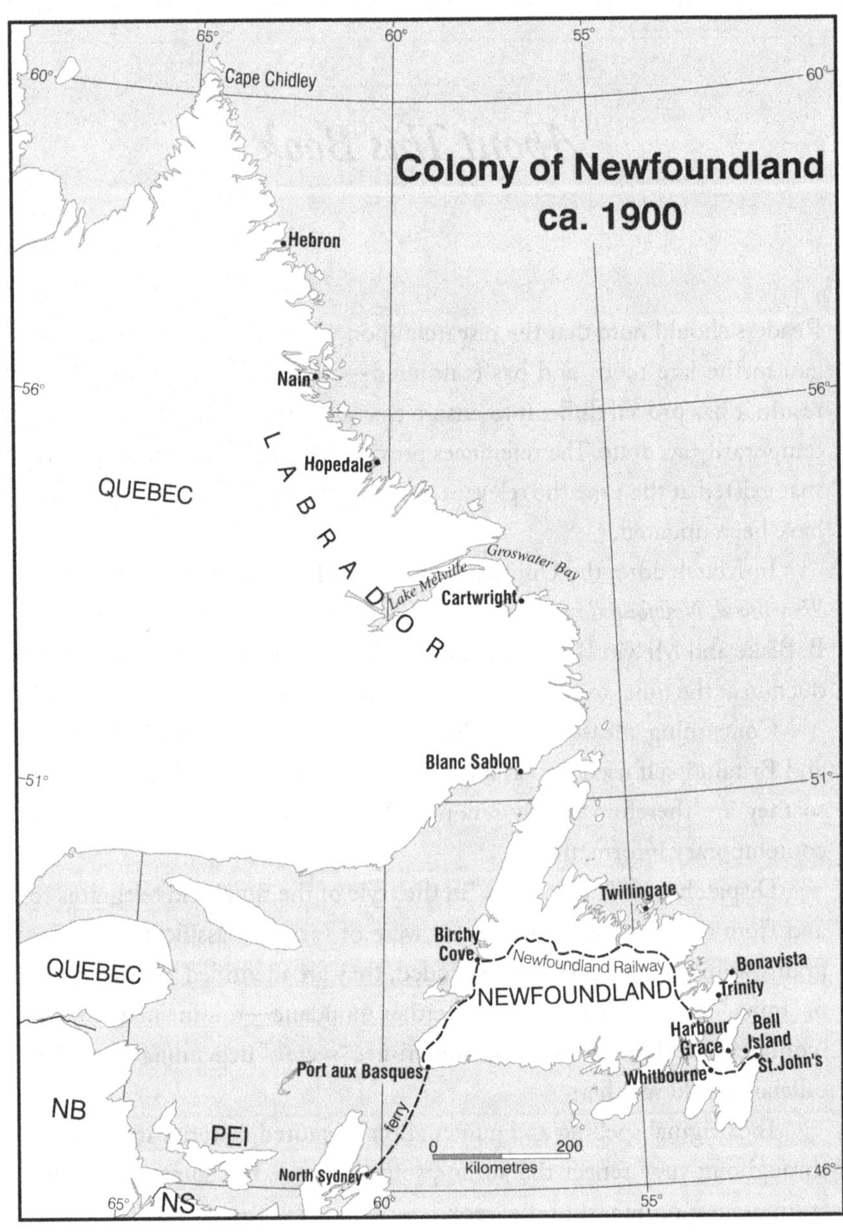

(Map by C.M. Conway)

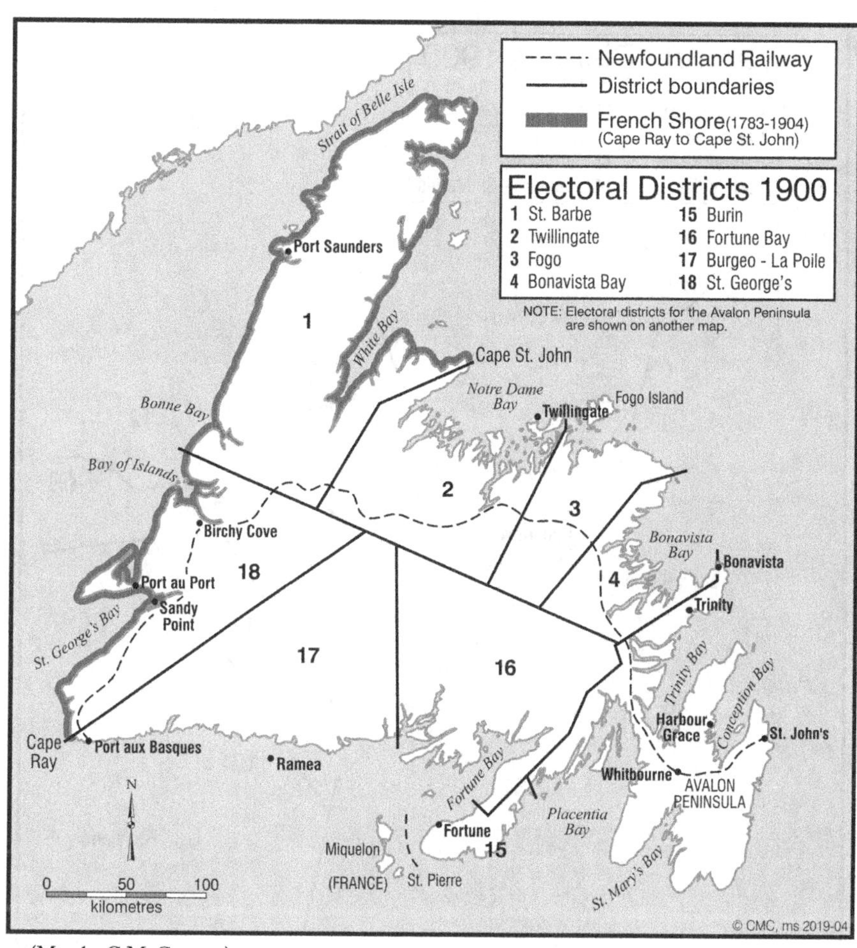

(Map by C.M. Conway)

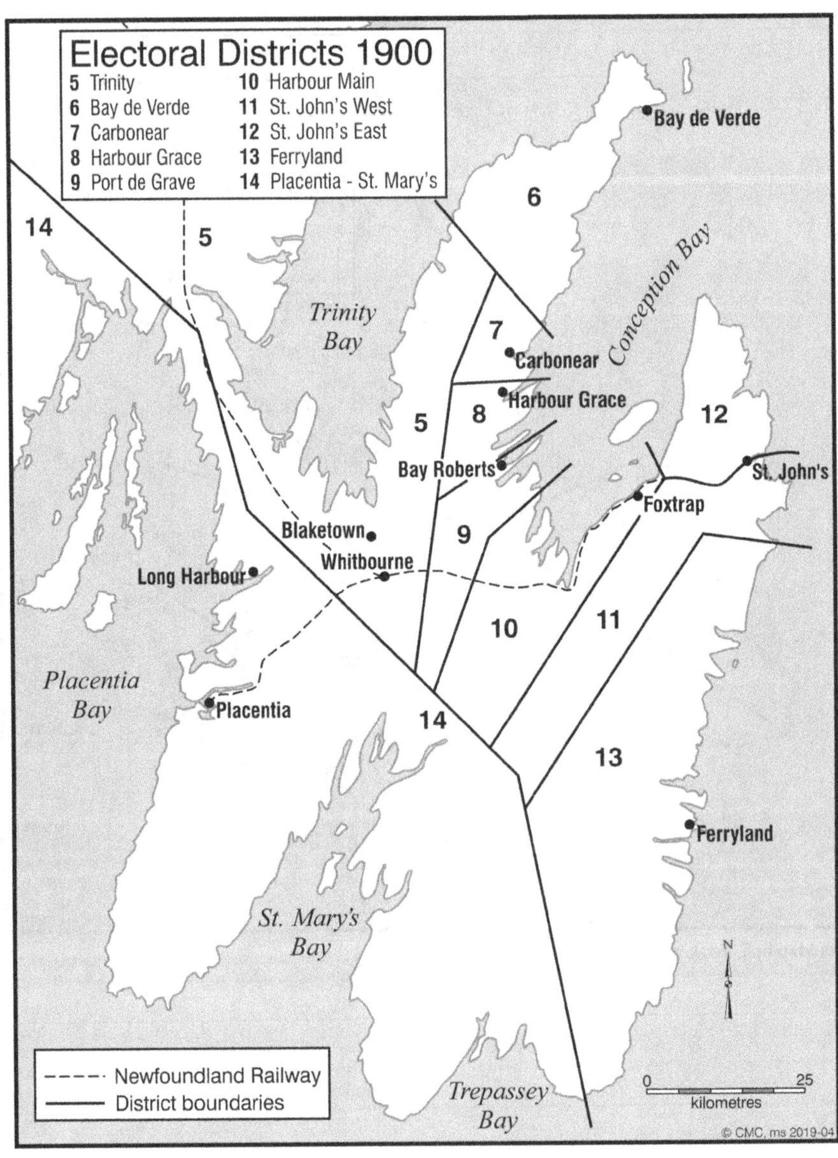

(Map by C.M. Conway)

Introduction

A book of this nature needs some explanation. On a general level, there is the question of whether there is value in the genre of political biography in and of itself. More specifically, why should there be a political biography of Robert Bond? He was and remains an admired figure in the political history of Newfoundland*—but is another such volume needed?

During the nineteenth century, biographies were generally devoted to "the great and the good": prominent individuals, usually male, who had exercised considerable influence in the public sphere and beyond. The overall tone was serious and uncritical, and these volumes often contained information that remains of value. A reaction gathered force in the late nineteenth century, continuing into the twentieth, that insisted that public figures—and indeed the subject of any biography—had to be placed in context and examined as truthfully as possible, without moralizing or cover-ups. Nevertheless, there remained a persistent debate, especially in literary circles, about the potential intrusiveness of biography: were not people, alive or not, entitled to some degree of privacy? And there has been discussion, as well, about the value of "psycho-biography," in which subjects were subjected to Freudian analysis, an approach that was popular in the mid-twentieth century.[1]

For all that, biography has remained an immensely popular genre. Over the past century its scope has markedly widened, with far greater attention being given to women and to people (often obscure) who formerly would have been ignored. Biographers have also become more critical of their subjects, seeking to evaluate what their contributions may have been. Over the past twenty years or so, certainly, historical biography has

* Throughout this book, I use "Newfoundland" rather than "Newfoundland and Labrador," which did not become the province's official name until 2001.

undergone "a renewal" and the phrase "the biographical turn in history" has been used.[2]

Yet biography has been, and still is, seen by some historians to be a problematic genre—in John Tosh's words, one that "has no serious place in historical study"[3]—and it has generated an extensive bibliography. Ben Pimlott (a practitioner) argues that biography is "the least confident form of political writing" and though "avidly consumed . . . the least analysed."[4] The case against historical biography is that it can easily cause the historian to overestimate the contribution of a given individual, and to see the subject as in some sense representative of the milieu in which that person functioned. Further, by concentrating on an individual, the biographer may discount group dynamics and the overall social and economic forces that conditioned society in a given period.[5] Biography can also, it is argued, oversimplify the complexities of political events. Pimlott adds that a biographer may well try to do as well for the subject as the facts allow.[6] As a result, by and large academic historians tend to shy away from biographies (or are ambivalent about them)—though they are quite prepared to contribute to such works as the *Dictionary of Canadian Biography* (*DCB*) or the *Oxford Dictionary of National Biography*. Much of the reason for this can be placed on the dominance of the "new social history," here in Canada and elsewhere, from the 1970s, with its emphasis on the group and on social class rather than on the individual.

These are scholarly debates—and biography is not limited to scholars. The field continues to attract writers of ability and distinction who are outside the world of academe. There is a widespread understanding that, as the Victorian sage Thomas Carlyle wrote in 1830, "History is the essence of innumerable biographies"—a well-known and frequently repeated statement. But the individual life has to be interpreted for the present, since only in this way can biography explain both the person and the setting—how the subject was part of the history of the time. There must also be an analysis of motive and intention, and of the interaction between the individual and those who surrounded him or her. How did people in the past perceive the future? Surely that, too, is an important factor. Historians cannot ignore personalities and individual life histories, but they must see them in context.

This study assesses the political career of Robert Bond, who became a central figure in the public life of Newfoundland soon after his first election in 1882 at the age of 25. He was prime minister from 1900 to 1908, and retired from public life in 1914 at the relatively young age of 56. He is remembered, by those who care about such things, as the best and the brightest of his comparison group—other first ministers of his period—and as the man who might (just might) have saved Newfoundland from the humiliation of surrendering responsible government in 1934. This book tries to evaluate his contribution and asks whether his posthumous reputation is warranted. Was he, in actual fact, as I was once told, "Newfoundland's only statesman"?

My interest in Robert Bond derives from my being an historian of Newfoundland politics. Hence, this book focuses on political analysis. It also attempts to explain both what happened in the colony's public life during Bond's adult lifetime and his important role.[7] I do not address in any detail Bond's private life, the establishment of the town of Whitbourne, or his building of an increasingly elaborate house, The Grange, in that community. These matters could not be ignored, obviously, but in this study they are secondary.

Bond as a public figure needs to be fairly assessed. He was honest and principled, but could be insufferable, autocratic, and hot-tempered. He had a genuine devotion to, and belief in, Newfoundland as a viable country with considerable economic potential—hence, for all his fiscal conservativism, his support for building an expensive railway. He insisted that the imperial government in London should treat Newfoundland as an equal to the other colonies of settlement, in all respects. He worked hard and his abilities were recognized. What he lacked was flexibility and an understanding—though the realization may have arrived later in life—of the limitations necessarily imposed by the imperial and international contexts within which the colony had to operate. In addition, he certainly overestimated the colony's overall economic potential and its strategic value to the British Empire. In short, Bond's contribution was important, but it should not be exaggerated.

Bond's reputation has been enhanced by several factors. J.R. Smallwood (Newfoundland's first provincial premier, 1949 to 1971) was, as a young man, very conscious of Bond's existence. He claimed to have listened to Bond in the House of Assembly before the Great War, when Bond was Leader of the Opposition—Smallwood must have been quite young—and he certainly met him in 1919 and 1925.[8] He frequently referred to "the great Sir Robert Bond" and saw to it that a bridge was named after him.[*] A railcar ferry followed. More important has been the generally negative impression of his successors in office, principally Edward Morris and Richard Squires (his predecessors, perhaps unfairly, have received relatively little attention). The evidence given to the Newfoundland Royal Commission in 1933 provides a relevant snapshot: many of the witnesses expressed the view that Bond's resignation as prime minister in 1908 had been an important turning point for the worse; the overall assumption seems to have been—in retrospect—that once Bond left office, the colony was on the road to disaster.[9] William J. Browne, who sat both in the House of Assembly and the Canadian House of Commons, thought that Bond was "the greatest political figure in the past one hundred years" and that his exit "meant a radical departure from the careful and conservative manner in which . . . [he] had conducted our national affairs."[†]

This is a defensible if oversimplified position. Newfoundland's collapse during the Great Depression was primarily due to a large public debt, mostly representing problematic attempts at economic diversification and the cost of the Great War. Bond refused to try to become his country's saviour in spite of repeated calls to return to public life. Instead, he prevaricated and remained on the sidelines, removed from the political fray that he had come to loathe, reclusive as he always had been. Indeed, seclusion at Whitbourne may well have enhanced his later reputation.

The person from this period who has received the most attention in

---

* Bond was also the only person to be awarded a full-page photograph in Smallwood's *Encyclopedia of Newfoundland and Labrador* (volume 1). The bridge is in central Newfoundland.

† Browne, *Eighty-Four Years*, 189. Even Governor Sir Charles Harris thought, in 1918, that Bond appears "to stand head and shoulders above any Newfoundland politician whom I have seen of late years" (Harris to Long, secret, March 23, 1918, CO 537/1167).

recent years, in fact, is William Ford Coaker (1871–1938), who founded the Fishermen's Protective Union (FPU) in 1908, entered politics in 1913, and became Minister of Fisheries in 1919. Academic historians and others have been fascinated by his rise from relatively humble origins to positions of considerable influence as a union leader, politician, and merchant. Several works related to Coaker are mentioned in the bibliography, though the basic source remains Ian McDonald's 1987 account, as well as Melvin Baker's entry in the *DCB*.[10]

Over the past fifty years, the history of pre-nineteenth-century Newfoundland has been subjected to a severe and long-overdue revisionism that has debunked many of the once-prevalent theories about the country's European origins and its treatment by the British government,[11] which were espoused by late nineteenth-century historians such as the highly influential Daniel W. Prowse and by the prolific Moses Harvey.[12] Their accounts, which mixed pride ("Britain's oldest colony") with accusations of imperial neglect and abuse, were the orthodoxy in Robert Bond's day. For their generation—and for later ones, as well—Newfoundland's history was seen as one of struggle: against prohibitions on settlement, against imperial hostility and marginalization, and against the constraints imposed by ancient fisheries treaties with France and the United States. But they felt that these disadvantages would be overcome. The valuable resources that were assumed to exist in Newfoundland's interior and elsewhere would be developed, and the colony would become respected and important. The island's strategic significance would be recognized and the colony would conquer its past.[13] Bond certainly accepted this version into the 1920s, and the idea that Newfoundland's history has been one of constant struggle still persists.

Contemporary academic historians have largely rejected this interpretation. They are not Whigs (like Prowse) and have taken a critical and comprehensive approach to the history of both Newfoundland and Labrador. Even so, some areas of post-1815 history have done better than others. The loss of responsible government in 1934 and the highly contentious "confederation period" between 1946 and 1949 have both received a great deal of attention, as has (more recently) the First World War.[14] But historians and others have also debated additional matters: pre-confederation economic diversification initiatives, the credit or "truck" system, the apparent failure to tackle the problems of the all-important fisheries, and the experience of Indigenous peoples.[15]

So this book does not cover untravelled ground—far from it. A fair number of historians, myself among them,[16] have looked at Newfoundland during Robert Bond's lifetime, and at Bond himself. In terms of general surveys, there have been valuable contributions by S.J.R. Noel, Patrick O'Flaherty, and Sean Cadigan.[17] Noel's seminal account of twentieth-century politics has been known for many years and retains considerable value. O'Flaherty's narrative of this period was published in 2005, and Cadigan's accounts followed in 2009 and 2013.

O'Flaherty was a professor of English who specialized in eighteenth-century literature, but he had a strong historical bent—like Ronald Rompkey, whose biography of Wilfred Grenfell (*Grenfell of Labrador*) is now the standard work—as well as a fascination with the history of his native province. His is the most passionate and detailed of the recent surveys of this period; it forms part of his dense but highly readable three-volume history of Newfoundland from the country's beginnings. O'Flaherty was a Newfoundland patriot who abhorred—but sought to understand—the surrender of responsible government in 1934 and the flirtations with confederation that had preceded it. Robert Bond does not escape censure—he was "suspect," O'Flaherty says, because he was willing to consider confederation.[18]

Sean Cadigan is a prolific environmental and social historian. His major theme in *Newfoundland and Labrador: A History* (as far as this period is concerned) is that efforts to develop landward resources were largely mistaken, and that the colonial government would have done better to concentrate on the fisheries and the sea. This is an entirely plausible argument but somewhat discounts the contemporary fascination with railways and the "hidden resources" of the interior, which Bond fully shared. In *Death on Two Fronts*, an innovative book, Cadigan concentrates on William Coaker and the FPU, and seeks to draw a line connecting the 1914 *Newfoundland* sealing disaster, the outbreak of the First World War, and the collapse of responsible government. Robert Bond plays a brief walk-on role. The argument here is clearly important and accurate, Cadigan holding that Coaker, in time, became one of the "long-coated chaps" he had once despised, and that he failed to bring in the class-based politics he had originally advocated.

William Coaker's career has long been a central preoccupation for Melvin Baker, who has made a significant contribution to our understanding of this period.[19] He has also written on the history of St. John's and on various aspects of Newfoundland history in the nineteenth and twentieth centuries. He joined Peter Neary in writing two important biographical articles on Robert Bond and consulted with Ted Rowe about his recent biography of Bond, which is solid, accurate, and well-researched.[20]

Other authors also deserve mention. There have, for instance, been recent investigations of Newfoundlanders of Irish descent in this period and beyond. Carolyn Lambert has made valuable contributions to this history, both in St. John's and in Newfoundland more generally.[21] She has provided detail about bishops John Mullock, Thomas Power, and Michael Howley, stressing the imperial loyalty of the Catholic population and its endorsement of Newfoundland nationalism. Patrick Mannion has taken a later but overlapping period, starting in 1880, and has also found that Catholics of Irish descent in Newfoundland generally valued their freedoms within the British Empire and were ambivalent about the prospect of Irish independence. These are valuable contributions. Kurt Korneski has taken a different perspective. Considering the colony as a whole, he has taken a fresh and original look at several of the crises and problems that characterized this period, for instance the south coast bait trade, the west coast lobster fishery, and railway building.[22] He has successfully added a deeper social dimension and new interpretations to relatively familiar incidents. There have been additional significant contributions to the historiography, of course, too numerous to list here: many of them appear in the bibliography.

The other Atlantic provinces have tended to concentrate on their own histories and that of the Maritimes, though there were efforts some years ago to encourage a genuinely regional historiography.[23] This is a lost cause and it has to be accepted that Newfoundland and Labrador and the Maritimes will develop (and have developed) separate accounts of their pasts, linked though their histories may be. Historiographically and politically, the term "Atlantic Region" is little more than a convenience.

Thus Newfoundland and Labrador remains distinct from the adjacent areas of Canada and it has developed its own history. And if academic interest in Newfoundland's history is not what it once was, there is intense curiosity among the general public. Social media groups, discussion clubs, and websites prosper, as do established institutions like the Newfoundland and Labrador Historical Society and the Wessex Society. The province has an aging population, and it seems that many Newfoundlanders and Labradorians want to connect with a past that has either disappeared or is disappearing—numerous outport settlements have gone, and a far-flung diaspora continues to grow.

There also persists a curiosity about Robert Bond, who remains an important figure in historical memory. If this book can help place him in context and provide a fair assessment of his political career, it will have done its job. He should neither be idealized nor vilified, but seen for what he was.

NOTES

1 Lee, *Biography*, 57–63, 72–88.

2 Possing, "Biography," 7. See also Snowman, "Historical Biography."

3 Tosh, *Pursuit*, 75.

4 Pimlott, "Political Biography," 214.

5 See, for example, Riall, "Shallow End," 375–97; O'Brien, "Political Biography," 50–57; and Whitaker, "Writing About Politics," 7–8.

6 Berger, *Canadian History*, 222; Pimlott, "Political Biography," 221.

7 Morgan, "Writing Political Biography," 33–34.

8 Smallwood, *I Chose Canada*, 157.

9 Hiller, "Corruption and Collapse," 84–85.

10 See McDonald, "*To Each His Own*."

11 Two examples: Peter E. Pope, *Fish into Wine*, and Bannister, *Rule of the Admirals*.

12 G.M. Story, "Prowse, Daniel Woodley," *DCB* 14:850–54; Aldrich, "Harvey, Moses," *DCB* 13:455–57; and Armour, "'Castles in the Air'." Both Prowse and Harvey were prolific authors, but see particularly Hatton and Harvey, *Newfoundland,* and Prowse, *History of Newfoundland.*

13 Bannister, "'Sport of Historic Misfortune'," 263–314.

14 Works covering these topics include Overton, "Economic Crisis"; Letto, *Newfoundland's Last Prime Minister*; Neary, *Newfoundland in the North Atlantic World*; Patricia R. O'Brien, "The Newfoundland Patriotic Association"; and Mike O'Brien, "Producers versus Profiteers."

15 For these matters, consider Alexander, "Development and Dependence" and "Newfoundland's Traditional Economy"; Ommer, *Merchant Credit;* and Kennedy, *Encounters.*

16 See particularly "The Political Career of Robert Bond," "Robert Bond and the Pink, White and Green," and "A History of Newfoundland."

17 Specifically, Noel, *Politics in Newfoundland;* O'Flaherty, *Lost Country;* and Cadigan *Newfoundland and Labrador* and *Death on Two Fronts.*

18 O'Flaherty, *Lost Country,* 163.

19 For a list of Baker's publications, visit his homepage: www.ucs.mun.ca/~melbaker/.

20 Baker and Neary, "Bond, Sir Robert," *DCB* 15:122–30. See also Rowe, *Robert Bond: The Greatest Newfoundlander.*

21 See, for example, Lambert's thesis, "Far from the Homes of Their Fathers" and "This Sacred Feeling," 124–42.

22 In particular see Korneski, *Conflicted Colony.*

23 Hiller, "Is Atlantic Canadian History Possible?" 16–22.

CHAPTER ONE

The Personal and Political Background

Robert Bond was born in the scruffy port town of St. John's, Newfoundland, in February 1857. According to the census taken that year, the town and its "suburbs" had a population of about 24,800, of which over 73 per cent were Roman Catholics of Irish descent.[1] This was not far off the size of Halifax, Nova Scotia. But a visitor in 1872 called the town

> a queer place . . . full of heights and hollows, corners and angles, and not so substantial in its buildings. . . . The better class of houses are of brick, some faced with plaster, too many with an old, unwashed appearance. . . . The larger shops are very respectable and do a deal of quiet business. . . . You walk on rough cobbled pavements, and climb steep, foul by-ways, with rocks cropping up in the middle of them. You see rickety houses all out of the straight, shored up with long poles. . . . Down at the shore the fishermen are drying and mending their nets, and at wooden stands erected on the wharves people are buying cod, salmon and halibut.[2]

Yet improvements lay ahead. It remained "a queer place," but ten years later Thomas Talbot claimed that the town was "scarcely inferior to any town or city in British North America."[3] He may well have been exaggerating. A visitor in 1886, possibly exaggerating in the other direction, described St. John's as "a unique little town . . . at once filthy and picturesque. . . . The streets of St. John's are narrow, ragged, and wind about in a tortuous manner, highly perplexing to the stranger, who loses his way

John Bond (1805–1872) and Elizabeth Parsons Bond (1822–1900), parents of the seven Bond children, undated. (ASC, RBP 12.02.002 and 12.02.005)

frequently and brings himself up in quarters of unimaginable filth, tumble-down hovels. . . . A more unsavoury place cannot be imagined."[4]

Whatever the state of the town, that is where the Bond family lived. Robert Bond's parents were both English and his father came from Devon, a county long connected with the Newfoundland trade. John Bond (1805–72) was a Methodist and a merchant. He was the eldest son of William Bond, a papermaker living in Kingskerswell, Devon, by his second marriage. The family had Newfoundland connections. Both of William's sons by his first marriage became mariners in the Newfoundland trade, and one of them—another William—became business agent in St. John's for Samuel Codner, who originally came from Kingskerswell. Codner ran an extensive business, specializing from the 1820s in the importation of "Bridport goods"—nets, seines, lines, ropes, and sailcloth. John Bond, it seems, came to join his half-brother in St. John's during the early 1820s, and worked for Codner until the business closed in 1844.* He then became the agent for William Hounsell and Company, also of Bridport,† becoming a partner in 1856.[5] He traded on his own account from 1866, as well as acting for Hounsell's. The R.G. Dun commercial agency noted that "John

* Handcock, "Codner," *DCB* 8:164–67. An evangelical Anglican, Codner is best remembered for founding the Newfoundland School Society in 1823 (*ENL* 5:99).

† In 1863, Hounsell's had a "Bridport Warehouse" at Riverhead in St. John's and advertised seines, nets, twines, cordage, canvas, hooks, boots, shoes, ale from London and Dorset, cider, Hamburg bread, and American flour (*Public Ledger*, May 29, 1863). Elsewhere they sold coal, paint, varnish, glass, and linseed oil.

Bond continues the business in his own name" and "is much respected as a man of business and otherwise."[6]

In 1847, John Bond married Elizabeth Parsons (1822–1900), then living in Maidstone, Kent, who was fifteen years his junior. Little is known about her background.[*] There were seven children born between 1849 and 1859. Two girls, Julia and Elizabeth, died soon after birth, in 1849 and 1852 respectively; William died in 1871, aged 18, and Henry in 1878, aged 23. Samuel died at the age of 2 in 1861. Only two of the children can be said to have lived full lives—George John (1850–1933) and Robert.

John Bond died suddenly on June 11, 1872. He had not been well—he had heart problems, apparently—and his wife had feared that "if he got in one of his tempers" it might be the end.[7] He left an estate valued at $65,000.[†] The business was wound up, and the house and mercantile premises at 435 and 437 Water Street (at the bottom of what is now Springdale Street) were taken over by P. and L. Tessier.[‡] There was also a house on Portugal Cove Road, where John Bond had acquired property in 1853. This, too, was sold after his death.[8] Elizabeth Bond did not return to England, possibly because her sons continued to live in Newfoundland; Elizabeth lived with George and Robert at Richmond Hill (or Richmond Cottage) in the west end of the town, which George had bought in 1875.[§] John Bond's widowed niece, Sarah Roberts (née Sambell) came out from Plymouth to be Elizabeth's companion and to keep house. She would remain in Newfoundland until her death in 1924.[9] Circa 1886, Robert, his

---

* The obituary in the *Evening Telegram*, August 17, 1900, gives Kingskerswell as her birthplace. But the tombstone erected after her death says that she was born in Kent (Sir Robert Bond Collection (RBP), photo, 12.02.049).

† John Bond's will and other documents (RBP 1.01.010., 1.02.001) and George Bond to Robert Bond, June 20, 1872 (RBP 1.02.006). In 2019 dollars, the estate's value would approximate $1 million.

‡ The property was also known as the Angel Estate (Devine, *Ye Olde St. John's*, 75–76).

§ The house was demolished in 2017, amid justified controversy. George Bond sold the property in 1879. He married Lucy Macpherson of St. John's in 1881 and moved to Nova Scotia ten years later.

mother, and Sarah moved into an attractive house that still stands (now 2 Circular Road).

Robert Bond was 15 years old and at school in England when his father died. Indeed, his parents had just returned to St. John's from a visit there, leaving him at the Wesleyan Collegiate Institute (from 1888, Queen's College), just outside Taunton in Somerset. They had visited London, Bristol, Plymouth, and Kingskerswell.[10] The news reached him rapidly and his brother George later wrote at length.[11] There was no question of Robert returning to St. John's. By this time, he had spent five years at St. Andrew's School in St. John's* and a year at the General Protestant Academy there.[12] He was not the first boy from St. John's to be sent to Taunton; at least two others were attending the school at the same time. The college register shows a significant number of enrollments from overseas: "We have boys here from all parts, Africa, West Indies, Australia, France, Brazil, Newfoundland, and almost any place you could mention."[13] The register noted that Robert knew no Latin or French, but had some Spanish and was "good" in history, geography, and English (but "Arithmetic to Practice)."[14] He remained at the Wesleyan Collegiate Institute until mid-1874, and during the school holidays got to know his relatives in Kingskerswell and Plymouth, and the Hounsells in Bridport.

Robert Bond in 1880, aged 23. (ASC, RBP 12.01.002)

Once he returned to St. John's, Bond—who very much disliked the way in which his father's estate had been handled—was clearly expected to stay with his mother, at least in the short term. Of his two older brothers, Henry was ill—he died four years later—and George had decided to become a Methodist minister; he graduated from Mount Allison Wesleyan College (now Mount Allison University) in 1874. George, too, returned to St. John's after completing his studies,

* Little is known about this school, but the name suggests a Presbyterian affiliation.

and was ordained in 1876. George's decision to continue with the ministry after his father's death seems to have upset Robert; he gave up any thoughts of a naval career[15] and began to train for the law with William Vallance Whiteway (1828–1908).[16] Their careers were to be entwined until Whiteway's death more than thirty years later.

Whiteway was an English West Countryman who had come to Newfoundland as a merchant's apprentice before switching to the law. He entered politics in 1859. In 1874, when Bond joined his firm as a trainee, he was one of the three House of Assembly members for Trinity Bay and had just become solicitor general in Frederic Carter's[17] Conservative government. Able and hard-working, he was clearly poised for greater things.

Whiteway's influence on the young Robert Bond was probably significant. Whiteway believed that there was more to Newfoundland than fish and seals, and he promoted the colony's mineral and agricultural potential. He supported the idea of building a railway across the island—a survey was carried out in 1875—and was convinced that future prosperity depended on the railway, interior settlement, and on modifying French fishing rights on the "Treaty Shore," which extended from Cape St. John to Cape Ray (around Newfoundland's northeast and west coasts). Bond shared these views, and he would also have been exposed to the issue of American fishing rights in Newfoundland waters under an 1818 Anglo-American treaty (which became a major issue during his premiership) because Whiteway prepared the case that Newfoundland presented to the Halifax Fisheries Commission in 1877. The tribunal assessed the financial compensation that the United States would pay for fishing privileges in British North American waters under the Treaty of Washington (1871); Newfoundland emerged $1 million richer. Whether Bond directly assisted Whiteway is not known, but he would certainly have been introduced to

William V. Whiteway (1828–1908) in 1869, aged 41. He and Robert Bond were to have a long and tense relationship. (LAC, Collections Canada, Mikan 3471458)

the international complexities involved. In short, it is probable that Bond received both a political and a legal education in Whiteway's office—he once said that his political involvement began in 1878.[18] During this period, Bond also began to explore Newfoundland on hunting trips on the Avalon Peninsula and on prospecting expeditions to the west coast, and he developed a passion for the outdoors.* He once told the Assembly that for ten years he had spent two months annually travelling in the interior—north, south, east, and west.[19]

As it happened, Bond did not qualify as a lawyer and never practised law. Political enemies in future years claimed that he had either failed the examination or did not have sufficient ability to face it. Bond himself said that the reason was medical,[20] but one has to suspect that there were other factors. Certainly, with his inheritance and as a single man living with his mother, he did not need the money that the law would have brought him. He also saw a future in the development of the colony's resources. So instead of combining law and politics, a common practice, he chose politics alone, entering the fray in the 1882 general election. Whiteway—now Sir William—had succeeded Frederic Carter as premier in 1878 and was looking for a second term. Not long after, Bond started to invest in and develop the wilderness area around the community now known as Whitbourne.

Robert Bond was Whiteway's political protégé. Twenty-five years old in 1882, he was well-educated and well-travelled. He read widely, enjoyed outdoor pursuits, and was developing into a colonial nationalist. That is to say that, while he identified himself as British and took a strong interest in his British ancestry, Bond was very much attached to Newfoundland. Nationalism of this sort, increasingly prevalent in the settlement colonies, has been described somewhat negatively as "a qualified and ambiguous force, a local patriotism seeking self-rule and self-respect, but unwilling to break its links with 'the Mother Country'."[21] The essence of it was that, like many of his fellow countrymen, Bond saw himself as both British and a Newfoundlander—but Newfoundland was home, it was where he

* There are diaries of hunting trips in 1875 and 1876 in RBP 2.02.001. Bond was on the west coast in 1879, 1880, and 1881 ("Notes on the Bay of Islands and Humber Sound," n.d., RBP 2.02.005).

belonged, and he fully supported Whiteway's ambitions for the colony's future.

Newfoundland's population in the early 1880s was about 197,300, a small number of people inhabiting a huge territory.* One of the largest islands in the world, Newfoundland has an area of more than 111 million hectares. At the time, very few of its inhabitants lived in the interior; they were spread out along the island's lengthy coastline (though concentrated in the southeast) and dependent on the cod and seal fisheries that were central to the colonial economy. This was a marine society, tied to the Atlantic Ocean and the trade with Britain, southern Europe, the West Indies, and South America. Labrador was the island's extensive northern dependency, with a sparse permanent population, many of them Inuit, Innu, or Métis. Its interior boundary was undefined until 1927, the only point of agreement being that the "coast," which had been originally placed under Newfoundland jurisdiction in 1763, extended from a point near Blanc Sablon, in the Strait of Belle Isle, to Cape Chidley in the north. The territory had no representatives in the colonial legislature. For most Newfoundlanders, Labrador was a place to fish: according to the 1884 census, 1,150 vessels were engaged in the Labrador fishery, and some 17,600 men, women, and children went north each fishing season as passengers. Such administration as existed was left, for the most part, to the Moravian Mission in the north, and elsewhere to other churches, the Hudson's Bay Company, and magistrates from Newfoundland who ventured out during the fishing season. Labrador's relationship with the island resembled Newfoundland's relationship with Britain in the eighteenth century.†

Religious denomination was of central importance in Newfoundland, as elsewhere. The 1884 census shows that about 40 per cent of its population was Roman Catholic, mainly of Irish origin and living for the most

---

* The population figures are rounded and taken from the 1884 *Abstract Census and Returns*.

† The 1884 *Census* did not separate out the Inuit living north of Hamilton Inlet, but listed 130 "Indians" (Innu) for Labrador, surely an underestimate, and eight hundred "Indians" for the colony as a whole. This total must include the Mik'maq of southern and western Newfoundland.

part in St. John's and on the southeastern Avalon Peninsula. The Protestants were mainly divided between the majority Anglicans and an increasing number of Wesleyan Methodists (the Bond family among them), who made up about 40 per cent of all Protestants. There was a small but influential Presbyterian congregation in St. John's, with roots in Ulster and Scotland, and a few members of other Protestant denominations. From the mid-1880s, the Salvation Army began to have a significant influence.

Not surprisingly, religious and ethnic affiliations had an important impact on political life. In 1855, after internal tussles and quarrels with the British government, Newfoundland had adopted the system of responsible government that was becoming the norm in British colonies of settlement. This meant that the colonial government—officially called "the Executive Council"* and headed by the premier—led a majority party that was responsible to a House of Assembly (which initially consisted of thirty seats). There was also an upper house, the appointed Legislative Council. In effect, the system was internal self-government†; external relations and defence continued to be controlled from London. Moreover, the British-appointed governor retained significant discretionary powers and frequently used them. He was expected to send regular reports to the Colonial Office in London, and all colonial legislation had to be confirmed there. Newfoundland's was not a senior governorship and it did not pay very well. The result was that the colony tended to have governors who were either at the end of their careers or on their speedy way up the ladder. Nevertheless, the governor was an important figure with considerable influence.

Britain maintained a military garrison in St. John's until 1870, a naval squadron visited each year, and Newfoundland was very much a part of what has been called "the British world." The colony was proud to be part of the British Empire and this sentiment was shared by those of both English and Irish heritage. Indeed, local patriots saw John Cabot's 1497 voyage and his supposed landfall at Bonavista (or possibly somewhere else in Newfoundland) as its founding moment. The British Empire had begun

---

* In this volume, it is often referred to as simply "the Executive."

† For additional information about the workings of the government, see the Appendix.

in Newfoundland, it was claimed, and Robert Bond firmly accepted this assertion.

The Liberal party that took power in 1855, following the introduction of responsible government, was a coalition of convenience between elements that had felt excluded from place and influence by an Anglican establishment. The impetus behind the campaign for responsible government had come from Roman Catholic politicians backed by the Roman Catholic hierarchy, but they had needed additional support. They found it among Methodists and other dissenting Protestants, who felt equally marginalized, if not more so. Whether John Bond, Robert's father, supported these political changes is not known; though a Methodist, he was also a merchant—and many merchants had significant reservations about these developments, fearing political instability and sectarian strife. All that can be said is that John Bond did not play a significant role in politics at any stage of his life, though he did meet others for discussions about local affairs at the Market House.[22]

The Liberals formed the first two governments after 1855. Though still a significant force, they lost power in the early 1860s to the mainly Protestant Conservatives. Two basic issues were settled during the 1860s that

The Colonial Building, seat of the Newfoundland legislature since 1850, shown here in the mid-1880s. ("Newfoundland Scenery," photograph by S.H. Parsons, ASC, Coll. 199)

were to have long-lasting implications. First, following a bitter and violent political crisis in 1861, it became accepted that denominationalism would have to be entrenched in public life. The unwritten rule was that each denomination should be fairly represented in the legislature, the government, and the public service. Together with the introduction of a fully denominational school system in 1874, this did much to allow political debate to turn toward broader issues. There was strong criticism of this fundamental (if tacit) agreement over the years, especially from outside observers, and it certainly caused inefficiencies and additional expense, but it proved to be a sensible solution to a problem that faced most, if not all, British North American colonies.[23]

The second issue was whether or not Newfoundland should join the Canadian confederation, a project that was under serious discussion on the mainland from 1864. Confederate and Anti-Confederate parties—led by Frederic Carter and Charles Bennett, respectively—cut across existing party lines. It was accepted that there had to be an election on the question, and it was hard-fought. Almost all Liberals and a substantial number of Conservatives joined the Anti-Confederates, who won a landslide election in 1869.[24] This result removed confederation as a realistic option for the foreseeable future, but it never went away. Confederation lurked in the background as a distinct possibility, but it was a highly sensitive issue and support for, or even flirtation with, the idea could be seen as disloyalty. The consensus was that the colony would remain an independent entity within the British Empire and manage its domestic affairs as it thought fit. Whiteway was a Confederate in the 1860s and remained one, but Robert Bond always saw confederation as a last resort. First and foremost, Bond was a Newfoundland nationalist.

By the mid-1870s, the earlier party divisions had reappeared. The Conservatives returned to power in 1873–74; early in 1878 Whiteway became premier. He won a low-key general election that November with a majority of eleven seats, in part because the Liberal opposition was disorganized and ineffective. Indeed, the Liberals were fading as an independent political force. They had achieved much of what they had fought for and were generally supportive of Whiteway's policies.

If the colony was to remain independent, then the economy had to be strengthened and diversified and its strategic advantages and resources had to be emphasized and asserted. An independent Newfoundland could not remain an underdeveloped backwater almost totally dependent on the troubled salt-fish trade. Optimistic Geological Survey of Newfoundland reports by Alexander Murray[25] and James Howley[26] seemed to indicate that there were other land-based resources to exploit. There was a real prospect, they argued, of developing agriculture, forest, and mining industries. Frederic Carter had known all this, but he was instinctively cautious and also skeptical about the potential of railway building, that potent symbol of mid-nineteenth-century "progress." Whiteway was more willing to take risks. Thus, during his first term in office, he pressed ahead with a programme that had railway building at its heart—a line across the island to a terminus at St. George's Bay on the west coast. This would open the interior to economic development and, in addition, the railway might also form part of an express "Short Line" route linking Europe and North America.* Newfoundland had strategic importance, the government argued, in relation to both transatlantic travel and imperial defence, given its position in the northwest Atlantic as the most easterly point in North America and the key to the St. Lawrence. Therefore, building a dry dock in St. John's also made eminent sense and the port should be developed into a naval base rivalling Halifax.[27]

The British government was not encouraging. The Admiralty did not see the need for another naval base in the northwest Atlantic. The imperial government's central concern, rather, was the seasonal fishing right granted by eighteenth-century treaties to France on "the French Treaty Shore." It was an issue with which Robert Bond would be engaged for much of his political life. Interpretations of this "right" varied. In summary, France held that it possessed an exclusive right of fishery along the defined area of

---

* This idea was first proposed by the Scottish-Canadian engineer Sandford Fleming in 1865. Fast steamers would connect Ireland and Newfoundland; passengers would then cross the island by train and take steamers to Cape Breton and the mainland rail network. In various formats, the scheme was under discussion—off and on—until 1914.

coastline, and it could control or exclude all other users. Newfoundlanders argued that the right was "concurrent"—anyone could fish there as long as the French were not interrupted. The British government prevaricated but gradually moved nearer to the Newfoundland position.

"The French Shore question," as the difference of opinion was usually called, had been the major local issue in the year of Bond's birth.[28] In 1857, the new Newfoundland government was faced with a draft convention that defined how the French Shore was to be shared. Local opinion thought it was far too favourable to France, and the resulting outcry produced what became known locally as Newfoundland's "Magna Carta." In April 1859, Colonial Secretary Henry Labouchere wrote that the governor could give "such assurance as you may think proper that the consent of the community of Newfoundland is regarded by Her Majesty's Government as the essential preliminary to any modification of their territorial or maritime rights."[29] This phrase from "the Labouchere Dispatch" was to be quoted back to the British government on many occasions, and Bond was among those who did so.

With reference to the railway, the imperial government decided that a terminus on the French Shore was impossible. It did concede, however, in the face of strenuous French objections: the appointment of magistrates on the Shore, the stationing of constables and granting of land (though restrictively worded), and political representation for the area.[30] These were significant gains, in that the British government had finally recognized the legitimacy of settlement on the French Shore. But given Britain's continued opposition to a terminus there, and local concerns about the cost of railway building, the Whiteway government decided to make a start by building a narrow-gauge line along the east coast from St. John's to Hall's Bay, which was expected to become a significant mining centre.* In 1880, the legislature passed a Railway Act approving the scheme in principle, the Liberals supporting the government. Tenders were called and a location survey begun—at which point the doubters woke up and serious debate erupted.

---

* See Martin, *Once Upon a Mine*, Chapter 2. Hall's Bay is an inlet of Notre Dame Bay on the northeast coast.

The first issue was whether it was wise to embark on railway building at all, given the expense involved. A petition to the legislature signed by more than seventy businessmen requested in vain that further discussion should be postponed until the electorate had been consulted.[31] The second issue was the agreement made in 1881 with a New York-based syndicate, represented in Newfoundland by A.L. Blackman, which took the name "Newfoundland Railway Company." Within five years, the company was to build the St. John's–Hall's Bay narrow-gauge line, with branches to Brigus, Harbour Grace, and Carbonear, in return for a subsidy that would reach $180,000 a year when the line was completed. In addition, they would receive land grants of 5,000 acres per mile, to be taken in alternate blocks along the line or elsewhere if acceptable land was unavailable. The government would advance $90,000 for the right of way, and the company would deposit $100,000 as security. The contract was based on precedents elsewhere and was, on the face of it, not unreasonable. However, there was justified suspicion that the company did not represent enough capital to carry out the contract. James S. Winter, a government member, voiced this question in the Assembly, as did the Speaker, Alexander J.W. McNeily.[32] Eight members of the Assembly and four Legislative Councillors voted against the contract, most of them soon becoming part of an emerging opposition to Whiteway's policies.* There were reports in the press that a "New Party" was taking shape.[33]

The company floated mortgage bonds in London and paid the deposit. Work on the line began in August 1881; the following year, two other schemes were revealed. First, the Newfoundland Railway Company petitioned the legislature for incorporation as the "Great American and European Short Line Railway Company." Its ambitious and expensive proposal envisaged a standard-gauge line from a point in Bonavista Bay to Cape

---

* In the Assembly: James Winter, Stanley Carter, Augustus Goodridge, William Donnelly (surveyor general), Daniel Greene, Alexander McNeily, Lewis Tessier, Michael Dwyer; in the Council: Stephen Rendell, John Warren, John Winter, Robert Thorburn. The President of the Council, Edward Morris, also spoke against the contract. Some of these men would remain significant political figures.

Ray, a ferry to Cape North, and new railways in Nova Scotia, where the company was already incorporated. In Newfoundland, the company wanted land grants and a guarantee on a $5 million issue of mortgage bonds. The legislature balked at the guarantee but was willing to provide the land and the incorporation.* This response was not what the company had hoped for and its enthusiasm for Newfoundland rapidly diminished. The second scheme was the construction of a St. John's dry dock. This contract was awarded to the railway company's former chief engineer. The government agreed to endorse a first mortgage and pay a subsidy for forty-five years, but the legislation was almost defeated in the Legislative Council.

As the 1882 election approached, a new political configuration became clearer. The Whiteway Conservatives and the Liberals became allies, though the parties did not formally merge, and this new entity became known as the "Party of Progress."[34] Against them was the "New Party," sometimes called the "Anti-Endorsation Party" because it opposed Whiteway's supposed willingness to endorse or guarantee any bonds that the railway syndicate might send his way. The New Party claimed that it could accept the Hall's Bay railway as long as the contract was strictly enforced. It lacked a strong and effective leader, however, and found it difficult to counter the Whitewayite argument: progress and development were being opposed by adherents of an old order that deserved to be swept away. It was also difficult to promote what was essentially a negative message, which voters could only contrast with the government's optimism.[35] The *Evening Mercury*, for instance, founded that year as a Whitewayite newspaper, predicted that Newfoundland's "rich lands and forests will be opened up, and the solitudes of the interior will be made to blossom like the rose. Our people, many of them now existing in semi-starvation round the bleak shores of the island, will find happy homes and plenty down the great iron highway."†

* The Colonial Office refused to recommend final assent until it was clear the works were intended for the French Shore.

† *Evening Mercury*, August 21, 1882. The paper's first editor was the Reverend Moses Harvey (*ENL* 2:849–50), about whom see F.A. Aldrich, "Harvey, Moses," *DCB* 13:455–57 and James E. Armour, "Castles in the Air," 160.

Protestant politicians living in St. John's frequently ran in outport districts because of the capital's heavily Roman Catholic character. Thus Whiteway, an Anglican resident of St. John's, had represented Twillingate and Fogo before shifting to Trinity Bay in 1873. Both were Protestant constituencies. In 1882, Whiteway invited Robert Bond to join himself and Joseph Boyd (also new to electoral politics) on the government ticket in Trinity Bay, an important district with a substantial population of about 17,000. Bond accepted this offer and declined an invitation to run in the new district of St. George's Bay on the west coast, since it was accepted that a Catholic should run there.

The government slate was known by early August, but it was the custom in Newfoundland and elsewhere that formal canvassing did not start until the candidates had received signed requisitions from various parts of the district. These requisitions asked a preferred candidate to run, and he* was expected to make a suitable reply. In 1882, Whiteway used the opportunity to expound on the railway policy, as well as the need to fully develop the French Shore and expand the telegraph system. He also vowed that he would never endorse Short Line bonds, nor discuss confederation unless the people demanded it.[36] Bond somewhat pompously said that, "With me the people's welfare shall be the supreme law, and our country's advancement the first consideration."[37] The government slate was opposed by three New Party candidates, of whom the most important was Stephen R. March, a member of a prominent Old Perlican family and a merchant with an extensive business in the district.[38] There was also one independent candidate, James Watson, who ran a business in Hant's Harbour.†

Bond delivered his first campaign speech in early October. It was to be expected, he said, that there would be "opposition to progress" coming from the New Party, which stood for "stagnation and retrogression." It was their policy, such as it was, that would lead to confederation with

* The 1877 Election Act provided that only male British subjects could vote or run as candidates.

† Watson had been on the Whiteway ticket in the two previous elections and was probably dropped because he had New Party sympathies.

Canada—not building a railway. The Whiteway party wanted to raise the country from "the embryonic state in which she has been for years . . . the Country is at least a century behind the rest of the civilized world." The railway would help create "a hive of industry" and raise "politically and socially our unfortunate people, the fishermen and . . . [bring] this island home of ours before the public as one of the world's greatest mining regions. . . . Gentlemen, a New Era is dawning upon Newfoundland."*

This was standard Whitewayite propaganda, and it worked. Voting took place on November 6; Whiteway headed the poll with 1,176 votes, Boyd was second with 849, and Bond third with 812.† However, the returning officer wrote that it had been "the worst managed Election I ever knew. No person acting to meet every difficulty, no working Committees or active working men. Everything appeared to be left to chance. . . . But why did not one of each of the candidates of your party remain in each of the most disaffected sections of the District?"[39] Sourly, the opposition *Evening Telegram* claimed that the Whitewayites had purchased votes at 20 shillings each. And there seems little doubt that the promise of railway jobs was used to bolster political support, paid for with the security deposit required by the Newfoundland Railway Company contract.‡

Overall, Whiteway won twenty-six seats to the New Party's five, with two independents also elected.[40] He was supported by eleven of the fifteen Catholic seats and fifteen of the eighteen Protestant seats, and had formed the first truly interdenominational governing coalition in the colony's history. Further, he had demonstrated that Water Street could not necessarily control the legislature, and that the "Policy of Progress" commanded widespread support—not only among voters in general, but also from the churches, many outport merchants, and smaller businessmen

* "Sir Robert Bond's first political speech, 1882," is in a campaign notebook in RBP 3.01.004. The *Evening Mercury* called the speech "masterly" (October 5, 1882).

† *Newfoundlander*, November 7, 1882. Open voting lasted until 1887.

‡ *Evening Telegram*, November 7–8, 1882. The company was allowed to withdraw the deposit (Whiteway in Assembly, March 14, 1883; *Evening Mercury*, March 16, 1883).

to whom large expenditures on public works spelled increased sales and the chance of lucrative contracts. Nonetheless, deep political divisions remained. At the age of 25, much younger than was usual, Bond was entering a difficult and fractious political world. He would remain there for more than thirty years.[41]

NOTES

1 *Abstract Census 1857*, 2–9.
2 Quoted in Paul O'Neill, *The Oldest City*, 58–59.
3 Baker et al, *Ireland's Eye*, 6–10.
4 Portia, "A Trip to Newfoundland" (1886) in Rompkey, *Garrison Town*, 80–81.
5 Appointment of John Bond as agent, October 11, 1844 (RBP 1.01.003).
6 R.G. Dun Collection, LAC, 61.
7 Elizabeth Bond to George Bond, April 13 [1872] (Rev. George John Bond Collection (GJBP), 5.03.001).
8 Registry of Deeds, St. John's.
9 Rowe, *Bond*, 19.
10 Robert Bond to George Bond, June 3, 1872 (RBP 5.01.001).
11 W. Hounsell to Bond, June 12, 1872; George Bond to Bond, June 20, 1872 (RBP 1.02.005, 1.02.006).
12 Wishart, "The General Protestant Academy," 27–32.
13 Robert Bond to George Bond, June 3, 1872 (RBP 5.01.001).
14 Queen's College Registers, 1843–1887. I am grateful to the College for access to this source.
15 On these points, see Elizabeth Sambell (Plymouth) to Bond, April 3, 1873 (RBP 1.02.008).
16 Hiller, "Whiteway, Sir William Vallance," *DCB* 13:1089–95 and *ENL* 5:564–66.
17 Hiller, "Carter, Sir Frederic Bowker Terrington" *DCB* 12:161–65 and *ENL* 1:363–65.
18 Rowe, *Bond*, 22.
19 Bond in Assembly, March 21, 1889 (*Evening Mercury*, April 1, 1889).
20 *PHA*, February 21, 1911, 185.
21 Hyam, "The British Empire," 58, and Eddy and Schreuder, *Rise of Colonial Nationalism*. Newfoundland is not mentioned in this book.
22 Devine, *Ye Olde*, 18.
23 See Fitzpatrick, "Render unto Caesar."
24 Hiller, "Confederation Defeated" in Hiller and Neary, *Newfoundland*, 67–94.

25 Hughes, "Murray, Alexander," *DCB* 11:630–33 and *ENL* 3:656.
26 O'Flaherty, "Introduction," in Howley, *Reminiscences*. Also *ENL* 2:1093–95.
27 For the landward development shift, see Korneski, *Conflicted Colony*, 71–100.
28 The standard work is Thompson, *French Shore Problem*.
29 *ENL* 3:199–200, also Thompson, *French Shore*, 37, and Olaf U. Janzen, "The French Shore Dispute," in English, *Barrels to Benches*, 1–23.
30 Hiller, "Appointing Magistrates," 39–58. For the railway, see Hiller, "The Railway and Local Politics in Newfoundland, 1870–1901" in Hiller and Neary, *Newfoundland*, 123–47.
31 *JHA* 1881, 45; *Public Ledger*, March 22, 1881.
32 In the *DCB*, see Hiller, "Winter, Sir James Spearman," *DCB* 14:1073–76, and Story, "McNeily, Alexander James Whiteford," *DCB* 14:730.
33 *Harbor Grace Standard*, July 30, 1881, and *Terra Nova Advocate*, August 8, 1881.
34 *Patriot*, October 15, 1882.
35 *Public Ledger*, September 26 and 29, 1882.
36 *Evening Mercury*, September 9, 1882.
37 The requisitions (August to September 1882) can be found in RBP 3.01.02 and 3.01.03. Bond's reply, September 25, 1882, is in RBP 3.01.03.
38 *ENL* 3:452.
39 G.H. Cole, Trinity, to Bond, November 14, 1882 (RBP 3.01.005).
40 *ENL* 1:693–94.
41 Kerr, "Social Analysis," 13–14.

CHAPTER TWO

Turbulent Times, 1882–1885

The later nineteenth century was a difficult period for much of the Western world. Economists speak of a "long depression" (or "recession") extending from the mid-1870s to the late 1890s, which was characterized by falling prices and sluggish economic growth. The impact on Newfoundland was described by David Alexander:

> Newfoundland's traditional economy underwent a crisis in the late 1880s and 1890s. Export prices for salt codfish sank from $3.82 a quintal in 1880/84 to $2.89 in 1895/99—a collapse of around 32 per cent. Production volumes also fell from about 1.5 million quintals in 1880/84 to some 1.2 million in 1895/99—a 20 per cent decline. Accordingly, industry gross earnings sagged from $5.6 million to $3.6 million—a decline of 36 per cent. . . . The traditional economy [had] reached a limit to its extensive growth.[1]

There was heavy outmigration from Newfoundland in these years—between 1,500 and 2,500 persons annually—and population growth slowed. Fish exporters faced severe competition from France and Norway in European markets and became understandably nervous and uneasy. In addition, the cold temperatures that characterized the nineteenth century made cod stocks less productive. This factor, combined with a population that was only slowly increasing, meant that the average annual catch per fisherman by 1880, according to one source,[2] was only one-third what it had been in 1800. In addition, the seal fishery was in slow decline and

Water Street and Duckworth Street, St. John's, in the mid-1880s. ("Newfoundland Scenery," photograph by S.H. Parsons, ASC, Coll. 199)

employing far fewer people than it had at its mid-century peak. Social tensions in some parts of the colony increased, especially in years when there were poor fisheries, low prices, and a lack of employment in other sectors. As we have seen, the first response to this dismal situation was railway building. But there were many who feared the expense that came with this solution, and who thought that the first priority of any government should be the problems faced by the fish trade. The new-fangled departure—railway building—was unfamiliar and problematic, posing a challenge to the traditional economy.*

The recently elected legislature, of which Robert Bond was a new member, opened on February 15, 1883. Bond did not play an especially prominent role. He presented and spoke to petitions from his district—a necessary task, since petitions were, in the absence of elected local government, a way in which local people made known their needs. He chaired several committees and supported Whiteway's resolution for a survey of the state of the fisheries as a preliminary to comprehensive protective legislation. He did

* This is one of the themes in Kerr, "Social Analysis." See, for example, 81.

not believe the fisheries to be inexhaustible, he said, and the depletion of salmon and sea trout stocks were a case in point:

> The present Government had initiated many good measures since its coming into power; it had done more for the fishing classes of this country than any other in its history. . . . It had always kept its eye fixed upon the great object of all good Administration—the development of the material prosperity, and the promotion of the commercial advancement and general well-being of the community. He was glad to see another progressive measure following in the train of many predecessors.[3]

This speech was uncontroversial, and he does not seem to have spoken on possibly the most contentious piece of legislation in the session. That was a bill to approve a contract with J.E. Simpson and Co. of New York to build a substantial dry dock in St. John's; it superseded the legislation passed in 1882. The bill's passage indicated that New Party activists were accurate to question the Newfoundland Railway Company's financial stability and its commitment to Newfoundland.

Another indicator was the very slow pace of railway construction. The government withheld the subsidy due on July 1, 1883, because the railway company was not meeting its liabilities. In 1884, the company closed down, declaring bankruptcy early in 1885. The colony was left with 84 miles of track between St. John's and Harbour Grace that had cost about $1.7 million. The government had provided about a third of this in the form of subsidies, right-of-way payments, and an advance on the unbuilt Carbonear branch. Management of the line was assumed by the company's receiver, the merchant banker Francis H. Evans, who had arranged the original bond flotation in London. Disputes and expensive legal actions between the company and successive governments would rumble on into the late 1890s.

In spite of these problems, the government seemed secure enough, though its opponents were regrouping. Since Whiteway's party was now allied with the Roman Catholic Liberals, New Party stalwarts such as

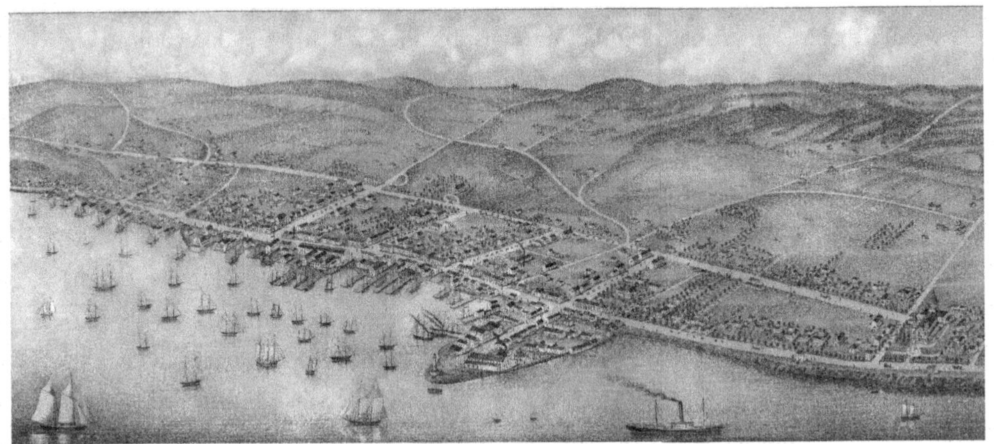

"Panoramic View of Harbour Grace" by A. Ruger, 1879. (Centre for Newfoundland Studies, Queen Elizabeth II Library, Memorial University)

Alexander McNeily and Donald Morison (a young lawyer who was James Winter's law partner[4]) decided to play the sectarian card. All three men were active members of the Loyal Orange Order. In the spring of 1883, its Grand Lodge agreed (on McNeily's motion) to form a political committee. Later in the year, it circulated resolutions to the twenty-one lodges that then existed in the colony, calling on Protestants to unite lest the Order, or Protestantism, be threatened. Morison toured the northern bays to recruit new members and engender a feeling of Protestantism endangered.[5] Then an incident at Harbour Grace unexpectedly gave this fledgling movement an enormous boost. It also, indirectly, helped speed Robert Bond's climb up the political ladder. This was the famous "Harbour Grace Affray," a violent confrontation between Orangemen from the Harbour Grace area and Roman Catholics from nearby Riverhead.

Local Lodge members did not celebrate on the usual date for Orangemen's Day (July 12), since it was in the middle of the fishing season. Instead, they met to parade in winter—those from Harbour Grace on December 26, St. Stephen's Day.* In 1883, several hundred Orangemen paraded through the town accompanied by the British Society band,

* The most recent and thorough account of the confrontation is in Keough, "Contested Terrains," 29–70. Newfoundland Orangemen paraded either on December 26 or on Candlemas Day, February 2.

following a service at the Methodist church. They were confronted at Pipetrack Lane by about 150 men from Riverhead, who thought that the Orangemen intended to march through "their" territory, which may well have been the case. Shots were fired and twenty-three men were wounded, five of them fatally (four Orangemen and one man from Riverhead). Thirty-four men were arrested, twenty-seven of them Roman Catholic. Eventually the Protestants were cleared and nineteen Riverhead men went to trial. Sectarian and ethnic tensions were immediately inflamed. In the absence of the governor, the Administrator (Chief Justice Carter) reported "a bitter feeling on both sides, and a line of demarcation drawn in social intercourse which has not for many years existed between the respective parties at Harbour Grace and adjacents: in fact, there is more or less of the same feeling generally in the Colony."[6]

The causes of the disturbance can be—and have been—endlessly debated. Sectarian tensions had been building in the area for some years and violence was not unknown, encouraged no doubt by poor economic conditions. The population on the north side of Conception Bay had declined steadily in the late nineteenth century, the Labrador fishery had failed, and there was widespread suspicion among Roman Catholics that Protestant merchants, who dominated the trade, favoured Protestant fishermen. In addition, missions by anti-Protestant Redemptorists from the United States—invited by the local bishop to shore up Roman Catholic unity—were clearly a contributing factor. But whatever the exact causes may have been, the political and social implications were potentially toxic and threatened the Conservative-Liberal alliance.

A tense peace prevailed in the immediate aftermath. In St. John's, the 1884 legislative session was largely business as usual. There was little discussion of what the Throne Speech called the "lamentable events" at Harbour Grace. Bond led the debate on the Speech, and in careful language deplored what had happened before moving on to safer territory, the state of the fish markets and the potential of the interior.[7] But the lull ended with the session. On May 9, the trial of the nineteen Riverhead men who were charged with murder began. Whiteway led the prosecution with James Winter, the solicitor general, who was also the Grand Master of the Orange Order. Catholic lawyers handled the defence, including Robert J. Kent, who was both the Speaker of the House and the Liberal leader.[8] HMS *Tenedos* was on hand in St. John's harbour, in case of disorder. The Admiralty had reluctantly sent the vessel, agreeing only because the British government wanted to ensure the completion and local acceptance of a new French Shore agreement that was then under negotiation.

After forty-seven days, during which witnesses for both sides flatly contradicted each other, the defendants were acquitted.* There followed an explosion of Protestant indignation that clearly threatened the government's stability. But the Whiteway party held together, thanks to some skillful manoeuvring by the senior Catholic on the government side, the ambitious (and recently knighted) Sir Ambrose Shea,[9] with the co-operation of Robert Kent. Whiteway appears to have contained his own Orange supporters.† There was, however, widespread apprehension that there would be more violence, and the government managed to arrange for the *Tenedos* to be stationed at St. John's for the winter.

Sir Ambrose Shea (1815–1905) in 1885. An influential figure, Shea emphasized the importance of reciprocity with the United States. (McCord Museum, II-77257.1)

The Riverhead men faced a second trial in the fall of 1884. On January 22, 1885, they were once again acquitted. Public meetings at Harbour Grace and Carbonear condemned the verdict as "an outrageous miscarriage of justice" and demanded that defence witnesses be tried for perjury.[10] There was much

* The jury was composed of Roman Catholics.

† Two Orange circulars, dated October 4 and November 21, 1884, are in RBP 3.03.001. They argue that as a result of the coalition, "virtual control" of the colony had been placed in Catholic hands and a "Protestant Union" was needed.

speculation about what would happen when the legislature opened in February. Feelings in the Harbour Grace area remained inflamed, in part because of friction between local Orangemen and the Redemptorists, who were once again visiting from the United States and reportedly using strong language about Protestantism and its origins.[11] In the St. John's area, a referendum on applying the Permissive Act to control the sale of alcohol took on a sectarian tone because many Roman Catholics opposed the legislation as inadequate and unfair.*

Thus the Throne Speech of February 12, 1885, carefully regretted the continuance of "that disturbed condition of feeling resulting from the calamitous event which took place at Harbour Grace."[12] Substantive debate on the Speech did not begin until February 19; on the 23rd, Alfred Penney, the Whitewayite member for Carbonear and also a member of the Orange political committee, unexpectedly moved an amendment (drafted by McNeily). It spoke of the Affray as an "unjustifiable outrage" and attributed "disturbed feelings" to "the disgraceful failure of justice at the recent trials." The amendment's seconder, Jabez Thompson (originally from Harbour Grace), told the House that a great crime remained unpunished.[13] Ambrose Shea intervened and the House adjourned.[14]

Debate on Penney's amendment resumed on February 26. Both Whiteway and Shea argued that the House could not criticize a judgment of the Supreme Court. The amendment could have been defeated then and there—but five Orangemen on the government side might well have then gone over to the opposition, leaving Whiteway as a sitting target for Protestant accusations of Catholic bias. So Whiteway moved his own amendment, to the effect that "disturbed feelings" continued because of "a widespread conviction" that there had been a failure of justice. After considerable debate in Committee, the Penney amendment was defeated and Whiteway's carried—all Protestants in favour (including Bond), all Catholics against. Out of Committee, Shea moved that the offending section of Whiteway's amendment should be deleted, and Penney once again moved that his amendment should be accepted. Both motions were

* *Evening Mercury*, February 5, 1885; *Terra Nova Advocate*, February 11, 1885. The imposition of the Permissive Act was defeated, 2,261 to 1,379.

defeated.* Robert Kent announced his resignation as Speaker and the Catholic members of the House, including Shea, moved across the floor to sit as a separate group.†

The new Speaker, elected unanimously on February 27, was Robert Bond. This was clearly Whiteway's doing. While promoting a Methodist made good political sense, there was also general agreement that Bond was well qualified.[15] The House over which he presided consisted, according to his calculations, of twelve Whiteway supporters (Conservatives), thirteen Catholic Liberals, and six New Party members.‡ In theory, Whiteway could have resigned and forced an election—assuming that the governor would have granted a dissolution—but he stayed in office, knowing that the Liberals would support essential legislation. It was clear, however, that the minority government could not survive for long. Whiteway's support was unstable, given a recent alliance between the New Party and the Orange political committee that made the Orangemen in his party an unreliable fifth column.[16] Particularly problematic was the position of James Winter, a prominent Orangeman who had been a vocal critic of the railway contract. It was widely thought that Winter was on the government side only because Whiteway had promised him a cabinet post. So the general consensus was that, although the Whiteway government might get through the session, it would certainly be killed in an election. Thus the 1885 session, racked by sectarian tension and political uncertainty, proved to be difficult. It certainly tested Bond's abilities as Speaker.

The Colonial Office pressured Whiteway to introduce legislation allowing the government to ban processions. This bill eventually passed, but it was not popular with Orangemen. So it was perhaps to help assuage

---

* *JHA* 1885, 20–23. Shea's motion was defeated twelve to eighteen (Bond included); Penney's eleven to nineteen (including Bond and Shea).

† Assembly debate, February 26, 1885 (*Evening Mercury*, February 27 and 28 and March 2 and 3, 1885). Bond was a member of the committee that drafted the Address in Reply.

‡ This is according to a list of members dated February 27, 1885 (RBP 3.04.001). The *Evening Mercury (*March 7, 1885) calculated thirteen Whiteway supporters, thirteen Liberals, and five New Party supporters.

Protestant anger that Whiteway also introduced a representation bill, which increased the number of Protestant seats by three. The Liberals did not oppose it and this, too, passed into law.* Much more provocative were petitions from Harbour Grace and Carbonear, as well as a Jury Amendment bill introduced by the leader of the New Party, Augustus F. Goodridge,[17] but drafted by Winter. These were linked, in that they reflected continued Protestant anger at the result of the trials. The Harbour Grace petition, presented by Winter on April 14, asked that the legal cases resulting from the Affray should be transferred to a non-partisan tribunal, possibly in Britain—or, failing this, that the jury law should be amended in such a way as to allow special juries for criminal cases, as well as civil cases.

In a strange passage of events, the New Party members decided not to vote on the motion to receive the petition. Instead, Goodridge moved adjournment, seconded by Kent, which killed the petition.[18] Bond then consulted various authorities about the handling of petitions, knowing that Penney intended to introduce a similar one from Carbonear. He advised Penney to send the petition back to have objectionable language removed, which he did; a revised Carbonear petition was introduced on April 29. Kent objected that this petition could not be accepted because it criticized the administration of justice. Speaker Bond sustained the objection, a ruling that was controversial—even though it was upheld by the House on appeal (eighteen to eight)[19]—and did not sit well with opponents of the government.

Goodridge did introduce his Jury Amendment bill, however, which narrowly passed second reading during a marathon session on May 5, supported by Protestants and opposed by Catholics. Although Whiteway voted for second reading, he was obviously not happy with the bill and blocked its progress by successfully moving a six months' hoist. He noted that the difference between petty and special jurors was £500, not intelligence—and if justice had not been done, it was the result of perjury. The law should not be changed, he argued, if the sole object was to convict

* Assembly debates, April 14 and 20, 1885 (*Evening Mercury*, April 16, 17, 21, and 23, 1885). In an Assembly debate on March 26, 1884, Penney had criticized the distribution of seats (*Evening Mercury*, March 31, 1884).

men awaiting trial, which was apparently what the Orange political committee wanted.[20]

The session ended on May 6. James O. Fraser,[21] the surveyor general (about to retire from politics), wrote to congratulate Bond on "the distinguished discharge of Mr. Speaker's duties by you. Coming after such a Speaker as Mr. Kent, and coming, too, midst what may be called a thick political snow-storm, you stood clear of danger, and, certainly, have come out with first-class credentials."[22] There was lingering controversy, though, over how Bond had handled the Carbonear petition, which would become an issue later in the year.

The political crisis forced an election in 1885, a year earlier than expected. The Assembly was dissolved on July 7 and Whiteway eventually set the voting day for October 31. The Orange-New Party alliance adopted the name "Reform Party" and set out to organize a pan-Protestant campaign that would remove Whiteway and his supporters from political life—Whiteway having made it clear that he did not intend to retire. Winter had resigned from the government in early June, intending to lead the Reformers, and started to campaign. It seemed that there would be three parties contesting the election, two of them—Whiteway's Conservatives and the Reform Party—fighting over the Protestant districts.

During the course of this manoeuvring, both McNeily and Winter criticized how the Carbonear petition had been handled. Bond could be thin-skinned and had (like his father) a hot temper. He wrote a long, irate letter to the *Evening Mercury* taking aim at Winter, charging him with insinuating in his speeches and through the Reform Party newspaper (*The Watchman*) that the ruling was biased and had been made "at the instance of Sir William Whiteway." They were false allegations made by "a venal slanderer," said Bond, insisting that at every step he had followed rules and precedents.[23] Winter regretted Bond's use of "coarse and violent language" and denied ever having stated that the ruling was partisan—but he continued to believe that it was mistaken.[24] There the matter rested, a testy exchange in the midst of a disagreeable political situation.

Whiteway's party was obviously weak, bereft of much mercantile and Orange support and all Roman Catholic backing. His manifesto called for Protestant unity in the face of the miscarriage of justice in the Harbour Grace trials, but promised justice for all, railway building, and a continuation of the policies of Hoyles* and Carter.[25] The Reformers campaigned for Protestant union under the slogan "No Amalgamation With the Roman Catholics," raising a virulent sectarian smokescreen to cloud their fundamental purpose, which was to get rid of the Whitewayites. As for the Liberals, their key figure was Ambrose Shea, who had taken over the leadership from Kent. He apparently believed that the Reformers would beat Whiteway's party but would not have enough seats for an overall majority, so Liberal support would be crucial. Moreover, Shea was angling to be appointed governor of Newfoundland in place of Sir John Glover, who had left the colony in June, seriously ill (he died on September 30, 1885). A deal with the Reformers, so he thought, would do him no harm. By late August, even the Catholic *Advocate* was making polite remarks about non-Orange members of the Reform Party, and urging the election of Liberals pledged to co-operate "in whatever arrangements may be made after the elections."[26] The Reform manifesto contained (in the small print) a promise that Catholics would be given "a full measure of justice in relation to their political and civil rights,"[27] which, as the *Evening Mercury* pointed out, implied an interdenominational government in due course.[28] Shea had made his deal and he delivered the Catholic vote to Reform in predominantly Protestant districts.

Before election day arrived there was a further development. Late in September, Whiteway threw in the towel and made his own deal with the Reformers: the two parties would combine after all. Whiteway must have understood that his political career was over for the time being, and there was another factor. If Carter, the Chief Justice and Administrator, were to replace Glover as governor, then Whiteway could move to the bench. They both telegraphed London, pressing Carter's claims, and Carter also wrote on his own behalf, stressing his long service and how his appointment could solve internal problems.[29] The Colonial Office was non-committal, no doubt because Shea was, in fact, being seriously considered for the post.

---

* Jones, "Hoyles," *DNB* 11:431–34 and *ENL* 2:1098–1101. Sir Hugh Hoyles was Carter's predecessor as premier.

The agreement between the Whiteway and Reform parties did not mention the governorship, of course, but listed those who would run for the "amalgamated party" in each district; it also provided that those not chosen would be "favorably considered." Whiteway agreed not to stand as a candidate and to being replaced as premier before the election by the inexperienced but generally acceptable Robert Thorburn,* a prominent Presbyterian and St. John's businessman who had been a member of the Legislative Council (MLC) since 1870. Winter would become attorney general. After the election, the Executive would consist of Thorburn and Winter, a Catholic and a Methodist nominated by Whiteway, and two Protestants and a Catholic nominated by Thorburn. Whiteway would be offered a seat on the Legislative Council and the Chief Justiceship, if and when the latter became vacant.[30] Not all of Whiteway's supporters accepted this arrangement—including Bond.† The new administration took office on October 12, just under three weeks before the election.

Bond was demonstrating that, although he might have entered political life as Whiteway's protégé, he retained his independence. He remained Whiteway's political ally and supporter, but quite clearly disliked the compromises and deals made in 1885. In public, though, he remained an unrepentant Whitewayite. In a lengthy draft address—"To the Electors of Trinity Bay, 1885"—the district in which he expected to run again, he applauded the record of the Whiteway administration, as well as his own contributions, and described the Harbour Grace riot as "a crime which for blackness and foulness has never been surpassed in the whole history of crime." Its perpetrators had got off. That said, he had no time for the New Party or its Reform successor. Had Reform members been genuine and sincere defenders of Protestant rights, they would have co-operated with

* Hiller, "Thorburn, Sir Robert," *DCB* 13:1031–33 and *ENL* 5:375–76. Thorburn was also acceptable to Winter and Goodridge.

† Bond said that he was the only party member to oppose this "division of the spoils," but in a letter to the *Evening Mercury*, October 13, 1885, Alfred Morine said there were others. Whether all these details are accurate is uncertain. For instance, Bond claimed in a March 3, 1887, speech that Whiteway had resigned unconditionally (RBP 3.06.003).

Whiteway rather than attacking him, and the abortive Jury Amendment bill had been nothing more than a political card designed to embarrass the government. "Alas that political trickery and usurpation should be baptized with the sacred name of religion."[31]

The Whiteway-Reform agreement awarded Trinity Bay to Thorburn and two other Reform candidates, so Bond was forced to look elsewhere. He was approached to run in both Brigus-Port de Grave and Fortune Bay. He eventually chose the latter, influenced by that district's previous member, James Fraser (who had been appointed postmaster general) and by James L. Syme, an MLC and the agent in St. John's for Newman and Co., a firm with immense influence in the one-member district. Bond was returned by acclamation. Later, there was a controversy about whether he had run as an independent or as a Reform supporter. Bond claimed, angrily and consistently, that he had gone as an independent, and had made this clear to party managers and everyone else. However, this position does not seem to have been clear to Thorburn, Fraser, Syme, or the Newman firm, and he was accused of having taken the seat under false pretenses.[32] Two Anglican clergymen in the district supported Bond's version of events,[33] and Chief Justice Carter described Bond as "a Whiteway man and a very respectable and intelligent young man, albeit a Methodist."[34] Alfred B. Morine—of whom much more later—probably got it right when he speculated[35] that Bond would not run except as an independent, and that the Reform party let him go to Fortune Bay because they feared his opposition elsewhere, hoping after the election to wheel him into line.

The 1885 election was a curious affair. The various inter-party deals meant that nine of the eighteen districts were uncontested and that, where there were contests, they were one-sided. It was a "fixed" election, which returned twenty-one Reformers, all Protestant, fourteen Liberals, all Roman Catholic, and one independent in the person of Robert Bond.* Shortly thereafter, Thorburn offered Bond the Speakership, mentioning that "members of your denomination" were "strong supporters of the New Government." Bond hesitated, since he had not campaigned with a view "to self-interest or the acceptance of any office." And when Thorburn

* This is according to *ENL* 1:695, and my own calculations in "A History," 372.

invited him to a Reform party meeting, he refused on the grounds that he could not unite with a "Sectarian Government." His attendance, he felt, would not be honourable and would place both him and Thorburn in a false position.[36] Bond did not accept the Speakership, remained an independent Whitewayite, and refused to be co-opted. This was no doubt because of policy issues, but what he thought of Whiteway's political manoeuvres is another question. Indeed, the events of 1885 may well have planted doubts in his mind about how far politicians can remain true to their stated principles. Bond eventually learned about the need for flexibility, but throughout his career he remained stubborn on some issues, fixed in many of his opinions, and difficult to persuade.

Not yet 30 years old, Robert Bond had been in politics for only three years—busy and difficult ones, in many ways—but there can be no question that he was seen as a coming man in the colony's small political world. Following the 1885 election, the prospect of a smooth ascent toward the Executive under Whiteway's patronage appeared to have exploded, but Bond was now more readily able to shape his own future while remaining loyal to Whiteway's policies. His erstwhile patron had gone into political exile, making it quite obvious that he would prefer to be chief justice if he could not have the premiership, and the government had passed into the hands of those who were at best skeptical about the policies promoted by the previous administration. Bond now sat on the opposition side of the House, a party of one, and his political future was difficult to predict.

NOTES

1 Alexander, "Newfoundland's Traditional Economy," 23–25.

2 Rose, *Cod,* 284–86.

3 Assembly debate, April 19, 1883 (*Evening Mercury*, April 27, 1883).

4 *ENL* 3:620.

5 A.B. Morine in Assembly, February 28, 1887 (*Evening Mercury*, March 4, 1887) and Senior, "Origin and Political Activities," 148.

6 Carter to Derby, conf., February 2, 1884 (CO 194/207, 71–72).

7 Bond in Assembly, February 14, 1884 (*Evening Mercury*, February 15, 1884).

8 Hiller, "Kent, Robert John," *DCB* 12:482–83.

9 Hiller, "Shea, Sir Ambrose," *DCB* 13:942–47.

10 *Evening Mercury*, January 27, 1885.

11 *Evening Mercury*, January 5, 6, and 24, 1885; *Terra Nova Advocate*, February 4, 11, and 21, 1885.

12 *JHA* 1885, 13.

13 For Penney, see *ENL* 4:247; for Thompson, *ENL* 5:373.

14 Assembly debate, February 23, 1885 (*Evening Mercury*, February 25, 1885).

15 *Evening Telegram*, February, 28, 1885; *Evening Mercury*, February 27, 1885.

16 *Evening Mercury*, March 3, 1885.

17 *ENL* 2:559.

18 *Evening Mercury*, April 15, 1885; *Evening Telegram*, April 15 and 16, 1885.

19 *Evening Mercury*, April 30, 1885; Bond, letter to *Evening Mercury*, August 28, 1885; *JHA* 1885, 127–28.

20 *Evening Mercury*, May 4 and 6, 1885; *JHA* 1885, 128–39.

21 *ENL* 2:395.

22 Fraser to Bond, May 6, 1885 (RBP 3.04.03).

23 *Evening Mercury*, August 28, 1885; RBP 3.04.010.

24 Winter, letter to *Evening Mercury*, August 31, 1885.

25 Manifesto, July 10, 1885, folded into the October 24, 1885, edition of the *Evening Mercury*.

26 *Terra Nova Advocate*, August 16 and September 9, 12, 23, and 30, 1885.

27 *Watchman*, September 11, 1885.

28 *Evening Mercury*, September 17, 1885.

29 Carter and Whiteway to Stanley, tgms., October 2, 1885 (CO 537/120, 103–5); Carter to Stanley, conf., October 11, 1885 (CO 194/208, 90–93).

30 *Evening Mercury*, October 9 and 12, 1885; A.B. Morine, letter to *Evening Mercury*, October 13, 1885; Carter to Stanley, conf., October 15, 1885 (CO 194/208, 90–93); speech by Bond, April 20, 1886, reported in *Evening Telegram*, April 21, 1886.

31 "To the Electors of Trinity Bay, 1885," notebook in RBP 3.04.009.

32 *Evening Mercury*, April 17 and 28, 1886; Bond in Assembly, April 19, 1886 (*Evening Mercury*, April 27, 1886); letter from John Syme, *Evening Mercury*, May 3, 1886.

33 Letters in *Evening Telegram*, May 13, 1886.

34 Letter by Carter, November 24, 1885 (Provincial Archives of Newfoundland and Labrador [PANL], GN 3/13.)

35 Morine to Bond, April 20, 1886 (RBP 3.05.003).

36 Thorburn to Bond, November 13, 1886; Bond to Thorburn, November 14, 1886; Thorburn to Bond, January 1, 1886; and Bond to Thorburn, January 4, 1886 (RBP 3.04.012).

CHAPTER THREE

Waiting for Whiteway, 1885–1889

Politically isolated as he seemed to be, Robert Bond soon found that the new Reform Party government was less stable and less firmly wedded to its stated aims than it had initially appeared. It was rocked by the first major crisis with which it had to deal—the award of the governorship to a sitting member (for St. John's East) who was also the Liberal leader, Sir Ambrose Shea. And it faced a more fundamental problem to which it never found an adequate solution: how to formulate and persuasively present to the electorate a convincing and realistic development policy that was different from the one advanced by the Whitewayites.

In retrospect, this was a key moment, when an alternate vision of Newfoundland's future path might have been defined, promoted, and implemented. Men who were skeptical about expensive landward development schemes had won the government. Robert Thorburn, James Winter, and other Reform Party supporters were clearly concerned by the financial implications of railway building, and they thought that serious attention needed to be given to the fisheries and the fish markets. They were prepared to build roads and promote agriculture, and they certainly took steps toward creating a new policy direction. But overall, the Reformers missed their chance; they eventually fell back on railway building, though they did combine it with a distinctly more vigorous fisheries policy. Given economic circumstances, political pressures, and the personalities involved, their failure is understandable but possibly unfortunate. The clash over development policy had begun in the early 1880s, if not before, but it had become clouded by sectarian, partisan, and local issues. The result was that a necessary debate about the best way forward never really took place. The implications for Newfoundland's future were profound.[1]

The governorship issue blindsided the government and caused it some real political damage. Seventy years old, Shea had been a prominent figure in Newfoundland politics for many years. He favoured the colony joining confederation, supported the Whiteway agenda, and (like Bond and others) wanted to see closer trade links between Newfoundland and the United States. Knighted in 1883, he now wanted the imperial preferment that he thought he deserved. He had helped keep the previous Whiteway government in power, which had improved the chances of a new French Shore agreement (at least temporarily). In 1885, he had gone to Washington on behalf of the Chamber of Commerce to discuss the possible renewal of the fisheries clauses of the Treaty of Washington (1871), which had been due to expire that July. Shea had then gone on to Ottawa and, acting as a go-between, had helped prevent a serious fisheries crisis through the arrangement of a modus vivendi.* He was therefore very much *persona grata* at the Colonial Office, especially since he had let it be known that, if appointed governor, he would support confederation. After the 1885 election, Shea set off to London to press his claims; by the end of the year it was known that he had won the appointment. He arrived back in St. John's soon after.[2]

For the Colonial Office to appoint as governor the colony's most prominent Catholic politician and the leader of an opposition party—when the government was entirely Protestant and heavily Orange, and sectarian tensions were still high—was peculiarly obtuse and insensitive. Premier Thorburn immediately protested and threatened resignation, and Chief Justice Carter was deeply offended. Shea set off for London once again, pursued by more protests. In early February his name was withdrawn.[3] He returned to the colony bitterly disappointed and resentful, treating his constituents to a venomous speech alleging that he was the victim of Orange bigotry.[4] Bond and others saw Shea's rejection as an

* Brown, *Canada's National Policy*, 16–19. The modus continued American fishing privileges in British waters until January 1886, on the understanding that President Cleveland would recommend to Congress a commission on the fisheries question.

insult to native Newfoundlanders and the consequence of prejudiced political intrigue.* Roman Catholics were particularly upset and there was bitter criticism from Liberals in the Assembly.[5] The construction of an interdenominational government had to be postponed. Thorburn could not fill all departmental positions and he faced the possibility that the Liberals could make common cause with Bond and others. The new Reform government was suddenly not as strong as it once had seemed.

Making matters worse, Whiteway had not been sidelined into the Supreme Court and his supporters (Bond among them) were still at large. Moreover, the Reform Party also had to deal with tension between its mercantile and Orange wings and, as events unfolded, between political pragmatism and conflicting principles. How could anti-Catholic rhetoric be reconciled with the obvious necessity—if Reform was to survive—of creating a genuinely inclusive party? If Reformers were failing at this, then one reason was because the party lacked strong leadership. Though decent and straightforward, Robert Thorburn was a compromise figure who was unsuited to being premier. James Winter was ambitious and clever, but lacked the backbone and single-minded determination necessary for political success—his previous behaviour over the railway contract was evidence enough of that. The real talent lay outside the Reform Party—with Shea, Whiteway, and Bond, as well as newcomer Edward Patrick Morris (still in his twenties, Morris had been elected at the top of the poll in St. John's West†). Another real, though subversive and unpredictable, political intellect was Alfred B. Morine,‡ a Nova Scotian adventurer who had suddenly resigned as editor of the *Evening Mercury* to run,

* *Evening Telegram*, January 29, 1886, and *Terra Nova Advocate*, January 30, 1886. Bond remained in touch with Shea and awarded him a state funeral in St. John's upon his death in 1905. It was the first of its kind in Newfoundland.

† Hiller, "Morris, Edward Patrick, 1st Baron Morris," *DCB*, www.biographi.ca/en/bio/morris_edward_11E.html. The *Evening Telegram* (October 3, 1885) claimed Morris was an independent candidate, others thought he was a Liberal.

‡ *ENL* 3:618–20. Originally a journalist, Morine was recruited by Moses Harvey. He took over the *Evening Mercury* in July 1883 and left the paper in 1885 (Armour, "Castles in the Air," 165).

Alfred Bishop Morine (1857–1944), initially a supporter but soon an opponent and effective critic of Robert Bond. Originally printed in H.Y. Mott, *Newfoundland Men* (Concord, New Hampshire, 1894). (ASC Coll. 327, 1.01.011)

unsuccessfully, in Bonavista Bay. The same age as Bond, Morine would become a controversial presence in Newfoundland political life; all three younger men would be centrally important in public life for years to come.

If the Reform Party faced difficult internal problems, it also had to deal with some problematic external issues. First, the United States' abrogation of the fisheries clauses of the 1871 Treaty of Washington had serious implications for exports to that market, even though those exports were not large. More important, this event had once again raised the contentious question of American rights in Newfoundland and Canadian waters (unclearly defined in the 1818 Anglo-American treaty). The agreement with which Shea had been associated was no more than a temporary fix.

Second, in 1884 the British and French governments had concluded a draft convention that redefined British and French rights on the Treaty Shore. After the election, the Colonial Office pressed for Newfoundland agreement to the final version, signed by the British government in November 1885. France had made some significant concessions (from its point of view), recognizing a concurrent fishery, an exclusive colonial right to freshwater fisheries, and the permanence of existing settlements along the Treaty Shore, and allowing industrial development in some areas. However, the agreement gave the French exclusive use of some harbours and Britain agreed to recognize the *de facto* state of affairs regarding the actions of French naval officers within territorial waters. In addition, the French could purchase bait on the south coast—and *that* proved to be a central problem.[6]

The importance of the bait issue needs explanation. Increasingly, American, French, and Canadian fishing fleets had moved their activity to the offshore banks, where they used long lines of baited hooks to catch cod. The bait was usually herring, capelin, or squid, according to the season, and was purchased from inshore fishermen in both Canada and Newfoundland, sometimes using cash, sometimes by barter. In current terminology, the bait supply was "outsourced." Bait fishermen were quite happy with this arrangement, since it gave them ready income, and the inshore and offshore fisheries had become to some extent interdependent. The main Newfoundland baiting areas were along the southern and southeastern shores of the island, between Bonne Bay on the west coast and Conception Bay on the east coast. Colonial governments saw this trade both as a problem and as a bargaining chip. Easy access to local bait supplies could only assist French competition in the fish markets; at the same time, bait could be a way to bargain for closer trade relations with the North American mainland.*

Whiteway had clearly viewed the draft French Shore agreement as another step along the long road leading to eventual French withdrawal, a process in which he had been involved for some time. The effective opening up of the west coast, which would allow railway building (among other things) was a considerable gain and certainly worth the concession of south coast bait. He agreed that bait export to foreign fishing vessels should be strictly controlled by the colony and that legislation was needed, but reckoned that the French deal was acceptable.

The new Reform government, however, took the position that France could not be allowed access to bait unless it reduced or eliminated the subsidization of its fisheries. This had taken the form of "bounties" that the French government paid to French outfitters engaged in the Newfoundland, Iceland, and North Sea fisheries; there was an additional bounty on fish exported to foreign markets. The system was extended to St. Pierre and Miquelon in 1881.[7] The result, as seen in St. John's, was that the French bank fishery was artificially large, which in turn increased the amount of cheap French fish finding its way to European markets (particularly to Italy). Newfoundland exporters experienced serious losses as a

* There is a good account of the south coast bait trade in Korneski, *Conflicted Colony*, 15–46.

result.* The only way to retaliate, it was argued, was to cut off the supply of bait to French banking vessels. The British government had hitherto opposed such legislation—and since the French government viewed the draft agreement's bait clause as a *sine qua non*, confrontation loomed.

When the legislature opened (February 11, 1886), the Reform government had to show its hand. It announced that there was to be a commercial audit of the public accounts (which led to a loan bill and the colony's first direct overseas bond issue), and that a Joint Select Committee would consider the draft French Shore agreement.† Supervised agricultural districts would also be created.[8] The opposition was skeptical. Ambrose Shea forced a debate on the state of the colony by calling for a resumption of work on the northern railway with a branch line to Placentia (an important Roman Catholic district).[9] This alone, he argued, would create desperately needed employment and stimulate farming. But Thorburn and his allies held that the existing railway had had little economic impact and had been far too costly. To complete the railway as envisaged in Shea's resolutions would simply drive up taxes and the debt. A branch line to Placentia might be feasible, but the country should be opened up by building roads.

Bond spoke eloquently in support of Shea's resolutions, stressing the prevalence of destitution and unemployment, and the crying need to develop the valleys of the Gander, Gambo, and Exploits rivers.[10] The Reformers defeated Shea's resolutions, supporting others introduced by Thorburn that spoke of the need to sort out the colony's difficulties with the railway company and to stimulate agriculture by road building.‡

Though he was an agricultural enthusiast, Bond opposed many of the suggestions coming from the government side, including its 1886

---

* For example, one commentor claimed that Munn and Co. of Harbour Grace experienced an average annual loss of $50,000 between 1882 and 1894 (letter to *Evening Telegram*, October 23, 1897).

† Thorburn, Assembly debate March 2 (*Evening Mercury,* March 3, 1886) and Assembly debate, March 8 (*Evening Mercury*, March 10, 1886). The committee included members of both houses of the legislature.

‡ Shea's resolutions were debated on March 19, 22, 23, 24, and 25 (*Evening Mercury*, March 23 to 25, 27, 29, 30, and 31, April 1 through 6, 1886).

agricultural legislation. As he said in the House in March 1886, the prevailing destitution was indeed caused in part by commercial depression, but more important was the fact that

> there are too many people depending upon one industry; there are too many hungry mouths and there is too little food to feed them. What is the remedy? Why, sir, there are large stretches of fertile land awaiting culture. What is wanted, then, is that the Government should hold out liberal inducement to our people to settle upon the land and devote their attention to agriculture. In this country there would appear to be a prejudice against this employment. Yet, sir, it holds a high place amongst the pursuits of men; it is the art of arts. . . . I shall ever do all in my power to encourage agriculture, for I think it will eventually prove to be an industry of immense value to our people.[11]

Bond could not support the government's bill because it did not apply to the whole island, was confined to two agricultural districts, and its beneficiaries had to be genuine paupers. This was impractical and unfair.[12] Three years later, opposing a bill to establish a Board of Agriculture and a model farm, he argued that the way forward was to establish and encourage agricultural societies.*

One of the 1886 bill's problems, from Bond's point of view, was that his district, Fortune Bay, would not gain anything from it. In fact, because the government was determined to pass legislation allowing it to control or prohibit the export and sale of bait to foreign fishing vessels, his constituents could lose money. The debate on the Bait bill was held in camera, but it was no secret that Bond opposed it. Because Fortune Bay was the centre of the south coast bait trade, French, American, and Canadian vessels spent large amounts of money there and paid light dues. The trade employed between 1,600 and 2,000 people; if it was stopped, they would be destitute.

* Bond in Assembly, March 20, 1889 (*Evening Mercury,* March 28, 1889). His views would change. When prime minister, Bond created a short-lived model farm and, in Opposition after 1909, he was critical of agricultural societies.

This was unjust, Bond said, and he predicted that the legislation was unenforceable—it would be impossible to target the French alone while supplying Americans and Nova Scotians. In any event, the French could get bait in St. George's Bay on the Treaty Shore, or at St. Pierre and Miquelon. He argued further (and less convincingly) that the legislation would not give any advantage to Newfoundland fish in European markets.[13]

Bond predicted, as well, that the British government would not let the bill go forward—and he was correct. It was denied Royal assent. The British government was not yet convinced by the colony's case for imposing bait restrictions, saw trouble ahead with France, and had received protests from Canada expressing concern that the bill could be used both to damage its Atlantic fishery and facilitate a separate reciprocity agreement between Newfoundland and the United States (which Bond advocated). The Canadian government was implacably opposed to this option; as a result, not surprisingly, confederation re-emerged as a possible solution.

In June 1886, the opposition side of the House was strengthened by the return of Alfred Morine in a Bonavista Bay by-election in which he had defeated a government minister seeking re-election.* This event probably stimulated Reform interest in a rapprochement with the Liberal members, since it indicated a possible resurgence of the Whiteway faction. After lengthy and difficult negotiations facilitated by the Roman Catholic bishop,† the government reconstructed itself and the old Liberal party effectively disappeared. Robert Kent resigned his seat and Ambrose Shea distanced himself from active party politics, though he was willing enough to cooperate with the Reform government and look after his own priorities. Two Catholic Liberals joined the government side, others were given jobs, and it

* *Evening Mercury*, June 14, 1886. Ministers had to be re-elected on accepting office. The *Evening Mercury* (June 7, 1886) reported that Bond was going to help Morine's campaign.

† In his memoirs, Governor William Des Voeux (who had arrived in April) claimed he was also involved, although his official report said his efforts had "not largely contributed." (Des Voeux to Granville, August 2, 1886 [CO 194/209, 151]; Des Voeux, *My Colonial Service*, 2:137, 157; Hiller, "Des Voeux, Sir George William," *DCB* 13:269–70).

was accepted that there would be a railway branch line (originally called "a road") to Placentia and a substantial amount spent on building sewers in St. John's.[14] Most, but not all, Liberals bought into this arrangement. Some members of the Reform Party's Orange wing were unhappy, but the Grand Lodge resolved that given the "crying needs of the country" it was appropriate to acknowledge "the expedient coalition of parties which has been made." Donald Morison resigned as Grand Master.[15]

This amalgamation finally ended the political aftershocks of the Harbour Grace Affray (the charges still pending against those arrested were dropped). It also marked the end of the Reform Party's attempt to create a prudent, cautious, fiscally responsible administration. Combined with economic misery—1886 was another bad year in the fishery—it forced the government to undertake expensive public works and extensive road building.

The first business of the legislature when it opened on February 17, 1887, was to pass another bait bill and send an address to the Colonial Office requesting allowance.[16] The debate on these matters was held behind closed doors.[17] Bond voted against the Bait bill, using arguments similar to those of the previous year, and urged that if it did come into force, those who suffered should be compensated.[18] The bill passed and Thorburn then departed for London with Ambrose Shea to press for Royal assent (and to attend the first Colonial Conference), leaving James Winter in charge of government business.[19]

On the opposition side of the House there remained several former Liberals plus Bond, who was backed by the irrepressible Morine and by Kent's St. John's East successor, Thomas J. Murphy. The newcomer had announced in the House that he was joining "Mr. Bond's party who, at present, are the sole representatives of progressive politics in this country."[20] These three members always voted together, occasionally joined (depending on the issue) by Edward P. Morris and

James Winter, undated. (PANL, VA 19-89)

others. They were energetic and lively, and peppered the government with questions. Their attacks focused on the alleged hypocrisy of the amalgamation, as well as on over-expenditure on public works (especially the Placentia line), neglect of the northern districts (and Fortune Bay) in favour of St. John's and the southeastern districts, and the failure to extend the railway north and adopt what they considered to be a sensible agricultural policy.[21]

Bond received great credit (at the time and later) for introducing a bill, seconded by Morris, to adopt voting by secret ballot. Other parts of the "British world" had implemented the practice between the 1850s and the early 1870s—the United States took its time—and Bond was correct when he said that Newfoundland was the only British colony retaining open voting. Quoting at length from a speech in the British House of Commons made by his hero, William Gladstone, Bond argued that voters were pressured by their suppliers and that there was "coercion" from road board chairmen, government officials, and clergymen. Canvassing was "a system of organized pressure," and some people—tradesmen and shopkeepers for example—often did not vote at all.[22] Winter complained that Bond had not consulted the government but sensibly did not oppose the bill. Instead, he proposed three bills to deal separately with the ballot, electoral corruption, and the trial of controverted elections. Bond was appointed to the Select Committee that worked on this legislation, which passed in late April.[23] He also supported resolutions introduced by Morine to implement manhood suffrage in place of the existing franchise, which had a property qualification—only 64 per cent of adult males in Newfoundland had the vote. This proved to be too radical a proposal for the Assembly, which defeated it (seventeen to eight).[24] In 1889, Bond initially supported another attempt by Morine to introduce manhood suffrage, but in the end he voted against the bill when Morine accepted an age limit of 25.*

Morine (an Anglican) and Bond (a Methodist) also called for "free, public, and non-sectarian education" through an amendment to an Education bill (at the time, schools were run by the major churches). They were the

---

* Bond in Assembly, April 5 and 12, 1889 (*Evening Mercury* April 13 and 23, 1889). Bond originally favoured the exclusion of illiterates; when this was rejected, he adopted the age of 21.

only members to vote in favour. While both men believed in what they were saying—Methodists had generally supported public education—they must have known that the idea would never be accepted or even seriously discussed. The move was probably an attempt to embarrass the government, given that the Orange Order had supported the idea in the past and the Reform Party had flirted with it.[25] In addition, both men opposed the Placentia branch line and refused to attend a dinner honouring Thorburn for being awarded a knighthood while he was in London.[26] Thorburn had also obtained Royal assent to the Bait Act, helped by Shea and supported by Governor Des Voeux. The British government had accepted, reluctantly, that there was no chance of the Newfoundland government changing its policy and that consequently the French Shore negotiations would go nowhere.

Sir William V. Whiteway in later life. He was knighted in 1880 for his role in the North Atlantic Fisheries arbitration, 1877. (PANL, VA 19-98)

As if to emphasize the point, both houses of the legislature, opposition members included, endorsed the report of the Joint Select Committee on the draft French Shore agreement, which had been under consideration for over a year. This report argued that if the French were allowed to control the principal harbours on the Treaty Shore, French naval officers would have too much power. It also found no real concessions for Newfoundland—and, given the climate of the times, it argued that the provision for permanent access to bait was impossible.[27] Together, the rejection of the agreement and the passage of the Bait Act ushered in a new and tense period in Anglo-French relations concerning Newfoundland. From the French point of view, this was a declaration of unarmed war.

During the summer of 1887, Bond and Morine approached Whiteway, now nearly 60 years old, about his political future. Was he returning to public life or not? If so, when would he make his move and would he lead a party?[28] In late September, Whiteway formally announced that, given the sorry state of the country and the Reform Party's broken promises, he felt it necessary to "unfurl the banner of progress . . . at the earliest possible opportunity."[29] So a Whiteway party was to reappear. Bond was probably clarifying the battle lines in time for the next election, but Morine had another agenda. He saw himself as the guardian of Canadian interests in Newfoundland and was in frequent contact with senior federal Canadian Conservatives, who were concerned about the implications of the Bait Act and disturbed by Newfoundland's recent tendency to assert its independence in external affairs. The best way to neutralize the colony was to bring it into confederation, and Morine actively busied himself with this issue, especially after news leaked out about meetings in London between Shea and the American minister there.[30] The Thorburn government did decide to ask imperial permission to negotiate an independent reciprocity treaty with the United States, but by mid-1887 arrangements were well advanced for a British-American conference at Washington to try and settle the fisheries question. Newfoundland was not allowed direct representation but was permitted to send an agent. The job went to Winter; Sir Charles Tupper, then Canadian High Commissioner in London, was to represent Canada. Morine suggested that Tupper should visit St. John's on his way to Washington, advising him that "Winter is your man and [has] got his price."[31]

Tupper arrived in St. John's in October 1887. His visit was inconclusive, though the terms he outlined for confederation were more generous than those of 1869. Whiteway and Bond made positive noises—the former saying he would support confederation on good terms, the latter apparently agreeing with him—so Tupper did not anticipate opposition from that quarter.[32] But the Reform government was divided and unprepared; if Winter and his associates were enthusiastic, the Thorburn wing was skeptical. And the issue was, after all, political dynamite. The new governor, Henry Blake, reported that the Thorburn ministry "appeared to shrink from any expression of opinion whatever."* The matter did not develop further until Tupper and Winter were able to talk privately in Washington and sort out who would get which positions. The Canadian government was persuaded that confederation might be carried, and agreed to send an invitation for a formal conference when Winter gave the signal.

Morine kept quiet until early March 1888, when the invitation to send a delegation to Ottawa arrived.[33] This event precipitated a political crisis that is difficult to unravel because Bond and Morine later published divergent accounts. Bond's version was that he had had suspicions and saw a conspiracy that he did not want to be involved in. However, he was prepared to use the delegation and the timing of its trip to Ottawa as a wedge issue that could split the government and cause its collapse.† Hence Bond's statement to the House that, although he was an anti-confederate, he believed that given the sorry state of the country, a delegation should immediately go to Ottawa to ascertain proposed terms of union, which would have to be an improvement on those of 1869.[34] The motion was voted down and the Assembly decided that the timing should be left to the government. But it was indeed the case that the Reform government was deeply divided and, internally, hotly disputing the timing of a delegation—some members even arguing that there should be no delegation at all without legislative approval.

In Morine's version of events, Bond was not opposed to confederation, Whiteway remained in favour, and they both approved of his continued contact with Winter—indeed, he had been authorized to tell Winter that even if he left the government on the timing issue, the Whiteway party would support him for the rest of the session. Then, according to Morine, Bond backtracked and began talking to the anti-confederate wing of the government.[35]

* Blake to Holland, conf., October 10, 1887 (CO 880/11, 1). Blake had replaced Des Voeux earlier in the year. Ambrose Shea replaced Blake as governor of The Bahamas.

† Bond, letter to the *Evening Telegram*, November 22, 1888. By this time, the *Telegram* was supporting the Whitewayites.

For the moment, though, Bond and Morine remained political allies. The question of an Ottawa delegation remained the subject of much speculation, and politicians were inevitably conscious that 1889 was an election year. The nascent Whiteway party had not yet settled its position on central issues, and there is no doubt that Bond was becoming increasingly mistrustful of Morine and his influence over Whiteway (who, he later wrote, had become blinded by Morine's "sophistry"[36]). Matters came to a head in the late summer, when everyone's minds were no doubt sharpened by an approaching by-election in Bonavista Bay. When the Whiteway party met on September 1, 1888, there was a confrontation between Bond and Morine. If the latter's account is accurate, Bond's purpose (with Whiteway's acquiescence) was to make the party overtly anti-confederate, thus he put forward a resolution to the effect that there could be no amalgamation with Winter and his colleagues while a coalition with the anti-confederates remained on the table. Morine thereupon left the Whitewayites, reminding Bond and Whiteway of their earlier confederate statements, and calling the whole affair "a piece of double-dealing."[37] Bond then refused to join the delegation that was scheduled to leave in mid-September. For their part, the Canadians were unwilling, perhaps unfairly, to negotiate with a purely exploratory delegation, and the confederation initiative collapsed.[38]

Whiteway decided not to run in the Bonavista by-election, though he was importuned to do so; indeed, some thought that the vacancy had been created for him. But given Morine's defection, it was no longer a safe district—in addition, Donald Morison (at Morine's behest) had entered the contest as an independent.* In response, the Whitewayites decided to enlist their leader's law partner, George M. Johnson.[39] Bond, Whiteway, and others went north to canvass, the party clearly thinking that this, the first election to the Assembly using the secret ballot, was important to its future. Johnson, however, was badly defeated, the *Evening Telegram* blaming the Orange vote and government and mercantile influence. The *Evening Mercury* saw it as an ignominious defeat for the

* Though the *ENL* (1:696) says he was a Reform supporter.

Whiteway party, as many others must have done, as well.*

At the start of 1889, then, the Whiteway party had only two confirmed members in the Assembly—Bond and Murphy—though Robert J. Parsons, Jr., who had taken Ambrose Shea's seat in St. John's East, was sometimes associated with them. Outside the House, the party had about a dozen members. The potentially valuable Morine was gone, and former Liberals in opposition were still officially independent.† Clearly, Bond was not yet seen as a party leader, nor did he see himself as such, and so the new party could not fully emerge until Whiteway's active return. A letter to the *Evening Mercury* suggested that Bond, now 32, had achieved political prominence much earlier than usual because of political factors, not because of experience or public service, and that he tended to be imprudent and vindictive.[40] Those who agreed had their views confirmed soon after the legislature opened in mid-February 1889. Thorburn made condescending remarks about Bond's commentary on the Throne Speech, saying that it was "nicely delivered" with "unexceptionable" diction, comparing it to "the well-prepared essay of a schoolboy." Bond responded angrily. Thorburn should have used "the language of a gentleman," he said, but clearly did not know any better and so made himself ridiculous. He was "the most incompetent man who has ever occupied the Premier's chair." Commenting on this intemperate language,‡ the *Mercury* suggested, mischievously, that Bond had been unable to control his temper since the Bonavista by-election.[41]

Two other examples of thin-skinned anger and impetuousness during this long session can be mentioned. In mid-April, the Acting Speaker, Patrick Scott, denied calling Bond "stupid" (as reported in the *Evening Telegram*) in relation to a point of order. Though Bond admitted that he

---

* *Evening Telegram*, October 25, November 12 and 13, 1888; *Evening Mercury*, November 12 and 16, 1888. The result was Morison, 921; Johnson, 453; Wyatt, 14.

† The *Evening Telegram* (February 14, 1889) counted nineteen government members, eight "Loyal Neutrals," three independents and three members of "Bond's Opposition."

‡ The exchange occurred on February 20 and was reported in the *Evening Mercury* on February 22 and 23, 1889.

himself had called Morison "deaf and stupid," he stubbornly continued to insist that the Acting Speaker had insulted him. All MHAs supported Scott.[42] The second instance occurred when Bond accused Winter of trying to bribe Parsons and Murphy to vote with the government on railway issues. This was a serious matter and the House went into a Committee of Privilege, examined witnesses, and reported that the accusation was "a gross calumny," implying that Murphy—who had started the affair—had made a false statutory declaration. Bond had not done his homework and had to eat his words.[43]

These unfortunate incidents did not enhance Bond's reputation, nor did they ruin it. Bond did introduce useful legislation to protect caribou numbers on the island,[44] at the behest of Whiteway and others, and continued to press for financial compensation for constituents who suffered because of the Bait Act, which had been enforced from 1888 and had hurt many south coast fishermen.[45] Bond also joined in the universal indignation at French behaviour on the Treaty Shore—of which more below—and served on the Joint Select Committee to draft an address to the Crown that passed at the end of the session.[46]

Though an advocate of railways, Bond strongly opposed the government's intention to re-start work on the line north to Hall's Bay. The situation in 1889 was that the Newfoundland Railway Company, though in receivership, owned and operated the incomplete line that then existed (excluding the Placentia branch). It had not continued the line to Carbonear and clearly had no intention of building to the north. Because the company had failed to complete its contract, the Reform government decided to stop paying the subsidy for which it was liable. The resulting court case found its way to the Privy Council, which in 1888 ruled that the subsidy had to be paid on the completed portion of the line but that the government could counter-claim for damages, which it decided to do. It then turned its attention to the incomplete Hall's Bay section and called tenders, none of which were accepted. And at that point it decided to make a survey of the route and begin the work itself. Winter introduced the new policy to the Assembly in a long speech on May 7.[47]

The debate exhibited a range of conflicting views on the railway experience since 1880. In his response, Bond was careful to reiterate his support, in principle, for a railway that would open the interior and link Newfoundland's east and west coasts. "As a country, we have been favoured with as large a share of blessings as ever fell to the lot of any community," he said. With the fisheries and the development of agriculture, forestry, and mining, a foundation would exist for "a prosperous and contented community." But, he argued further, the government's proposals were clearly linked to the approaching general election and tenders had been called only to provide ammunition for the claim against the railway company. Moreover, he felt that government should not be doing the work—if it built the whole line, the result would be bankruptcy and confederation on Canada's terms. It was far better to subsidize a private company, the formula used in the 1881 Blackman contract. He also stressed the absence of a settlement scheme, which he thought to be of central importance. The interior's fertile and mineral-rich areas had to be settled—that was, surely, the object of the exercise—and the result would be traffic for the railway.[48]

Predictably enough, the government majority endorsed Winter's proposals and the survey and railway work went ahead. It was a remarkable shift for a party that, four or five years earlier, had severely criticized railway building and denounced the Whiteway agenda. There can be little doubt that the change was largely due to the severe decline in fish exports during the 1880s—especially after 1887, when exports fell by 22 per cent (and remained low until the end of the 1890s). This placed a severe strain on the colonial economy and its banking institutions, leaving the government little option but to create work.[49]

THE 1889 ELECTION

Once the session was over, politicians prepared for the general election scheduled for November 6. There was little difference between the two parties running candidates. Both pledged "no confederation," railway building, local government reform, and increased expenditure on education. Whiteway added an undertaking to modify the Bait Act to promote a bait trade that could be of value to fishermen.*

This was, however, the first general election to use the secret ballot and there was a significantly expanded (male) electorate. The government party, so it seems, took little account of these changes and decided to stand on its record, which was by no means negligible. It expected that the usual pattern of pressure and patronage, assisted by the work available on the Hall's Bay railway and in St. John's, would deliver the votes and a majority. The approach of its opponents was very different. How far Bond was involved in election planning is not known, but there can be little doubt that he was influential.

First, the Whiteway party appropriated the "Liberal" name. After the retirements of Ambrose Shea and Robert Kent, the old Liberal Party—with roots going back to the early days of representative government—had become leaderless and divided. Not all the remaining Liberals joined the Whitewayites, but the name was available and potent—and it could now be made non-denominational (having been previously associated with Roman Catholics). Second, the party adopted a populist stance that a Reform newspaper thought "socialistic and communistic."[50] Party slogans summed up the approach: "Rally Around the Friend of the Workingman and the Apostle of Progress"; "Vote for Whiteway and $1.25 per Day"; "No More Starvation Wages"; "No More Emigration."[51] This approach was combined with attacks on "fish-flake insolence" and the mercantile system in general, which had some bite as the price of fish—particularly for Labrador cure—slipped.

The election result surprised everyone—it was a landslide for the Whiteway Liberals. The Reform Party salvaged only five seats† and all the members of the Executive were defeated. Thorburn came last in the poll in Trinity Bay, where Whiteway, Bond—who had abandoned Fortune

* Whiteway's manifesto appeared in the *Evening Telegram* on June 22, 1889. He then went to London, returning in late August. Thorburn's manifesto was published in the *Evening Mercury* on July 24, 1889.

† Morine was elected as a member for Bonavista

Bay—and a local candidate won with large majorities.* Overall, the Whiteway party took twenty-eight seats, and there were three independents.[52] Commentators put the results down to the impact of the secret ballot, the power of Whiteway's promises, and the Reform government's flirtation with confederation. There was some justifiable shaking of heads. The *Newfoundland Colonist* pointed out that the majority contained many inexperienced and "unknown" men, adding that "this looks more like the wave of a social revolution than a mere political change."[53] The *Evening Mercury* was more positive. Whiteway had

> a splendid opportunity . . . for the exercise of his statesmanship. . . . He has awakened great expectations. . . . [The electors] expect him to introduce a new era of happiness and prosperity—to banish poverty—in fact, to make all things new. . . . It is a heavy contract. We sincerely hope that Sir William may be able to carry it through. If he does, Newfoundland shall raise a statue to his memory as the greatest benefactor of the country.[54]

As for Bond, he had established his position as an important and influential player. A colonial nationalist who was primarily anti-confederate, he supported railway building, had great faith in the country's resource potential, and had supported progressive political reforms such as the secret ballot and manhood suffrage. He also supported—with great caution—non-sectarian education. He was a hard-liner on French Treaty Shore issues, ambivalent about the effectiveness of the Bait Act, and convinced that Newfoundland should have its own, separate reciprocity treaty with the USA. It has been remarked that, "for Bond, somewhat paradoxically, nationalism and reciprocity went hand in hand."[55] The quest for a treaty with the Americans was to become so dominant in Bond's future political career that it is worth pausing to ask why he pursued this goal so single-mindedly.

---

* Kenneth Kerr sees this as a very significant victory for the "new economy" over the old (Kerr, "Social Analysis," 92).

Newfoundland's trade with the United States was relatively small and imbalanced. The US took only about 9 per cent of the colony's exports while supplying about 26 per cent of its imports. Yet many St. John's businessmen saw the American market as "a sort of El Dorado," to quote R.A. MacKay.[56] Yet, given American protectionism and the political influence of the New England fishing industry, improving access was problematic. Bond and his allies must have hoped, however, that the prospect of a separate trade treaty without Canadian encumbrances would attract American administrations (he was right)—and there was also the alluring possibility of American investment in Newfoundland industries. Diversification into mining, forestry, and other industries would demand external investment and, from Bond's perspective, it was better to have American involvement than Canadian, since the latter might, ultimately, lead to confederation. Such investment would also strengthen the colony's independence. Almost certainly influenced by Ambrose Shea, Bond was attracted by the prospect of a closer trade association with the continental economic superpower.

THE AVALON INTERIOR

It was during the 1880s that Bond began his long association with the interior of the Avalon Peninsula, a tangible demonstration of his faith in the colony's economic potential. Early in 1884 he went into partnership with Alexander M. Mackay, the Newfoundland superintendent of the Anglo-American Telegraph Company and, at the time, a Whiteway supporter.[57] They purchased eight square miles of land from the Newfoundland Railway Company; when surveyed, it was named the "District of Avalon Township." At the time, the railway had just reached Harbour Grace Junction, where a branch line to communities on the north shore of Conception Bay began. Two years later, Bond and Mackay formed the Townships Timber and Land Company; their original holding was transferred to it in 1887. By that time, the company had bought another sixteen square miles from the Railway Company, and had obtained (from the government) timber rights over an additional twenty-three square miles. Bond was the company's president and the other directors were, originally,

Whitbourne ca. 1900, by which time a small industrial centre had grown up in the area once known as Harbour Grace Junction. (PANL, VA 19-61)

Mackay, Whiteway, Moses Monroe,[58] and William J.S. Donnelly.[59] The company's purpose was to establish a township, set up a lumber business, and sell land to settlers.*

A township began to grow up at Harbour Grace Junction, not far from the Reform government's agricultural settlement at Dildo Pond (renamed Blaketown, after the governor, in 1888), which Bond had trenchantly criticized in the Assembly. Bond had a "hunting lodge" there, which in time became a substantial dwelling house with elegant grounds that he named "The Grange." Neither settlement was represented in the legislature. In 1889, probably prompted by a petition from the Junction asking for money to build a road,[60] Bond introduced uncontroversial legislation to rename Harbour Grace Junction after Sir Richard Whitbourne

* "Prospectus . . . ," November 26, 1886 (ASC, Whiteway Collection 2.01.001; RBP 2.07.003). Interestingly, all the original directors except Bond and Whiteway were supporters of the Thorburn government (Rowe, *Bond*, 44).

(1561–1635)—"He was the first to say a good word for [Newfoundland] and to bring the possibilities of the country before the world"—and to include both it and Blaketown in the Trinity Bay electoral district. This enabled these places, which had a combined population of about 440, to receive road and school grants in the usual way.*

Bond wanted to show that it was possible to live and prosper in Newfoundland's interior. "This Island was intended for something more than a mere fishing station," he told the Assembly in 1884. People should "rest assured that the balances of this country's future are in the interior. There lie wrapped up in the folds of an eventful futurity the influences which will most principally affect our interests as a colony."[61] Whitbourne was intended to demonstrate the truth of his convictions.

NOTES

1 Korneski, *Conflicted Colony*, 90–91.

2 *Evening Telegram*, December 28, 1885; M. Harvey to Whiteway, January 1, 1886 (RBP 3.05.004); Minute by Herbert, January 1, 1886 (CO 194/208, 375). There is further correspondence on this matter in CO 537/120.

3 Stanley to Shea, February 2, 1886 (CO 194/209, 22).; Stanley to Carter, tgm., February 5, 1886 (CO 537/120, 125).

4 "Speech of Sir Ambrose Shea at the Star of the Sea Hall, February 26, 1886" (ASC, Whiteway Collection 8.01.001).

5 Scott in Assembly, March 8, 1886 (*Evening Mercury*, March 10, 1886).

6 Derby to Glover, June 12, 1884 (*JHA* 1886, Appendix, 550–68) and Thompson, *French Shore*, Chapter 3.

7 La Morandière, *Histoire de la Pêche*, 1115, and Loture, *History of the Great Fishery*, 131.

8 Assembly debate, March 12, 1886 (*Evening Mercury*, March 18, 1886).

9 *Evening Telegram*, March 12, 1886 (*JHA* 1886, 50–52).

10 Bond in Assembly, March 22, 1886 (*Evening Mercury*, March 29, 1886; *Evening Telegram*, April 1, 1886).

11 *Evening Mercury*, April 22, 1886.

---

* Bond in Assembly, April 29, 1889 (*Evening Mercury*, May 6, 1889). Bond said he had taken a "census" himself (Cell, "Whitbourne, Sir Richard," *DCB* 1:668–69).

12 Assembly debate, April 16, 1886 (*Evening Mercury*, April 22, 1886, as per cutting in RBP 3.05.005).
13 Assembly debate, March 11, 1886 (*Evening Mercury*, March 13, 1886). See also Bond in Assembly, March 2, 1887 (*Evening Telegram*, March 9, 1887).
14 Morine in Assembly, March 2, 1887 (*Evening Mercury*, March 4, 1887).
15 Loyal Orange Association, Special Session held in the Orange Hall, Carbonear, August 31, 1886, and in Victoria Hall, St. John's, commencing September 7, 1886 (Loyal Orange Association, St. John's, n.d., in RBP 3.05.001).
16 *JHA* 1887, 9–26.
17 *Evening Mercury*, February 19 and 22, 1887.
18 Amendment to the Address in Reply, March 4, 1887 (*JHA* 1887, 36).
19 *Evening Telegram*, February 22, 1887.
20 Assembly debate, February 22, 1887 (*Evening Mercury*, February 25, 1887, and *ENL* 3:655).
21 See, for example, Bond in Assembly, February 22 and 28, 1887 (*Evening Mercury*, February 24 and March 1 and 2, 1887).
22 Bond in Assembly, March 10 (*Evening Mercury*, March 12, 1887; *Evening Telegram*, March 11 and 16, 1887).
23 Winter in Assembly, March 14 (*Evening Mercury*, March 16 and 19, 1887) and *JHA* 1887, 157.
24 Morine in Assembly debate, March 23 (*Evening Mercury*, March 26, 1887).
25 Assembly debate, March 24 (*Evening Mercury*, March 26 and 30, April 1, 1887).
26 *Evening Telegram*, April 2 and 25, 1887.
27 *JHA* 1887, 164.
28 Bond and Morine to Whiteway, July 25, 1887 (RBP 3.06.004).
29 *Newfoundland Colonist*, September 22, 1887; *Evening Telegram*, September 21, 1887.
30 Tansill, *Foreign Policy*, 263, 265–67.
31 "Ellesmere" to *Evening Telegram*, September 20, 1888; "J.B." to Bond, October 27, 1888 (RBP 30.07.002). Much of what follows is based on Hiller, "A History," 155ff.
32 Morine, letters to the *Evening Mercury*, October 18 and November 22, 1888. The *Evening Mercury* supported the Thorburn government.
33 *Evening Mercury*, March 9, 1888.
34 Bond in Assembly, April 9, 1888 (*Evening Mercury*, April 12 and 13, 1888).

35 Morine, letter to *Evening Mercury*, November 22, 1888.
36 Bond, letter to the *Evening Telegram*, November 22, 1888.
37 Morine, letter to the *Evening Mercury*, November 16, 1888. See also *Evening Mercury*, September 14, October 10 and 31, and November 1, 16, and 17, 1888.
38 *Evening Mercury*, September 12, 1888.
39 *ENL* 3:119–20.
40 Letter from "Observer," *Evening Mercury*, February 21, 1889.
41 *Evening Mercury*, February 25, 1889.
42 *Evening Mercury*, April 16, 1889, and Assembly debate, April 15, 1889 (*Evening Mercury*, April 24 and 25, 1889).
43 *Evening Mercury*, May 16, 18, 21, and 25, 1889.
44 See Bond's speech on March 21, reported in the *Evening Mercury*, April 1, 1889.
45 Bond in Assembly, February 27, 1889 (*Evening Mercury,* March 11, 1889). Also see Hiller, "A History," 161–70.
46 *JHA* 1889, 224–49 (May 31 and June 1, 1889). The debate was not published.
47 Reported in the *Evening Mercury*, May 14, 1889.
48 Bond in Assembly, May 9 and 15, 1889 (*Evening Mercury*, May 16 and June 3, 1889).
49 Chu, "Too Big to Fail?," 168, 173.
50 *Evening Mercury*, October 1, 1889, and *Newfoundland Colonist*, October 8, 1889.
51 *Evening Telegram*, August 28, 1889, and other dates.
52 *ENL* 1:696–97.
53 *Newfoundland Colonist*, November 12, 1889.
54 *Evening Mercury*, November 12, 1889.
55 Reeves, "Aping the 'American Type'," 45.
56 MacKay and Saunders, "Economy of Newfoundland" in MacKay, ed., *Newfoundland*, 146, and Appendix, Tables 6 and 13.
57 Baker, "Mackay, Alexander McLellan" *DCB* 13:651–53 and *ENL* 3:413.
58 Baker, "Monroe, Moses" *DCB* 13:451–54 and *ENL* 3:599.
59 *ENL* 1:635.
60 Assembly debate April 4, 1889 (*Evening Mercury,* April 10, 1889).
61 Bond in Assembly, February 14, 1884 (*Evening Mercury*, February 15, 1884).

CHAPTER FOUR

In Government: Fisheries and External Affairs, 1889–1893

The installation of the new Whiteway government was messy and confused. Though the Reform Party had been trounced at the polls, it decided to stay on until the end of the year. This was an unusual situation, and the referee was Sir Terence O'Brien, the colony's new governor.

Then 58, O'Brien had arrived the previous January. He was to stay on in Newfoundland for a remarkably long time, in what turned out to be his last posting.[1] He had served in the Indian Army, later in Mauritius, and also as governor of Heligoland. His appointment to Newfoundland was unfortunate, since he was never comfortable with the conventions and requirements of responsible government. After the 1889 election, he insisted that the Reformers should make no unnecessary appointments or expenditures, since none of its ministers had seats in the legislature.[2] Whether this was constitutionally correct was uncertain. O'Brien seems never to have appreciated that governors were generally not criticized for taking ministerial advice, nor that rejecting miniserial advice could lead to involvement in local politics—from which governors were supposed to remain detached.[3]

Governor Sir Terence O'Brien (1830–1903), ca. 1892. (PANL, A 19-73)

Even so, affairs might have run relatively smoothly had not gangs of men, taking Whiteway's election promises at face value, descended on St. John's looking for work. The bewildered unemployed were shunted between a resentful Thorburn, an annoyed and embarrassed Whiteway, and a non-plussed O'Brien. Whiteway pressured the lame-duck government to provide employment on public works; eventually it agreed to increase the workforce on the Hall's Bay railway. Then O'Brien, wanting to ensure that jobs were not allotted on a partisan basis, insisted that the Whiteway should be allowed a representative on the railway commission that was managing the project. Thorburn quite justifiably protested, to no avail. Party feeling, wrote the governor, was "being raised to a pitch, stretched to a length, and lowered to a depth, in language and tone, as I would scarcely believe possible."[4] Finally, and with ill grace, the Thorburn government resigned on December 16.[5]

Augustus W. Harvey (1839–1903), the voice of Water Street in Liberal administrations after 1889, undated. (PANL, VA 19-93)

Whiteway now became premier and attorney general. He was the only member of the new administration who had held executive office before. Bond was appointed colonial secretary, a senior and influential post. In essence, he was the minister responsible for internal affairs.* Other members of the Executive included Edward Morris and A.W. Harvey, a Member of the Legislative Council and very much a Water Street figure, both without portfolio.[6] As for the Reformers, they re-branded themselves as the "Patriotic Association," wound up the *Evening Mercury* and launched a new paper, the *Evening*

* Rev. Walter Smith thought that, next to the premiership, colonial secretary was "the most exalted and responsible position in the colony." He was glad it was held by "a fellow countryman." (Smith to Bond, December 18, 1889, RBP 3.08.010). It has been called "a catchall department" (*ENL* 3:584).

Herald, which was initially edited by Morine, who had no difficulty changing political sides. The paper's purpose was "to hold up to public execration the misdeeds of which the Whiteway Administration will undoubtedly be guilty."[7] The new government's opponents were not going away to lick their wounds.

The legislature met for the first time on March 6, 1890. The opposition, led by Morine and Morison, mounted a spirited attack on the government, and Morine (not surprisingly) took particular aim at Bond. The session had hardly begun when yet another crisis over the French Treaty Shore put the government on the defensive and handed the opposition a gift.

THE LOBSTER MODUS VIVENDI

Provoked by the Bait Act and the failure of the 1885 draft agreement, the French had become more aggressive in asserting their assumed rights on the Treaty Shore. Particularly contentious at this juncture was the claim that French operators could catch, process, and can lobsters. Maritimers had launched the lobster industry on the west coast during the 1870s; by 1888 at least thirty-three "factories" (canneries) operated there.[8] The French entered the business in a smaller way in 1883, an action that precipitated a serious controversy. The Newfoundland position was that the French had a concurrent right to take codfish only—not lobsters, which were crustaceans—and that they most certainly did not have the right to establish factories. The French argued that they could indeed take lobsters—or anything else in the sea, for that matter—and that British factories were illegal under the treaties because they were "fixed establishments" and violated the exclusive French right of fishery.

The issue came to a head in 1888, when two Newfoundlanders began building a lobster factory at Hauling Point, White Bay. A French naval officer stopped them, stating that his government had given the site to a French company. A British officer then ordered the men to remove their property and the French began constructing their own building.[9] This caused huge local indignation, and in 1889 the legislature protested to the British government. But there was uncertainty in London about whether or not the French lobster fishery was legal, and arbitration was thought inevitable. After his

A lobster factory at Brig Bay, on the Northern Peninsula, undated. (Courtesy of Kurt Korneski)

election victory, Whiteway was asked to go to London for discussions on the issue, but he refused to leave his inexperienced colleagues until the first legislative session was over. The British decided that postponement meant a modus vivendi, which stipulated that the status quo as of July 1, 1889, would be maintained and disputes settled by naval officers. The Whiteway government reiterated the protest concerning the French right to lobsters, but agreed to accept the modus if its effective date was changed to January 1, 1890. That would allow several factories opened late in 1889 to continue operations. The French would not go this far: they countered that new establishments could be allowed only if the respective naval commanders agreed, on a factory-for-factory basis. Fearing that further consultations would lengthen negotiations beyond the expected life of the existing French government, the British signed the revised modus on March 11, 1890.*

---

* Hiller, "History," 195–97. In private correspondence, Lord Salisbury (the British prime minister) referred to "this grotesque lobster difficulty. To think that we should be still be paying, in hopeless weary negotiations, the penalty of Bolingbroke's abortive intrigues a hundred and eighty years ago. Oh! Why was Newfoundland created? Or why have the fish not the good sense to frequent a warmer place?" (Salisbury to Knutsford, private, December 10, 1889, Salisbury papers, D 32/80). The lobster dispute is covered in Korneski, *Conflicted Colony*, 131–58.

This was an unexpected shock, and it made the colonial government vulnerable to accusations that it had not been sufficiently vigilant. Strong protests followed, asserting that to acknowledge France's concurrent right to lobsters, even temporarily, would prejudice future negotiations, and that to allow the French an equal number of factories was out of all proportion to their "usufruct" on the Shore. Further objections related to infringements on Newfoundland's territorial integrity were also raised.[10] The Assembly discussed the revised modus in closed session and passed resolutions condemning it as "most objectionable." Opposition members tried to insert much stronger wording, signalling that they would play the patriotic card and embarrass the government as much as possible.[11] No wonder that Whiteway lamented that, for the first time, the French Shore question had become a party issue.[12] A Joint Select Committee (which included Bond) drafted yet another address to the Crown, which was passed at the end of the session.[13] Bond's view of the French issue was fuelled by local nationalism and by the prevailing interpretation of Newfoundland history that would find expression in the works of Moses Harvey and Daniel Prowse. This interpretation completely rejected the French argument that France had once owned the island of Newfoundland and that its rights on the French Shore were exclusive— because in 1713, under

Bonne Bay on Newfoundland's west coast in the 1880s. (LAC, Collections Canada, Mikan 3249455)

the Treaty of Utrecht, France had ceded only its land on the island to Britain, leaving the fishery as part of its "ancient sovereignty." Bond would have none of this. "What a preposterous assertion! France never had and I trust never will have any sovereignty over this island." English sovereignty, he argued, dated to the voyage of "the old Bristol navigator John Cabot" in 1497, and it was formally entrenched by Sir Humphrey Gilbert in 1583. The French were only tolerated intruders. Further, the 1713 Treaty had granted only a concurrent right of fishery to France in what was clearly British territory. The Treaty of Paris (1814) represented "the last favourable opportunity that England had of doing justice to the people of this ancient and loyal Colony. The opportunity was allowed to pass, the interests of the people of this Colony were neglected, their complaints were unheard and for the 26 years following the British Gvt even omitted to send a man of war to protect the rights and interests of its subjects." In short, Newfoundland had always been English or British and the French claims were exaggerated nonsense.* This version of events now seems tendentious and inaccurate, but it served to bolster both resistance to France and local nationalism. It also demonstrated a certain ambivalence in the imperial relationship—pride in the empire and having British heritage, but resentment at perceived imperial neglect. The difficult French Shore issue would soon become a major fault line between Bond and Whiteway who, being English-born, was always more amenable to compromise—and who was, in some respects, more realistic.

Meanwhile, the Patriotic Association was doing its best to stir up "great and unreasonable excitement"† and francophobe patriotism. A meeting at the Athenaeum in St. John's attracted about a thousand people,

---

* This summary is based on an incomplete handwritten speech that is clearly from this period (RBP 7.13.001).

† O'Brien thought (probably mistakenly) that many Catholic clergy led their flocks to believe that England was an oppressor and sympathetic to American interests (O'Brien to Knutsford, secret, March 28, 1890, in CO 194/214, 255–65). For Bishop Power's involvement, see *Evening Telegram*, March 20 and 27, 1890; *Newfoundland Colonist*, March 21, 1890; "Newfoundland Notes" in (London) *Canadian Gazette*, 15:368 (April 24, 1890), 79.

and it was followed by a large and noisy meeting in Bannerman Park on March 26 (some merchants even giving their employees a holiday so they could attend). Whiteway later referred to "the 'hullobaloo' [*sic*] in Bannerman Park, the march of the great anti-French party through the town with drums and fifes and tin-kettles and cries of 'Down with the French,' 'The French must go,' and the like."[14] Members of the Executive pointedly stayed away. As Bond later said, "The French fishery claim is a matter that affects the interest of the whole people of this colony, and to make it a party question . . . is an injustice to the people and an unpatriotic course to pursue."[15] Patriotic Association resolutions authorized a committee to organize the defence of the colony's rights, to draft a memorial to Parliament, and to send delegates to England and Canada.[16] A month later, Winter, Morine, and Patrick J. Scott left for London, and Morison and others for the mainland. Governor O'Brien reported that the delegates were "the emissaries of the defeated mercantile minority, the necessary funds being subscribed by that body."[17] He later forwarded a petition to the Crown with 12,000 signatures.[18]

The lobster affair was not the only controversial French-related issue with which the legislature had to deal. In 1888, the previous government had legislated the abolition of cod traps, a change that was to come into effect in the 1890 fishing season. This had been done, in part, to satisfy demands from the French, who refused to allow the use of traps on "their" shore—they often hauled up and sometimes destroyed traps set by Newfoundlanders. W.H. Whiteley,[19] a Liberal backbencher who ran a substantial fishing operation at Bonne Esperance on the Quebec North Shore (and who has been credited with inventing the cod trap), introduced a bill, supported by the government members, to repeal the act. Bond argued that its enforcement would cause considerable hardship and proposed that, in place of the legislation, a "local option law" and regulations on mesh size should be introduced.[20] Whiteway held that the government could not take away a means of making a living. If it did, it would have to support fishermen, which could not be afforded. In any event, the government had the right to legislate for the fisheries, as long as such legislation applied to all parties. It was not for the colony to introduce exemptions deriving from imperial treaties.[21] The Colonial Office insisted that clauses should be inserted excluding the French Shore. The government refused, the bill was reserved,[22] and the existing legislation was not enforced.

The other delicate issue was the Bait Act. Whiteway's position was that, although the legislation irritated the French, it had not damaged them in any material way—but it had impoverished Newfoundlanders.[23] This was not the view of the Commercial Society, which held the act had been "beneficial," a position represented within the government by A.W. Harvey.[24] A compromise was reached—or so Winter interpreted it.[25] Thomas Bennett,[26] the magistrate at Harbour Grace, was sent to the south coast to conduct a formal inquiry. While it was ongoing, the government prohibited supplying bait to St. Pierre. Foreign and Canadian vessels entering Newfoundland waters to purchase bait were allowed to do so under licence, but only after they posted a $1,000 bond. Without such a system, Bond explained, the Bait Act could not be effective, since supplies taken by Americans and Canadians often found their way to St. Pierre.[27] This change in policy did not require new legislation, and to an extent reflected the position adopted by Bond after the passage of the Bait Act in 1887. But there was a considerable amount of sniping about it in the House, and the Canadian government was furious.

When the 1890 session closed in early June, Whiteway and Harvey left for England, and Bond and George Emerson* set off for the French Shore.[28] The latter expedition may have been prompted, in part, by Bond's correspondence with the Reverend Michael F. Howley, at that time the Roman Catholic Vicar General of St. George's.† A Newfoundlander by birth and an energetic, outspoken, and mercurial figure, Howley took it upon himself to represent the interests of the west coast population. In April that year, he had written to congratulate Bond on his "firm and splendid stand," adding that "timidity has been our bane all thru on this

* A lawyer and later a judge, George Emerson was the Speaker at the time (*ENL* 1:775).

† *ENL* 2:1095, and Crosbie, "Howley, Michael Francis," *DCB* 14:512–14. Howley was the brother of the government's Geological Surveyor, James P. Howley. Michael Howley is discussed in Lambert, "This Sacred Feeling," 124–42.

F.S. Question."[29] On the lobster issue, he urged a fight and a local investigation: "I know of course that poor John Kent with Count Gobineau once came here, in '54, on such an expedition, but nothing came of it. There was too much champagne in it. . . . Do look to this like a dear good honest man. Save us! We trust in you. Poor Newfoundland. How she is strangled in her efforts for life."*

There was also the bait question to investigate. The French now saw St. George's Bay as an alternative source of bait, as Bond had predicted. On May 22, a French officer (in uniform and with a sword, it was noted) had landed to demand the removal of forty-odd herring nets set by locals. This was done—for approximately twenty-four hours, while the French caught what bait they could. Howley appears to have been behind a public meeting at Sandy Point on May 24, which resolved that residents should not have to pay Newfoundland taxes unless they were provided with adequate protection and given some compensation.[30] Although a resulting tax revolt was not widespread, some people did initially refuse to pay duty on goods arriving from Halifax.[31] Much of the upset (and some reports may well have been exaggerated) probably derived from the French taking their own herring rather than buying it. But the opposition jumped on the incident, and Morison and Michael Carty[32] (the local MHA) began taking evidence for compensation claims.[33]

On their trip, Bond and Emerson, accompanied by the governor's private secretary, visited harbours between La Scie and St. George's Bay, taking evidence at each place.[34] They heard about the herring incident†—the magistrate said that local people lost no more than 40 barrels and that the May 24 protest meeting at Sandy Point had not been well attended. More important, they heard about how the modus vivendi was working. The operator of a lobster factory at Port Saunders, for example, complained of French harassment abetted by the British navy. At St. George's

* Howley to Bond, May 9, 1890 (RBP 6.02.004). The Gobineau/Kent commission took place in 1859, not 1854. See Wilkshire, *A Gentleman in the Outports.*

† In 1891, Judge Pinsent carried out a full inquiry into claims filed by the fishermen in St. George's Bay (PANL, GN E/17, "Records and Report of the St. George's Bay Inquiry [1891]").

James Baird (1828–1915), the protagonist in the famous case of Baird vs. Walker., undated (PANL, VA 23-96)

Bay, they heard about the closure of a lobster factory at Fishell's Brook, one of the two that the French had wanted shut down.* The factory was owned by Edward Le Roux but mortgaged to James Baird, a St. John's businessman and a prominent member of the Patriotic Association.[35] The British Commodore, Sir Baldwin Walker, had ordered Le Roux to close, saying he would do his best to get him compensation. Le Roux had agreed—but Baird told him to keep operating until closed by force. On June 25, Walker landed three marines and closed the factory. Baird immediately dispatched Morison to gather evidence for an action against Walker. In mid-July, Baird filed a writ for trespass, claiming $5,000 in damages.[36] By this time it was generally known that the naval officers had no statutory authority to enforce either the treaties or the modus because the British Parliament, by mistake, had repealed the relevant act (28 Geo. III, c. 25). Thus another complication was added to the lobster imbroglio: the need for new enforcement legislation, which would have to be dealt with in London if it was not passed by the colonial legislature.

THE DELEGATES IN LONDON

Their investigation completed, Bond and Emerson went on to London. When Whiteway had arrived there some weeks earlier, he had found that not only had the unofficial "People's Delegates" met with some popular success, but that there was a widespread impression that Newfoundland was in a state of virtual insurrection.[37] The unofficial delegates were to some extent responsible for this, but lurid and inaccurate press reports

---

* The French ignored the other sixteen factories built since July 1889, in return for permission to build one new French factory. By the end of the season the French had six factories, the British had seventy-five (Walker to Watson, July 18, 1890, *JHA* 1891, Appendix, 570–72).

were equally to blame.[38] The British government viewed the delegates as extremists[39] and hoped to make some headway with the "official" representatives—after all, Whiteway had been reasonably flexible in the past. However, the Patriotic Association had put Whiteway's government on the defensive, and both Harvey and Bond were hardliners on French-related issues. The position now taken by the Newfoundland government was that a partial arbitration on the lobster question alone was undesirable. Instead, all matters in dispute should be arbitrated as a first step toward placing a value on French rights—that is, arbitration should be preliminary to French withdrawal. Further, Newfoundland would concede bait to the French only if they reduced or eliminated their bounties. (The British government thought bait concessions might be used as compensation for French withdrawal.[40]) In addition, the colony wanted the French to agree to a British consul at St. Pierre. After some discussion, the British ambassador in Paris was instructed to approach the French government with the Newfoundland proposals.[41] The reply was not encouraging: France would consider only a reversion to the failed convention of 1885 or arbitration on the lobster question alone.[42]

While in London, the Newfoundland government delegates raised two additional issues unrelated to the French Shore dispute. First, they asked the imperial government to guarantee a $10 million railway loan. Their argument was that Newfoundland's development had been held back by "past policies and present treaties," and this would be a way for Britain to make amends.[43] The British reaction was, not surprisingly, to link the request to the French problem. Whiteway was told that a guarantee would have to be part of a general settlement of the French fisheries question.[44] As T.V. Lister of the Foreign Office put it: "No assistance of this kind can in any case be given to the Colony, unless Her Majesty's Government receives the full concurrence and support of the Colonial Government . . . in whatever measures and negotiations may be found necessary to put the questions connected with the French rights of fishery on a more satisfactory footing."[45] The delegates thought this attitude showed "an absence of interest in the welfare and advancement of the Colony."[46] However, the financial atmosphere was unfavourable, given the inflammatory and exaggerated messages about the French Shore that were in circulation in London, as well as rising public debt and the problems associated with the Newfoundland Railway Company. The London and Westminster Bank, which took care of the colony's financial business in London, would not lend any more than £50,000. Much more was needed.

RECIPROCITY TALKS, 1890

The second issue the delegates wished to discuss was a separate reciprocity treaty with the United States. Since the expiry of the fishery clauses of the Treaty of Washington in 1885, Newfoundland had been party to a temporary agreement between Canada and the United States. For some time there had been discussion of Newfoundland negotiating its own treaty, rather than having to tag along with Canada, whose relations with the United States were difficult and strained. The Newfoundland government had raised the matter earlier in the year[47] and the delegates now restated their case: they wished to give American vessels the same bait privileges as Newfoundlanders; in return, the US would admit Newfoundland fish and other products duty free.[48]

Here there was finally some movement. The Colonial Office thought that permission to open talks would mitigate disappointment at the lack of progress on French fisheries issues (but did not want to consult Canada on a matter "in which, strictly speaking, Canada has no claim to interfere"[49]). The colonial secretary, Lord Knutsford, told the British prime minister, Lord Salisbury, that he did not want the delegates to return "absolutely empty handed"—Newfoundland should be allowed "to make a separate and independent Treaty as to fishery with the United States.... This would go far to compensate them for the failure of arrangements with the French. I do not see that Canada has any ground for interfering in such a question."* As one official put it, the proposal was for "a simple arrangement not complicated by the numerous questions between

* Knutsford to Salisbury, August 24, 1890 (Salisbury papers, class E.305). He added, "Sir W. Whiteway is the most loyal man, next to Sir [R.] J. Pinsent, in Newfoundland."

Canada and America which increase the difficulty of any agreement between them—and in this case Nfdland [*sic*] has something definite to offer which Canada does not possess."[50] The Foreign Office agreed and Bond set off for the United States on September 10, authorized "to communicate . . . the views of the Colonial Government" to Sir Julian Pauncefote, the British minister in Washington.[51] In a later speech,[52] he described his understanding of his role—that he had official recognition from both the British and Newfoundland governments. Pauncefote, however, later wrote that Bond "seemed to me very quiet and reasonable when here and never pretended to me for a moment that he had any authority to negotiate with Mr. Blaine."[53]

Bond arrived in Washington to find that Pauncefote was at his summer residence and did not intend to return immediately, so he submitted a lengthy statement.[54] Pauncefote arranged for him to meet the American secretary of state, James G. Blaine, on October 7. Bond was assured that any proposals he submitted would receive Blaine's "most careful attention." Bond then went on to promote his cause in New York, Boston, and elsewhere in New England. He also visited Pauncefote, who put the Newfoundland proposals in the shape of a draft convention. It provided American ships with free access to purchase bait in exchange for duty-free entry into the US of Newfoundland fish, fish oil, and crude minerals. After amendments suggested by Bond, Pauncefote submitted the draft convention to Blaine on October 18.[55] Bond then made his way back to St. John's, pausing to make his case once more to businessmen in New York, Boston, Gloucester, and Cape Ann.[56] Whiteway and Harvey had still not returned from London; they did not arrive in St. John's until late November, an absence of almost five months.

The Canadian government was well aware of what was going on. Newspapers reported Bond's movements and Morine (now studying law in Halifax) had sent an urgent telegram to Sir Charles Tupper.[57] Canada was already upset that the Bait Act was being applied to Canadian vessels, despite assurances to the contrary apparently given by Thorburn and Shea in 1887. And it reacted to Newfoundland's American reciprocity initiative with implacable hostility, seeing the Harrison administration in

Washington as anti-Canadian and strongly resenting the highly protectionist McKinley tariff (1890). Moreover, reciprocity was a central issue in Canadian politics, and the Conservative government was strongly opposed to commercial union or unrestricted reciprocity. Canada also feared discontent in the Maritimes, especially in Nova Scotia, where Premier W.S. Fielding, who had won the 1886 provincial election on a separatist platform, strongly favoured reciprocity. Newfoundland could not be allowed to achieve outside confederation what the Maritime provinces could not achieve within it. Lord Stanley, Canada's governor general, wrote that

> Blaine is playing a deep game with us, in which your Newfoundland negotiations have accidentally helped him. . . . We felt here that if you departed from the traditional policy of dealing on one footing with all North American Colonies, there would be great danger that they would be tempted to break off from Confederation under the inducements possible under the McKinley Bill.[58]

As the result of strenuous Canadian protests, Pauncefote was instructed to proceed slowly with the Newfoundland convention and ascertain whether Canada could be included.[59] Blaine said he would only deal with Canada on a separate and wider basis. Pauncefote was told that the two conventions should proceed *pari passu* but, given Canadian protests, he was eventually instructed to suspend negotiations altogether.[60] The affair might have ended at this point, had not the Colonial Office passed on a message to Bond from Blaine, asking him to return to Washington to supply statistical information.[61]

Bond was enroute back to the United States when the decision was made to suspend negotiations. At a meeting with Pauncefote on November 28, Bond was told that Canada was "much annoyed" and would probably try to stop ratification. Moreover, Pauncefote had not been empowered to conclude a convention—all he could do was receive Newfoundland's proposal and hear what Blaine had to say. Bond recorded his reaction in his diary: "Then, I replied, my Government has been deceived by the Colonial Office."[62] The next day, Bond and Pauncefote met with Blaine. Pauncefote later suggested that Canada should also make a proposal, but Bond forcefully responded that Canada should not be mixed up in the Newfoundland negotiation—and in any case, this would annoy Blaine.

Having had no news of Blaine's response to the November 29 meeting, Bond again called on Pauncefote (December 11), who told him there was nothing to be done. Bond noted that Pauncefote had probably been told "not to exert himself concerning this matter" and that "I am being played false." By this time, in fact, the Newfoundland government had been told that no convention could be concluded until Canadian interests had been fully considered.[63] Pauncefote asked Blaine whether Bond needed to stay longer. In response, Blaine asked Bond to call on the morning of December 15. He did so without Pauncefote, who assumed the meeting would be a formality.* The following excerpts are from Bond's account of what transpired:

> I regret he [Blaine] said to learn that you are going to leave here so soon. Do you feel safe in so doing? I asked what he meant. Well he said you appeared anxious . . . to bring about a treaty . . . , if you are still of the same mind I cannot understand your leaving here just now. You told me that you are not in sympathy with the Dominion of Canada and that you do not desire the treaty to be considered as appealing to Canada and I gave you my candid opinion relative thereto. . . . To be plain, can you trust Sir Julian Pauncefote to carry out your views? Are you aware that he is working in the interest of reciprocity for Canada? This is private, remember. I . . . replied that from certain things Sir Julian had said I was afraid that the Colony would be sacrificed to Canadian interests. Then he said you do not desire your

* In a speech on March 6, 1891 (*Evening Telegram*, March 13, 1891), Bond stated that it was he who arranged the meeting with Blaine (RBP 7.04.001).

> proposal to be considered in relation to Canada. Certainly not I replied. I have been anxious to conclude an arrangement with you and still am anxious before leaving here.

Bond then reviewed the "confederation plot" of 1887–88, the defeat of confederate sympathizers in the 1889 election, and

> our statement to the Colonial Office that we desired to conduct our affairs apart from Canada, of the struggle that is now being made for independence and the fact that if a treaty with this country [the US] was accomplished the question of Confederation would be dead. I produced a telegram from London to the *Montreal Star* stating that Sir Charles Tupper was watching these negotiations and [*illegible*] to show that Sir Charles' Agent Morine was the author of all the adverse [*criticisms?*] that had appeared in American papers. At the conclusion of my remarks he said "My God if you are sure that England will ratify a treaty entered into by your Colony, and will be reasonable in conceding certain things that I shall have to ask for, otherwise I cannot pass a treaty through Congress, in one hour from now we can fix the whole business. He hereupon locked the door and we proceeded to discuss the Draft Convention.

The discussion went on until 6 p.m. and for much of the next day. They finally concluded a draft convention, which Blaine said he would sign. Bond took a copy to Pauncefote, explaining that

> as the agreement had been arrived at while he (Sir Julian) was not present that I had asked Mr. Blaine that the approved Draft might be discussed with him (Sir Julian) before official notice was taken of it. . . . I then by permission proceeded to read it. Sir Julian exhibited much excitement and annoyance and . . . said "I cannot do anything in this

> matter, in fact I cannot recognize these negotiations as official in any way."

A tense exchange followed. Bond angrily asked whether it was possible that "all my trouble is in vain" and whether the British government was going to "further trifle with the feelings of an outraged people." Pauncefote insisted that he "must not know anything about this interview of yours or this document and if Mr. Blaine sends me this as an amendment upon the Draft that I sent to him I will telegraph it home. That is all that I can do." Pauncefote went on: "I am exceedingly sorry for you in this matter for I know how you have laboured and had it not been for your efforts nothing certainly would have been arrived at for I had no authority to do anything. To tell you the truth I never expected the matter would come to anything." Bond replied: "Sir Julian, matters are much worse than I had any thought of. The Imperial Gvt. has willfully been misleading my Gvt. from first to last." Bond then left for Halifax, travelling via Boston. He telegraphed Whiteway, noting that "Blaine has accepted my draft. Fish and copper free. . . . To my dismay Pauncefote refused to sign Treaty. . . . I have had to contend against English scheming and Canadian rascality all through but I have conquered thank God unless England vetoes my work."*

The official position in London was that the convention was temporarily suspended while Canada explored whether it, too, could negotiate a reciprocity agreement. This was hardly likely and constituted an effective veto, which placed Newfoundland at loggerheads with both the imperial

* Pauncefote's official account of these events, and the text of the draft convention, can be found in Pauncefote to Salisbury, December 26, 1890 (*JHA* 1891, Appendix, 535–39). On Blaine's motivation, see Hiller, "A History." 215–17. Pauncefote thought that the draft treaty would have been thrown out by Congress (Pauncefote to Salisbury, private, February 6, 1891, Salisbury papers, A 78, 15).

and Canadian governments.* Relations between all three were further inflamed by the Bait Act, the lobster question, and the need to provide naval officers with statutory power to enforce the treaties and the modus, given the likely outcome of the Baird vs. Walker case. Not inclined to be co-operative, the Whiteway government refused to pass such legislation locally,[64] which made imperial action probable. "Where are we then," wrote Bond to Whiteway, "and whither tending?"†

Bond was hurt, outraged, and embarrassed by the failure of the reciprocity endeavour. He blamed both the British and Canadian governments for it, and he apparently managed to persuade his colleagues of the justice of his cause—even Whiteway, who had never been especially keen on reciprocity, believing that a deal with France was more important. In summary, and at the risk of oversimplification, two narratives emerged about what had happened in Washington. Bond's version, adopted by the Newfoundland government, was that he had possessed official status during his visits, that there was nothing irregular about his talks with Blaine, and that the British government had betrayed the colony first by refusing to accept the December draft convention and then, at the insistence of the Canadian government, by refusing to ratify a second draft, which Blaine transmitted in January 1891. The British version was that Bond had not possessed official status and that all he was supposed to do on his first trip to Washington was submit proposals to Pauncefote and Blaine and, on his second trip, supply the information that Blaine had requested. He held no power to negotiate or conclude a convention. As for its failure to ratify what had been negotiated,

* Knutsford was sympathetic to Newfoundland on the reciprocity issue and thought Canada had adopted a "dog in the manger policy." Salisbury overruled him: "It is evident that we cannot sign the Convention about Nfland [*sic*] until we have satisfied Canada." Salisbury seems to have been primarily concerned with opinion in the British Parliament (Knutsford to Salisbury, December 27, 1890, and Memorandum by Salisbury, December 1890, Salisbury papers, E 323, and typed volume).

† Bond to Whiteway, June 23, 1891 (RBP 8.03.011). Bond was quoting the title of an 1886 publication by Moses Harvey.

the British government had to take into account the reactions of other members of the Empire, as well as the convention's possible impact on British interests. British officials would have agreed with the *Evening Herald* and the opposition that Bond had misled both his colleagues and the legislature.

It was perhaps unfortunate that, at this time, there existed no definitive statement of the limits on the colonial treaty-making power. It was not until 1895 that Lord Ripon officially laid down the principle that no colony could accept concessions from a foreign power that were hostile to other parts of the Empire, and that concessions made by one colony had to apply to other British states and to those entitled to "most favoured nation" treatment.[65] Nevertheless, Knutsford thought that his consent to Bond's "informal and unofficial" visit to Washington had been made under well-recognized conditions.[66] As he said in the House of Lords:

> There is no objection in principle to a separate negotiation between a foreign power and an individual Colony with the sanction of Her Majesty's Government. . . . But the mere fact of consent being given . . . is always subject to a well understood and well recognized principle . . . that when the draft terms have been settled . . . , then Her Majesty's Government must consider those terms, and see how far they affect other interests. . . . That is to say, the leave to negotiate does not carry with it an obligation or an engagement to sanction the arrangement when made.[67]

Unable to persuade the imperial government to change its decision, the Newfoundland government decided to retaliate by refusing bait licences to Canadian vessels. This was done ostensibly on the grounds that Canadian vessels had been supplying the French with bait, but it was really an attempt to force the Canadian government to withdraw its objections to the convention[68]—a faint hope. The Canadians exploded into activity, urging the British government to force the Newfoundland government to honour its promises and withdraw the restrictions, or to repeal the Bait

Act by imperial legislation.[69] At the same time, Senator G.W. Howlan of Prince Edward Island was sent to St. John's to discuss outstanding problems and the possibility of confederation.[70]

Howlan arrived to find that Whiteway and other leading politicians were about to sail for England on French Shore business, so he joined them on the voyage. Perhaps because Bond was absent and Morine present, their shipboard talks appear to have been amicable. Howlan was hopeful about the prospects for confederation in his reports back to Ottawa.[71] But as Whiteway—who referred to Howlan as "a smart old man . . . [who] appeared very enthusiastic"[72]—wrote to Sir John A. Macdonald, existing disputes would have to be settled and bitterness allowed to subside before the question could proceed, and the voyage did little to achieve those ends.[73]

THE IMPERIAL ENFORCEMENT BILL

The party that Howlan had joined was charged with trying to prevent the passage of imperial legislation to provide naval officers with the necessary statutory authority to enforce the French treaties. Given the colony's unwillingness to pass such legislation locally, the British government had concluded that there was no other alternative than doing it in Parliament—treaties with France had to be enforced or there might be serious trouble on the French Shore. Lord Salisbury genuinely feared that British and French naval squadrons might clash, which could have serious ramifications at a time when Anglo-French relations were under strain. "It is needless to say that all the risks of war are with us," he told the cabinet.[74] Moreover, the Newfoundland Supreme Court had found in favour of James Baird in his case against Commodore Walker, Chief Justice Carter ruling that there could be no act of state to justify the trespass.*

On March 19, 1891, Knutsford had introduced a bill in the House of

* O'Brien to Knutsford, tgm., March 18, 1891 (CO 194/18, 262). The British government had hoped for a compromise out-of-court settlement engineered by Whiteway.

Lords that simply revived previous enforcementu legislation (1824).* The news reached Newfoundland the same day. The Assembly formed a Select Committee (which included Bond) to meet with a similar committee from the Legislative Council. Together they crafted a joint resolution asking for the "coercive legislation" to be delayed until the British Parliament had heard the colony's views. Morine said that the opposition would co-operate.[75] Over the next few days, the legislature decided to send a bipartisan five-member delegation to London, consisting of three MHAs and two MLCs—the party that Howlan joined.

The delegates had curious terms of reference: when a majority of them agreed to a way in which the affair could be settled, that plan was to be recommended to the Newfoundland legislature—each delegate was bound by the majority decision and pledged to use his best efforts to secure its adoption.[76] The members were to be Whiteway, Emerson, and Harvey, representing the government, and Morine and Moses Monroe representing the opposition (Harvey and Monroe were members of the Legislative Council).[77]

The delegation was preceded by a petition from the legislature protesting the revival of the 1824 act because it was "of an arbitrary and oppressive character" and an "instrument of coercion."† The petition also objected to the recent Anglo-French decision to arbitrate on the lobster question alone. The government indicated that it would neither participate nor be bound by the result.‡ There were meetings expressing indignation in St. John's and elsewhere, and Governor O'Brien reported that

* The text of the bill, as well as an account of the confrontation, can be found in Thompson, *French Shore,* Chapter 6 and Appendix 3. See also *JHA* 1891, Appendix, 643–52.

† *JHA* 1891, 90–92. The legislation was popularly known as the "Coercion Bill"; the name had great contemporary resonance, especially among people of Irish descent, given Gladstone's "Coercion Bill" of 1881.

‡ O'Brien to Knutsford, tgm., March 23, 1891 (CO 194/218, 295). The Colonial Office thought that a comprehensive arbitration, as favoured by the colony, would be dangerous. See the Minute by Anderson, March 10, 1891 (CO 194/218, 214).

there had been a "most revolutionary debate" in the Assembly that had included cries of "Down with England" and allusions to the United States that were greeted with cheers. He had heard of a proposal to fly the Stars and Stripes outside the Colonial Building. "From Whiteway downwards they have an idea, which nothing can get out of their heads, that Her Majesty's Government is the enemy of the Colony, and has always sacrificed its interests for every secondary consideration." Of the delegation, he noted that Whiteway was going to England against his will and seemed "rather sorry for himself, especially to have to go in such company." Harvey and Emerson were "quite mad," Monroe "a most objectionable individual," and Morine "about as disreputable, unscrupulous, and slippery a character as I have ever heard of. . . . He is clever, and will try and lead, and as there is a mortal hatred between Whiteway and him, with Monroe into the bargain, I should not be surprised if ere they got home there was a row." O'Brien thought Morine, Monroe, and Emerson were birds of a feather—they wanted to make it appear "at the next elections that they were the defenders of the Colony."[78] For all his prejudicial exaggerations, there was some truth in what he had to say.

The delegation left on April 6. Bond stayed behind, in charge of government business. The issue of enforcement legislation would cause the first significant dispute between him and his erstwhile patron—but it is difficult to sort out what exactly occurred in London and it would be argued about for years. The delegates arrived on April 17 and the next day met Lords Salisbury and Knutsford.[79] They found, of course, that they had to provide alternative proposals to counter the British government's decision to legislate. According to Whiteway, all their contacts, whether Liberal or Conservative, agreed that "our only chance of doing anything

HMS *Cleopatra* in 1893. The vessel was one of the naval corvettes that patrolled Newfoundland waters, Commodore Curzon-Howe in command. (PANL, VA 91-19.3)

was by adopting a course which would in some way provide for present carrying out the Treaties, execution of the [arbitration] award & modus vivendi. We laid especial stress on the establishment of Courts instead of the Treaties being executed by Naval Officers. This seemed to attract Lord Salisbury's favour."[80]

The delegates were asked to put their views in writing, which they did. The reply was to the effect that the bill would go to second reading as scheduled, but that the delegates could speak at the bar of the House of Lords the next day.[81] Whiteway spoke for the delegation on April 23, 1891. His address contained many of the same points as the Newfoundland legislature's petition, but also made a proposal that had been suggested earlier: if the Newfoundland legislature passed temporary legislation for the 1891 season, then the imperial bill could be withdrawn and negotiations started for an acceptable replacement for local enactment, incorporating the use of courts.[82] "We were well recd.," wrote Whiteway in his execrable handwriting, "and at the close there was an unusual burst of applause (so they said most extraordinary for that House). I was shaken hands with by a lot I did not know and highly lauded more that I am afraid I merited. Be that as it may we made a very good impression."*

But the proposal made to the House of Lords (and in a formal letter[83]) had not been approved by the Newfoundland legislature, as required by the delegates' terms of reference. This was because the delegates wanted assurances as to the character of future permanent legislation, as well as overall agreement with the British government on a deal, which could then be sent to St. John's.[84] Whiteway later admitted that "we erred in not sending you our proposals to the House of Lords . . . but at the time driven into a corner we had no alternative but to act at once."[85] A telegram was finally sent to Bond on May 6. It outlined the proposals the delegates had presented, and asked the legislature to pass resolutions confirming them and undertaking to pass a temporary act.[86]

There followed a tense four days. Bond's first response was to consult

* Whiteway to Bond, April 27, 1891 (RBP 6.03.003). Morine later claimed that Whiteway's address was "prepared by me," and this could well be true (PANL, Morine fonds, MG 271.2, folder 6, draft history of Newfoundland).

Edward Shea, the president of the Legislative Council. He then cabled Whiteway to the effect that, in his and Shea's opinion, it would be preferable for the British Parliament to pass the temporary legislation. This was clearly impossible, as the delegates immediately pointed out. The proposals were then discussed by the Assembly in closed session, which resulted in a motion to defer the matter until further information was received.[87] Bond cabled (May 7):

> Long debate; legislature consider delegates exceeded their power in proposing legislation suggested, without first consulting them. Very strong feeling adverse. Requisite you give ample reasons. This message is sent at instance of House who do not desire it to form record in Journal.

The Deputy Speaker transmitted the text of the relevant motion.* The delegates replied the same day that unless the legislature approved the proposals there was no hope of defeating the imperial bill and the colony would not be supported by any political party. "If Legislature does not approve our proposals it aids opponents and leaves Colony friendless, losing everything." The Assembly discussed this telegram, again in closed session, and passed a motion stating that the delegates had not provided a satisfactory explanation and that the legislature could not assent to the proposals.[88]

On May 9, Whiteway received an anonymous telegram:

> House passed resolution yesterday declining to accede request delegates, government party voting solid. . . . Opposition voted sustain delegates. . . . Entire Legislative Council favor sustain delegation. Meantime at suggestion [J.S.] Pitts both houses meet informally eleven to-morrow discuss situation. Bond introduced the resolution in strong speech denouncing

---

* James A. Clift was appointed to act as Speaker on April 7, 1891; soon after, Clift became ill and W.H. Whiteley took over as Deputy Speaker, on May 6, 1891 (*JHA* 1891, 96 and 182, and *ENL* 1:451–42 and 5:562).

> proposition. [P.R.] Bowers and mercantile faction jubilant over turn of events.[89]

Whiteway angrily wired Bond asking him to confirm this report. "If Government party do not sustain me appears I was urged on this delegation to humiliate me." Bond replied:

> Perfectly true that I am opposed to legislation suggested but absolutely false that I introduced resolutions. Whole house unanimous on resolutions except [R.S.] Munn. Matter has not been discussed in Legislative Council. At personal odium am doing all in my power to have your proposal approved. . . . Have arranged a conference for this morning [May 9]. Do delegates think that passing proposed resolutions would seriously embarrass Imperial Government in passing bill?[90]

Whiteway responded that it would. According to Bond, the London delegates then sent a private telegram to J.S. Pitts in the Legislative Council, arguing that since Knutsford insisted on a permanent bill there would be no harm in adopting the delegates' proposals, and that their acceptance of them would win the support of the British press and the Liberal party.* As Bond had noted, an informal meeting took place on the morning of May 9 at which, according to the *Newfoundland Colonist*, the Legislative Councillors lectured the MHAs. That afternoon, the Assembly passed the necessary resolutions (seventeen to five) and sent them to the Council.[91] The rumour in St. John's was that Whiteway had told Bond that if the resolutions were not passed, he would return to Newfoundland, seek a dissolution, and go to the country on the issue.[92]

At this point, Whiteway had no reason to believe that Bond was telling him anything but the truth. In later years, he came to think that Bond had indeed led the initial opposition to the delegates' proposals and had drafted the resolutions of May 7, although he had not been the one to

---

* Bond in Assembly, May 12, 1892 (*Evening Telegram*, June 6, 1892). Whiteway claimed that the telegram to Pitts was signed only by Morine and Monroe.

introduce them in the House.[93] Bond certainly opposed the delegates' proposals and therefore any compromise with an imperial government, whose behaviour on the US convention issue he found unforgivable. He also, probably, disliked the arm-twisting London had used to try to obtain compliance on French Shore issues. Given his mood, he thought it better that the imperial government should force coercive legislation on the colony rather than the colony pass such legislation itself. "You may and probably do think it would have been better to consider whether we should not have let them pass the Imperial permanent bill," wrote Whiteway on May 11, "fighting against it step by step."[94] Emerson, too, wrote that he knew Bond would be surprised and annoyed.[95] In this context Whiteway's accusation is plausible, but there is much about this crisis that is unclear and unknown.

Whiteway and the other delegates argued that their decision was the only one possible. Had the legislature not passed the resolutions, "the Colony would have lost all its friends and we (I especially) should have been placed in a most humiliated position and all of us including yourselves discredited."[96] Morine was dispatched to Newfoundland to explain matters to the legislature, which he did on May 22. On May 26, a temporary enforcement bill passed third reading in a thin house. Bond and Morris conveniently had the flu.* (The British government then withdrew its bill, which had reached second reading in the House of Commons, where Whiteway was waiting to make an address.†) Wider disapproval was obvious: the previous day had been marked as the Queen's birthday‡ and although proclaimed a holiday, merchants kept their premises open; halyards were removed from flagpoles outside the Colonial Building, Chief Justice Carter's house, and Government House, where an attempt had been made to burn down the pole.[97]

---

* *Newfoundland Colonist*, June 20, 1891. The legislation extended through 1893. The text can be found in Thompson, *French Shore*, Appendix 5.

† *JHA* 1891, 203–18 and *Evening Telegram*, June 1 and 3, 1891. The British government anticipated a difficult debate.

‡ Queen Victoria's birthday, May 24, fell on a Sunday in 1891; the holiday was on Monday, May 25.

Morine did not return to London, though Whiteway thought he should either have done so or accepted what the other delegates decided.[98] Monroe "strove hard to get away" and Emerson left before the end of June "without intimating his intention of going"*—all of which left Whiteway and Harvey with the unpleasant task of negotiating the final version of the permanent enforcement bill with the British government. Emerson took with him an early draft, which was discussed by the Executive at home, and about which Bond transmitted comments and objections.[99]

In its final shape, the draft bill provided for the creation and appointment of judicial commission courts under whose authority naval officers were to act, and before whom all complaints were to be heard. The draft specified that the courts could only act in matters relating to the treaties, with appeal to the Privy Council.[100] It was a cumbersome measure that Whiteway admitted was "not all I could wish but I have got all I can."[101] Moreover, the French government announced that it would never accept the proposed courts' decisions nor proceed with the lobster arbitration unless permanent legislation of the kind originally introduced (and later retracted) into the British Parliament was enacted. For his part, Whiteway (and probably Harvey, as well) saw the final legislation as another positive step in asserting colonial and British sovereignty on the French Shore and removing the anachronism of "quarter-deck justice." Whether the other three delegates favoured the legislation was unclear. They "ought to have remained until the terms of the permanent bill were settled," complained Whiteway, "and it was cowardly of them to leave."[102] He came to suspect that party politics were involved, certainly as far as Morine and Monroe were concerned, and that Morine was scheming to bring down his government.

Accommodation on the permanent bill was accompanied by agreement, at last, on the loan guarantee, which Bond thought essential in the absence of reciprocity with the Americans.[103] The colonial government formally accepted the conditions the imperial government had laid down

* "Truth" to *Harbor Grace Standard*, May 4, 1901 (PANL, MG 213.29). In the same letter, Whiteway alleged that Emerson "was getting very unpopular in Placentia where there existed a meaningless anti-French feeling, and he was afraid of his coming election."

in February: co-operation on the French issue now meaning local passage of the permanent enforcement bill.[104] An imperial commission of inquiry was to visit Newfoundland in the spring of 1892, by which time, it was hoped and expected, such a bill would be law.

THE CONFRONTATION WITH CANADA

Whiteway and Harvey looked to other matters while in London, as well. They held talks concerning the possible purchase of the Newfoundland Railway Company and lobbied for ratification of Bond's reciprocity convention. They also met Sir Charles Tupper to discuss questions at issue with Canada, especially the bait embargo, but here there was no agreement. The Newfoundland government remained convinced that Canadians were supplying bait to the French. It also felt that the Dominion government had treated the colony badly over the proposed US convention. Though the British Law Officers (legal advisers to the Crown) advised that Newfoundland could not refuse bait licences to Canadian or other British subjects, the colonial government decided to enforce the Bait Act against Canadians until there had been a judicial decision.[105] The Canadian government viewed this action as illegal and a breach of faith, and argued that very few Canadians were selling bait to the French. It even went so far as to suggest—again—the repeal of the Bait Act by imperial legislation.[106]

On November 25, Governor O'Brien (who had failed to persuade the government to change course[107]) learned that Canada further intended to place duties on imports from the colony unless Newfoundland reduced its duty on Canadian imports.[108] The Newfoundland government refused, for revenue reasons, and warned that if a tariff was placed on Newfoundland fish, then additional duties would be placed on Canadian imports (then valued at $2.4 million annually[*]). O'Brien believed that Whiteway and Harvey were unhappy with this turn of events, but Bond and the hawks carried the day and a tariff war began on December 9, 1891. When complaints began, Bond counselled staying the course—to do otherwise

* O'Brien to Knutsford, conf., December 3, 1891 (CO 194/218, 754). Newfoundland exports to Canada were valued at $600,000 annually. Imports from Canada consisted mainly of foodstuffs, kerosene, and tobacco.

would "play into the enemy's hands."[109] On Christmas Eve, the Executive Council formulated all the colony's grievances against Canada: opposition to the Bait Act and the US convention, the exclusion of Newfoundland from reciprocity conferences, and the Canadian wish to use a Newfoundland asset for its own benefit.

The year 1892, as a result, began with the governing Liberal party under strain. Whiteway was by nature a moderate, a negotiator, and a compromiser. Bond was none of these by temperament and he was often backed by Harvey, who strongly supported the Bait Act and a separate reciprocity treaty with the US. Many other Liberals seem to have been equally adamant. The situation was fraught. The legality of imposing bait restrictions on Canadians was highly questionable, and then a Newfoundland Supreme Court judge ruled (in the case of the schooner *Howard Holbrook*) that the Bait Act itself did not empower the government to charge licence fees.* In an earlier case, the Court had also questioned the legality of surcharges on Canadian imports, causing clauses to be added to the government's revenue bill to legalize the extra payments *post facto.*[110] And then there was Morine who, law studies completed, had recently returned to St. John's after contesting a federal by-election in Queen's County, Nova Scotia. He was, of course, keeping the Canadians informed. The government of Sir John Abbott (now Canadian prime minister following John A. Macdonald's death in in June 1891) intervened. As a result, the offending clauses in Newfoundland's revenue bill were suspended until the British Law Officers made a decision on them. The retroactive legalization of duties could be allowed, they determined, but the licence fees could not.[111]

At the same time, the Canadian government proposed to Newfoundland a temporary agreement on these issues—meaning, in effect, reversion to the status quo of 1889[112]—pending a conference. A few days later, Morine (who still held his seat in the House of Assembly despite his recent activities elsewhere) moved resolutions approving fees imposed on

---

* O'Brien to Knutsford, tgm., March 30, 1892 (CO 194/221, 164). The American schooner *Holbrook* was arrested in 1890 for allegedly taking more herring than allowed by licence.

American vessels until reciprocity was achieved but calling for an end to the confrontation with Canada, since Newfoundland fishing vessels going to the Quebec North Shore might face problems as a result.[113] Bond defended the government, expressing skepticism about that threat,[114] and there seemed to be deadlock. Morine told the Canadian minister of justice, Sir John Thompson, that "the Labrador exclusion bill must be pushed, or these cattle down here will not give way."[115] So early in May, the Canadians announced that Newfoundland fishermen on the North Shore might be prohibited from using seines and cod traps.[116]

The Newfoundland government's first reaction was a counter-offer: Newfoundland would concede bait to the Canadians, remove import surcharges, and agree to a conference—but Canada's objections to the reciprocity convention had to be withdrawn.[117] What happened over the next few days is not known, but on May 20 Whiteway showed the Canadian message to his party and the next day a modus vivendi was accepted.[118] Surcharges on Canadian goods were lifted and Canadian fishermen received bait licences. The Colonial Office thought it would be a graceful act on the part of the Canadian government to drop the court actions for recovery of licence fees, but this it refused to do.*

It seems that two MHAs in the government party who had extensive interests on the North Shore—almost certainly William Whiteley and Samuel Blandford†—persuaded the other government members that the Canadian sanctions would be felt over much of the island, which might be politically fatal given that an election was on the horizon.[119] Morine was less modest: "Congratulations on brilliant result your policy," he wired Thompson. "Next your own wise conduct you owe conclusion to my efforts here. Seeing this, to aid me should be pleasure as well as duty."[120] A contributing factor may be that, by this time, the British government had

* Knutsford to Stanley, July 4, 1892 (CO 194/221, 458–59) and Stanley to Ripon, September 21, 1892 (PANL, GN 21/202). Whiteway's bitter letter to O'Brien on this point, dated June 7, 1892, was sent confidentially by the governor to Knutsford the next day (CO 194/221, 450–53).

† Blandford managed the Job Brothers establishment at Blanc Sablon (*ENL* 1:207).

firmly decided that it would not consent to the US convention.* Overall, this was a significant climb down from earlier positions, which many in Newfoundland disliked.

With unusual insight, O'Brien had written earlier:

> The Newfoundlanders are jealous of their independence, and feel that while they have it their claims are equal to those of any other Colony, they have waited long to have those separate claims recognized and they trusted that the hopes held out to them would be fulfilled, and that as they suffer more from Imperial obligations than any other of Her Majesty's colonial subjects, their vital interests would have had prior consideration, and not been made subservient to those of another Colony, no more independent than themselves, though one which from being more wealthy can afford to wait while delay means ruin to them.[121]

Whiteway expressed his own bitterness, as well:

> It would appear that Her Majesty's Government, whilst conferring upon this Colony a constitution, would desire to withhold from it those constitutional rights which are part and parcel of . . . that constitution. If this Colony is to be made wholly subservient to Canada, if we cannot be allowed to move without the consent of the Dominion Government, it would be well that we should know it . . . instead of living in an imaginary possession of rights we do not enjoy.[122]

Both men were saying that constitutional status did not necessarily translate into political stature, and that this reality was much resented locally.

The Canadian confrontation and, especially, the French treaties bill placed considerable strain on Whiteway's Liberal party, most of whose

* *Evening Telegram*, June 1, 1892. This was in reply to a Parliamentary question from Francis Evans, a Liberal MP since 1888.

members—with Bond at their head—supported a hard line against Canada and opposed the permanent enforcement bill that Whiteway had negotiated. Morine used these divisions to engineer a clever but ultimately futile plot. Using Rev. William Pilot*—Whiteway's relative by marriage—as an intermediary, he suggested an alliance between the opposition and the Liberals supporting Whiteway. Together they would work out an agreement with Canada, drop the US convention, and pass a French treaties bill. Whiteway would gain great credit with the imperial government, thus improving his chances of a colonial governorship, went the argument. Meanwhile Morine would have split the Liberals and created a ready-made confederate party (to be led by Winter)—even though it would mean he had to drop some allies in the process. The Canadian government knew all about this proposal and passed on to the Colonial Office Morine's suggestion that a word from London might help. None came and Whiteway rejected the offer, telling Pilot that he was bound to carry out his party's programme. †

WHITEWAY'S PERMANENT ENFORCEMENT BILL

It remains a mystery why Whiteway did not publicize the scheme right away. If he had, he might have done some damage to Morine during the debate on the proposed permanent treaties bill. That began with the submission of two reports from the 1891 London delegates. Monroe, Emerson, and Morine held that the final draft of the bill was unsatisfactory and

* *ENL* 4:299 and McCann, "Pilot, William," *DCB* 14:841–42. Pilot had acted as Whiteway's private secretary during the 1891 French Shore talks with the British government.

† *Evening Telegram*, May 25, 1892, and Morine to Thompson, tgm., April 18, 1892 (LAC, Thompson fonds, 18993); Stanley to CO, tgm., secret, April 20, 1892, and Knutsford to Stanley, tgm., April 25, 1892 (CO 537/113, 12–14). John Anderson (at the Colonial Office) thought the Canadian message "most mischievous" if only because "Morine is about as untrustworthy an adviser as could possibly be found" (Minute, April 21, 1892, CO 537/113, 12). Morine's version of events can be found in the Assembly debate for May 20, published in the *Evening Telegram*, June 30, 1892.

that there should be an attempt to get amendments.[123] Whiteway and Harvey recommended that the bill should be accepted.[124] This division had been known for some time, the bill's passage was obviously uncertain, and both Whiteway and Edward Morris would have welcomed postponement to 1893.[125] When the Colonial Office reacted negatively to postponement, Whiteway asked what the imperial government would do if the bill failed—would it be passed in Parliament? Unhelpfully, the British government refused to say, simply reminding Whiteway that the loan guarantee depended on the bill's passage.[126]

A reluctant Whiteway, fatigued from a long illness and a series of stormy party meetings, spoke in defence of the bill at second reading on May 12.[127] It was not presented as a government measure, on the grounds that French Shore matters should be non-partisan. Whiteway described the delegates' actions the year before and warned the Assembly that the bill contained the only terms acceptable to the British government. If it failed, there would be imperial legislation and the loan guarantee would be lost. The delegates had acted within their powers, he himself had done his duty, and defeat would bring the country into contempt.

Morine immediately spoke against him. The majority of the delegation could not be bound by the minority, he argued, especially since Harvey and Whiteway had failed to keep in touch with the other delegates after they had left London. "The delegation never sought to pledge this Legislature to the adoption of such a bill as the present one," Morine asserted. He objected to the court structure envisaged by the bill and argued that members should not be bribed by the loan guarantee. Far better to have temporary legislation, to keep the sore unhealed, than to accept a bill that Whiteway had no authority to introduce.[128]

Bond spoke after Morine. Having expressed his regret for having to differ from Whiteway, he argued that the delegation had misinterpreted its terms of reference and misled the legislature. On the first point, he noted that the delegates

> were not to approach the Imperial Government, but were to appeal to the British Parliament and people to try and prevent

> the passing of the Imperial Bill, and then report the result of their efforts to the Legislature. . . . He remembered the question being put as to what the delegates were to do after they had presented an address to the British Parliament. The answer was that it would be their duty to seek the aid of the press, and, if necessary, to stump the country, and thus lay our case before the British public in every important town in England.[129]

By proposing legislation to the British government without consulting the legislature, they had violated their instructions. On the second point, the delegates had persuaded the House that if it passed temporary enforcement legislation it would never have to pass permanent legislation, meaning that the temporary bill would be used for political purposes: to gain support in Britain and embarrass the British government. He went on to remind the House that the delegates' report had to be unanimous, with the minority bowing to the majority. Yet the legislature had been presented with two reports. Given that the majority was opposed to a permanent bill, that position should bind all concerned. Instead, there was a draft permanent bill before the House. "The proceeding was . . . most incomprehensible and unjustifiable." The delegates had indeed told the British government they would report back to the House in favour of a bill—"but the question arises, what bill?" The delegates had envisaged local courts staffed by local men with power to try both British and French subjects, with appeal to the Supreme Court. The draft bill had none of these features. Moreover, it was unworkable and would operate unfairly against Newfoundland fishermen. As for the loan—if it "was to be the price of the liberty of our people, the liberty to live upon their own soil, to fish within their own waters, to mine and till that which was theirs by birthright, let it go!"

So, which course should be adopted? Bond suggested a tactic that, twelve years later, was to be one of the bases of the ultimate settlement of the French Shore issue. Considering that there was no possibility that France would reduce or remove its fishery bounties and that "the present

Bait Act was at the bottom of the whole trouble," he proposed that the Treaty Shore should be dealt with separately. In order to allow time to negotiate a French withdrawal, he moved an amendment that the existing temporary enforcement legislation should be extended until the end of 1895, and that further consideration of the whole question should be referred to a Joint Select Committee. Bond "appreciated" that

> a pacific and conciliatory feeling towards the Imperial Government is the duty of the House and of the country, but it was not our only duty. We owe a duty to ourselves and to our native land. Surely there was no man so abject as to think that Imperial courtesy required him to hush up the grievances under which his countrymen were laboring, or to stifle his convictions respecting the matter. . . . Let us further appeal to the sympathy and honour of the Imperial Government and [the] great British public, to lessen, if it be not possible wholly to remove, the evils which threaten us.[130]

The debate lasted until past midnight the following day (May 13). When Whiteway responded to his critics, he knew that the bill was lost. Nevertheless, he mounted an able defence. Deserted, as he saw it, by Morine, Monroe, and Emerson, he and Harvey had become the delegation. What had been agreed upon prior to their departure was only that there would be courts. Knutsford had said, before Monroe left on June 6, that the imperial government would appoint its members. In Whiteway's view, all the delegates were bound by an undertaking to support a bill creating courts. "In one breath," he went on, "they were claiming as possessing constitutional government—the right to legislate in this matter, and promising to do so, and immediately afterwards, in the next breath, repudiating those promises and telling the British government to legislate." Morine's statement that he would rather have the 1824 act re-imposed was unbelievable, given the fuss mounted by his party in 1890. It was also disgraceful that Morine and Monroe apparently never intended to support a permanent bill. As for Bond, his insistence that the delegates should not have negotiated was "a singular proposition." How else was anything to be achieved? In addition, the loss of the loan guarantee was a calamity. The Assembly was discrediting itself and the colony.[131]

Whiteway then asked leave to withdraw the bill. The Speaker ruled that there had to be unanimous consent, which Morine and two others refused. As a result, the motion for second reading was put and defeated (twenty-three to eight), both Bond and Morris voting with the majority.[132] Bond's amendments carried (twenty-one to ten), and the Joint Select Committee was formed on May 16. Whiteway was originally named to it (as were Bond, Emerson, Monroe, and Morine), but he stepped down the next day and refused to speak to it.[133] Clearly humiliated and bitter about the whole affair, Whiteway then publicized Morine's plot to divide the government party. Morine unsuccessfully demanded that Pilot be brought to the bar of the House to explain himself to a Committee of Privilege. He also said, among other things, that he regarded Bond as the leader of a faction that was causing all the trouble in the colony by overriding Whiteway's "wise judgement" concerning the US convention.[134]

This series of events confirmed the Colonial Office's low opinion of Newfoundland politics and politicians. "Very odd things are done in Nfland," wrote Robert Meade, "but it is an entire novelty to find the Prime Minister moving a Bill and his Col. Secretary moving an amendment dishing it. The procedure would be more suitable in a Gilbert and Sullivan comic opera."[135] Bond's line of argument was thought "extraordinary."[136] A disgusted O'Brien reported that MHAs were fearful of voting for a "coercion bill," given that a general election was scheduled for 1893. He thought that Whiteway had done his best.[137]

Whiteway had predicted that permanent legislation would be passed in London, since the imperial government was determined to proceed with the lobster arbitration.[138] He was wrong. Appalled as officials were by the Newfoundland bill's defeat, they already knew that the French government would not arbitrate unless there was permanent legislation in place to enforce the award. France would not have accepted the draft bill as satisfactory, and would certainly not accept anything that was even more favourable to the colony. The only option, then, was for the British government to legislate. The House of Commons, however, had demonstrated some sympathy with the Newfoundlanders—especially the Liberal party—and the Conservative government knew there could be political trouble.[139] Moreover, an early dissolution of Parliament was expected, with a general election following (it took place in July) that was predicted to be very close (and was). The result was inaction on the Newfoundland question and the collapse of the planned lobster arbitration.[140] The French government refused to discuss withdrawal from the Treaty Shore, but Bond continued to think it was possible.

So what are we to make of this affair? First, it is clear that the delegates had all agreed in London to recommend temporary local enforcement legislation to the legislature pending agreement on a mutually satisfactory permanent bill. Bond had disagreed with this compromise, wanting to force the imperial government into unilateral coercion—as MHA Daniel Greene put it: "If chains were to be fastened on the colony, let John Bull be the blacksmith."[141] This was at least a straightforward, if obtuse, reaction. The same cannot be said for the actions of Morine, Monroe, and Emerson. The evidence suggests that they collaborated in the delegates' original offer to the British government but then left Whiteway and Harvey stranded. The Colonial Office understandably assumed that the latter had the authority to negotiate on behalf of the Newfoundland legislature and government, and reached an agreement with Whiteway that, while by no means ideal from the colony's perspective, at least enshrined the principle that courts rather than naval officers should adjudicate treaty-related disputes. The other delegates held that this final draft bill was so far removed from the delegation's initial proposal that it could not be supported. But it may well be the case that they never intended to agree to any locally legislated permanent bill, preferring limited-term temporary legislation that would provide the opportunity to exert pressure on the imperial government at regular intervals.

Bond certainly agreed with that approach, and there was force in the argument that permanent legislation was to the colony's disadvantage. Moreover, the Newfoundland government had never supported partial arbitration on the lobster issue, so its collapse was no great loss. Opponents of the negotiated permanent bill were quite right to say that it provided for a cumbersome legal regime that the French would never accept, and that would be seen within the colony both as insulting to local courts and as great an infringement on colonial sovereignty as the naval regime had been. Sir Baldwin Walker, the naval commodore, thought that the bill would have been unworkable; John Bramston at the Colonial Office had told Whiteway the same thing. However, Whiteway had been right in principle, he wrote, and the bill would have made a start in placing matters on a basis of civil authority:

> The naval officer is a necessity only in the absence of civil authority, and the French naval officer is an accident of that necessity owing to the British naval officers not being ubiquitous, but the French [naval officer has] no more authority in law upon the coast of Newfoundland than he has in the Thames.[142]

The bill was in reality a clumsy compromise between imperial and colonial agendas and its failure was unlamented. However, the affair drove a deep wedge between Bond and Whiteway, who never forgot nor forgave his humiliation. And it did nothing for the colony's wider reputation.

THE HALIFAX CONFERENCE

The agreement with Canada, reached before the permanent legislation debate, provided for a conference to discuss the outstanding difficulties between the dominion and the colony. Despite the divisive ill-feeling in Newfoundland, the conference went ahead, taking place in Halifax in November 1892. As the time for it approached, the *Evening Telegram* began to float pro-confederate articles, claiming that attitudes toward Canada were changing thanks to growing social and commercial links with the mainland, Canadian generosity in sending fire relief (see Chapter 5), and the growing realization that Newfoundland counted for little in London.[143]

The *Herald*, meanwhile, claimed that such articles were written by Whiteway to test public opinion and divide the opposition.[144] This tactic is not unlikely, since the two parties were vigorously contesting a by-election in Burin, where the confederate Sir James Winter was nominated by the opposition and the undistinguished Joseph Boyd[145] by the Liberals. Winter and Morine were again trying to form a confederate grouping and were alarmed that Whiteway might negotiate while in Halifax.[146] If the *Herald* can be believed, the government apparently thought that with enough public money scattered about and some not-so-subtle sectarian manipulation, Boyd might just win.[147] Shortly before voting day, however, the *Telegram* predicted that Winter would win, and it was correct.* This was a significant morale booster for the Tories, and the news cannot have been welcomed by the colony's delegates in Halifax, where the conference finished on the day the result was announced.

The conference had begun on November 9. Newfoundland was represented by Whiteway, Bond, and Harvey.[148] The Canadian government delegation consisted of three cabinet ministers: Sir Mackenzie Bowell, Joseph-Adolphe Chapleau, and Sir John Thompson. Confederation was not on the official agenda. On the first day, the delegates discussed the Labrador boundary issue and the Canadian complaint that Newfoundland officials imposed duties on goods destined for consumption in Canadian territory.† They then moved on to review the bait and reciprocity issues. Thompson argued that the Bond-Blaine convention would have discriminated against Canada and suggested that they all should agree that "Canada as well as Newfoundland should have the right to take part in such, or any negotiations which would affect the interests of both countries" and that "no convention should be concluded which both countries should not have the option to avail themselves of." Whiteway persisted in asking whether Canada would

* *Evening Telegram,* November 12, 1892. The vote was 799 to 529, with a sixty-seven per cent turnout (*Evening Telegram,* November 15, 1892).

† This summary is based on the "Report of a Committee of the Honourable the Privy Council, approved . . . on the 19th December, 1892" (copy in RBP 8.02.003). What became known as the "Labrador boundary dispute" began in the late nineteenth century. Canada held that Newfoundland was entitled to no more than a coastal strip; Newfoundland held that its territory extended, for the most part, inland to the height of land.

maintain its objections even if it failed to negotiate its own reciprocity agreement within a given time, but Thompson refused to be drawn.

Bond led off the next day. He claimed that Canada, in its own negotiations, had never shown any sensitivity to Newfoundland's interests, denied that the draft convention was discriminatory, and repeated that "Canada had no right to protest against an arrangement merely on the grounds that it gave to Newfoundland advantages which Canada had repeatedly attempted in vain." The rest of the day was unproductive and the exchanges at times testy. The following day (November 11), the two sides agreed to work together toward the establishment of a British consulate at St. Pierre, and the Newfoundlanders urged the Canadian government to help in the enforcement of the Bait Act against the French. The discussion then returned to the Canadian complaint that the enforcement of the Bait Act against Canadians violated assurances given in 1887. Bond argued that the promise was never made the subject of a Minute of Council and so was not binding on the Whiteway government. Thompson was clearly unimpressed by this line of argument. As for the convention, "Canada and Newfoundland now share the American market. By the adoption of the convention, it is proposed that Newfoundland should share it with the United States, and Canada be shut out."

Later that day, Bowell filed a statement that contrasted Canada's treatment of Newfoundland fishermen with the allegedly unfair treatment accorded to Canadians by Newfoundland. He then raised the question of confederation as the way to solve such "vexed questions" as were under discussion, arguing that it would benefit Canada, Newfoundland, and the Empire. Whiteway saw no harm in an informal discussion. "His views, personally, on this question were well known. He had always been in favour of confederation, and viewed it as entirely one of terms." Harvey strongly objected to any such discussion and it went no further until November 14, when Bond joined Whiteway in expressing a willingness to hear what the Canadian delegates had to say.* But nothing happened. The final hours of the conference were occupied by Canadian explanations as to why the bait licence cases would continue to be litigated, and by descriptions of the hardships suffered by Canadian fishermen. The two sides were unable to agree on a final statement. The Canadian delegates refused to accept that concessions offered by Newfoundland were actually concessions, while the Newfoundland delegates were upset at the Canadian continuance of the lawsuits and refusal to withdraw the protest against the reciprocity convention.

In the end, the conference achieved nothing apart from undefined joint action on a St. Pierre consulate and a vague Canadian undertaking to facilitate the operation of the Bait Act. It had been made clear to Newfoundland, in effect, that it had no lever to use against Canada. Bait could not be refused, tariff discrimination would be disallowed in London, and Newfoundland could only talk to the United States with Canadian permission. The Newfoundland government's disappointment was reflected in Governor O'Brien's comment that Canada had persisted in "a dog-in-the-manger policy, for having on former occasions excluded us from participation in her American Fishery Conventions she now steps in and insists on sharing our arrangements."[149] Thompson remarked dismissively that the Newfoundland delegation had only come to Halifax to get Canada's consent to the convention, while insisting on the right of Newfoundlanders to fish in Canadian waters. He thought that confederation would benefit Newfoundland much more than Canada and was unenthusiastic at the prospect. As for the Newfoundland delegates, he found Harvey intransigent, Whiteway

---

* Pencilled on Bond's copy of the proceedings is: "Such was the manner in which I was prepared to deal with it in 1892. . . . I claim for the people of this Colony the constitutional right of deciding the question for themselves. Before they can be called upon to decide, they must be placed in possession of the terms that Canada is willing to offer, and must also be permitted ample time to consider those terms" (RBP 8.02.003).

slippery,* and Bond vigorous but conceited.[150] Given this attitude—Thompson became prime minister in December, 1892—it is hardly surprising that relations remained difficult, even though prompt Canadian assistance after the St. John's fire (earlier in the year) was appreciated. The colony refused to join with Canada in combined negotiations with the US, noting that Canada had arranged a treaty with France while ignoring Newfoundland—an action showing "an unfriendly spirit as only making use of us to suit her own purposes."[151] Lord Stanley reported (having spoken to Thompson) that "of the three Newfoundland delegates . . . [Harvey] was irreconcilable throughout and very aggressive until the last day. At first they practically refused to do any business until we had promised to withdraw our opposition to their draft convention with the U.S." Nothing definite had been settled.[152] The Newfoundlanders, no doubt, felt frustration at not being able to enforce the Bait Act against Canadian vessels, but there was also a feeling that the act was unenforceable and had done little good.

During the 1893 session of the legislature, James Murray, the independent member for the south coast district of Burgeo-La Poile, moved that the act be repealed, noting that the opposition had "left for the coal hole."[153] It was not a surprising action, since the opposition was now led by the man (Sir James Winter) who had introduced the Bait Act in the first place but who now represented Burin, where the act was unpopular (although it remained a favourite of the St. John's merchants, whose party he now led[154]). It was an awkward position to be in.

When Murray's repeal motion reached the floor, with only three opposition members present, Whiteway moved that the Bait Act be suspended. In an interesting speech, he argued that the act and its ineffectual enforcement had merely irritated the French, who had renewed their bounties until 1902 and found bait supplies elsewhere. Overall, the act's results had not justified its costs, and it would be far better to licence all foreign vessels to gain some revenue and let the people sell herring.[155]

---

* Bowell, who had led the confederation discussions (such as they were), later commented that Whiteway "yielded more to the opinion of those who surrounded him than to his judgement" (Bowell to Morison, March 5, 1895, LAC, Bowell fonds).

Bond seconded the amendment, claiming that his attitude had always been consistent. He had opposed the original legislation and his predictions about its consequences had proved correct. "What he had always favoured was an enactment which would enable the Government to impose a license fee on French and Americans, and which would compel them to come into the bays of the colony."[156] The amendment carried and Morris introduced the necessary legislation.*

WHITEWAY'S PERMANANENT BILL—AGAIN

All this occurred after another acrimonious debate concerning permanent treaties enforcement legislation.† The new Liberal administration in Britain (led by W.E. Gladstone) had decided that unless Whiteway's bill (or a satisfactory substitute) was passed in Newfoundland, the imperial bill should be revived in preparation for an arbitration on the lobster issue. After several stormy cabinet meetings—from which Bond escaped to Whitbourne—the Newfoundland government offered a two-year extension of the temporary act passed in 1892, Whiteway dissenting. When this was refused by the Colonial Office, it pleaded that the Joint Select Committee appointed in the previous session had not yet reported, and postponed a decision. The report appeared on March 8, 1892. It summed up the arguments of the bill's opponents— that the bill was "an absolute departure from the basis of the Act which the Legislature understood it would be called upon to enact." The Committee would only support a bill that provided for locally appointed courts as well as compensation for those who might suffer as a result of an arbitration award. It also recommended a general, rather than a partial, arbitration, and that the appointment of a British consul at St. Pierre should be a precondition.[157]

Bond introduced and spoke to the report on March 9; the main debate took place the following day.[158] Whiteway defended himself at length, Morine put forward a different version of events, and both Morine

* Morris in Assembly, April 10 (*Evening Telegram,* April 21, 1893) and O'Brien to Ripon, conf., April 20, 1893 (CO 194/224, 431). O'Brien suspected (as did Morine) that the act would be ineffective.

† Much of the following account is based on Hiller, "A History," 260–64.

and Bond criticized the draft bill—the latter saying that Whiteway had made "a great mistake." Both houses passed the report with substantial majorities and the governor was asked to send a cable to London summarizing the report's recommendations and offering an extension of the temporary act to the end of 1895. At this point, the British government began to retreat. The Colonial Office offered to drop the imperial bill and postpone discussion of the points at issue until after the 1893 election, as long as the temporary act was extended as offered. Whiteway, who had been issuing solemn warnings that imperial legislation would follow the colony's failure to act, once again felt badly let down. He was so furious that he refused to bring in the extension bill, so Bond did it. It went through the legislature on May 22, opposed by Morine and a few others.* Whiteway abstained. The temporary act was never replaced by permanent legislation. It would continue to be re-enacted until the final settlement of the French Shore problem in 1904.

Governor O'Brien was predictably appalled and sounded off about Bond. He wrote to Lord Ripon:

> Mr. Bond's position is the worst and it is somewhat annoying to see him. He is one of the most egregiously vain men I have ever met, he is very narrow minded . . . and has had his head turned by his early success in local politics, and above all by the people in Washington, where he was made to believe he was an Ambassador. . . . He is a [illeg] at heart, but a hard-working and (for here) honest fellow, but is very self-opinionated believing that Newfoundland is the pivot of the world which is kept going by being greased with cod and seal oil. He poses as a great patriot and the press . . . calls him "our incorruptible commoner." He is very hot headed . . . [and] threw over his chief most shamefully when the treaty enforcement bill came on.[159]

---

* The renewal was presented in the form of a report from the Joint Select Committee. It was signed by only six of its members (*JHA* 1892, 162).

The governor also had little time for Whiteway, whom he thought grasping and weak, but he was quite right to think that the colony's aggressive stance on fisheries issues and the French Shore had brought few dividends. He also felt that a separate reciprocity treaty, assuming that such a thing was possible, would remain a pipedream as long as Canada remained intransigent and the British government placed Canadian interests ahead of those of Newfoundland.

The Bait Act had proved to be a weaker weapon than originally thought because it could not be enforced selectively, and in any case the French had found different sources and types of bait. Fish markets remained difficult, not only because of subsidized French exports but also because of large amounts of cod coming from Norway. In addition, France showed no willingness to negotiate constructively on French Shore issues and continued to take lobsters. Newfoundland had avoided inappropriate treaty enforcement legislation in London, as well as the clumsy bill that Whiteway had negotiated—temporary bills did make more sense—but the affair had severely strained relations with the British government and caused a rift in the Liberal party. All in all, the period had demonstrated Newfoundland's ambivalent position in imperial affairs, given that it did not possess the stature to back up its quite valid claims to equality of status with other colonies with responsible governments, and given the British government's insistence that French rights on the Treaty Shore, however they were defined, had to be respected.

NOTES

1 Hiller, "O'Brien, Sir John Terence Nicholls," *DCB* 13:774–76 and *ENL* 4:142.

2 O'Brien to Knutsford, conf., December 10, 1889 (CO 194/212, 391).

3 Minute by John Anderson, January 4, 1890 (CO 194/212, 422).

4 O'Brien to Knutsford, conf., February 24, 1890 (CO 194/214, 88).

5 This episode is described in Hiller, "A History," 187–89, and Harvey Mitchell, "Constitutional Crisis," 323–31.

6 Baker, "Harvey, Augustus William," *DCB* 13:451–54.

7 *Evening Herald*, January 3, 1890.

8 Korneski, "Development and Degradation," 36.

9 Thompson, *French Shore*, 58–61 and 97.

10 O'Brien to Knutsford, tgm., March 14, 1890 (CO 194/214, 178) and O'Brien to Knutsford, conf., March 15, 1890 (CO 194/214, 205–209).

11 *JHA* 1890, 25–28 and *Evening Telegram,* March 15, 1890.

12 Whiteway in Assembly, March 19 (*Evening Telegram,* March 21, 1890).

13 *JHA* 1890, 324, 207–13 and O'Brien to Knutsford, June 25, 1890 (CO 194/215, 90).

14 Typescript of a letter from "Truth" (Whiteway) to *Harbor Grace Standard,* May 4, 1901 (PANL, Whiteway fonds, MG 213.29).

15 Bond in Assembly, March 27, 1890 (*Evening Telegram,* March 30 and 31, 1890).

16 J.J. Rogerson and J. McDougall to O'Brien, April 24, 1890 (PANL, GN 3, 16).

17 O'Brien to Knutsford, April 25, 1890 (CO 194/214, 367).

18 O'Brien to Knutsford, May 27, 1890 (*JHA* 1891, Appendix, 560–63 and CO 194/214, 445).

19 *ENL* 5:562.

20 Bond in Assembly, March 27 (*Evening Telegram,* March 29, 1890).

21 O'Brien to Knutsford, conf., March 31, 1890 (CO 194/214, 288–93).

22 O'Brien to Knutsford, April 14, 1890 (CO 194/214, 334).

23 Whiteway in Assembly, March 19 (*Evening Telegram,* March 21, 1890).

24 Commercial Society resolutions, April 8, 1890, and encl. in O'Brien to Knutsford, April 10, 1890 (CO 194/214, 309).

25 Winter to Sir John Thompson, April 30, 1890 (LAC, Thompson fonds, 12311).

26 *ENL* 1:177–78.

27 Whiteway in Assembly, April 1 (*Evening Telegram,* April 8, 1890) and Bond to Cecil Fane, April 14, 1890 (*JHA* 1892, Appendix, 425).

28 *Evening Telegram,* July 7, 1890.

29 Howley to Bond, April 28, 1890 (RBP 6.02.004).

30 "Resolutions passed at a public meeting at Sandy Point, Bay St. George, on May 24, 1890 . . ." (PANL, GN 3, 16) and encl. in O'Brien to Knutsford, June 9, 1890 (CO 194/215, 37).

31 Commander D. Riddell to Commodore Walker, June 17, 1890, and encl. in Admiralty to CO, July 11, 1890 (CO 194/216, 153).

32 *ENL* 1:379. For the St. George's Bay dispute, see Korneski, *Conflicted Colony,* 101–30.

33 M.E. Dwyer to Bond, July 1, 1890 (PANL, S2/139) and Carty to O'Brien, July 21, 1890 (PANL, GN 3, 16). Commodore Walker's report can be found

in Walker to Vice-Admiral Watson, June 6, 1890, encl. in Admiralty to CO, July 8, 1890 (CO194/216, 114–24).

34 Diary of a trip to the French Shore, 1890 (RBP 6.02.006), and Cecil Fane to O'Brien, July 19, 1890 (CO 194/215, 148–79).

35 *ENL* 1:113–14, and Baker, "Baird, James," *DCB* 14:31–32.

36 O'Brien to Knutsford, conf., July 1, 1890, and July 15, 1890 (CO 194/215, 128, 143).

37 Whiteway in Assembly, February 20, 1891 (*Evening Telegram*, March 2, 1891).

38 *Canadian Gazette* 7:328, July 18, 1890.

39 Foreign Office (FO) memorandum, June 19, encl. in FO to CO, conf., June 21, 1890. CO 194/217, 227–36.

40 "Memorandum in re French Treaties, Newfoundland," July 21, 1890 (*JHA* 1891, Appendix, 569–70), and Whiteway and Harvey to Herbert, October 9, 1890 (CO 194/217, 725–28).

41 Salisbury to Lytton, September 24, 1890 (*JHA* 1891, Appendix, 575–79), and FO to CO, October 25, 1890 (CO 194/217, 342).

42 Ribot to Lytton, October 29, 1890, and Waddington to Salisbury, November 29, 1890 (*JHA* 1891, Appendix, 582–84, 594–96).

43 Whiteway, "Memorandum respecting the Development of the Resources of Newfoundland . . . ," July 21, 1890 (*JHA* 1891, Appendix, 493–95, and CO 194/217, 685).

44 John Bramston to Whiteway, July 31, 1890 (*JHA* 1891, Appendix, 495).

45 FO to CO, conf., August 6, 1890 (CO 194/217, 269–70).

46 Delegates to Knutsford, August 15, 1890 (CO 194/217, 709).

47 Minute of Council, February 27, encl. in O'Brien to Knutsford, February 28, 1890 (CO 194/214, 115–17).

48 "Memorandum with regard to the United States," July 12, 1890 (CO 194/217, 677).

49 CO to FO, August 18, 1890 (CO 194/217, 283–84).

50 Minute by Bramston, August 12, 1890 (CO 194/217, 280).

51 FO to CO, September 10, 1890 (CO 194/217, 312–14).

52 "Speech of Hon. Robert Bond, in the House of Assembly, on Friday, March 6, 1891 . . ." (RBP 7.04.001).

53 Pauncefote to Lord Stanley, private, March 27, 1891 (LAC, Frederick Arthur Stanley, 16th Earl of Derby fonds, MG 27-IB7).

54 Bond to Pauncefote, October 3, 1890 (RBP 7.03.002).

55 Pauncefote to Salisbury, October 30, 1890 (*JHA* 1891, Appendix, 506).

56 *Evening Telegram,* October 31 and November 6, 1890, and Bond to E. Thomas, President of the New York Produce Exchange, October 20, 1890 (RBP 7.03.003).

57 Morine to Tupper, tgm., October 15, 1890 (LAC, Thompson fonds, 12380).

58 Stanley to Knutsford, February 12, 1891 (LAC, Lord Stanley fonds, microfilm reel A446).

59 FO to Pauncefote, tgm., October 31, 1890; encl. in FO to CO, November 3, 1890; FO to CO, November 4, 1890 (CO 194/217, 394–99).

60 FO to Pauncefote, tgm., November 20, 1890 (CO 537/120, 220).

61 Knutsford to O'Brien, tgm., November 14, 1890 (CO 537/120, 195).

62 Diary of the second visit (RBP 7.03.004).

63 Knutsford to O'Brien, tgm., December 10, 1890 (*JHA* 1891, Appendix, 512).

64 O'Brien to Knutsford, tgm., December 5, 1890 (*JHA* 1891, Appendix, 597).

65 Keith, *Responsible Government*, 3:1119–20.

66 Knutsford to O'Brien, February 12, 1891 (*JHA* 1891, Appendix, 543–46).

67 House of Lords, February 17, 1891 (*Hansard*, 3rd series, 350:819–20).

68 O'Brien to Knutsford, tgms., March 18 and 24, 1891, and Minute by Anderson, March 19, 1891 (CO 194/218, 258, 259, and 297).

69 Stanley to Knutsford, tgm., April 23, 1891, and Tupper to Knutsford, April 28, 1891 (CO 880/12 [NA 151], 44 and 53).

70 Beck, "Howlan, George William," *DCB* 13:481–83.

71 Howlan's report to Abbott, June 16, 1891 (LAC, Bowell fonds, 4405–33).

72 Whiteway to Bond, private, July 6, 1891 (RBP 6.03.003).

73 Whiteway to Macdonald, May 3, 1891 (LAC, Bowell fonds, 4434–35). See also Mitchell, "Canada's Negotiations," 277–93.

74 Salisbury, cabinet paper on "Newfoundland," November 21, 1890 (NA, Cabinet Office (CAB) 37/28, 9082).

75 Assembly debate, March 19, 1891 (*Evening Telegram,* March 31, 1891).

76 Assembly debates, March 20, 23, and 24, 1891 (*Evening Telegram,* April 1 and 2, 1891) and *JHA* 1891, 62–74.

77 *JHA* 1891, March 26 and 31, 1891.

78 O'Brien to Knutsford, private, March 26, 1891 (CO 194/218, 344–45).

79 The Whiteway fonds at PANL contain a printed volume of the "Correspondence of the Newfoundland Delegates with Her Majesty's Government" and a notebook containing a basic record of the delegation's activities up to June 6 (MG 213.9, 213.10).

80 Whiteway to Bond, May 11, 1891 (RBP 6.03.003).

81 Whiteway to Bond, April 27, 1891 (RBP 6.03.003).
82 *Hansard*, 3rd series, 351:1135–50 (*JHA* 1891, Appendix, 653–71).
83 Delegates to Knutsford, May 1, 1891 (*JHA* 1891, Appendix, 624–29).
84 Delegates to Knutsford, May 6, 1891 (*JHA* 1891, Appendix, 631).
85 Whiteway to Bond, May 25, 1891 (RBP 6.03.003).
86 Bond in Assembly, May 6 (*Evening Telegram*, May 22, 1891) and O'Brien to Knutsford, tgm., May 7, 1891 (CO 194/218, 473). The text of this and other telegrams can be found in Whiteway, *Duty's Call*, 77ff.
87 Assembly, May 6, in the *Evening Telegram*; May 23, 1891 in *JHA* 1891, 185.
88 *Evening Telegram,* May 25, 1891 (*JHA* 1891, 191) and Whiteway, *Duty's Call*, 78–79.
89 Whiteway, *Duty's Call*, 79. For James S. Pitts, see *ENL* 4:315–17.
90 Ibid.
91 *JHA* 1891, 192–93; *Evening Telegram*, May 26, 1891; *Newfoundland Colonist*, May 11, 1891.
92 O'Brien to Knutsford, conf., May 11, 1891 (CO 194/218, 498); *Newfoundland Colonist*, May 11, 1891.
93 Whiteway, *Duty's Call*, 82. This was reported at the time in the *Newfoundland Colonist*, May 25, 1891.
94 Whiteway to Bond, May 11, 1891 (RBP 6.03.003).
95 Emerson to Bond, private, June 9, 1891 (RBP 6.03.004).
96 Whiteway to Bond, May 11, 1891 (RBP 6.03.003).
97 O'Brien to Knutsford, conf., May 26, 1891 (CO 194/218, 533–34).
98 "Truth" to *Harbor Grace Standard*, May 29, 1901 (PANL, MG 213.21).
99 Whiteway to Bond, July 19, 1891 (RBP 6.03.003).
100 The text can be found in Thompson, *French Shore*, Appendix 4.
101 Whiteway to Bond, private, July 21, 1891 (RBP 6.03.003).
102 Whiteway to Bond, July 19, 1891 (RBP 6.03.003).
103 Bond to Whiteway, June 23, 1891 (RBP 8.03.011).
104 O'Brien to Knutsford, tgm., July 20, 1891; Knutsford to O'Brien, conf., August 28, 1891 (*JHA* 1898, Appendix, 272–75); Minute by Anderson, n.d. [1895] (CO 194/233, 265–67).
105 Law Officers to Knutsford, May 11, 1891 (CO 194/220, 365–73); O'Brien to Knutsford, June 22, 1891 (*JHA* 1892, Appendix, 474).
106 Minutes of Canadian Privy Council, September 21 and November 21, 1891 (*JHA* 1892, Appendix, 478–80 and 493–96); Stanley to Knutsford, October 1, 1891 (National Archives, 151).

107 O'Brien to Knutsford, November 21, 1891 (*JHA* 1892, Appendix, 487–88).
108 O'Brien to Knutsford, conf., December 3, 1891 (CO 194/218, 754).
109 Bond to Whiteway, December 19, 1891 (ASC, Whiteway Collection 5.04).
110 O'Brien to Knutsford, tgm., April 28, 1892 (CO 194/221, 249).
111 Stanley to Knutsford, tgm., secret, April 4, 1892 (LAC, Abbott papers, 1519); Knutsford to O'Brien, tgm., April 29, 1892 (CO 194/221, 249–60); Law Officers to CO, May 18, 1892 (CO 194/222, 115–20).
112 Knutsford to O'Brien, tgm., March 30, 1892 (*JHA* 1892, Appendix, 507).
113 *JHA* 1892, 47–49.
114 Bond in Assembly, April 5, 1892 (*Evening Telegram*, April 19 and 20, 1892; *JHA* 1892, 51).
115 Morine to Thompson, April 23, 1892 (LAC, Thompson fonds, MG 28-D).
116 Stanley to O'Brien, tgm., private, May 11, 1892 (PANL, GN 25, 1).
117 O'Brien to Stanley, tgm., personal, May 12, 1892 (PANL, GN 25, 1).
118 O'Brien to Knutsford, tgm., May 21, 1892 (CO 194/221, 369).
119 O'Brien to Knutsford, conf., May 28, 1892 (CO 194/221, 403–405).
120 Morine to Thompson, tgm., May 31, 1892 (LAC, Thompson fonds, 19386).
121 O'Brien to Knutsford, conf., April 1, 1892 (CO 194/221, 176).
122 Whiteway to O'Brien, May 4, 1892, encl. in O'Brien to Knutsford, conf., May 30, 1892 (CO 194/221, 285).
123 *JHA* 1892, Appendix, 540–42 (*Evening Mercury*, May 5, 1892).
124 *JHA* 1892, Appendix, 543–45.
125 O'Brien to Knutsford, tgms., April 20 and 29, 1892 (CO 194/221, 239 and 271).
126 O'Brien to Knutsford, private tgm., May 9, 1892 (CO 194/221, 289) and Knutsford to O'Brien, tgm., May 11, 1892 (CO 194/221, 291).
127 Assembly debate, May 4 (*Evening Telegram*, May 25, 1892) and May 12 (*Evening Telegram*, June 4, 1892).
128 Morine in Assembly, May 12, 1892 (*Evening Telegram*, June 6, 1892).
129 Bond in Assembly, May 12, 1892 (*Evening Telegram*, June 6, 1892).
130 Bond in Assembly, May 12 (*Evening Telegram*, June 8, 1892).
131 Whiteway in Assembly, May 13 (*Evening Telegram*, June 17, 1892).
132 *Evening Telegram*, June 18 and 20, 1892; *JHA* 1892, 122–23.
133 *JHA* 1892, 124, 127, and 137; O'Brien to Knutsford, conf., May 30, 1892 (CO 194/221, 409).
134 Assembly debates, May 20, 24, and 25 (*Evening Telegram*, June 27, 29, and 30, 1892; *JHA* 1892, 145; *Evening Herald*, May 23, 26, 27, and 28, 1892).
135 Minute by Meade, May 13, 1892 (CO 194/221, 334).

136 Minute by Anderson, n.d. (CO 194/221, 341).

137 O'Brien to Knutsford, conf., May 16, 1892 (CO 194/221, 344–46).

138 Whiteway in Assembly, May 13 (*Evening Telegram*, June 17, 1892).

139 Minute by Anderson, May 14, 1892 (CO 194/221, 336).

140 Minute by Anderson, August 19, 1892 (CO 194/222, 422).

141 Greene in Assembly, May 13 (*Evening Telegram*, June 9, 1892). For Greene, see *ENL* 2:722.

142 Walker to Vice-Admiral Hopkins, June 7, encl. in Admiralty to CO, June 20, 1892 (CO 194/223, 263–69) and Minute by Bramston, July 7, 1892 (CO 194/223, 261).

143 *Evening Telegram*, September 6, 1892; see also September 10, October 14 and 19, and November 1, 1892.

144 *Evening Herald*, October 21 and December 16, 1892.

145 *ENL* 1:237.

146 Hiller, "A History," 255–57.

147 *Evening Herald*, November 5, 11, 12, 16, and 19, 1892.

148 *Evening Telegram*, October 12, 1892.

149 O'Brien to Ripon, secret, January 1, 1893 (CO 194/224, 25).

150 Waite, *The Man from Halifax*, 422–23.

151 O'Brien to Ripon, tgm., March 7, 1893 (CO 194/224, 300), and O'Brien to Ripon, conf., March 8, 1893 (CO 194/224, 310). See also O'Brien to Ripon, June 19, 1893 (CO 194/224, 621–22).

152 Stanley to Ripon, private, November 19, 1892 (BL, Ripon papers, 4637:2).

153 Murray in Assembly, March 20 (*Evening Telegram*, April 11, 1893).

154 O'Brien to Ripon, secret, March 27, 1893 (CO 194/224, 398–400).

155 Whiteway in Assembly, March 22, in the *Evening Telegram*, April 11, 1893 (*JHA* 1893, 48).

156 Bond in Assembly, March 22 (*Evening Telegram*, April 13, 1893).

157 "Report of the Joint Select Committee of both Houses . . . on French Treaties Question" (*JHA* 1893, 9–23).

158 The debate was reported in the *Evening Telegram*, March 11, 13, 15, 16, 18, 20, and 22, 1893.

159 O'Brien to Ripon, private, February 14, 1893 (BL, Ripon papers, 43557: 141).

CHAPTER FIVE

Domestic Affairs: From Railways to the Bank Crash, 1890–1894

The emergencies involving the French Treaty Shore, Canadian relations, the fisheries, and reciprocity with the United States dominated political life during the Whiteway government's first term. But there was important domestic legislation as well, during the early years especially, and it reflected a policy based on railway building and economic diversification. The Whiteway programme promised jobs and prosperity, and that is what mattered to the electorate. Governments had to apply a careful balance, however, and the Liberals managed to pull this off. Anti-French policies—which were rarely unpopular outside the south and west coasts—had to be balanced with pro-American initiatives such as reciprocity, while economic diversification promised good things for everyone. A "new economy" was to be realized, or so it seemed.

RAILWAY BUILDING

One aspect of this possibly brighter future was the incorporation of a company that wanted to build a railway from Quebec City to the Labrador coast as part of a transatlantic system.* This was the first such proposal to mention Labrador, which was why, despite Whiteway's and others' strong support, Bond strongly opposed any such legislation—he thought

* *Canadian Gazette* 15:365, April 3, 1890, 2, and 15:387, September 4, 1890, 541. The *Gazette* also reported that a Toronto group, the Sault Ste. Marie and Atlantic Railway Co., was interested in a railway to Hamilton Inlet (14:361, June 3, 1890, 535).

the advantages of such a route should come to the island. He was a believer, he said, "in the idea that Newfoundland would be a future link in the chain of communications between Europe and America." Further, he went on, "Newfoundland would yet form part of the grand route between Asia and America. . . . The time would come when England would regard this island as the Gibraltar of North America, [part of] a highway connecting her with her western dominion." The idea was "by no means utopian."[1] He wanted a direct express rail line across Newfoundland and was to pursue this unlikely concept for years to come.

The Labrador scheme was indeed utopian and never materialized. More important and immediate was the question of the unfinished Hall's Bay railway. The government called tenders, as promised, and then negotiated a contract with Robert G. Reid and George H. Middleton of Montreal.* It provided that the contractors would be paid $15,600 per mile in colonial debentures over five years and between 40 to 60 miles were to be built annually.[2] The deal passed the House rapidly on June 6, 1890.[3] The contract represented a change in the colony's approach. The assumption hitherto, as in the Newfoundland Railway Company agreement, had been that the contractor would both own and operate the railway in return for subsidies. The 1890 Reid-Middleton contract stipulated that the railway would be owned by the colony, but said nothing about operation. This was a possible

Robert G. Reid (1842–1908), the builder of most of the Newfoundland Railway. Originally printed in H.Y. Mott, *Newfoundland Men* (Concord, New Hampshire, 1894). (ASC Coll. 327)

* The contract is in *JHA* 1891, Appendix, 407–31. F.H. Evans, receiver of the Newfoundland Railway Company, commented that "all I can say is that for any contractor it is a leap in the dark which nobody who had money to lose would meddle with" (Evans to Whiteway, March 27, 1890, ASC, Whiteway Collection 1.11.001).

mistake and the cause of much future acrimony. However, Reid was an experienced and reliable Scottish-Canadian engineer and railway builder who, like Middleton, had worked on the Canadian Pacific Railway (CPR). He was also closely connected to W.C. Van Horne,* Thomas Shaughnessy,[4] Donald Smith, and other prominent Canadian businessmen. The government had chosen well, in that Reid could be relied upon to deliver what he had agreed to. But the arrangement launched a long and fraught relationship between the Newfoundland government and the Reid family, which would last into the 1920s and beyond.†

Work started, in a small way, during the fall of 1890; more than five hundred men were employed by May, 1891. The government understood that railway building and land settlement would be expensive, but as Bond told the Assembly in April 1891:

> If we are to progress as a colony, we shall have to increase our public debt. Unless we are to remain in the unfortunate condition in which we found ourselves to-day, with hundreds of the population fleeing from the land in every steamer that leaves our shores, we must borrow and expend money in developing those resources that we believe the country possesses; in establishing new industries, that will give employment to our surplus fishing population, who now emigrate or starve.[5]

He went on:

> What was the railway going to do for our people? It was going to take from our coast our surplus fishing population and plant them in the interior of the island to develop our latent resources. . . . The earning power of the people has not increased during the last thirty-three years, because they

* Van Horne supplied a testimonial: "In our experience he [Reid] has had no superior" (Van Horne to Middleton, tgm., May 1, 1890, PANL, S2/38).

† Cuff, "Reid, Sir Robert Gillespie," *DCB* 13:859–62. Middleton dropped out in 1892 (*ENL* 3:534 and *ENL* 4:568).

> depended on one industry—the fishery; but when the railway was built across the country they would be able to open up other industries. . . . He had no sympathy with those people who were continually croaking about the condition of the country, crying aloud "retrench!" "halt!" and all that buncombe [*sic*]. Groaning over the past was not the way to bring about a better condition of affairs.

The government had already decided that the railway should extend across the island to the west coast; in 1890, James Howley was instructed to survey a route over the height of land. He protested, but Bond insisted.[6] Then, just in time for the election in 1893, the legislature approved two other contracts with R.G. Reid (Middleton had by this time dropped out of the partnership). It was announced that the projected line to Hall's Bay would be abandoned; instead, Reid would continue the line from a point near Bishop's Falls on the Exploits River to the west coast with a terminus at Port aux Basques (which was outside the French Shore), on the same general basis as the 1890 contract. Second, Reid would operate the railway beyond Whitbourne for ten years in return for fee simple land grants of 5,000 acres per mile.* Whiteway described his vision of "trains ladened with minerals, timber and agricultural produce, passing from the smiling fields and gardens of the West, on their way to market in the metropolis. That was what he believed would be seen here ten years from this date."[7] The railway would keep Newfoundland independent and make it "one of the richest and choicest jewels in the Crown of Her Majesty." Bond did not speak in this debate; the legislation passed rapidly.

Not surprisingly, the French government made inquiries and the Colonial Office reacted strongly. John Anderson at the Colonial Office immediately suggested that the railway could be used as a lever to extort a permanent enforcement bill—after all, Reid might acquire large tracts of land on the Treaty Shore and the imperial government would need the

* Morine later wrote that the operating period was far too short, but that Reid did not want it to be any longer at that time (PANL, Morine fonds, draft history, folder 12).

power to protect French rights.[8] The result was a threatening dispatch: unless the colonial government postponed all railroad activity on the French Shore until permanent legislation was in place, the railway legislation would be disallowed.[9] With uncharacteristic tact, Governor O'Brien showed the dispatch only to Whiteway, who pointed out that the terminus (Port aux Basques) had been chosen precisely because it was *not* on the French Shore, so the French would not be disturbed in any way. As planned, the line would touch the Shore only at Birchy Cove (now Curling) and St. George's; the French used neither place.[10] O'Brien added that disallowance in an election year would end any chance of permanent legislation.[11] The Colonial Office retreated, contenting itself with reminders about the prohibition on absolute land grants within a half-mile of the shoreline.[12]

By this time the public debt had reached approximately $6.5 million and was obviously set to climb further. Railway building was expensive. To summarize: early in its term, the government had made urgent efforts to obtain an imperial loan guarantee (as outlined in Chapter 4). The Colonial Office was prepared to consider the question, but the precondition was a commission of inquiry to investigate the colony's agricultural and mineral resources, the financial situation in general, and the condition of settlers on the French Shore. It was also made clear that the British Parliament would be unlikely to agree to a loan guarantee unless the colony co-operated on French treaty matters, and there would have to be some supervision of how the money was spent.[13] This offered small help to a government facing a financial crisis. Whiteway and Harvey had been unable to raise an adequate loan in London in 1890. The fish trade was experiencing difficulties, especially in Portugal, and large amounts of fish were left unsold. Both the local banks—the Union and the Commercial—were facing a liquidity crisis because of slow exchange payments from abroad due to currency crises in Europe and South America and the absence of government loan funds on deposit.[14]

In February 1891, the government again formally asked Britain for help in the form of a guarantee on a loan of £150,000.[15] This was effectively refused. The Newfoundland government resented the conditions being insisted upon and was reluctant to co-operate in a French Shore agreement.* Whiteway complained (privately) that the British government "sits heavily upon us," giving no assistance whatsoever—was the colony being forced into confederation?[16] In the end, rather than agree to the strings Britain was attaching to a loan guarantee, Whiteway arranged for the railway contractors to place the $250,000 security for which they were liable in the Commercial Bank.[17] The government also refused to make the loan correspondence public, which caused considerable annoyance in London.[18] However, as we have seen, once a pact had been reached in London on a permanent French treaties enforcement bill, there was agreement on the guarantee, which Bond thought essential.[19] The colonial government accepted the conditions laid down in February[20] and an imperial commission of inquiry was scheduled to visit Newfoundland in the spring of 1892. But no permanent enforcement bill was passed and thus no loan guarantee was forthcoming. The colony was left to manage the cost of the railway on its own.

At the same time, another growing expense was the increasing investment in education that the government thought necessary. At the time, the school system was run by the larger churches. Their superintendents reported to the governor-in-council until 1898, and thereafter to the colonial secretary. Bond took education seriously, asserting that "the foundations of the commonwealth, to be firm and lasting, must be built on the cornerstone of religion and education."[21] A Select Committee on Education was appointed in 1890; among its members were senior Liberals including Whiteway and Bond. It organized a prize essay competition for teachers, and recommended (among other things) greater uniformity across the school system.[22] The result was the appointment of nine education commissioners who were given wide powers to supervise and regulate the school system. Further legislation in 1893 created the Council for Higher Education, which implemented common external

---

* O'Brien to Knutsford, conf, February 12, 1891 (CO 537/120, 254). Sir Robert Herbert at the Colonial Office went so far as to suggest that the imperial government should take over the French Shore as security for a £2 million loan (Minute, March 4, 1891, CO 537/120, 250).

examinations in Grade 6 and higher.* The vote for education was increased and incentives provided for teachers to improve their credentials. The three denominational superintendents—Catholic, Anglican, and Methodist—remained powerful figures, but this education legislation was the most important for fifteen years or more. Serious problems persisted, such as denominational duplication, but a fundamental problem had been addressed. Bond also supported the Newfoundland Teachers' Association, which was founded in 1890 and held one of its early meeting at Whitbourne in late July 1891. (That settlement, meanwhile, was expanding thanks to the construction of a sawmill, and Bond was building what the *Evening Telegram* described as a "palatial" two-storey residence.[23])

Other positive legislation reduced the (male) voting age to 21—Bond's initiative—and encouraged shipbuilding and the cultivation of flax and hemp. The legislature grappled unsuccessfully (at Morris's behest) with the issue of local self-government, providing for the election of road boards but failing ultimately to enforce the legislation. It also had to deal with two disasters. The first occurred in Trinity Bay, Bond's district, in February 1892. The ice (and thus seals) had come into the bay earlier than usual. The morning of February 27 was fair with little wind, and about two hundred men went out in small boats to hunt. Around midday, however, a northeasterly gale set in and those out in boats found it difficult to get to shore. Twenty-four men drowned or died. The government sent steamers to help, but they were unable to get through the ice and into the bay. The legislature adjourned in sympathy, started a subscription fund, and appointed a committee (chaired by Chief Justice Carter) to manage the expenditures. Lord Knutsford sent £10. Bond was later criticized, unfairly, for not reacting faster and more effectively.[24]

---

* *ENL* 5:103. There were Education Acts in 1891, 1892, and 1893. See McCann, "The Politics of Denominational Education" and "Denominational Education" in McKim, ed., *Vexed Question*, 30–79.

THE GREAT FIRE, 1892

The second disaster to visit the colony was the great fire that swept through much of St. John's on July 8, 1892. Eleven thousand people were directly affected (almost 10,000 were left homeless*) and property loss was put at $13 million, of which only $4.8 million was covered by insurance. The government hastily erected sheds in Bannerman Park and provided more than one hundred tents. Chief Justice Carter, Administrator in the absence of Governor O'Brien, appointed a Relief Committee on July 11 (which included Whiteway and Morris but not Bond) to administer the funds that soon began to arrive. The Canadian government sent $10,000, as did Ontario. Nova Scotia sent more than $20,000, Halifax $13,000, and Montreal, $39,500. The imperial government provided £15,000. Naval ships arrived to give what help they could. In England, O'Brien and others raised £20,000.†

St. John's after the great fire of July 8, 1892. (ASC, Coll. 137, 5.01.010)

The colonial government was faced with the question of how to handle rebuilding the town. The Thorburn administration had provided St. John's with a municipal council of seven members (five elected

* For a description of the fire, see *ENL* 2:108–11. Afterwards, the homeless who could not find lodging numbered 1,536, of whom 1,021 were housed in tents. Others were billeted around Quidi Vidi Lake and at the Parade Rink, railway depot, and drill shed. It was estimated that 1,572 buildings were destroyed (*Evening Telegram,* September 1, 1892; *Evening Herald,* September 19, 1892).

† Baker, "The St. John's Fire," 3–4; *Canadian Gazette* 20: 496 (October 6, 1892), 1. In March 1893, the Relief Committee reported cash donations of $361,136 and estimated the value of donated goods at $84,915.20 (*JHA* 1893, Appendix, 357).

and two appointed by the government of the day). Earlier in 1892, the legislature had passed an extensive Municipal Act, which consolidated existing pieces of legislation and closed tax-avoidance loopholes. The St. John's municipal council remained very much under the government's control, however, since it could not widen streets without the government's approval and had to use the surveyor general's office for all land arbitrations.[25] Moreover, the council was in debt to the colonial government and was running a deficit. Some people believed that the extent of the fire was due to the council's incompetent administration of the volunteer fire department.* The council also harboured a number of prominent Tories, which did not sit well with a Liberal government.

Another complication was that much of the land in downtown St. John's was owned by absentee landlords and leased to mercantile and other tenants. Collectively, tenants were obviously reluctant to begin rebuilding unless they could be assured of long leases and fair rents. The 1892 Municipal Act had gone some way in this direction—stipulating that landlords would be liable for taxes unless they granted leases for 75 years or longer—but in the aftermath of the fire, backed by the council, tenants began to agitate for a local landlord and tenant act based on 1881 Irish legislation (which had established a land court). Whiteway was the agent for several absentee landlords, however, and would not agree.[26]

Taken together, these factors meant that the colonial government and not the municipal council became largely responsible for rebuilding St. John's. Initially, the government insisted that it (not the council) should survey the burned area and that no rebuilding should take place until the survey was completed. If streets were to be widened, then it would provide the money for compensation. The hope was that the funds would come from a loan to be floated at low interest with an imperial guarantee.

---

* A report found that "the brigade is disgracefully equipped. They have not a solitary modern appliance capable of saving life, or even contend[ing] with any serious fire." ("Report of John R. McCowan re Fire Department," *JHA* 1893, Appendix, 270). As colonial secretary, Bond was responsible for the inquiry. A new fire department was created in 1893 and placed under the control of the Newfoundland Constabulary in 1894.

A week after the fire, the request went to London, with a further provision that part of the money would be used to purchase landlords' property on the south side of Water Street and create a harbour trust.* The British government was not unsympathetic, but once again the negotiations broke down—hence the gift of £15,000 in October.†

On July 20, a Tenants' League was formed, headed by Moses Monroe, a prominent Tory. It demanded that the legislature should be convened to establish a land tribunal, retroactive to the date of the fire. Whiteway resisted such pressure until the survey was finished, at which point it was clear that a loan guarantee would not be granted in the immediate future.[27] Thus the legislature did not meet until August 11. The government had decided by then that it did not have the money to finance any extensive street widening or straightening. For example, it refused to allow the widening of Water Street to 70 feet (21 metres), insisting that 60 feet (18 metres) was sufficient, and there was no talk of purchasing the properties on the harbour side of the road. Legislation passed during this session deprived the St. John's council of its powers relating to rebuilding and street widening, vesting them in the colonial government. The opposition protested, but Morris held that the council was incompetent and that its total abolition would be a popular move.[28] Other bills lowered tariffs on supplies needed for rebuilding, encouraged landlords to give 99-year leases, and provided for the replacement of public buildings destroyed in the fire. An opposition motion for a land court was defeated. Morris introduced resolutions concerning a harbour trust; they were referred to a Select Committee, of which Bond was a member.[29] He did not play a significant role in the session, however, voting with the government on all occasions and leaving the main business to Whiteway, Morris, and Surveyor General Henry Woods.[30] His interventions were short, such as one in support of

* Carter to O'Brien, tgm., July 14, 1892 (CO 194/223, 29–30). It was suspected that some landlords had trespassed on Crown land in the area.

† The negotiations are not described here. The problems were (a) whether there should be an inquiry into the colony's finances; (b) whether conditions should be attached (for example, a permanent French treaties enforcement bill); and (c) whether such a loan could be used to purchase land titles.

the creation of what became Bond Street—possibly named after him—from a series of smaller, disjointed lanes.[31]

Clearly, Bond's focus at this time was on Whitbourne, on the failed reciprocity treaty, and on an investigation into the colony's telegraph system, which he chaired. This closely involved Alexander Mackay, a prominent local figure who was also the superintendent of the Anglo-American Telegraph Company, which held a local monopoly on transatlantic communications and owned the wires connecting Newfoundland to the mainland as well as maintaining a telegraph service on the Avalon Peninsula. Beginning in 1877, the colonial government had begun to build its own lines elsewhere on the island; these, too, had been constructed and were now managed by the Anglo-American Telegraph Company.* Mackay was a Legislative Councillor and a Tory supporter, but he was close to Whiteway (a fellow Mason), who had appointed him to the Fisheries Commission and made him a governor of the Savings Bank. Mackay had also been one of the original directors of Bond's Townships Company. The inquiry into the telegraph system undoubtedly placed further strain on the relationship between Bond and Whiteway, especially as its report concluded that Mackay had allowed government accounts to become entangled with those of the telegraph company, as well as with his own personal bank account, and that he had misappropriated public funds. Not surprisingly, Mackay lost his government responsibilities and his relationship with Bond became strained.[32]

THE 1893 ELECTION

The 1893 legislative session prepared for the coming general election with the new railway contracts and by providing for a $100,000 loan to be spent on "railway connecting roads"—that is, roads to connect outlying settlements with the railway. There would be plenty of jobs available. Bond, approached to run in several districts, decided to run once

---

* McCarthy, Galgay, and O'Keefe, *The Voice of Generations,* 85–88 and 111–12. After 1893, Reid built a telegraph line along the railway (as far as Whitbourne) to which the government lines were connected. All business was transferred at Whitbourne, causing higher charges.

again with Whiteway in Trinity Bay. "We understand each other now," he wrote,

> and I shall support him, but, if I thought for one moment that my return depended upon my support of the man and not of his policy I would wash my hands clean of politics immediately. My experience of political life has not been such as to induce me to sacrifice principle to the slavish following of any man. I should be better off in pocket, health and comfort if I were to drop out tomorrow, but there is a work of pacification [?] to be done, as well as a progressive policy to be sustained and I purpose remaining in the political arena for the present.[33]

The Tories—or the Patriotic Association, the official name remained uncertain—found themselves leaderless, since Winter had become a Supreme Court judge after a single session in the Assembly.* They would have done well to appoint Alfred Morine as Winter's replacement, but the leadership went instead to a pair of prominent St. John's businessmen, Walter Baine Grieve[34] and Moses Monroe. The *Evening Telegram* called them "the two firmest advocates of plutocracy in Newfoundland today,"[35] which foreshadowed the anti-merchant cries that came to dominate Liberal propaganda.

In a speech at Broad Cove in July, Morris attacked his opponents as the "Starvation," "Chinese Labour," or "Ropewalk" party, an allusion to one of Monroe's businesses and his allegedly exploitative tendencies.† "Tory grabbers," "hereditary Tory oppressors," "the 30 cents a day party" were other choice epithets. In contrast, Bond—who apparently was ill during the late summer[36]—was dubbed "the incorruptible commoner," Morris "the Scarsfield of the West End," and Whiteway "the Apostle of

---

* *Evening Telegram*, May 25, 1893. It is surprising that Whiteway did not appoint himself; he may have wanted Winter out of the legislature.

† *Evening Telegram*, July 31, 1893. Earlier, the *Telegram* had written of "the grinding oppression of the poor girls in the Ropewalk" (April 8, 1893).

Progress."* The voters had to choose between the Workingmen's Party or the Merchants' Party, said the Liberal manifesto, which celebrated the Liberal record and promised, among other things, to complete the railway, encourage land settlement, revise the tariff in favour of the poor, and promote local industries.[37] To help matters along, employment on the railway rose to an unprecedented 2,000 men in November 1893. An appalled Governor O'Brien reported that

> some 12 to 1,500 men are employed cleaning gutters and at all sorts of trivial work in St. John's to get votes. The other day they were taken off their work bodily first to give Bond an ovation at the Railway Station and then Whiteway at the Wharf when they started electioneering. . . . When Whiteway was going away he made a speech and said he went with a clean breast—a voice from the crowd exclaims Yes, with a clean chest too—not bad for the Colonies.[38]

The opposition manifesto predictably attacked the government's record, alleging extravagance and citing a long list of broken promises, the mishandling of French Shore issues and the Bait Act, and giving Reid a railway operating contract that handed over far too much land. Otherwise, its promises were similar in many ways to those of the Liberals. If elected, the Grieve-Monroe party would continue railway and road building, encourage local industry and agriculture, extend the telegraph system, build lighthouses and fog alarms, and reform the school system and the civil service. It was, in fact, the "Labour-Giving Party."[39] The *Evening Herald* ridiculed Whiteway's "Chariot of Progress," derided the Liberals' claim to be a workingmen's party (it contained eleven merchants, eleven lawyers, and three doctors),[40] and claimed that it defended merchants. It also made great play with money allegedly grabbed from public purse by sundry Liberals—"Bond's grab" was estimated at $15,000.[41]

* Whiteway (aged 65 in 1893) was also popularly called "the G.O.M" (Grand Old Man), a reference to W.E. Gladstone in Britain.

The *Daily Tribune*—a new and short-lived daily—called the election "a disgraceful battle with soot bags; and the biggest sweep is expected to win."[42] O'Brien reported a "most keen [contest], the open bidding for votes most unscrupulous, and the means adopted, as also the foul and personal abuse used is . . . unknown in any other part of the world." As for policies, "both parties appeal to figures as to the extravagance of their opponents in the past and both make promises which will entail similar extravagance in the future."[43] The historian Daniel Prowse agreed, calling it an "indecent carnival of scurrility."[44] It was accepted, as well, that the character of the election was influenced by the fact that it was the first held under both manhood suffrage and the secret ballot. The Newfoundland correspondent of the *Canadian Gazette* commented on the absence of any "great political issues . . . and only when Newfoundlanders have found a larger national life . . . can we expect to see some more real ground of battle between the opposing parties than the facial peculiarities of Mr. A, the social delinquencies of Mr. B, and the benefactions . . . which might be expected to follow Mr. C's return."[45]

This was not altogether fair. There were differences between the parties, though they were obscured by partisan propaganda and local gossip. The Liberals had some claim to be called "the Party of Progress" and had a history to back it up. Their opponents had no comparable record and the legacy of the Thorburn government was, at best, mixed. There was also the question of confederation, always a potent factor—but with Morine now a prominent Tory, this was put in the background. Nevertheless, the Tories took five seats from the Liberals (though both Grieve and Monroe were defeated). The final result was twelve Tories to twenty-three Liberals, with one independent. It was a comfortable majority, but the Tories had done surprisingly well. Overall, the government vote was 39,505, the opposition vote 35,434. And, as the *Evening Herald* pointed out, the Tories had won 75 per cent of the Protestant vote.*

In Trinity Bay, Whiteway headed the poll, with Bond and James

* *Evening Herald*, November 23 and December 26, 1893. The independent member was James Murray in Burgeo-LaPoile, who received 607 votes. Robert Thorburn was defeated in Bonavista—as a Liberal.

Watson not far behind.* It was a hard-fought contest, however. The Conservative slate was led by Grieve and did respectably.† An issue used against Bond was his allegedly incompetent handling of the government's response to the Trinity Bay disaster in 1892.[46] Bond took the accusation head on at a crowded meeting at Trinity, where he apparently spoke for three hours. Grieve refused an invitation to attend. According to the laudatory report in the *Evening Telegram*:

> Mr. Bond . . . amid loud and prolonged cheering . . . kept his audience spellbound. He was prepared for every emergency and with great force and success he carried war into the enemy's camp upon the Trinity Disaster Question with thrilling effect. He described the directors of the Newfoundland Sealing Company, amongst them Pitts, Monroe and Grieve sitting for some five hours deliberating how much they could wring from the Government for the hire of the "Labrador" while their fellow men were perishing on the ice, and actually insisting upon the payment of one thousand dollars before they would allow their steamer to leave. The effect of this will never be forgotten . . . they rose in a body and cheered Mr. Bond when he concluded.[47]

Bond's adversaries went further than levelling these accusations, however. Merchants put pressure on their dealers, and there was active opposition from Anglo-American Telegraph employees at Heart's Content, almost certainly because of Bond's pursuit of Alexander Mackay.[48] Correspondents also told Bond that he was not popular among his fellow Methodists—one J. Sullivan did not know why, except that "you were too liberal minded for their narrow views."[49] It seems that most members of the newly arrived but popular Salvation Army voted for the Conservatives, as well. "Do not give them a cent for a road to their cemetery," counselled an informant.[50] Bond also heard rumours that if

* For the 1893 results, see *ENL* 1:698–99. Watson was a merchant in Trinity.

† Grieve had contested Trinity Bay in 1889 and in a January 1890 by-election.

Whiteway had not actually canvassed against him, he had certainly not canvassed *for* him.[51]

Bitterness did not evaporate with the publication of the election results. Mackay launched a libel suit against the *Evening Telegram,* which had accused him of tampering with messages during the election and abusing his position as manager of the Anglo-American Telegraph Company for party purposes. Morine and Morison complained about corrupt practices in Bonavista district, and alleged threats that they would not be consulted about public expenditures there.[52] O'Brien thought that this was Morine causing trouble—"as clever, unscrupulous and cunning a rascal as can be found anywhere." He also heard that election petitions were being prepared: "It will be a case of the pot and kettle . . . if it comes to an issue, and very dirty water will be stirred up."[53]

There were indeed very stormy times ahead, but the fourth Whiteway administration began predictably enough. There were further appeals to London to accept the 1890 reciprocity convention,[54] and the Colonial Office remained insistent about permanent French treaty enforcement legislation, on which Whiteway prevaricated. In the Executive Council, Bond predicted that the agreed bill would certainly be defeated. Other members—Morris, for example—pointed out that the reciprocity issue made co-operation with London difficult, and that there was still time left on the temporary act. Negotiations about amendments that just might make permanent legislation palatable proved inconclusive.[55] By late March, the British government had decided that unless the colony acted quickly, legislation would have to be passed in London.*

ELECTION PETITIONS AND THE AFTERMATH

These familiar debates and disputes were rudely interrupted on January 6, 1894, when Tory supporters filed nine petitions in the Supreme Court disputing the election of sixteen Liberals—including the entire Executive

---

* Ripon to O'Brien, tgm., March 22, 1894 (CO 194/229, 403). The Foreign Office went as far as to suggest turning the French Shore into a crown colony (FO to CO, secret, February 15, 1894; CO 537/120, 298; Minute by Anderson, February 23, 1894, 294–95).

except Harvey—and James Murray, the only independent member. Filed on the last day allowed by law, the petitions in every case alleged bribery and other corrupt practices. The action was taken under the 1889 Corrupt Practices Act, which had transferred the adjudication of disputed elections from the Assembly to the courts, and which had never been tested.[56] Why the Tories took this action is unclear. The *Evening Telegram* put it down to envy and vindictiveness,[57] which may indeed have been part of the motivation. The Tories had done respectably in 1893. But depending on how the courts interpreted the act, the Liberals could be embarrassed and undermined—creating a chance for the Tories to take over the government either temporarily or more permanently through by-elections or a general election. What is obvious is that the Tories were not motivated by an altruistic desire for electoral reform; indeed, their candidates and members knew "the system" (and had used it) as much as their opponents had.

The first trial began on February 13, involving the Liberal members for Bay de Verde district: Surveyor General Henry Woods and George Moores. The judge was none other than Sir James Winter. The legislature opened two days later, with Augustus Goodridge leading the opposition. The Throne Speech was cautiously optimistic. Bond spoke at length in defence of the government's record and policies, concentrating on the railway, which he asserted was providing employment and slowing emigration, and which had "broadened and enlarged" people's views. He also expanded once again on Newfoundland as part of a transatlantic transportation route. More pertinently, he added: "We have hitherto never been able to take our true position as a colony of the British Empire. We had been for years a mere fishing station, and nothing more, but the time had now come when the old system of things should be abrogated."[58] Morine thought all this to be mere kite-flying.

The House spent most of its time during March discussing supply and ways and means, far earlier in the session than usual. At the end of the month, Judge Winter delivered his decision in the Bay de Verde case. It was a political depth charge: both Woods and Moores were found guilty of corrupt practices, unseated, and disqualified from running in by-elections for the current Assembly. Specifically, Woods (a prominent Methodist) had given employment on public works without proper governmental sanction and authority, and with a view to influencing voters; jobs had also been procured in St. John's for local residents and various promises made to individuals to obtain their votes. Moores had been a consenting party and active helper.[59]

This may well have been, as John Anderson remarked at the Colonial Office, "a case of Satan rebuking Sin"[60]—but the judgment triggered a major political crisis. The House was without a quorum from March 28 to April 10, while the government and the governor debated what would happen next. It was clear to everyone that if Winter's interpretation of the law was followed by the other judges, then all the election petitions would succeed. This was a bitter and unexpected prospect. The government argued, with some justification, that Liberal candidates had conducted their campaigns much as usual, and that the only difference between government and opposition candidates was that the former actually had money to spend, while the latter could only promise it. It was also contended that the judgment, in effect, prevented authorized public expenditures between a dissolution and a general election, thus frustrating the intentions of the legislature.[61] *The Times* pointed out that the judgment undermined "ingrained custom." Since 1832, voters had been "educated in the belief that some substantial benefit to themselves or their immediate surroundings is always of right connected with their exercise of the franchise." Voters looked on elections as "pay time."[62] James Murray had no apologies. The one chance poor people had of getting something from the government was in an election year, he told the House, and they could not be blamed for getting it in a fair and honest way, nor should members be blamed for distributing the road and district grants—which were, after all, the people's property. The system had existed "from time immemorial,"[63] and road work was always done in the fall.

Once again, Governor O'Brien was the umpire in a constitutional conundrum. His attitude was shaped by a military dislike of devious political ways, his personal aversion to what had occurred during the 1893 election, condescension toward colonials, and his reading of Alphaeus

Todd's *Parliamentary Government in the British Colonies.** This book saw a governor as the "pledge and safeguard against all abuse of power" and "the especial guardian of the law."[64] In A.B. Keith's words, it presented a governor as "a benevolent genius presiding over the destinies of the country and exercising the same sort of influence that . . . was exercised by the Sovereign in the Mother Country."[65] Thus Todd thought that a governor was not obliged to sustain a particular party in power and was justified in refusing a dissolution when requested for political ends—and that both courses of action were permissible particularly when he believed that a takeover by the other party would be beneficial. In other words, a governor did not have to be politically neutral.[66] So when an angry and rattled Whiteway told O'Brien that he intended to repeal the Corrupt Practices Act and indemnify all past actions that might have infringed it, the governor said he would refuse assent. He could not approve any measure that would stop the election trials and clear the accused, since he would then be participating in party politics. He also did not want to grant the government a dissolution, for which Whiteway began to press.[67] Remarkably, O'Brien felt that his position reflected his impartiality. Further, he pressed the government to ensure, whatever happened, that the supply bill would pass—the 1893 act had already lapsed and revenue legislation would expire on June 11.

O'Brien would have had to obey the Colonial Office, if it instructed him to accept the Liberal government's advice. What is astonishing is the amount of leeway that he was allowed. Officials in London were obviously influenced by the governor's reports (mainly derogatory), tired of years of confrontation over French Shore issues, and generally unsympathetic to local concerns and sensibilities. Nevertheless, there were some officials who thought that the less O'Brien interfered, the better. There was also unease about the permanent treaty enforcement bill and about supply. The governor was instructed to refuse an immediate dissolution. If the House passed legislation cancelling the Controverted Elections Act, he should

* Alphaeus Todd, *Parliamentary Government in the British Colonies* (1880). English born, Todd had become Canada's dominion librarian (Hodgins, "Todd, Alphaues," in *DCB* 11:883–85).

assent. If such a bill failed, Whiteway should be allowed a dissolution. And if Whiteway resigned, then O'Brien should form a new government that would have the right to a dissolution if it asked for one. As a matter of propriety, the current government should grant supply.[68] The governor did not pass on these instructions to Whiteway and the government; if they had known about them, matters would almost certainly have turned out differently.

Whiteway's next move was not to repeal the Controverted Elections Act, but to ask O'Brien for a dissolution. This he was loath to grant, encouraged by the Tories who claimed they would eventually get a majority.[69] Finally, the government sent an ultimatum: if O'Brien refused a dissolution, they would resign without passing the supply bill.* On April 11, members of the government submitted their resignations and O'Brien asked Goodridge to form an administration, which he agreed to do as long as the legislature was prorogued.[70] The Assembly resumed sitting the same day. Seconded by Morris, Bond moved resolutions rescinding earlier motions to grant supply and establish a Ways and Means Committee, which were carried by a strict party vote and later approved by the Legislative Council. Bond spoke for over two hours. The behaviour of the opposition, he said,

> bore the impress of bitter vindictiveness. It masquerades in the guise of duty. Duty is a good thing. The condemnation of evil is so noble a virtue that even an excess of zeal in its service may be pardoned or admired. *Amor patriae* is a thing so glorious that poets will hymn its praises. . . . But he had heard that respected brands are sometimes placed upon spurious articles. Duty is sometimes but the livery of an unholy

* O'Brien to Ripon, tgm., April 9, 1894 (CO 194/227, 468); for details of the interchanges, see O'Brien to Ripon, conf. (CO 194/227, 469–75). Interestingly, Harvey appears to have lobbied against a dissolution (F.J. Hopwood to Bramston, April 4, 1894, CO 194/227, 455–57). One of Whiteway's correspondents wrote that he was very disappointed that "Mr. Bond does not rally to you" (A.W. Whiteway to W.V. Whiteway, April 11, 1894, ASC, Whiteway Collection 5.04.001).

> purpose . . . and *amor patriae* assumes different faces—sometimes the image of a patriotic and noble-hearted Emmet, and sometimes that of a despicable and soulless Piggott. Have we not examples of this daily before us?

He then attacked Winter's judgment, which had asserted that spending public money authorized by the legislature and carried out by the Executive Council was "illegal and corrupt." The debate continued:

> MR. MORINE – The hon. gentleman was mis-stating Judge Winter.
>
> HON. COLONIAL SECRETARY – Was perfectly correct in what he had stated. . . . The House has been acquainted of the novel position of a Judge on an election petition rendering penal the expenditure of public moneys authorized by this Legislature, assented to by Her Majesty and carried out in the only way that it could be carried out, viz: by order and under the direction of His Excellency's Council.
>
> MR. MORINE – That was not what you said before.
>
> HON. COLONIAL SECRETARY – What I have said I have said, and it will appear upon the records of this House.[71]

Winter, he argued, had presumptuously infringed the prerogatives of the Assembly and offended the basic principle of responsible government—"our rights as a legislature under the Constitution that we possess." The petitions had been filed surreptitiously; if the government could have filed counter-petitions, they would have unseated every member of the opposition. Morine and Morison had arranged for Bonavista electors in St. John's to be taken back to the district; Goodridge had treated and intimidated voters in Twillingate; Munn had done the same in Harbour Grace; Monroe had handed out liquor in St. John's West. The opposition's ill-advised actions would have serious consequences and "destroy the credit of this colony abroad and blight the fair name of his native land."

The governor had refused a dissolution and could be "indiscreet enough to permit [the Opposition] an opportunity of forming a Government." This was an "extraordinary possibility," since they should not be trusted with public money.

Morine replied at even greater length, defending Winter's decision,[72] and the debate continued until after midnight, the galleries packed with Liberal supporters who greeted the resolutions with "tremendous applause." The Colonial Building grounds were crowded with noisy members of the "lower classes," organized, the governor suspected, by Morris and his friends.[73] Bond's speech was apparently widely discussed in St. John's,[74] so much so that the *Evening Herald*—which often took aim at him—felt it necessary to ridicule both the speech and Bond himself:

> Mr. Speaker,
> I do not rise to waste the night in words;
> Let that plebeian on my right [Murray]
> Blow his trumpet: 'tis not my trade,
> As I was brought up with a silver spoon,
> And to wear a fur-trimmed coat,
> But here I stand for right—the right
> To win by purchased votes,
> Though none, it seems, dare stand
> To take a tilt at me
> Friends, countrymen—slaves!
> They charge me false!
> Unseated, indeed! I defy you to it,
> I, the curled darling of "the People's House."
> My sweat's my own; and I,
> Who bought it with public funds,
> Would like to see the Court that will
> Attempt to keep me out of here!
> Smile on, you old bald-headed Tories.
> I scorn your election petitions; paltry tricks.

Listen to these "whereases," mark them well;
They seal your doom; the Governor's too!
Here I stand and scoff you! Here I fling
Hatred and defiance in your face!
Your leader's merciful—very; but if he
Dares to touch a hair of Bond, I will
Knock him higher'n a kite,
For I am the best little man that walks
The streets of the city, and don't you forget it!
You would have my seat, but your best men
Cannot take it. Back, slaves!
I have a ticket to Whitbourne in my pocket![75]

On April 13, the House passed an address to the governor asking for a dissolution.[76] The next morning, O'Brien swore in the new government. When the Speaker arrived with the address, he refused to receive it. In the afternoon, the House debated a motion of no confidence in the Goodridge administration, whose members entered the chamber to jeers. "Think of it, people of Newfoundland," cried Whiteway, "A.B. Morine is your ruler."[77] Discussion had not ended when Black Rod knocked on the door to summon members to the Legislative Council for the prorogation. In what was possibly a unique defiance of constitutional practice, he was kept waiting until the motion passed, a half-hour later. This proceeding invalidated the vote: the Liberals should certainly have acted faster.

The situation, then, was that the Liberals had lost power to a minority government whose existence depended on the governor, who himself faced a dilemma. There was no hope that the Goodridge administration could get a budget through the existing legislature, and Whiteway would not even try unless a dissolution was granted. Moreover, the governor was unwilling to take any action that would stop the election trials. The new Tory government urged O'Brien to maintain it in power by extending the prorogation—which had been granted, initially, for a week only—adding the argument that ice and bad weather in the northern bays would make spring electioneering impossible and effectively disenfranchise those constituencies. It then added a quite bizarre suggestion that the revelations of the election trials and a difficult financial situation showed the need for a thorough investigation of the colony's affairs by an imperial royal commission. Since the Liberals would oppose any such inquiry, the current government should be kept in power, the money bills being extended, if necessary, by imperial legislation.[78] O'Brien liked this idea but it was swiftly rejected in London.[70] This news, and the failure to tempt a few Liberals to cross the floor,* led the governor to decide on a dissolution. The Goodridge ministry resisted; after some argument, O'Brien agreed—against the advice of Chief Justice Carter[80]—to extend the prorogation for a month.[81]

The Trinity Bay election petition came up before Carter on April 30, though all the politicians were preoccupied by the by-election called for Bay de Verde, with voting on May 22. This was a remarkably virulent contest. Newspapers hurled brickbats at each other and at rival politicians. The *Evening Herald* went after Bond as the son of a merchant "who gained his wealth when oppression and wrong were rife. Robert Bond has hoarded up that ill-gotten wealth and neither man, woman or child ever gained a dollar from him." He had never invested "in the general business of the country, but gained his spurious reputation of 'Patriot' for being the least disreputable member of the Whiteway party."[82] The *Herald* began to call him "Pat" Bond—alluding to the *Evening Telegram*'s constant harping on the "incorruptible commoner's" patriotism. Bond attended the court daily between April 30 and May 9 and then left town, claiming business at Whitbourne. But he campaigned hard (as did Whiteway) for the Liberal candidates in Bay de Verde. It was a very close race. When the results were declared, only sixty-six votes separated the first and last place candidates. One Liberal and one Tory were returned.[83] The Liberal *Telegram* called it a "Brilliant Victory"; the Tory *Herald*, "a moral victory."[84]

---

* It was later alleged that Monroe offered to drop the election petitions as long as the Liberals agreed to continue subsidizing his ropewalk. Emerson called this the "worst scandal ever known" (Emerson to Bond, tgm., nd. [1894], RBP 3.13.012).

In the Trinity Bay case, the elected members were accused of arranging free train travel to Whitbourne and back for voters working in St. John's, and "refreshments" while they were there. Second, it was alleged that the Liberal candidates had authorized additional and unapproved expenditures on various public works; third, that they had decided, to their electoral advantage, how employment and patronage related to the construction of roads, bridges, and other work was to be allocated. Bond's behaviour first came under scrutiny on May 10,[85] but he did not appear until May 31, no doubt because of the Bay de Verde by-election. The first part of his evidence concerned his role as the Executive member on the Board of Works, which was one of the colonial secretary's responsibilities. Bond described the road-building programme in the district, many of them "railway connecting roads" that had been specifically authorized by the government and legislature. "Decidedly and emphatically" he avowed:

> No money was allocated by me for the purpose of influencing votes. I never attempted to influence a man's vote in my life except by fair talk. No condition whatsoever was at any time attached to any allocation. . . . I did not authorise the conveyance of any voter to any booth and have no knowledge as to who did authorise it.

Responding to accusations that he provided "refreshments" for voters at Whitbourne, where he had spent polling day, he stated:

> Most decidedly, I did not authorise anyone to procure refreshments for others that [polling] day. . . . I told [people] it was contrary to law and that if I gave even a glass of cold water it might affect my election. . . . [Lemuel] Simmonds came to my cottage at Whitbourne . . . and told me he had provided refreshments for several men and that he had not been paid for so doing. He said the object of his visit was to seek my advice . . . and I may state that the people of Whitbourne and different places come to me on all sorts of topics. . . . If they

> want medical aid or anything else they come to me. . . . I asked him who authorised him to feed those parties and he said a man named Coughlan . . . I said to him, "your course is to send a bill to Coughlan demanding payment."

There followed extensive questioning and debate concerning the expenditure of road grants, how elections expenses were divided, and how election day was managed at Whitbourne.

This ended Bond's evidence. The hearing did not resume until June 14, when the defence returned to the weighty matter of employment on a road between Deer Harbour and Thoroughfare on Random Island. More evidence was also given about election day at Whitbourne and how men were hired to work on railway connecting roads. Whiteway closed the case for the respondents on June 26 and 27 with a lengthy statement. He formally denied all the charges made in the petition, pointed out that the Thorburn government had also built railway connecting roads, and that such work had always been done in the fall. He swore that the relevant 1893 legislation "was not introduced into the Legislature with a view to the employment of people before the elections. . . . That Act was introduced in pursuance of the policy of the Government."

Judge Little, who had replaced Carter by this time, did not deliver his decision until July 25. Concentrating on the public works expenditures, he held that once the legislature had been dissolved on August 13, 1893, the respondents were no longer representatives but candidates. As such, they should not have continued to manage the financial affairs of the district, since this gave them an unfair advantage. Nevertheless, Whiteway and Bond had continued to allow various unauthorized expenditures when the only body that could provide legal authorization was the governor-in-council. They had improperly assumed that they could continue to manage the district's financial affairs, and that "the exercise of this patronage, the affording of this employment . . . must have exercised considerable influence on the minds of the recipients of such substantial benefits. The subtle influence of money or cash favors is far reaching and potent." Little did not dispute that Whiteway and Bond had acted honestly and in the usual way, but the law was the law. Thus he unseated the two most senior members of the House of Assembly and disqualified them from re-election to the current House. Watson, obviously marginal, was simply unseated.*

The trials dragged on, but politics did not stand still. Though the Bay de Verde by-election had returned an additional Tory, it had been a hard fight, so the government decided that, if possible, it would postpone all the other by-elections until November and the re-elections on acceptance of office until October. There were precedents for the latter, since it was legal to hold acting appointments for six months. The postponement of by-elections was more questionable. The relevant legislation stated that vacancies should be filled "at the earliest practicable moment." Acting Attorney General Donald Morison construed this phrase to mean "the earliest convenient moment"—and it was obviously most inconvenient to hold by-elections before the end of the fishing season. O'Brien was rightly dubious about this interpretation of the law, but the Colonial Office advised him to accept it.

This was a vital reprieve for the Tories. It was becoming clear by mid- to late May that it would be some time before enough Liberals were unseated to give them a majority in the Assembly, and also that the revenue bill would probably expire before that occurred. Whiteway evidently thought that the legislature would have to be convened. Unwisely, he showed his hand by letting it be known that he would not accept office or pass supply unless promised the dissolution that would end his trial (among others), and that if he won the ensuing election, he would refuse to serve under O'Brien.[86] The prospect of Whiteway and Bond sitting in the Assembly "with a rope around their necks" so appalled the governor that he decided to prorogue the legislature until such time as there was a Tory majority, and to allow the revenue to be collected without statutory authority.[87]

---

* See the report in the *Evening Herald*, July 25 and 26, 1894. Writing in the *Montreal Gazette*, Moses Harvey called this "the worst case which had yet come to light" and asserted that Whiteway and Bond had spent approximately $50 per vote (*Evening Herald*, August 18, 1894).

As the revenue bill's expiry date approached (June 11), the Whiteway press, already incensed by the by-election postponements, worked itself into a state of near-hysteria. The *Evening Telegram* accused Goodridge of harassing women on Rennie's Mill Road,[88] and urged importers to seize their goods without paying duty.[89] On June 14, no doubt to encourage the others, two Liberal members (George Emerson and James McGrath) marched at the head of a crowd down to a wharf where cargo was being guarded by Customs officials. Emerson seized a package consigned to him while McGrath and others wrestled with the Customs men, and made off in a carriage belonging to the unseated member for Burin (Dr. James Tait). The *Telegram* congratulated Emerson "for his manly and courageous attempt to vindicate the law of the land" and invited importers to follow his example the next day: "There will be hundreds of citizens present to help."[90] The storming of the sheds was frustrated by mounted policemen who arrived before the main crowd of demonstrators, which was headed by Whiteway. After much speech-making, the demonstrators dispersed. The government was restrained from vengeance and the only case to reach the courts was against McGrath, for assault. That staunch Whitewayite, Judge Prowse, fined him a token $2 and entered into a long disquisition on Tory iniquity.[91]

A more respectable line of attack was taken by several pro-Whiteway businessmen who applied in the Supreme Court for writs of mandamus that would order Customs authorities to show cause why their merchandise should not be delivered. The cases never came to a final issue thanks to the legal ingenuity and delaying tactics of Morine, who managed to spin out the proceedings until, at the end of July, the government side had a majority in the Assembly. He was handsomely recompensed ($934.75).[92] Moses Harvey thought that "it will be remembered as the greatest legal combat on record, and one that presented a fund of amusement for which the whole community feels grateful."[93]

All this was grand political theatre. An American visitor to St. John's wrote in July that the political situation was regarded "facetiously rather than otherwise, as the following copy from a poster in a conspicuous part of the town [see page 148], serves to indicate."

LOST
STOLEN OR STRAYED
Between the Colonial Building and the Government House
A RESPONSIBLE GOVERNMENT.
The finder will be suitably rewarded on returning the same
To a Sorrowing Public.[94]

The legislature met at last on August 2, the Liberal opposition being led by Daniel Greene. Thanks to the defection of one Liberal (William Woodford[95]), the sides were fourteen Conservatives to ten Liberals. The business of the short session was almost entirely devoted to passing the necessary money bills and indemnifying actions taken after the previous legislation had expired. There was also a loan bill.

Passing legislation was not a problem in the Assembly, but it was in the Legislative Council. Grieve and Monroe had taken vacant seats there, giving each party five firm votes. Of the remaining members, two were absent for the summer, one was President (and thus had no vote), and two were uncertain. O'Brien had wanted additional appointments, but the Colonial Office had refused. Thus when the legislation reached the Council, there was a real chance that Harvey and others could carry wrecking amendments. One of the uncertain members was persuaded to stay away, but the other, also elderly, had been persuaded to support the Liberals. In the nick of time, an absent Tory member was located on the west coast. He cabled his resignation, a replacement was appointed within an hour, and the day was saved for the Tories.[96] No wonder that the government petitioned to have the co-operative O'Brien's term as governor extended.[97]

Bond seems to have retreated from the public eye during the summer, though ritual abuse continued in Tory newspapers.* He is not mentioned in connection with pro-Whiteway rallies held in St. John's during August; he finally reappeared when the long-delayed by-elections began. The Goodridge government had laid the groundwork by removing many

* *Evening Telegram,* August 16 and 21, 1894. It was reported that Bond was to establish a tobacco factory at Whitbourne (*Evening Telegram*, August 14, 1894).

Liberal-appointed officials and road board members, by suspending or dismissing civil servants thought to have campaigned for Liberal candidates in 1893, and by voting generous sums for public works.* Whiteway thought these actions unprecedented. At the end of August, he issued a manifesto urging voters to support his candidates and reject those of the "Tory Mercantile Party." He lambasted the Supreme Court decisions, his political opponents, and Water Street merchants in general, promising a general election "BEFORE THE END OF THE PRESENT YEAR."[98]

The first by-election was in Burgeo-La Poile, James Murray's former seat. The proclamation issued on August 18 set September 11 as polling day. The government must have known that the steamers plying the south coast had already left St. John's, so there was a real danger that the Liberal candidate would miss nomination day. In the end, the candidate travelled through Halifax. Bond went to the district via Placentia and was campaigning there (as were Morison and Morine) by early September.[99] The Tory candidate won by seventy-eight votes.[100] Re-elections required upon taking office (Morine, Morison, and Duder) were held in Bonavista and Fogo and also went in favour of the government.[101] Bond campaigned in Fogo and then in Twillingate, where the Liberal candidate won.[102] He went on to Trinity Bay, where the vote was held on October 16. The government mounted a vigorous campaign and there were complaints of widespread skulduggery. However, the Liberal candidates managed to hold on to the three seats, though with severely reduced majorities. O'Brien, back from a trip to England and rooting for the Tories, complained to the Colonial Office that two hundred men had returned from Labrador on election day and had not been canvassed.[103] Overall, the Liberals won fourteen seats during the fall by-elections, and the Tories two. The final standings in the Assembly were twenty-three Liberals and thirteen Tories.†

---

* *Evening Telegram*, August 15 and 18, 1894. See also Whiteway to O'Brien, tgm., October 15, 1894. "This coupled with other summary dismissals indicates condition partisan political tyranny unprecedented" (PANL, GN 25/1).

† Bond campaigned in Burin after Trinity Bay, but not elsewhere. The by-election results are in *ENL* 1:699–700. Monroe and Grieve were both defeated, in Trinity Bay and Placentia-St. Mary's, respectively.

Bond's campaigning had been effective. The Little Bay Political Committee attributed Giles Foote's return in Twillingate to Bond's "eloquent address," and asked him to stand for the district at the next general election.[104] A correspondent from New Harbour (Trinity Bay) praised his "wonderful energy and hard work. . . . I for one Newfoundlander will never forget the noble work done this campaign by yourself."[105] Another congratulated Bond for "having cut off the head of the Monster Toryism. . . . Oh what a victory and what a people is ours!"[106] Alfred Seymour attributed both the Twillingate and Trinity results to Bond—"every young native voter will be with you, you can have no idea how proud we all feel of you."[107] "You, the Patriot of our dear old Terra Nova."[108] "You have won the greatest political battle that was ever fought in Newfoundland."[109] Whiteway asked Bond to come into St. John's from Whitbourne for a demonstration in his honour, but he declined—the strain of the past three months, he said, had made him ill.[110] A demonstration there was, however, with bands of men and boys parading the streets, and a torchlight procession with fireworks marched to the houses of Whiteway and Harvey.[111]

There was no rejoicing at Government House, where O'Brien found himself in a "whirlpool of dirty hot water." He attributed the results to poor strategy by the Tories, a general dislike of Morine, the "socialistic doctrines" and anti-merchant rhetoric used by Whiteway, Bond, and others, and the belief among the "lower orders" that the Liberals had been punished for providing money and work. His analysis was not inaccurate. He also expressed grave misgivings about the colony's future. The government faced a very serious financial situation and tense rumours about the state of the two private banks, the Union and the Commercial, were widespread. "The entire business community are in a state of panic, as are those who have shares in the banks and other commercial enterprises." Colonial bankruptcy seemed a real possibility.[112]

THE BANK CRASH

There had been speculation about the banks for some time, since they had significantly increased their loan business at a time of economic difficulty.[113] In addition, the refusal of supply, political instability, and bad publicity had reduced confidence in the colony. Reid, for example, was finding it difficult to sell his railway bonds on the London market, and prices of all Newfoundland issues had declined.* A bank manager reported in June that he had never received so many inquiries about the state of local firms. Whiteway had not helped matters, it was reported, when he tried to force the government-owned Savings Bank to pay a government debt of $664,000 to the London and Westminster in return for colonial debentures. The money would have had to come from the Savings Bank's deposits in the private banks, whose liquidity would be seriously compromised as a result. The Goodridge government cancelled the arrangement, but the Savings Bank board (on which the Liberal members had not yet been replaced) nevertheless ordered the banks to pay up and Whiteway went in person to demand the money. It seemed that he was deliberately trying to precipitate a commercial crisis that would force the recall of the legislature. It was rumoured, reported O'Brien, that "through rage and vindictiveness, Sir W. Whiteway has gone off his head."[114]

Despite the results of the by-elections, the Goodridge government—now in a minority again and facing a dismal financial and economic situation (there had been a poor Labrador fishery)—did not resign. It wanted to hang on, it seems, until at least the spring of 1895. It argued that it could retain power until it was defeated in the Assembly. Then, if it advised a dissolution, stay on until a general election took place, which the Tories thought they could win. Moreover, the government said, it was in a far better position to deal with the impending crisis than their opponents were.[115] All of this was highly questionable, but O'Brien, for his part, had no wish to see the Liberals in power, was uncertain whether he should impose spending controls, and would have liked a warship in the harbour.

Amid rancour, argument, panic, and paralysis, the colony ran onto the rocks. A well-founded rumour circulated that the London and Westminster Bank was going to refuse further credit to the Commercial Bank (which had already curtailed its business), and would not float the loan

* John Fretwell pointed out (to Ripon, November 30, 1894) that Newfoundland 3.5 per cent bonds had fallen to 89 cents on the dollar (CO 194/229, 688). On Fretwell, see *ENL* 2:423 and *Canadian Gazette*, vol. 23, passim.

authorized by the legislature in August. It was widely understood that either one of these eventualities would have disastrous results. Refusal of credit would force the Commercial Bank to call in its loans, which in turn would cause the suspension of many firms and a run on the other banks. Not floating its loan would force the government to take funds out of the Savings Bank to repay debt interest due on January 1, 1895; this would require the Savings Bank to withdraw deposits from the private banks, which would cause them to call in loans, with similar results. James Pitts had warned O'Brien that if the government made such a call, and if the banks were unable to make advances to merchants against their stocks of fish—some 400,000 quintals valued at £350,000—trade would come to a standstill.[116] He suggested that the situation was so serious that the Liberals should allow the Tories to stay in office until a loan was floated, and there was talk of a delegate going to London to negotiate with financiers.

A.W. Harvey, a member of the government, thought that such a deal would not be possible. Liberal party members had not met since the by-elections, and while he and Whiteway might agree, Bond and Emerson (dubbed "the irreconcilables") certainly would not—and Morris was (as always) on the fence.[117] Then on Saturday, December 8, news arrived that owing to the suspension of operations by Prowse, Hall, and Morris (a London discount house doing business with St. John's firms), the London and Westminster had refused to accept any further bank or commercial exchange from Newfoundland.

The result was immediate. E.J. Duder and Co. ceased doing business the same day, followed quickly by Goodridge, Steer, Job, and Baine Johnston.[118] It was widely expected that the Commercial Bank would close its doors on Monday the 10th, and that the Union might soon follow. The governor urged a coalition government. Goodridge and Morine said they would talk to Harvey and Greene,[119] but there was no result. The government also asked the Colonial Office about the possibility of a $1 million loan to the Savings Bank (technically an advance on the loan authorized in August), and agreed to accept an inquiry.[120] The reply was uncompromising: the British government could not intervene except after the full inquiry by a royal commission that had been requested by

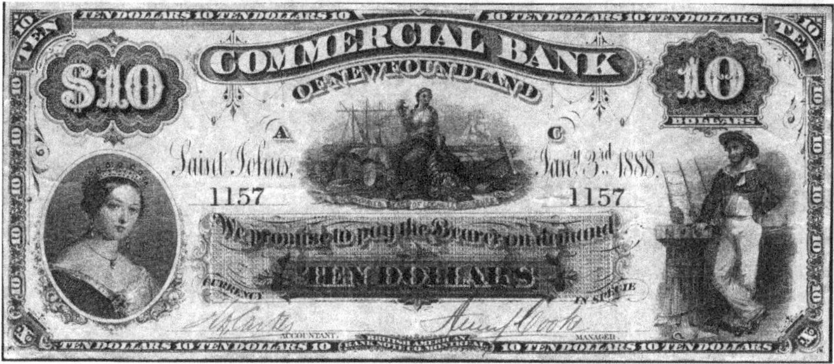

Notes of the Union and Commercial banks. (Bank of Canada Museum)

both the government and the legislature, which should be convened without delay.[121]

On "Black Monday," December 10, deprived of credit in London and with its customers unable to repay their overdrafts in anything but codfish, the Commercial Bank closed its doors. To avoid a run, the Union Bank soon followed.[122] Crowds filled the streets, too shocked to be violent, vainly looking for exchange for their suddenly worthless banknotes.* More firms stopped business; by the next day, more than half of the larger merchant houses had closed down. The Savings Bank, its assets tied up in the two failed banks and unsaleable colonial debentures, was also in a precarious position (though it managed to get $1 million from the Union

* The two banks had notes in circulation with a face value of approximately $1.4 million (JHA 1894–95, 16). The *Daily News* reported on December 13 that Union notes were circulating "fairly freely" at face value.

People gather on Duckworth Street, bewildered by the Bank Crash of December 10, 1894. (City of St. John's Archives, 02-07-058)

Bank). The colony faced bankruptcy. On December 11, a deputation—Whiteway, Bond, Emerson, Morris, and Woods— called on the governor and demanded that he dismiss the government. It was in a minority, many of its members had connections with the failed banks, and Goodridge had closed his business.

The governor first told the government to open the legislature, but further discussions with Harvey and Greene confirmed that a coalition was impossible. The government therefore finally resigned[123]—but not before drawing salaries and other fees from the depleted Treasury.[124] A Liberal ministry took office on the 13th, led by Daniel Greene, obviously shadowed by Whiteway, Bond, and others.[125] HMS *Tourmaline* sailed for St. John's from Bermuda.[126]

To many observers, it seemed that Newfoundland was now finished as an independent country. It had embarked on an expensive railway policy, running up a debt whose payments could not be met, given the overall economic situation and the difficulties in the fish trade. Its government's financial position was at best shaky. The colony remained at loggerheads with Canada, reciprocity with the United States seemed impossible, and there was no prospect of a deal regarding the French Shore. Opinion in London was unsympathetic: the colony's continued opposition to confederation seemed incomprehensible and its convoluted behaviour over the French Shore reprehensible. The political crisis of the early 1890s seemed to show that constitutional change had to happen. It did not, and much of the credit has to go to the government that took over in December 1894.

NOTES

1 Bond in Assembly, May 30 and 31 (*Evening Telegram,* June 10, 13, 1890).

2 *Evening Telegram,* June 4, 1890.

3 Assembly debate June 6, in the *Evening Telegram,* June 20, 1890 (*JHA* 1890, 192).

4 For Shaughnessy, see Regerh, "Shaughnessy, Thomas George, 1st Baron Shaughnessy," *DCB* 15:923–27.

5 Bond in Assembly, April 24, 1891 (*Evening Telegram,* May 12 and 13, 1891).

6 Howley, *Reminiscences,* 1085–86.

7 Whiteway in Assembly, May 17 (*Evening Telegram,* June 30, July 1, 1893).

8 FO to CO, June 15, and a Minute by Anderson, June 16, 1893 (CO 194/226, 270–72). Also see Chapter 4.

9 Ripon to O'Brien, July 17, 1893 (CO 194/226, 270).

10 O'Brien to Ripon, conf., November 17, 1893 (CO 194/225, 99–100).

11 O'Brien to Ripon, conf., August 10, 1893 (CO 194/224, 737–38).

12 Ripon to O'Brien, secret, September 21, 1893, and conf., September 20, 1893 (FO to CO, November 20, 1893, and CO 194/226, 375–77).

13 Knutsford to O'Brien, tgm., January 23, 1891 (*JHA* 1891, Appendix, 540).

14 O'Brien to Knutsford, conf., February 9 and 12, 1891 (CO 537/120, 241, 254); Whiteway in Assembly, February 20, 1891 (*Evening Telegram,* March 2, 1891).

15 O'Brien to Knutsford, conf., February 3, 1891 (CO 537/120, 221).

16 Whiteway to E.B. Pennell, February 17, 1891 (CO 537/120, 251).

17 Hiller, "A History," 228.

18 O'Brien to Knutsford, tgm., February 15, 1891 (CO 537/120, 262).

19 Bond to Whiteway, confidential and personal, June 23, 1891 (RBP 8.03.001).

20 O'Brien to Knutsford, tgm., July 20, 1891; Knutsford to O'Brien, conf., August 28, 1891 (*JHA* 1898, Appendix, 272–75). Also Minute by Anderson, n.d. [1895] (CO 194/233, 265–67).

21 Bond in Assembly, May 1, 1891 (*Evening Telegram*, May 19, 1891).

22 The committee's report is in *JHA* 1891, Appendix, 447–56.

23 *Evening Telegram*, July 31, August 3 and 23, and September 9, 1891.

24 *JHA* 1892, 7–8. The account of the tragedy from the *Trinity Weekly Record* can be found at http://ngb.chebucto.org/Articles/dis-trinity-bay-disaster-1892.shtml. See also RBP 4.11.010 and Michael Harrington, "Offbeat History," *Evening Telegram*, February 26 and May 2, 1979.

25 *ENL* 2:646.

26 Baker, "Absentee Landlordism," 13–14.

27 Baker, "Absentee Landlordism," 15.

28 Morris in Assembly, August 16 (*Evening Telegram*, September 8, 1892).

29 *JHA* 1892, second session, August 11 through 26, 1–32. The debates were published in the *Evening Telegram* when it reappeared in September.

30 For Woods, see *ENL* 5:617.

31 Oliver, "The Rebuilding of the City of St. John's," 120.

32 The report of the inquiry is in *JHA* 1893, Appendix, 395–432.

33 Bond to Dr. Anderson, August 29, 1893 (RBP 3.12.013).

34 For Grieve, see *ENL* 2:747.

35 *Evening Telegram,* June 7, 1893.

36 *Evening Telegram*, August 26, 1893.

37 *Evening Telegram*, September 23, 1893.

38 O'Brien to Bramston, conf., October 21, 1893 (CO 194/224, 779–80).

39 *Evening Herald*, September 16, 1893.

40 *Evening Herald*, October 7, 1893.

41 *Evening Herald*, September 29, 1893.

42 *Daily Tribune*, November 4, 1893.

43 O'Brien to Ripon, secret, November 4, 1893 (CO 194/225, 85–89).

44 Prowse, *History of Newfoundland*, 531.

45 *Canadian Gazette* 22:554, November 16, 1893, 155–57.

46 John F. Gash to Bond, November 13, 1893 (RBP 3.12.010).

47 Undated *Evening Telegram* cutting (RBP 3.12.014).

48 W.R. Smith to Bond, December 4, 1893, and Thomas Connor to Bond, November 25, 1893 (RBP 3.12.010).

49 J. Sullivan to Bond, November 24, 1893. See also W.A. Oke to Bond, n.d. [1893] (RBP 3.12.010).

50 H.C. Morris to Bond, November 11, 1893 (RBP 3.12.010).

51 Bond to R.H. O'Dwyer, February 27, 1894 (RBP 3.13.001).

52 The letters, dated November 17 and 30, were enclosed in O'Brien to Ripon, December 1, 1893 (CO 194/225, 127–28).

53 O'Brien to Bramston, private, December 2, 1893 (CO 194/225, 125–26). See also O'Brien to Ripon, conf., December 5, 1893 (CO 194/225, 150–52).

54 O'Brien to Ripon, tgm., January 3, 1894 (CO 194/227, 5) and O'Brien to Ripon, conf., February 8, 1894 (CO 194/227, 62–90). This contains a 28-page Minute of Council.

55 For example, O'Brien to Ripon, conf., February 2, 1894 (CO 194/227, 93–95).

56 O'Brien to Ripon, conf., January 13, 1894 (CO 194/227, 15–20).

57 *Evening Telegram,* January 12, 1894.

58 Bond in Assembly, February 22 (*Evening Telegram,* February 24, 1894).

59 Certificate of Judge Winter, March 31, 1894, encl. in O'Brien to Ripon, conf., April 2, 1894 (CO 194/227, 235–37).

60 Minute, March 28, 1894 (CO 194/227, 407).

61 O'Brien to Ripon, conf., April 2, 1894 (CO 194/227, 432–33).

62 *The Times,* January 24, 1894 (encl. in O'Brien to Ripon, secret, January 30, 1894, CO 194/227, 41).

63 Murray in Assembly, February 21 (*Evening Telegram*, February 23, 1894).

64 Todd, *Government,* Chapter 1 and 432, 460.

65 Keith, *Responsible Government* 1:148.

66 Todd, *Government,* 571.

67 O'Brien to Ripon, conf., April 2, 1894 (CO 194/227, 432–37).

68 Minutes by Anderson, March 29; by Bramston, March 29; by Meade, March 30; and by Buxton, March 31, 1894. Memorandum by Ripon, April 1; Ripon to O'Brien, tgm., April 3, 1894 (CO 194/227, 413–20).

69 O'Brien to Ripon, tgm., April 4, 1894 (CO 194/227, 464).

70 O'Brien to Ripon, conf., April 14, 1894 (CO 194/227, 535).

71 A copy of the speech is in RBP 3.13.005 (*JHA* 1894, 43–48).

72 See *Evening Telegram,* April 16, 1894.

73 *JHA* 1894, 45–49; O'Brien to Ripon, conf., April 16, 1894 (CO 194/227, 540). See also *Evening Telegram* April 12, 1894, and *Evening Herald,* April 17, 1894.

74 R.P. Mackenzie to Bond, April 12, 1894 (RBP 3.13.002).

75 *Evening Herald,* April 19, 1894.

76 *Evening Telegram,* April 20, 1894.

77 *Evening Telegram,* May 2, 1894.

78 "Reasons urged by Mr. Goodridge's Government for non-dissolution of the Legislature," encl. in O'Brien to Ripon, conf., April 17 , 1894, and O'Brien to Ripon, tgm., April 17, 1894 (CO 94/277, 496, 555–60).
79 Ripon to O'Brien, tgm., April 18, 1894 (CO 194/227, 564).
80 Carter to O'Brien, n.d. [1894] (PANL, GN 1/3/A) .
81 Hiller, "A History," 280.
82 *Evening Herald*, May 3, 1894.
83 *ENL* 1:699.
84 *Evening Telegram*, May 23, 1894, and *Evening Herald*, May 24, 1894.
85 This account is based on a transcript of the evidence, sixty-five pages in length, in RBP 3.13.004 and 3.13.006, and an untitled bound volume in the A.C. Hunter Reference Library, St. John's. See also Hiller, "The Trinity Bay Election Trial," 215–29.
86 O'Brien to Ripon, conf., May 19, 1894; tgms., May 29, 30, 1894 (CO 194/228, 30–33, 35–37, 41, and 86).
87 O'Brien to Ripon, conf., June 2, 1894 (CO 194/228, 94–97).
88 *Evening Telegram*, May 30, 1894.
89 *Evening Telegram*, June 9, 1894.
90 *Evening Telegram*, June 14, 1894.
91 These events are described in O'Brien to Ripon, conf., June 18 and June 30, 1894 (CO 194/228, 156, 185 and *Daily News*, June 15, 18, 1894).
92 O'Brien to Ripon, conf., June 25 30, 1894 (CO 194/228, 179 and 185); various newspapers, memorandum "In Re Mandamus proceedings," and Morine's account (RBP 3.13.007).
93 *Montreal Gazette*, reprinted in the *Evening Herald*, August 18, 1894.
94 Reprinted in the *Evening Herald*, August 24, 1894.
95 *ENL* 5:614.
96 Hiller, "A History," 285–86.
97 O'Brien to Ripon, July 26, 1894 (CO 194/228, 257).
98 Whiteway, "To the People of Newfoundland," August 29, 1894 (RBP 3.13.009).
99 *Evening Telegram*, August 20, 25, and 30; September 1, 3, 4, 6, 8, and 10, 1894.
100 *Evening Telegram*, September 14, 1894; *ENL* 3:634.
101 *Evening Telegram*, October 5, 1894.
102 *Evening Telegram*, October 22, 1894.
103 O'Brien to Ripon, November 2, 1894 (CO 194/228, 414–15).

104 Address from the Little Bay Political Committee, October 22, 1894 (RBP 3.13.010).
105 G.E. Bearns to Bond, n.d. [1894] (RBP 3.13.012).
106 H.C. Morris to Bond, October 15, 1894 (RBP 3.13.012).
107 Seymour to Bond, October 27, 1894 (RBP 3.13.012).
108 William Godden to Bond, November 19, 1894 (RBP 3.13.012).
109 H. O'Dwyer to Bond, November 1, 1894 (RBP 3.13.012).
110 Whiteway to Bond, tgm., November 15, and reply, November 15, 1894 (RBP 3.13.012).
111 O'Brien to Ripon, secret, November 17, 1894 (CO 194/228, 471–72).
112 This summary is based on O'Brien's secret and confidential dispatch to Ripon, November 17, 1894, and on his private letters to Anderson, November 16 and 19, 1894 (CO 194/228, 440–41, 442–45, 464-65, 471–72).
113 Chu, "Too Big to Fail?," 180, 188.
114 O'Brien to Ripon, conf., May 7, 1894; see also O'Brien to Ripon, conf, April 24, 1894 (CO 194/227, 590).
115 O'Brien to Ripon, tgm., November 28, 1894 (CO 194/228, 477).
116 O'Brien to Ripon, conf., December 10, 1894 (CO 194/228, 520–21); *ENL* 4:315–17).
117 Ibid.
118 *Evening Telegram*, December 26, 1894.
119 O'Brien to Ripon, conf., December 10, 1894 (CO 194/228, 514).
120 O'Brien to Ripon, tgm., December 10, 1894 (CO 194/228, 498–99).
121 Ripon to O'Brien, tgm., December 11, 1894 (CO 194/228, 494).
122 O'Brien to Ripon, conf., December 10 and 11, 1894 (CO 194/228, 514–15, 564–65).
123 O'Brien to Ripon, conf., December 22, 1894 (CO 194/228, 570–77).
124 O'Brien to Ripon, secret, December 19, 1894 (CO 194/228, 564).
125 O'Brien to Ripon, tgms., December 12 and 13, 1894 (CO 194/228, 534–36).
126 Admiralty to Colonial Office, December 12, 1894 (CO 194/229, 204).

CHAPTER SIX

The Crisis Years, 1894–1897

The Liberals faced an extraordinarily difficult situation. The colony was near financial collapse and the party was divided between those who were legitimate members of the Assembly and those who lurked outside. All Liberals opposed British intervention, if this could be avoided, but (like the Tories) they were divided over confederation with Canada. The question, therefore, was how could Newfoundland get out of the existing confusion to best advantage, in terms of both party warfare and national benefit. For the Liberals, there was also a real political problem: any solution would demand retrenchment and cutbacks, but how could this be made palatable to an electorate that would vote once again in 1897?

THE GREENE GOVERNMENT

The legislature met on December 15. The Throne Speech included these words:

> The great eagerness to acquire wealth by trading on credit has unquestionably been the cause of the present crisis, and the solidity of our character and the purity of our name have been sacrificed to it. . . . It should be remembered that the legitimate province of credit is to diffuse capital, and not to create it. It has been the false views prevailing on the subject, which, carried into the banking system, have done such business.[1]

A.W. Harvey rightly saw the crash as a delayed result of the economic depression of the 1880s, which had drained mercantile capital. He pointed also to a "reckless" local press and to political instability[2]—which, of course, had been assisted by the mercantile party. On December 17, the legislature formed a Joint Select Committee to investigate the closed banks.

One of the new government's first actions was to find money to pay the debt interest, which was due on January 1, 1895. It did this by using $250,000 that the Union Bank had on deposit at the National Bank of Commerce in New York.[3] The government also inquired whether, if the legislature agreed to a royal commission, the British government would provide immediate financial assistance and what the scope of such an inquiry might be.[4] That the Colonial Office refused to make any commitment other than to appoint a royal commission if requested is indicative of its attitude.[5] Its view was that a Newfoundland bankruptcy might have advantages. In the first place, it was argued, a grant-in-aid would merely throw good money after bad, and a long-term loan would not bring about any permanent improvement. John Anderson pointed to the large increase in the debt since 1890, as well as to the deficit financing that had characterized the colony's affairs. In his view, Newfoundland could not be trusted to run its financial affairs properly. He noted "that the Colony which [in 1891] was in such straits as to ask for an immediate loan of £150,000 should since then have entered upon such a work [as the railway], shews sufficiently the financial ideas of the men who then as now have been responsible for its government."* In the second place, if the colony did go bankrupt, the imperial government could step in as receiver and decide whether Newfoundland should become a crown colony or a Canadian province.[6] Britain could then handle French Treaty Shore matters unilaterally. The best policy, then, was simply to wait and turn down appeals for financial help.[7]

Locally, the restoration of a circulating medium was urgent. The situation was eased by the speedy appearance of Canadian banks in St. John's—the first representatives arrived on December 16—and R.G. Reid persuaded

---

* Memorandum by Anderson, n.d. (CO 194/228, 498–99) and Minute by Anderson, December 12, 1894 (CO 1194/228, 515–18). John Anderson (1854–1918) may have briefly visited Newfoundland in 1901. Sir John Anderson from 1901, he later became governor of the Straits Settlements and then of Ceylon.

the Bank of Montreal, with which he was closely connected, to open a branch in St. John's.[8] Canadian currency became legal tender in Newfoundland early in 1895. The government considered issuing treasury notes in exchange for Union and Commercial currency, but in the end decided to guarantee local banknotes at a value to be decided.[9]

That value depended on the Joint Select Committee, which reported on December 27, ten days after it was formed.[10] Its conclusion was that the stability of the Union Bank had been damaged by heavy losses on large overdrawn accounts, but that it was solvent and should be able to pay its creditors in full.* The Commercial Bank, on the other hand, was bankrupt, its books were a mess, and it should be liquidated. The Committee recommended that the government guarantee Union notes at 80 cents to the dollar, and Commercial notes at 20 cents.[11] A reluctant O'Brien was instructed to assent to the legislation once it was passed in late December.

This decision was widely unpopular. Most notes circulating outside St. John's were those of the Commercial Bank (the magistrate in Harbour Grace told Whiteway to expect rioting).[12] People in St. John's held Union notes, for the most part, but indignation was equally widespread. A mass meeting of more than 3,000 people, held outside the Colonial Building on January 1, resolved that the situation was unjust and that all noteholders should be paid full value. The meeting also protested the appointment of trustees for the banks by the government rather than the Supreme Court, and urged the appointment of an imperial royal commission of inquiry.† Petitions to that effect went to the legislature and to the governor,[13] and the *Evening Herald* campaigned in favour.[14] The response from London was that a royal commission could only be sent if requested by the full legislature, not by the government alone, and there could be no

---

* Chu argues that both banks were insolvent (Chu, "Too Big to Fail?," 180, 186).

† O'Brien to Ripon, conf., January 4, 1895 (CO 194/230, 75). "The applicants for a Royal Commission," commented Anderson in London, "appear to think it would go out laden with bread and butter and various other good things for promiscuous distribution, and their demand that the bank notes should be guaranteed in full is not very consistent with their demand for retrenchment" (Minute, January 15, 1895, CO 194/228, 590).

pledges in advance about what might happen as a result—a clear hint that constitutional changes might be made.[15]

The Liberals were divided about the desirability of a royal commission. Some (including Bond) opposed the idea outright. Others (including Harvey) were prepared to give conditional support: the inquiry should be seen as preliminary to a loan guarantee, and there had to be an assurance that there would be no interference with the constitution.[16] This was hardly likely to happen. With the internal division unresolved, there was no royal commission and the imperial government's financial help came in the form of a relief fund administered not by the Newfoundland authorities, but by the former chairman of the British Board of Customs, Sir Herbert Murray.[17] "Mrs. Britannia, the generous old dame," sniped the *Evening Telegram*, "has taken pity upon us, and, not to be outdone by 'Brother Jonathan,' has adopted this method."[18] This was a reference to the sympathy and aid coming from Newfoundlanders and others in New England, which had sparked discussion of annexation to the United States. But, as the *Evening Herald* remarked, that, too, was impossible—and since no prominent person stepped forward to lead such a movement, the idea commanded little respect.[19] Nevertheless, the newspapers gave the possibility of annexation to the US a considerable amount of attention, and contrasted American generosity with British stinginess. A more realistic option was confederation with Canada, which soon became a subject of vigorous debate.

On New Year's Eve, the rotund governor's blood pressure was raised to a dangerous level by the passage of a bill to remove the electoral disabilities imposed on those members unseated in 1894—both O'Brien and the opposition called it "the Whitewash Bill." Recoiling at the prospect of Whiteway and his colleagues returning to the government, the governor referred the matter to London. He was instructed to assent,[20] which he did reluctantly, remarking that the bill could be seen as a Liberal victory over himself and the Supreme Court. In fact, the bill was a sensible move, since it paved the way for a more experienced government and the re-establishment of some semblance of stability.

THE WHITEWAY GOVERNMENT AND CONFEDERATION

Greene resigned on February 1, 1895, and decided not to join the new government that Whiteway agreed to form. It took Whiteway a few days to form the Executive, given the political manoeuvring involved and the fact that five members on the final list did not have seats in the legislature. The new government was finally announced on February 8.[21] Whiteway took a seat on the Legislative Council, but on February 27 won a by-election in Harbour Grace. Morris and Woods found vacancies in their former districts; Bond and Emerson went to the Council.

The financial outlook remained grim, and the colony's future was at best uncertain. The British government remained adamant that there could be no direct financial assistance without a formal inquiry, which the Liberals did not want. The Canadian government refused loans to the colony and to the Savings Bank. In these circumstances, there seemed no other option but to explore the possibility of confederation.[22] On March 1, the Canadian government agreed to receive a delegation,* though it was as unenthusiastic about the discussions as the Newfoundlanders. Canada was also facing financial difficulties, was distracted by the Manitoba schools question, and could not afford to offer terms that might exacerbate financial problems or cause further federal-provincial friction.

The Newfoundland delegation's departure was delayed when Bond and Whiteway both caught "severe colds"—and the latter something worse: it was reported that Whiteway was suffering from "severe nervous depression and internal complications caused by overwork and excessive mental strain."[23] Consequently, the delegation was led by Bond; the other members were Morris, Emerson, and William Horwood.† The Canadian

---

* Aberdeen to O'Brien, tgm., March 1, 1895; "Documents Relating to the Proceedings of the Conference at Ottawa upon the Subject of Confederation with Canada" (Hereafter "DRPC"), p. 4 (RBP 8.02.013); *JHA* 1894–95, Appendix, 369–432. Newfoundland suggested meeting at Saint John or Fredericton; the Canadians chose Ottawa.

† Horwood had been colonial secretary in the Greene administration. The membership of the delegation was suggested by Whiteway (Whiteway to Bond, 21 March, 1895 (RBP 8.03.020) and *ENL* 2:1039).

prime minister, Sir Mackenzie Bowell, had intimated that he would accept a bipartisan delegation, but this was not to be. As a result, the opposition resolved not to be bound by any recommendations made by the delegation and retreated into self-righteous neutrality.[24]

However, the opposition did not go so far as to support the vigorous anti-confederate campaign, which reached a crescendo in March. The most prominent member of that group was probably James Murray, who published a magazine called the *Anti-Confederate*. Other businessmen and local farmers were sympathetic, and there were large meetings in St. John's.[25] Murray and others argued that Canada and Newfoundland had nothing in common: trading patterns would be upset, food prices would increase, Crown lands would be alienated to strangers, and the island depopulated.[26] Moreover the current problems were merely temporary. When the delegation left St. John's on March 27, Murray led a demonstration of about five hundred people at the wharf. They jeered the delegates and carried a Union Jack, the "native flag" draped in crepe, as well as a banner with a map of Newfoundland on one side and a seal on the other.[27] The annexationists paraded with a band.*

The Newfoundland party arrived in Ottawa on April 3. At a banquet soon after, Bond spoke warmly about Canada and Canadians, but made it clear that the delegation was not begging for help on bended knee. Canada was not negotiating with a financial and economic basket case, but with a fellow member of the British Empire that possessed valuable assets. Newfoundland was not "that wretched, worthless island that some would have you believe." It had great economic potential in its forests, minerals, and agricultural land, and its people were "hardened by the storms that rage along our coast [and] would be able and willing to defend our common country should occasion ever require it." He continued:

> We are anxious to learn what Canada is prepared to offer us. . . . If we are offered that which will enable us to build up a community that will withstand the winds and storms of

* But O'Brien reported that the steamer left amid "complete silence" (O'Brien to Ripon, conf., April 4, 1895, CO 194/230, 473).

> the future, then Newfoundland will come in and join you, and aid you too, in completing a structure which, bound together by the bonds of patriotism, will add greater prestige to that Empire upon which the sun never sets.*

The talks began on April 4. The Canadian federal government was represented by Bowell, Sir Adolphe-Philippe Caron (Postmaster General), George E. Foster (Minister of Finance), and John Haggart (Minister of Railways and Canals). The Newfoundland delegation (not unreasonably) based its initial proposals on the terms discussed with Sir Charles Tupper in 1887–88, and on the further, if less formal, discussions held with Senator Howlan in 1891; it hoped for generosity and flexibility. The Canadians refused to accept the earlier talks as precedents because they had been unofficial,[28] and they were understandably cautious.

The central problem was the Newfoundland debt, which now stood at approximately $15.8 million.† Canada offered to assume $10.3 million, based on $50 per head of population (the same allowance provided to Prince Edward Island in 1873) and pay "a yearly allowance" of $465,000. It would maintain services that "fall under the head of general or Dominion services" as well as steamship connections. There would also be a militia grant of $40,000 per annum. Newfoundland would be represented in Ottawa by four senators and ten members of Parliament. Newfoundland fishermen would receive no special treatment, despite Newfoundland's request for it.[29] There was no mention of the railway. The Canadian representatives argued that Newfoundland was being treated fairly compared to other provinces, and that a larger allowance would be rejected in Parliament and cause federal-provincial problems. Moreover, Canada would be a net loser, when all payments were tallied, to the extent of $657,000 annually.

The Newfoundland delegation was therefore faced with a situation where, as a new province, it would lose the Customs revenues on which it

---

* *Montreal Gazette* report, printed in the *Evening Telegram*, April 23, 1895 (RBP 8.03.021). The banquet was on April 9.

† This figure includes the funded and floating debt plus contractual obligations relating to the railway.

had traditionally relied, be forced to service a debt of about $5.4 million, be responsible for providing services it estimated would cost more than $700,000 annually—and would also pay for the completion of the railway. The delegates argued strenuously for better terms, but it was clear that the Bowell government was not willing to take any risks, financial or political, to bring Newfoundland into the Dominion. It is a measure of the colony's predicament that the delegation (but not the Newfoundland government as a whole) seemed, by April 10, to have been close to accepting the Canadian terms,[30] even though they implied a massive reorganization of internal services and the imposition of municipal and local taxation. But they held that Newfoundland could not do this and service the remaining debt. It was therefore decided to appeal to London for financial help. Lord Aberdeen, Canada's governor general, told the Colonial Office on April 11 that there was a "prospect of reaching basis of agreement" but that

> much . . . if not everything, will depend on whether HM's Govt will supplement allowance to be given by Canada to Newfoundland. If this is done, Newfoundland delegates are prepared to give an undertaking that their Govt will pass the last permanent [French Shore enforcement] Bill submitted by HM's Govt to the Newfoundland legislature.*

The talks were suspended on April 16 to await a decision from London.[31] The delegates arrived back in St John's five days later.

It had been predicted that financial aid might be necessary, but the nature of the draft terms of union and the amount of money requested caused officials in London to become decidedly unsympathetic. The idea of Britain contributing to the annual subsidy was rejected out of hand. John Bramston noted that the proposal amounted to "an offer by Newfoundland to pass a permanent act if England will grant her an annual

---

* Aberdeen to Ripon, tgm., April 11, 1895 (Ripon papers, British Library, Add. Mss., 43558, 68:125). Aberdeen also forwarded a message from Foster to the effect that it was important for the imperial government to "give practical sympathy" (Ibid., 126; the telegram is also in CO 537/113, 89).

sum forever in aid of the expenses of Government," and he predicted that the House of Commons would object.[32] In general, the impression at the Colonial Office was that Canada was driving an unnecessarily hard bargain and should improve the financial terms.[33] There was a similarly negative reaction to a later Canadian proposal that the imperial government might provide a lump sum of approximately £1 million to pay down the Newfoundland debt, or at least guarantee a loan for that amount—but mitigation of the debt problem, it was thought, would set an impossible precedent. In summary, the British government now took the position, as Sir Robert Meade put it, that "desirable as Confederation is, one can pay too high a price for it." Tellingly, he added that for a fraction of this sum, Newfoundland would accept "some form of control"[34]—and that is what was really wanted. Thus on May 9, the Colonial Office told Aberdeen and O'Brien that the established policy would be followed: the British government could not take any action concerning Newfoundland without a full inquiry.[35]

On May 1, Whiteway had told Bowell that his government could not accept the proposed terms of union unless Canada assumed the full Newfoundland debt, completed the railway, and provided an annual subsidy of $650,000.[36] In response, Canada offered $6,000 a mile toward the cost of the railway and a subsidy increase of $35,000 (bringing it to $500,000 per annum).[37] The colonial government turned this down and began to look for another solution. A few days later, Morris reported to the legislature. The delegation, he said, had not expected the 1888 discussions to be repudiated, and the refusal to assume the entire public debt had made agreement impossible.[38] In Montreal, Bond stated that the Canadian government had taken advantage of the colony's predicament to try and drive a hard bargain and that the repudiation of the 1888 offer justified "mistrust." He added that the completion of the railway had also been a problem, alleging that the Canadian government wanted it either stopped or completed at Newfoundland's expense.[39]

BOND SAVES THE DAY

Why was Bond in Montreal? He had been asked by the government to try and raise a loan of $2.5 million to pay the interest that would be due on the debt at the end of June and eliminate the floating debt. He was accompanied by R.G. Reid. They had left St. John's on May 11, the day Bowell's last offer arrived, and reached Montreal on May 15. Reid was being paid in Newfoundland bonds and so had a vested interest in the government's stability, but he also had many contacts in the Canadian financial world.[40]

The first approach was made to the Bank of Montreal, which had already advanced $700,000 to the Newfoundland government and was initially unwilling to go further. Eventually it offered to loan half the amount of the interest due—if the London and Westminster Bank (or another respectable source) provided the balance. Bond also talked to Hanson Brothers, a brokerage firm linked with merchant banks in London and the agent for Coates, Son and Co. in particular, who made an offer on May 18. Bond found that offer unacceptable and left for Boston. He rapidly learned that Newfoundland bonds were unsaleable either there or in New York—"All declare that the credit of the Colony has been ruined by the dispatches sent from St. John's to the press." Pressure mounted when a telegram from Whiteway stated that the Savings Bank was near collapse because of a run caused, Bond and Whiteway thought, by Tory scaremongering. If no help were forthcoming, it would close and the "prospect for loan would be ruined." On May 22, however, Hansons asked Bond to return to Montreal, and colonial survival seemed possible. Bond told Whiteway to calm down—he hoped to have a loan for the colony arranged by May 24 and would do his best to get a temporary loan for the Savings Bank: "Give me time and stop cursed press reports and I will put things straight."

Back in Montreal, Bond closed the deal on May 30, after extensive negotiations. Hanson Brothers had brokered a loan agreement with Coates, the issue to be handled by Glyn, Mills, Currie & Co.* He had to accept a low price, but managed to increase the amount of the loan to

* Hanson Bros. to Bond, May 23, 1895, lists the conditions (RBP 9.01.05).

£550,000. He also had to agree to an austerity programme: expenditure was to be reduced by $500,000 and revenue increased by $180,000. The government had little option but to accept the terms.

There remained the Savings Bank problem, which proved to be more difficult. Reid was prepared to provide a temporary loan, but the Bank of Montreal refused the money. He was apparently "very much annoyed" and on May 25 the bank allowed $50,000. Hansons agreed to provide a short-term loan of $100,000 at 5 per cent, to be guaranteed by "the Government of Newfoundland and you personally," and the Savings Bank was to deposit $200,000 in Newfoundland government bonds as additional security. Bond agreed to provide the personal guarantee. The process was completed on May 29.*

Apart from the press reports, Bond blamed his problems on "the strongest Canadian influence here and in London." Newfoundland had got a reprieve and congratulatory messages began to arrive. Bond then left for London via New York, arriving on June 12. There followed a considerable amount of negotiation over the loan prospectus; final signatures were delayed until June 20. Tenders opened on June 24 and the loan was oversubscribed. Bond also managed to arrange—eventually—a loan for the Savings Bank of £170,000 at 3.5 per cent.

Besides the loan business, which took most of his time, Bond talked with Sir Francis Evans—as he now was—about the possible sale of the Newfoundland Railway Company. Reid was anxious to consolidate its lines into his system, which was only sensible. However, Evans wanted $1.6 million, which Whiteway found unreasonable, and he refused the idea of a lease. As a result, the situation remained stalemated.[41] Morris and Horwood had written to urge Bond to press for the appointment of Whiteway as governor when O'Brien left that summer. They certainly did not want Sir Herbert Murray, who was rumoured to be in the running—"a very undesirable man." Both they and Whiteway also feared that Winter would try to get the appointment, and they certainly wanted that

* Hanson Bros. to Bond, two letters, May 29, 1895. Also Bond to Hanson Bros, two letters, May 29, 1895, one of which gave the personal guarantee, the other on behalf of the Savings Bank (RBP 9.1.020).

stopped.[42] Bond raised the matter at the Colonial Office but did not get very far. His main business there, however, was to deal with the repercussions of the government's austerity measures.

The Newfoundland legislature did little business during April and May. It did not really resume business until June 12, when it rapidly passed a loan bill, extended the French Treaties Act, and expunged from the *Journals* all the certificates resulting from the election trials. It then turned to retrenchment. The start of the financial year was moved to July 1, import duties were raised 5 per cent across the board (with heavier taxes on luxuries), and the supply bill detailed a series of drastic spending cuts. The governor's salary was reduced from $12,000 to $7,000—more than 40 per cent—and the three Supreme Court judges suffered a combined reduction of $2,600 in their salaries. O'Brien protested vigorously, believing these changes were the result of political vindictiveness, pure and simple. Whiteway wrote that "the old fellow is doing all in his power to thwart us in every way he can."[43] As a result the Colonial Office reserved the legislation applying to the judges—which was indeed controversial—but Bond, still in London, was able to persuade officials that the salary cuts were not a result of spite but part of a general, graduated reduction of all civil service salaries ranging from one-tenth on the lowest to one-fifth on the highest. Bond also took the opportunity to inform them at length about O'Brien's behaviour since 1893, and he won the main point. The governor was instructed to assent. But the new Conservative colonial secretary, the "radical imperialist" Joseph Chamberlain, sent a strong dispatch calling the bill "dangerous and objectionable."[44]

Bond left Liverpool on July 16—he sang solos in two concerts during the voyage home—and arrived in St. John's a week later. On the evening of the 26th, there was a demonstration in Bond's honour. The press reports diverged significantly, the *Evening Telegram* calling it "A Monster Gathering," while the *Evening Herald* reported a sparsely attended "fizzle."[45] There was a parade to Bond's house on Circular Road, where Whiteway and Morris moved a resolution of welcome and congratulation.[46] Bond then spoke at length. When he had left Newfoundland in May, the options had seemed to be either confederation or reversion to crown colony status. Canada's terms, however, were "derogatory to the present and future of the colony" and giving up responsible government was "a cruel and humiliating" alternative. He had been dogged throughout his mission by "literary assassins residing in this city" (he exonerated Moses Harvey), who had done all they could to prevent him arranging the loans by sending defamatory cable dispatches to newspapers in Canada, the United States, and England. The Savings Bank was safe and secure, he assured the crowd. "We have passed through our dark hour; already the morning is beginning to appear. . . . The autonomy of the country has been saved; it is now in your keeping, and it rests entirely with you, my friends, as to how long we shall retain it."

The events of 1895 passed into political legend. Bond had not only saved the country and the Savings Bank, but he had pledged his own resources to do it.* Writing to his mother after the demonstration, a correspondent called him "the pride and hope of his countrymen!—every Man, Woman and Child for generations to come will revere his name."[47] J.B. Howson of Little Bay referred to him as "the saviour of this dear but downtrodden Little Island! May God ever bless you!"[48] In the popular mind, clearly, Bond had established his credentials as able, patriotic, unselfish, and as a politician who not only had great faith in the country's future but was also sensitive to the needs of the ordinary citizen. No wonder that the *Evening Herald* remarked that while Whiteway's star was setting, Bond's was rising.[49]

RECOVERY AND A NEW GOVERNOR

Governor O'Brien left the day after the demonstration. He was glad to go. His time in Newfoundland had been "perhaps the most unprecedented and unpleasant tour of service that has fallen to the lot of any Governor of H.M.'s Colonies to deal with and certainly the most troublous of my life."[50] There were laudatory articles in the *Herald* and highly critical ones in the *Telegram*, including the rhyme that follows.

---

* Bond was eventually paid $2,000 plus expenses (Whiteway to Bond, September 8, 1896, RBP 9.01.028).

Arise, old land, once more arise,
Breathe free once more without disguise,
His seat he has vacated.
Perverted judgement sat enthroned
Within the cranium Britain loaned
To rule old Newfoundland.[51]

Governor Sir Herbert Harley Murray (1829–1904), undated. (PANL, VA 27-52)

His replacement was not Whiteway, but Sir Herbert Murray. The press generally welcomed the appointment when it was announced in September, since Murray was thought to have handled the relief fund well. As some suspected at the time, he would prove to be as troublesome as his predecessor—with whom, of course, he had stayed at Government House. As a result, the government continued to face problems both locally and at the Colonial Office, where the influential Joseph Chamberlain, a political heavyweight—unusual for that portfolio—proved to be an energetic and forceful minister with little sympathy for colonial sensibilities. He viewed Newfoundland as a nuisance colony with an incompetent and inefficient government, and he had no qualms about intervening when he thought it necessary.

Bond's next task, having recovered his breath, was to find a seat in the House of Assembly. It was arranged that Jabez Thompson, editor of the *Twillingate Sun*, would resign his seat in that district and become the magistrate at Brigus.[52] Requisitions addressed to Bond began to arrive; the top of one of them bore the signature of William F. Coaker, with whom Bond was to have a long, fraught, and very difficult political relationship.[53] Bond toured the district with Thompson, was elected by acclamation on September 16, and remained a member for Twillingate for the rest of his political career—which is curious, since he could easily have switched back to Trinity Bay, his home district. Why he did not do so is unknown.

The Liberal government had two years until the next election (1897). But given the conditions imposed by lenders and the general shakeup of business resulting from the bank crash, which had hurt many voters and commercial firms, its options were limited. The economy remained uncertain and fragile, and there was now Governor Murray to deal with (he arrived in November 1895). A widower in his late 60s, Murray was autocratic by nature, had no previous colonial experience other than the relief appointment, and saw himself more as a headmaster than as a governor presiding over a responsible government. He and Bond seemed to get on with each other, however. In December, Murray praised both Bond and Receiver General Patrick Scott, "who really have the Finances of the Colony in their hands and seem very well disposed if they are not hampered by others."[54]

The first fight between governor and government was over the Legislative Council. Using Bond as an intermediary, Murray insisted that former directors of the defunct local banks had to step down from the Council. Criminal charges had been laid against them, alleging conspiracy to circulate false bank statements, and they were technically under arrest. James Pitts and Robert Thorburn apparently resigned without protest, but A.W. Harvey, a member of the Executive, had to be persuaded to do so by Bond—and he was very bitter about it.[55] Next in Murray's sights was Bond's old antagonist, Alexander Mackay. A cloud had been hanging over him for some time, and it now became known that he had been heavily overdrawn at both banks. Murray told Mackay that he should resign; when he did not, the governor began to investigate how he might be removed. There is indirect evidence that Bond helped Murray build his case.[56] Mackay was compulsorily removed from the Council in May 1896.

The government did not protest these actions, but it did become upset early in 1897 when Murray unilaterally recommended the appointment of two new Legislative Councillors. He was working within a curious wrinkle in the local constitution, which provided that members of the Council had to be appointed by the Crown and selected by the governor, not necessarily by the current colonial government—though this had always been the practice. Murray wanted, he said, to change the Council from "a mere office of Registry" into an active defender of respectability and probity against what he saw as the excesses of the House of Assembly.[57] Murray refused to sign the government Minute protesting that his action was improper, and referred the matter to London. Bond asked the Colonial Office to listen to authorities on constitutional law, Whiteway suggested other candidates, and Sir Francis Evans was brought in to make representations.[58] In the end, the Colonial Office accepted that Murray had violated both established practice and his instructions, and that to force appointments was politically unwise. Whiteway worked out a compromise in London in 1897; it was a tussle that the local government had won in principle.

It is not known why the 1896 legislative session opened late (not until June 11). During the session, Bond vigorously (and at length) defended his actions in arranging the 1895 loans.[59] The budget increased the 1896–97 expenditure by about $230,000 to cover additional debt interest and grants for roads and education. The tariff remained largely unchanged.[60] The only piece of legislation to cause serious problems was a bill to incorporate the Reid-owned St. John's Street Railway Company, which was given the authority to build such a railway in the town "and the country adjacent thereto," with a boundary set at 20 miles (32 kilometres). There were immediate protests from the Newfoundland Railway Company, which mounted a spirited lobby in London.[61] The bill was reserved, but eventually Chamberlain decided that assent would be given.[62] This development concentrated minds; in short order, the company agreed to sell out for £325,000,and abandoned its seemingly endless litigation.* The colony finally possessed a unified railway system with a single tariff operated by R.G. Reid, who had clearly indicated that he and his sons were interested in diversifying and expanding their Newfoundland interests.

* Murray to Chamberlain, conf., December 11, 1896 (CO 194/235, 80). Formal assent to the bill was given once the transfer of assets was completed (October 1897). There were those who thought that the bill was designed from the outset to force the company to come to terms (Minute by Anderson, August 18, 1896, CO 194/234, 352).

More problematic was the government's handling of the prosecutions of the former bank directors, which prompted severe criticism from Murray and the Colonial Office. It seems clear enough that Whiteway was reluctant to proceed expeditiously with the charges, since many of the defendants were his friends, acquaintances, or colleagues (it was a small society). The proceedings did not end until late 1897. To cut a long story short, true bills were obtained against the directors of the Commercial Bank, but the Supreme Court judges refused to hear the case—two judges because they had been shareholders and one because he had been involved as a lawyer in earlier stages of the process. Whiteway belatedly asked the Colonial Office to find an outside judge, which it did. The result was an acquittal, since conspiracy could not be proved, and the Union directors never had to stand trial at all. The local establishment was no doubt glad to have the matter buried, if not forgotten.[63]

The following year, 1897, was dominated by two issues: the miserable state of the economy and the general election scheduled for the fall. Merchants had large stocks of fish on hand but faced weak markets. They also now had to deal with Canadian banks that were new to the Newfoundland fish business and reluctant to provide generous credit—unlike the defunct local banks, which had been set up to do just that. Merchants complained once again about "unfair" competition in European markets and asked both for the re-imposition of the suspended Bait Act as well as new reciprocity talks with the United States. There was also concern about a recent commercial treaty giving Norwegian fish most-favoured-nation treatment in Portugal. The government was sympathetic. Unless competition was checked and new markets opened, stated a Minute of Council, there might be a repeat of the 1894 crisis.[64] However, it did not re-impose the Bait Act and, given Canadian opposition, there was nothing it could do about reciprocity with the United States unless the British government changed its attitude.

There were certainly political factors involved in the Bait Act decision, and Bond did his best to turn the issue against the Tories when the legislature met in March. His argument was sound. If Newfoundland was losing Mediterranean markets, he said, it was less because of French bounties and more because of an inferior cure and "the rushing of cargo after cargo into market. . . . What did it matter whether the Bait Act was enforced or not, if such a condition of things was going to exist!" The problem was local—and it was the responsibility of the merchants, who were represented by the Tory party.[65] Nevertheless, the opposition launched a sustained attack on the whole "policy of progress," which Morine and Morison charged had driven up the debt and increased taxation without delivering the promised diversification of the economy and populating of the interior. Moreover, these increased costs had to be met, ultimately, by the fish trade—which had to run up large overdrafts that merchants could not pay off because of the state of the markets. The government's policies had almost bankrupted the country.[66]

These were plausible arguments. Bond replied in typical fashion, attacking the Tory record and stressing the country's economic potential and resources, which only the railway could make accessible. The interior of Newfoundland had good agricultural land and the "coal area near Grand Lake" could now be reached—coal that would be used "in connection with smelting, manufactories, and other like purposes. . . . These were not mere visions or pictures of the imagination. What had happened in other countries was not impossible or improbable here."* He went on to defend other aspects of the government's programme and dismissed the charge that the "policy of progress" had broken the banks. The culprits were the Tory government of 1894 and the bank directors, most of whom were members of that party.[67] It was a spirited and combative performance.

Besides adding to the road and public works grants, widely seen as election bait, the budget made few changes to expenditures or the tariff in 1897. However, a bill did provide for more railway branch lines—to Carbonear, Brigus, Clarke's Beach, and Burnt Bay (now Lewisporte), which were expected to be popular with voters. Also with the election in mind, the government introduced legislation to amend the 1889 Elections Act,

* Bond in Assembly, March 24, 1897 (offprint in RBP 3.16.002). Sir Ambrose Shea wrote from London to congratulate Bond on this speech. There had been a choice, he said, between building the railway "and an exodus and the alternative could not be faced" (Shea to Bond, April 26, 1897, RBP 3.16.012).

obviously trying to prevent another round of election petitions. It narrowed the definitions of corrupt practice and agency, allowed the expenditure of public money during election campaigns, and made the filing of election petitions more difficult and expensive.[68] The bill passed against strenuous arguments from the opposition, which sent a memorial to the Colonial Office claiming that it legalized bribery. The bill was reserved.[69] Murray's commentary was scathing—"No Governor can ever before have written such a despatch about his Ministers," noted John Bramston—and the government's protests made no difference. The Colonial Office consulted the Law Officers and, on receipt of their report, disallowed the bill.[70] Such interference in a responsible government colony's internal affairs was highly unusual, if not unprecedented.

At the end of the session, Whiteway spoke at length in his own defence. He could not have known that it would be his last speech in the House of Assembly, nor that his effective political career was over.[71] Murray closed the session on May 12. He deviated from the approved script by refusing to voice approval for the branch railways, and he expressed hope that "the money thus voted for useful public purposes . . . will be wisely and impartially assigned, and that when so assigned it will not be used for mere electioneering purposes."[72] There is no question that he was a loose cannon. A visiting journalist wrote that Murray "fatally misunderstands the colony, its needs, and, more emphatically, its politics."[73]

In spite of all their problems, Newfoundlanders enthusiastically celebrated Queen Victoria's Diamond Jubilee in 1897, which coincided with the anniversary of the probable arrival of John Cabot (Zuan Caboto) four hundred years earlier. The government inaugurated a Jubilee Scholarship to assist students going on to higher education. Public debate about the location of the Cabot landfall was unavoidable. Moses Harvey argued for Cape Breton, but Judge Daniel Prowse, the pre-eminent local historian, plumped for Cape Bonavista and Bond followed suit. As the minister responsible for the postal service, he arranged (at Prowse's suggestion) for a commemorative stamp issue to mark the occasion. It was the colony's first such issue and consisted of fourteen handsome designs celebrating Cabot (with a Bonavista landfall), the Jubilee, and the colony's industries.

Ever difficult, Governor Murray attended various Jubilee events but refused to lay the foundation stone for Cabot Tower on Signal Hill. It was, he said, "not in accordance with Her Majesty's express wishes as to the method in which her Jubilee [was] to be celebrated."[74]

The official Newfoundland delegate to Jubilee events in London was Whiteway, who was elevated while there to the rank of Privy Councillor. Morris also attended,[75] but Bond stayed home. Both he and Morris played leading parts in a demonstration in late August, however, to welcome Whiteway back to the colony. According to the *Evening Telegram*, thousands of people turned up for

Cabot Tower, undated. (PANL, A 35-5)

Jubilee postage stamp issue, 1897. Robert Bond assisted in the design of this issue. Theses examples show Cape Bonavista, the official seal of the colony, and aspects of the economy. (Courtesy of Queen Elizabeth II Library, Memorial University)

the event, with bands, torchbearers, and banners. The speakers praised the "policy of progress" and predicted great things for the future.[76]

THE 1897 ELECTION

The demonstration was, in effect, the start of the Liberals' election campaign; polling day was October 28. An election committee had been formed earlier in the year, but it does not seem to have done much work. Whiteway later complained that Bond had done "literally nothing" to organize for the election, except to shower good things on his own district.[77] There were signs that the party was running out of steam. Bond had complained in January that he had to do the work of some of his colleagues, which kept him at the office from 10 a.m. to 7 p.m. daily, and that they failed to support "those who are giving their heart's blood to the public service."[78] The *Evening Herald* thought there were three Liberal factions, and it may well have been correct.[79]

In contrast, the Tories seemed to be relatively well-organized. They were supported by two newspapers and made concerted efforts to garner support in rural districts. Leading Tories in St. John's had been meeting weekly; in March, they decided to form supporters' clubs around the island.[80] The party was led once again by Sir James Winter, who had resigned from the Bench in November 1896 (giving a speech to the Bar in which he lambasted the Whiteway government). The party was able to use the still miserable economic times—1897 saw poor seal and cod fisheries—to scoff at Liberal policies which, its newspapers repeated, had caused the bank collapse and mercantile bankruptcies. The "policy of progress" had failed and it was time for a change. The Tory manifesto accused the government of deceiving the people, of mismanagement, and of allowing corruption in the public service.[81]

There can be no doubt that the Liberals faced a difficult campaign, given the hard times, the impact of the bank crash, retrenchment, and adverse reaction to its attempts to reduce smuggling. In addition, the government had reformed the poor relief system, which was not popular. The failure of its election bill meant that expenditures during the campaign period had to be watched carefully. The Liberals attacked the Tories

View of Twillingate, Nortre Dame Bay, 1908. Photo by William McFarlane Notman. (McCord Museum, photo 4575)

vigorously enough, taking specific aim at Morine, did their best to put a positive spin on the economic situation, and promised a large-scale colonization scheme for the interior and help for the fisheries.[82]

Bond left for his district in late September. The other Liberals running there were Donald Browning, a St. John's lawyer, and George Roberts, a local businessman and owner of the *Twillingate Sun.* A Northern Liberal Association had been formed in 1896 at Bond's suggestion (William Coaker was a leading light); it helped organize an enthusiastic parade when the candidates arrived at Twillingate on October 3:

> The Government candidates were met by ten fishermen representing the ten settlements on Twillingate Islands. Soon after a well-organized procession, numbering at least 500, proceeded to the Coastal Wharf and as Mr. Bond and his colleagues stepped on shore they were saluted with twenty-five guns. Fifty stalwart fishermen armed with guns formed a guard of honor and after the candidates had taken their seats in the waiting carriage, fired volley after volley along the line of march. The procession was headed by 500 staunch supporters

> of the Liberal Party. Then came a magnificent banner of Liberal blue with the following inscription in crimson and gold "The Northern Liberal Association," "Our Country and Liberty," and in the centre the coat of arms of Newfoundland surrounded by a wreath of laurel. Next came a carriage drawn by a number of young fishermen in which was seated Mr. Bond and his colleagues . . . then seven carriages containing the old Liberals who were unable to walk. . . . The grand parade occupied two hours or more and it was after six o'clock when it halted at Colbourne's Hotel.[83]

The Tory slate was led by none other than Morine, who was joined by Alan Goodridge (a young St. John's businessman)[84] and J.H. Taverner. The campaign was vigorous. There was no love lost between William Coaker—now in charge of the post and telegraph office at Herring Neck—and Morine, who had supported charges made by a local Tory merchant that Coaker and others had misused road board monies. (Prowse investigated and cleared Coaker, saying that the charges resulted from "personal and political ill-feeling."*) On voting day, Bond led the poll, followed by Browning—and then by Goodridge. The *Evening Telegram* claimed that Goodridge got in by a fluke, because illiterate voters simply marked the first three names on the ballot (they were in alphabetical order). In addition, votes had been lost because work had not begun on the Burnt Bay branch line—the labourers, living in the open, were discontented.[85]

The overall result, however, was a substantial Tory victory: they won twenty-three seats to thirteen Liberals. The Liberals held on to the six St. John's seats as well as Harbour Grace, Carbonear, the two seats in Twillingate, and one in Ferryland. Several prominent Liberals were defeated, including Whiteway, who had run in his old district of Trinity Bay. He and his government resigned on November 16.

A staggering reversal, it was perhaps understandable considering that, since 1893, the Liberal government (and the colony) had lurched from one crisis to the next against a backdrop of severe economic and financial

---

* The correspondence is in RBP 3.16.008; Prowse did find "great irregularity."

difficulties. Voters clearly wanted someone to blame and were in the mood for change. Though the Tories had been responsible for much of the instability that had characterized the previous four years, the electorate seemed willing to give them a chance to turn things around. And so the Liberals were faced with having to rebuild a badly damaged and divided party. For Bond, it was a crucial moment—would he, or would he not, finally abandon Whiteway?

NOTES

1 *Evening Telegram*, December 15, 1894 (*JHA* 1894–95, 5–7).
2 Harvey in Legislative Council, December 15, 1894 (*Evening Telegram*, December 19, 1894).
3 O'Brien to Ripon, conf., December 22, 1894 (CO 194/228, 573).
4 O'Brien to Ripon, tgm., December 18, 1894 (CO 194/228, 548).
5 Ripon to O'Brien, tgm., January 1, 1895 (CO 194/228, 551).
6 Minutes by Anderson and Bramston, December 10 and 12, 1894 (CO 194/228, 492, 515–18).
7 Ripon to O'Brien, tgm., January 1, 1895 (CO 194/228, 551).
8 *Evening Telegram*, December 17, 1894; *Evening Herald*, December 15, 1894.
9 O'Brien to Ripon, December 19 and 23, 1894 (CO 194/228, 559 and 581).
10 *JHA* 1894–95, 13–16.
11 Enclosure in O'Brien to Ripon, conf., December 31, 1894 (CO 194/228, 595; *JHA* 1894–95, 13ff.).
12 T.R. Bennett to Whiteway, January 1, 1895 (ASC, Whiteway Collection 5.05.001).
13 O'Brien to Ripon, tgm., January 3, 1895; to Ripon, January 4, 1895; to Ripon, conf., January 4, 1895 (CO 194/230, 16, 36, 73–75). Assembly debates, January 3 (*Evening Telegram*, January 16, 1895).
14 For example, in the *Evening Herald*, January 8 and 9, 1895.
15 Ripon to O'Brien, January 7, 1895 (*JHA* 1898, Appendix, 386).
16 O'Brien to Ripon, tgm., January 24, 1895 (CO 194/230, 135).
17 Hiller, "Murray, Sir Herbert Harley," *DCB* 13:749–51.
18 *Evening Telegram*, March 19, 1895.
19 *Evening Herald*, February 11, 1895.
20 Ripon to O'Brien, tgm., January 21, 1895; Minutes by Anderson and Meade, January 15 and 16, 1895 (CO 194/230, 39–40).

21 *JHA* 1894–95; *Evening Herald*, February 8, 1895.

22 This account is based on Hiller, "The 1895 Newfoundland-Canada Confederation Negotiations," 94–111.

23 *Evening Telegram*, March 6 and 21, 1895.

24 *Evening Herald*, March 14, 15, and 29, 1895.

25 *Evening Telegram*, March 20, 23, and 25, 1895.

26 *Evening Telegram*, February 13, 1895.

27 *Evening Herald*, March 27, 1895; *Evening Telegram*, March 27, 1895.

28 Morris in Assembly, May 16, 1895 (*Evening Telegram*, June 5, 1895).

29 "DRPC," 45–47 (RBP 8.02.013).

30 Saywell, ed., *Canadian Journal*, 216.

31 "DRPC," 13–14 (RBP 8.02.013).

32 Minutes by Bramston and Meade, April 11, 1894; the reply telegram, April 13, 1895 (CO 537/113, 84–88).

33 Minutes by Anderson, April 27, 1895; Ripon to Aberdeen, tgm., May 4, 1895 (CO 42/829, 862–64, 869–72, and 885).

34 Minutes by Anderson and Meade, May 4, 1895 (CO 537/113, 94).

35 Ripon to Aberdeen, tgm., May 9, 1895 (CO 537/113, 102); Ripon to O'Brien, tgm., May 9, 1895 (CO 194/231, 27).

36 Whiteway to Bowell, tgm., May 1, 1895, in Stanley, "Further Documents," 370–86.

37 Bowell to Whiteway, tgm., May 11, 1895 (*JHA* 1895, Appendix, 422, copy in RBP 9.01.018).

38 *Evening Telegram*, June 5, 1895.

39 *Montreal Star*, May 12, 1895, reprinted in the *Evening Telegram*, May 27, 1895.

40 The following account is based on "Loan Diary, 1895" in RBP 9.01.021.

41 Evans to Bond, June 21, 1895; Whiteway to Bond, June 25, 1895; Bond to Evans, July 5, 1895 (RBP 10.01.003, 9.01.05).

42 Morris and Horwood to Bond, June 29, 1895; Whiteway to Bond, June 29, 1895 (RBP 9.01.025).

43 Whiteway to Bond, June 29, 1895 (RBP 9.01.025).

44 Hiller, "A History," 314–16.

45 *Evening Telegram* and *Evening Herald*, July 27, 1895. This account relies on the report in the *Telegram*.

46 There is a copy of the resolution in RBP 3.14.005.

47 E. Carbery to Mrs. Bond, July 27, 1895 (RBP 9.01.033).

48 J.B. Howson to Bond, September 16, 1895 (RBP 3.14.010).

49 *Evening Herald*, July 24, 1895.

50 O'Brien to Chamberlain, conf., July 25, 1895 (CO 194/231, 320).

51 The verses are from the *Evening Telegram*, July 27, 1895, and the *Evening Herald*, July 26, 1895.

52 *Evening Telegram*, September 5, 1895.

53 The requisitions are in RBP 3.14.006, 007. See Baker, "William Ford Coaker," 223–66.

54 Murray to Chamberlain, December 18, 1895 (Birmingham University Library, Joseph Chamberlain papers, JC 9/4/1/1).

55 Murray to Chamberlain, secret, December 22, 1895 (CO 194/231, 525); Murray to Bond private, December 23, 1895 (RBP 3.14.004). See also *Evening Telegram*, December 28, 1895.

56 Bond to O'Dwyer and reply, January 17, 1896 (RBP 3.15.002).

57 Murray to Chamberlain, conf., February 3, 1897 (CO 194/237, 78).

58 The extensive correspondence can be found in CO 194/237, 238 and 239.

59 Bond in Assembly, June 17, 1895 (*Evening Telegram*, June 23, 1895).

60 Murray to Chamberlain, August 4, 1896 (CO 194/234, 388–95); Scott in Assembly, June 23, 1896 (*Evening Telegram*, June 29, 1896).

61 Evans to Chamberlain, July 1, 1896; Chamberlain to Murray, July 8, 1896 (CO 194/236, 289 and 299).

62 Chamberlain to Evans, October 22, 1896 (CO 194/236, 338).

63 Hiller, "A History," 323–26.

64 Murray to Chamberlain, February 4, 1897, enclosing a Minute of Council and a merchants' memorial (CO 194/237, 94–101); *Evening Herald*, January 5 and 29 and February 4, 15, and 18, 1897.

65 Bond in Assembly, March 24, 1895 (*Evening Telegram*, April 1, 1897, and speech offprint in RBP 3.16.002).

66 Morine and Morison in Assembly, March 20 and 23, 1897 (*Evening Telegram*, March 20, 22, 26, 27, 29, and 30, 1897); Morine in Assembly, March 26, 1897 (*Evening Telegram*, April 5, 1897).

67 Bond in Assembly, March 26, 1897 (*Evening Telegram*, April 8, 1897, and offprint in RBP 3.16.003).

68 Morris in Assembly, March 29, 1897 (*Evening Telegram*, April 12 and 13, 1897); Carter to Chamberlain, April 6, 1897 (CO 194/237, 194–202).

69 Morine in Assembly, March 29, 1897 (*Evening Telegram*, April 14, 1897). The memorial (April 6, 1897) is in *JHA* 1898, Appendix, 425–29. See also Chamberlain to Murray, tgm., April 24, 1897, *JHA* 1898, Appendix, 411.

70 There is a considerable amount of correspondence on this matter in CO 194/237 and 238, some of which was printed in *JHA* 1898, Appendix. See particularly Murray to Chamberlain, June 2, 1897, and Law Officers to CO, July 31, 1897 (CO194/239, 61–65).

71 Whiteway in Assembly, May 11, 1897 (*Evening Telegram*, June 1, 2, and 3, 1897).

72 *Evening Herald*, May 12, 1897; Murray to Chamberlain, May 13, 1897 (CO 194/237, 293).

73 Willson, *The Truth About Newfoundland*, 46.

74 *ENL* 4:414; *Evening Telegram*, June 17 and September 21, 1897. See also Jiri Smrz, "Cabot 400," 16–31.

75 *Evening Telegram*, June 26 and July 1, 1897.

76 *Evening Telegram*, August 25, 1897.

77 Whiteway, *Duty's Call*, 2.

78 Bond to Whiteway, January 28, 1897, draft (RBP 3.16.001).

79 *Evening Herald*, August 18, 1897.

80 *Evening Herald*, March 7, 1897.

81 *Evening Herald*, September 27, 1897.

82 For the Liberal manifesto, see the *Evening Telegram*, October 4, 1897.

83 Offprint from the *Twillingate Sun*, October 5, 1897 (RBP 3.16.005).

84 *ENL* 2:557–58.

85 *Evening Telegram*, January 18, 1898 (*ENL* 1:700–701).

CHAPTER SEVEN

Interregnum: The Railway Contract and the Premiership, 1897–1900

The Tory government led by Sir James Winter started out with energy and determination. Three years later, it collapsed. Its unity was shattered by internal rivalries and by major disagreements across the political spectrum concerning a new railway contract with R.G. Reid, which the government put through the legislature in 1898. The "Reid Deal," a defining and central factor in Newfoundland politics, was still being argued about years later. It raised important issues of principle about the viability of Newfoundland as an independent political unit, and about the relationship that should exist between the colonial government and a private enterprise. At what point do justified concessions become indefensible giveaways? As for the Liberal party, the period saw considerable internal uncertainty and disunity, which centred initially on the troubled relationship between Robert Bond and William Whiteway, and then on important differences between Bond and Edward Morris.

THE PROBLEMS OF THE LIBERAL PARTY

In retrospect, neither Whiteway nor Bond behaved with good sense after the 1897 election. The former was understandably upset by his personal defeat and by that of his party. He felt, he wrote later, "that my efforts, however well-intentioned, had not been appreciated, or had been misconstrued, or that possibly I might have put a higher estimate upon my work than others were willing to accord to it."[1] Bond must have known that this was his chance to take over, but he was cautious, knowing that the Liberals were still seen as Whiteway's party. He seems to have wanted Whiteway to decide what was to happen and remained characteristically distant. This was a mistake, since Whiteway resented the lack of personal consultation. He was a tenacious politician with strong opinions, unlikely to take kindly to playing a subordinate role to his erstwhile protégé or to retire quietly to his law practice. He did not hesitate to write pseudonymous letters to the press on public issues, often to the *Harbor Grace Standard*. In any event, Bond chose not to negotiate with Whiteway, formally or informally. The party was temporarily paralyzed.

Bond was forced to take action in late January 1898, when the elected Liberal members formally asked him to organize a party meeting to prepare for the opening of the legislature. This was at the last minute, and it was only then that Bond approached Whiteway—not personally, but in writing. Was it the case that he wanted to drop out of politics? Only if "you really do not intend to again lead the Party and intimate the same to me" would Bond consent "to assume the organization that is desired."[2] Whiteway replied that he was in no position to lead a party in the legislature and it was up to the elected Liberals to select a leader. That said, Bond's idea that he wanted to drop out of politics was mistaken, and he would not promise to stay out of public life in the future.[3] Whiteway reminded Bond that he had urged him to take the premiership*—but he was really saying that he would only accept Bond as the interim leader of "his" Liberal party in opposition, and that he might intervene at any time. This cast Bond as the leader within the legislature only and with limited authority outside it, subject to Whiteway's overall supervision. If this reading is accurate, then Bond's apparent hesitation and reserve becomes more understandable, if not excusable. Whatever the case, Bond headed the Liberal opposition when the legislature met on January 28, 1898.

THE RAILWAY CONTRACT, 1898

The Throne Speech promised a revision of the tariff, the introduction of stamp duty, the issue of treasury notes,† and an audit and appropriation

* There is no independent evidence that I know of to support this assertion.

† Murray said he would reserve any bill concerning treasury notes (Murray to Chamberlain, conf., January 31, 1898, CO 194/240, 62).

bill. In addition, the government proposed a royal commission of inquiry into the colony's affairs as a preliminary to an imperial loan guarantee, similar to the situation some years earlier. The railway system would be consolidated; the government would also pay bounties to sealing schooners and for land clearance and settlement.[4]

The colony's financial situation was still a major concern. Governor Murray concluded that the 1897–98 financial year would be one of the worst ever, leading to another round of comments at the Colonial Office predicting bankruptcy because of the burden of debt charges.[5] Murray reported in early January that the Newfoundland government was overdrawn at the Bank of Montreal, which had nevertheless agreed to make a $100,000 loan. In his view, a loan guaranteed by the imperial government would not be used for development, but to consolidate and reduce interest on the colony's bonds.[6] Bond thought that the financial situation was not as serious as the government believed. He argued the point in his speech on the Address in Reply, defending the Whiteway administration's record. In fact, Bond's papers contain a statement for December 31, 1897, showing a credit balance in the government's current account. He clearly did not believe that bankruptcy was looming ahead.*

Finances aside, the session was dominated by the storm over a new railway contract with R.G. Reid. That a new contract was under discussion was widely known, given the need to formally consolidate the railway system (supported in principle by both parties), the completion of the main line to Port aux Basques, and the obvious interest of the Reids in continuing and expanding their Newfoundland enterprises. Talks had begun with the previous government (but only about operating the line) and they continued with the new one.[7] The *Evening Telegram* reported in January that Reid had offered to operate the railway for twenty years in return for more land, which the newspaper thought would be a good deal. Murray, too, was well aware of the ongoing discussions.[8] Winter tabled the new contract on February 22. It went much further than anything the

* Bond in Assembly, January 31, 1898 (*Evening Herald*, February 2, 1898, and offprint in RBP 3.17.001). The statement was compiled by John Cowan, the Acting Minister of Finance, who later defected to the Liberals (*ENL* 1:553).

Throne Speech had foreshadowed or anyone outside government circles had expected. Reid would operate the railway for fifty years in return for fee-simple land grants of 5,000 acres per mile of track, in addition to the acreage to which he was entitled under previous contracts. At the end of the fifty years, the railway would become the property of his successors. For that "reversionary interest," Reid would immediately pay the Newfoundland government $1 million and return 2,500 acres per mile, half of his additional land entitlement. His holding was to include "the areas of land near Grand Lake in which coal has been discovered."

There was more. At government expense, Reid would build a new line from Topsail into the west end of St. John's, where he would build "a suitable and sightly depot" and establish his headquarters. The machine shops would be moved there from Whitbourne, and he would purchase the St. John's dry dock for $325,000. This would be useful because Reid also agreed to operate several coastal steam services for thirty years, as well as the ferry service from Port aux Basques to Cape Breton, receiving approximately $90,000 a year in subsidies. He would build and operate a street railway in St. John's, powered by electricity generated by his plant at Petty Harbour, and pave Water Street. Finally, Reid would take over the government-owned telegraph lines, operate them for fifty years, and "at the option of the Government" purchase them in 1904, when the Anglo-American Telegraph Company's monopoly expired.[9]

These were dramatic and unexpected new developments. Thirty-five years later, Morine summarized the thinking behind the contract,[10] with which he was closely associated, having sat in on the negotiations between Winter and Reid's eldest son, William D. Reid.[11] The economic depression persisted, and the completion of the railway had thrown 3,000 men out of work. Public finances were shaky, the railway line to Harbour Grace (now owned and operated by the government) was in poor condition and eating money, revenues were falling, and the government faced having to pay approximately $950,000 to cover debentures that had been called in. The government pressed Reid to create jobs by beginning the development of his land holdings, but Reid said he could not do this as long as the future of the railway was uncertain, given that his operating contract expired in 1904. Reid himself was in poor health, but his sons were keen to develop forest and mining industries—hence the offer to operate for fifty years. Ownership was added at a later stage of discussions. The $1 million would immediately help pay off government debt and, from Reid's point of view, ownership would simplify future incorporation and the raising of money. As for the other parts of the contract, Morine pointed out that the dry dock had lost money steadily and was probably worth less than Reid paid for it, and it made sense to make it part of a new St. John's terminus. Reid offered to provide a better coastal steam service than currently existed for a lower subsidy, and the same applied to the telegraph system.

These arguments were repeated and elaborated in the Assembly in more colourful language by Winter and Morine.[12] Then, on February 24, Edward Morris caused a political sensation by announcing that he and four other Liberals would support the new contract. It was later reported that Bond had initially offered to be bound by a majority of the caucus, but that Morris himself refused to be so bound once it was clear that the majority was hostile, and so he left the party with his followers.[13] Bond certainly told the party that he could not conscientiously support the contract.[14] Morris thought that the colony would be freed from

Sir Edward P. Morris (1859–1935), undated. (PANL, VA 33-59)

> the incubus of the operation of the railway and we secure the settlement and development of the country. . . . No man has more faith in this country and its resources than I have, but it won't do to spend our lives boasting about the capabilities of the country and permit the people of the country to be starving and perishing all around us. We have been hugging these phantoms to our bosom too long.

He ended his speech to the Assembly by claiming, no doubt to Bond's chagrin, that "the present contract will remain forever as the justification of the Whiteway Party."* It did not escape notice that Morris was a member for St. John's West, a district that would profit handsomely from the contract, nor that Whitbourne would suffer by the relocation of the machine shops. The Morris faction now sat separately from the Bond Liberals in the Assembly.

When he spoke at length against the draft contract on February 25, Bond characterized it as a miserable sellout of the colony's most valuable assets for a mere $1.45 million—assets that had cost over $18 million.[15] To argue, as did Winter, that the railway was of no value "as a commercial enterprise" was untrue. "Mr. Reid is a shrewd business man, a very shrewd man. He is not going to invest money in a property that is of no value 'as a commercial enterprise,' or in which 'he is certain to lose his money.'" If there was money in the railway, the dock, and the telegraphs for Reid, "there is also money in them for the people of this colony, therefore the Government should not barter them away." Then there was Morine's claim that if the contract did not go through, the colony would be bankrupt in six months. This was "simply and purely a scare," and it was ridiculous to suggest that passage of the contract would immediately help the colony's unemployed. He then launched into a review of Whiteway's railway policy, pointing out that in 1893 it was anticipated that the railway would be "self-supporting or nearly so" by the end of the operating contract, and this could still be the case. He went on:

> I am not prepared to thus barter away the property of the people of this country and of those who shall come after us. I have full faith in the brighter future that is in store for us, the gleam of which is already apparent. We hold this country in trust for future generations. Let us guard what we hold.

Reid was an admirable businessman, he continued, who should be encouraged, but the railway and other assets should be leased to him, not

* Morris in Assembly, February 24, 1898 (*Evening Herald*, February 28, 1898). Whiteway, in fact, disliked the contract.

sold: if they were sold, Reid could transfer his properties to others who might not be "of the same high character." Nor was it in the public interest to transfer the telegraph lines to a private party involved in trade and business. As for the dock—"I am strongly opposed to selling the dock and waterside premises in the neighborhood, because I consider it will be for the greatest good of the people for the Government to assist the expansion of trade." Steamship contracts should have been put out to tender and not simply handed to Reid:

> The crisis is a great one. The whole complexion of the destinies of the country depends on the action of the Government. By whom, by what influence, from what quarter, are its rich resources, its hopes, its fortunes to be controlled? That is the question we have now to decide.

The contract resolutions passed the House on February 25.* Governor Murray thought that government members had been frightened into compliance by the threat of colonial bankruptcy and that this, in turn, had strengthened the Reid bargaining position.† Related legislation was scheduled to follow, but the government needed Murray to sign the contract so that it could become law. He was reluctant to do so. By now Murray disliked both the government and the contract. He requested instructions from the Colonial Office, where news of the contract had been greeted with highly critical comments.[16] Murray forwarded a protest from the Most Reverend Michael Howley, now the Roman Catholic bishop of St. John's, who thought that the Savings Bank might be in danger,[17] and a memorial from the opposition, signed by Bond and Horwood, that listed their objections and suggested that there should be an appeal

---

* Michael Cashin (Ferryland) voted against the resolutions because he had promised Bond that he would do so, but thereafter voted in favour of the contract (*Evening Herald*, February 28, 1898). See Baker, "Cashin, Sir Michael Patrick," *DCB* 15:193–95.

† Murray to Chamberlain, conf., February 25, 1898 (CO 194/240, 111). Morine denied this (*Railway Contract*, 10).

Bishop (later Archbishop) Michael F. Howley (1843–1914), undated. (PANL, VA 35-11.4)

to the electorate.[18] Bond also contacted Coates and Co. in London, asking them to lobby Chamberlain to prevent assent, given that bondholders could be affected.[19]

Nevertheless, and on the grounds that this was essentially a local and internal matter, the Colonial Office told Murray he would have to sign the contract and assent to the bill, which went through the Assembly on March 3.[20] It passed the Legislative Council on March 7 in twenty-five minutes without opposition,[21] though Bishop Howley had threatened to use his influence to try and prevent this happening—"I am now prepared to go to any extremes." He and Bond also discussed whether the government could be brought down, either through Howley's actions or the governor's intervention. The contract, wrote Bond, "means ruin to the people of the Colony and is in itself nothing short of a swindle."[22]

The session closed on March 30. Apart from the sensational Reid contract, a body of other legislation, much of it constructive, had been dealt with. It addressed civil service reorganization, a new Audit Act, tariff increases, and the encouragement of agriculture. The government also managed to amend the Elections Act in a manner acceptable to the governor and the Colonial Office.[23] In addition, the legislature passed resolutions (supported by Bond) requesting a royal commission of inquiry as a preliminary to a loan guarantee.* The thinking, apparently, was that besides examining the financial situation, the commission would report on the colony's landward resources and the French Shore treaties, since these had allegedly hindered the colony's development.[24] Prompted by Murray, the Colonial Office saw this as a request for financial assistance pure and

* Assembly debate March 25 (*Daily News*, March 26, 1898); Council debate March 29 (*Daily News*, April 5, 1898); and Murray to Chamberlain, March 26, 1898 (CO 194/240, 299). The government wanted a $5 million loan (*Daily News*, April 2, 1898).

simple and turned it down.[25] However, it did agree to a royal commission into the operation and effects of the French treaties, which collected evidence in September 1898.*

The end of the session did not mean that argument over the railway contract was over. In late March, in a highly unusual move, Joseph Chamberlain sent a dispatch[26] summarizing in strong language the Colonial Office's view of the contract, even though it had been judged a local matter:

> Such an abdication by a Government of some of its most important functions is without parallel.
>
> The Colony is divested forever of any control over or power of influencing its own development, and of any direct interest in or direct benefit from that development. It will not even have the guarantee for efficiency and improvement afforded by competition. . . .
>
> I can only conclude that . . . they [the government] consider that it is beyond the means and capacity of the Colony to provide for the honest and efficient maintenance of these services, and that they must therefore be got rid of at whatever cost.
>
> That they have acted thus in what they believe to be the best interests of the Colony, I have no reason to doubt . . . [but] the fact that the Colony after more than forty years of self-government should have to resort to such a step is greatly to be regretted.†

He gave instructions that the dispatch should be published. Not surprisingly the government yelped, objected to the publication of any of the

* The report was favourable to the colonial point of view and was therefore never published.

† In the original draft, the last phrase read that such a step "can scarcely be considered creditable to those who have been responsible for its administration, or to those who have chosen and supported them."

railway correspondence, and fired off a lengthy riposte to both the dispatch and the opposition's memorial. The Colonial Office agreed only to a delay of publication.[27] The correspondence became public in July, and it played a significant role in the anti-contract agitation that gathered strength over the summer and fall, with which Bond was deeply involved. Morine later commented that although Chamberlain was a figure whose opinions were entitled to "profound respect," the dispatch was "lacking in truth and sense."[28]

In mid-June, Winter and Morine left for London to discuss the proposed royal commission, French Treaty Shore issues, trade relations with Portugal and the United States, and other matters.[29] They managed to get agreement to a Newfoundland commissioner being present at forthcoming reciprocity talks between Canada and the US. Wilfrid Laurier (the Liberal prime minister of Canada since 1896) accepted this—as long as the representative was Winter, which disappointed Morine.[30] There was, apparently, no discussion of the railway contract while the two men were in London.

On August 3, a public meeting in Harbour Grace resolved to ask Bond whether it would be worthwhile to agitate for an election on the contract issue. Bond put the question to Governor Murray. Was the matter finally and irrevocably closed, or would the imperial government receive and act on a petition from the electorate? Murray, who was sympathetic, replied that he read Chamberlain's dispatch as a decision not to interfere (which it was). He had consulted the Colonial Office before giving his assent, and he had learned that disallowance in London was highly unlikely. It was too late,[31] and he said the same to Bishop Howley.[32] Bond argued that the dispatch could be interpreted as a decision on a constitutional point, since final assent had not yet been given in London. He added, "I am quite confident that if it can be said with certainty that Her Majesty's disallowance would issue provided the majority of the Electors signified their desire to have the bill vetoed, four fifths of the Electors would hasten to make the request. . . . [I] desire to do my best to undo what I believe will prove most detrimental to the people of the Colony."[33]

Bond had convinced himself, it seems, that disallowance of the contract legislation could follow a petitioning campaign, or an anti-contract victory in a possible (but unlikely) general election. He was not deterred either by Murray's skepticism or by the colony having to compensate Reid. The campaign was also a way to galvanize and regroup a Liberal party that had been severely weakened by the 1897 election and the defection of the Morris faction. A Newfoundland Liberal Association was formed in July. It was a colony-wide version of the earlier Northern Liberal Association, so a skeleton organization was already in place.[34] The Liberals knew they could count on the support of Bishop Howley and Governor Murray. The governor's approaching retirement had been announced some weeks earlier,[35] but lame-duck status did not stop him from improper interference.

In the agitation that followed, Bond did not play a particularly prominent role, since the strategy, no doubt, was to present the campaign as a genuinely "national" protest. Whiteway was preoccupied with personal matters—his daughter had gone to South Africa to seek a cure for an unspecified but fatal illness and he was away for much of the latter part of 1898 and the first half of 1899. The leading public roles were played by Liberal-leaning pillars of the churches and the community. The first formal anti-contract meeting was held in St. John's on August 17; it resulted a petition with 350 signatures that asked for disallowance of the contract legislation and for Murray to be retained as governor (he was flattered).[36] Winter correctly understood that the Liberals hoped that Murray would dismiss the government and force an election.[37] Similar petitions soon poured in from around the colony; by early 1899, 22,774 signatures had been collected, which amounted to about 47 per cent of registered voters. A "monster meeting" took place in St. John's on October 4, chaired by Sir Robert Thorburn and attended by more than 1,300 people* including Bishop Howley, A.W. Harvey, and Protestant clergymen.[38] A "Citizens' Committee" requested Sir Francis Evans to

* According to Murray; the *Evening Herald* (October 5, 1898) put the attendance at 600.

lobby in London for disallowance, which he did.*

As for Governor Murray, he helped in several ways. When the publisher and editor of the *Evening Telegram*, the main anti-contract newspaper, were jailed for thirty days for contempt of court, he had them released.[39] More significantly, Murray forced Morine to resign from his portfolio and the government. The pretext was Murray's discovery, through a letter from the Liberal Association, that Morine had taken over as Reid's solicitor and had been acting in that capacity at the time of the negotiation and passage of the contract. The conflict of interest could not be condoned.[40] The subsequent protests from Morine and the government press had some justification. Murray had known of Morine's relationship with Reid since February[41] and other ministers had acted for Reid or other contractors, among them Morris, Whiteway, and Emerson.[42] Morine was right to accuse Murray of corresponding directly with the "agitators." He also pointed out that Murray was sending the anti-contract petitions directly to London without first showing them to the Executive Council, as he should have done.[43] Murray later told Bishop Howley that he had aimed to rid the colony of "the burden of the adventurer."[44] Instead, he only contributed to further political instability. Morine remained a significant player for many years to come.

The petitions did not persuade the Colonial Office either to extend Murray's term as governor or to disallow the contract legislation, and the dispatch so informing the governor of these decisions was another important statement about responsible government and the role and responsibilities of the imperial government.[45] But Murray could still force an election, and he wanted to do so. He set out his reasons in November, but in the end decided (in spite of pressure from the Liberal Association) not to act because he was about to leave the colony.[46] Had he stayed on, he would have told the government to resign or call an election. If it had refused, he would

---

* Evans to Chamberlain, November 7 and 23, 1898 (CO 194/242, 537, 549). Evans asked Whiteway whether, in the event of the government's dismissal, he would return and go to the country. Whiteway replied that Bond should be asked to form a government (Whiteway to Bond, conf., November 14, 1898, RBP 10.01.019).

have dismissed Winter and called on the Bond Liberals.[47] Murray finally left Newfoundland early in 1899. His successor was Sir Henry McCallum, a soldier who also had some fixed ideas about governance.[48]

Murray cannot be blamed for the government party's internal difficulties (though he certainly exacerbated them). The Conservatives' central problem was Morine's ambition to become premier, which was a very divisive issue. Murray reported that he was "paramount" in the ministry due to his "energy and force . . . he has ability of all kinds, but is too impetuous." The basic problem, in Murray's view, was that "few men like him, and still fewer trust him." Moreover, the merchants who backed the government financially and therefore had influence, had some confidence in Winter but little in Morine.*

It had been expected that Chief Justice Carter would retire, as he did in May 1898, and that Winter would succeed him, leaving the premiership to Morine.[49] Some party members objected to this plan, in part because Morine let it be known that he would invite Morris to join his government. Winter then abandoned the plan, so Judge Little became Chief Justice and Donald Morison the new assistant judge. But Morine refused to give up, raising a chorus of protest that eventually forced Winter to agree to resign as premier at the end of the 1899 session, by which point Little, too, would have retired. The deal was put in writing and signed by party members.[50] There was a period of calm until early 1899, when Morine began to suspect that Winter had no intention of stepping down. He held meetings with his followers, apparently spoke disparagingly about Winter, and twelve party members pledged their support. Colonial Secretary J.A. Robinson urgently cabled Winter—who was in Washington at the reciprocity conference—asking him for a firm denial that he would retire; in other words, to repudiate the agreement. Winter complied.[51] As a result, both parties were now split and there were four factions in the Assembly. And no conclusive resolution to the situation could occur until both Winter and the new governor were in St. John's. That happened in early March and the manoeuvres began.

---

* Murray to Chamberlain, February 27 and April 8, 1898 (Chamberlain papers, JC 9/4/1/14, 15). Murray thought that the mistrust derived from Morine's behaviour over the treaties legislation and his pro-confederation attitudes.

What was Bond's view of the political situation? In mid-February 1899, he wrote a private letter to Alexander Parsons, editor of the *Evening Telegram*. There was a Liberal party, it enjoyed the support of much of the electorate, and it formed the Official Opposition. The former "Whiteway Party," though, was "like the scattered leaves of autumn and to attempt to collect them would be a vain undertaking. Some are buried beneath treachery and fraud, others have found a resting place within the influence of the Government and the Monopolist [Reid]." Some true believers remained, and they would be "the nucleus of the Liberal Party that before very long will rule our native land." But Bond was not yet the leader of that party: "I am the Leader of the Opposition in the House of Assembly. The Liberal Party of the future has no Leader at the present time. . . . For the present I prefer to possess my soul in patience and watch the course of events. It is a great mistake to be precipitant."[52] Thus, in Bond's opinion, the Whiteway party was gone. There would be a new party, and it would be his, but he would bide his time. It did not turn out quite as Bond intended.

Winter was well aware of what was going on and knew that the Bondites might support him against Morine, if only to get the vital money bills through the legislature.[53] He also knew that Morine commanded substantial support, and those supporters argued that the original agreement should be honoured. Morine had done an immense amount for the party and he deserved his chance.[54] Indeed, on March 7, Winter received a memorial from eleven party members asking for Morine's reinstatement.* Fearing that the Morine and Morris factions might combine to defeat him, Winter met privately with Bond on March 11. The two men had never got on with each other and the encounter did not go well. Winter proposed a coalition of his and Bond's supporters, excluding the Morine and Morris factions. Bond was prepared to consider this option, but he

* The memo was signed by Woodford, Duder, Blandford, Lake, Callahan, Rogerson, Watson, Gibbs, Hayward, St. John, Bradshaw, and [illegible] (Morine to Winter, March 7, 1899). A "strictly private" letter from Berteau added Dawe, Kean, Mott—and even E.P. Morris—as other Morine supporters; "one of the Reids" attended a meeting, as well (Berteau to Winter, March 8, 1899). All letters in PANL, Winter fonds, 836.8.

had conditions. First, there should be an early general election. Winter refused: the result would probably be a Liberal victory and Governor McCallum had told him that an election had to be avoided. Second, Bond insisted that the new Reid contract had to be modified. Winter expressed astonishment: "I thought there was only one man in the world who [had] such a crazy idea and that is Bishop Howley." Bond referred to Chamberlain's dispatches and, as he later recorded in his notes, "contended at some length that he [Chamberlain] had clearly intended [?] therein that while Her Majesty's Government could not disallow the present bill, the power of ending the mischief rested in the people of the Colony. Considerable debate took place on this point." Third, Bond raised the issue of redress for officials who had lost their jobs through the change in government. And finally, he expressed concern that from the public's point of view, a coalition could well look like a Liberal endorsement of the Tory government and all its acts. For his part, Winter thought the main thing was to prevent Morine becoming premier, and that the best men on both sides had to unite to prevent it.[55]

Bond put Winter's proposals to "a committee of my party," which viewed the possibility of a Morine government "with alarm, believing that no greater calamity could befall the Colony at this time." Thus the Bond Liberals would give the government "independent support" with a single condition: that once all necessary legislation had been dealt with, the legislature would be dissolved. Alternatively, Winter could "resign the Government" after the coming session and help a new Liberal government persuade the governor to grant a dissolution. The Liberals also offered the following:

> Your party to receive at our hands a fair representation in the Government then to be formed and which would immediately appeal to the Country for endorsation. We shall of course consider ourselves bound to carry out such promises as the present Government may have made you concerning the Washington Commission and also to give you the reversion of the Chief Justiceship.

Considering, however, that even under these proposals a defeat in the House was possible, an immediate dissolution was the best way out—"if it can be secured."[56] In effect, Bond wanted the Winter Tories to hand the government over to him and the Liberals, Governor McCallum permitting; but McCallum proved very reluctant to facilitate a settlement by allowing a dissolution.

Winter was so serious about a coalition of some sort that he, Orangeman though he was, approached Bishop Howley indirectly, asking him to use his influence. Howley loathed Morine, and urged Bond to "put all feeling under foot and join with W. for the purpose of keeping that other party out. It would be fatal if they got even one day's power. I would not then . . . be too particular about any terms W. may demand. The game will be all in your hands."[57] The Liberal Association also wanted action. Would Bond lead a new Liberal party? Should there be a public meeting to try and force a dissolution?[58] Bond said he wanted to avoid any action that could reunite the Tories and advised against trying to create "a public movement." Bond and Winter exchanged further correspondence, but in the end the latter broke off the negotiations. In Winter's view, it would be wrong to inflict a general election on the public and the members of the Assembly. And in any case—and no doubt more importantly—policy differences could not be bridged. It would have to be a genuine coalition or nothing.[59]

Once again, the governor became the umpire in an unstable political situation. McCallum was not initially a political partisan but, like his predecessors (and successors), he had no previous experience of responsible government. An army man, he was level-headed but could be unnecessarily rigid. He thought that a dissolution because of a quarrel between Winter and Morine would be "ridiculous," and agreed that spring elections were undesirable given weather and ice conditions. Winter would have to meet the House. Moreover, he did not accept the opposition's view that the Reid contract warranted a dissolution, since it was not such a "grievous step" as had been represented. Indeed, McCallum viewed the contract much more positively than his predecessor. Writing to Bishop Howley later in the year, he stated that "it has its advantages . . . and that, if boldly and energetically worked it may yet prove of much benefit." Howley responded that the contract was "irremediably wrong, unjust, infamous . . . imposed upon an unsuspecting and betrayed people . . . you might as well ask me to hold myself impartial to the works of the spirit of evil."[60]

In the short term, McCallum acted as mediator and an agreement was patched up between the Tory factions. Winter would recommend Morine's reinstatement and retire as premier at the end of 1899; it was understood that Morine would be his successor. James Pitts* would replace Abram Kean (a Morine supporter) on the Executive Council to act as a "counter-lever," and Morine would not (while in office) act as a lawyer for the Reids.† Morine rejoined the government in mid-April as Minister of Marine and Fisheries.[61] But deep enmity between Winter and Morine remained, and the former was offended by a report on the agreement in the *Daily News,* holding that it was Morine-inspired and a piece of "outrageous folly."[62]

The legislature opened late (May 11, 1899), a date that coincided with a by-election in Placentia-St. Mary's, where William Donnelly, Minister of Finance and Customs, was running for re-election on taking office. (Bishop Howley used his influence against him and Donnelly lost to the Liberal candidate. Morine took over his portfolio.[63]) The legislative session was relatively short. The most contentious debate focused on Morine's budget, which imposed a 5 per cent surcharge on customs duties. McCallum had urged the government to impose higher taxation, with some reason.[64] Bond responded with an exaggerated attack on the government's financial record and could not avoid mentioning the Reid deal:

> [It is] a contract that has established in this colony a most grievous and oppressive monopoly, whose first fruits is the

* Pitts had been reappointed to the Legislative Council.

† McCallum to Winter with enclosures, April 13, 1899 (PANL, Winter fonds, 836.8); McCallum to Chamberlain, with enclosures, April 18, 1899 (CO 194/243, 144–52). Apparently both Morine and Morris urged Winter to reorganize the government in support of the contract (PANL, Morine fonds, draft history, Chapter 7, part 2, 5–6).

> expatriation of the flower of our population, and which I verily believe will ultimately result in the ruin of the commercial and other material interest of the colony. That hundreds of our young men have become disheartened and hopeless of the future of this colony since the creation of that huge monopoly and have left this island, is a fact, alas! too true to be gainsaid. . . . It is completely at the mercy of the winds and storms of adversity to which the colony is so liable. There is not the faintest hope of being able to raise further loans to meet deficits, and there is nothing before the Colony but to default, unless retrenchment immediate and thorough is undertaken by the Government.[65]

Once the session was over, there was a political pause until autumn by-elections scheduled for St. John's East and Fortune Bay (both vacancies caused by the deaths of incumbent members). This was an important test. A Liberal deputation assured Whiteway of the party's loyalty and asked him to continue as leader of the party outside the legislature. He declined, writing that he could not "undertake the work and to continue as leader," but he wished the party well. The letter was read out at a Liberal meeting on October 20. Bond was then requested to take over and he agreed.[66] This did not prevent the Tory press from claiming that Whiteway had been knifed. Certainly, there can be no doubt that Whiteway found political retirement difficult and deeply resented the way that Bond had treated him. Nevertheless, Bond was now formally in charge of the party both within the legislature and outside.

St. John's East was considered safe for the Liberals, but Fortune Bay was a different story. It had returned Tories in the two previous elections and, at Harbour Breton, the Newman company remained influential. The district became a battleground. The Tory candidate was John Furneaux,[67] owner of the *Evening Herald.* Morine was on the spot to run an energetic campaign, aided by one of the Reid brothers and the use of a government steamer. The Liberal candidate, James Way, was originally from the district. Bond canvassed on his behalf with two political colleagues. On the night before polling day, Bond and Morine held competing meetings at Harbour Breton.[68]

The Liberals won both by-elections,[69] a blow for the Conservatives. P.T. McGrath (editor of the *Evening Herald*) told Dr. James Tait that he "considered [the Fortune Bay result] the greatest victory ever gained by any opposition in the past." Reporting McGrath's words to Bond, Tait wrote: "He said they were 'cock sure' of Fortune and 'the defeat came to them as a thunderclap.'"[70] Another correspondent told Bond that if the Tories had won Fortune, they would have sprung a by-election at Twillingate, where a Liberal MHA had resigned to become Chief Clerk and Registrar of the Supreme Court.* Yet another recounted that Morris had "offered to bet me $50 on the result of Fortune Bay . . . I had to reduce it to $5 but offered to bet the result of St. John's East which he would not do."[71]

Not surprisingly, friction between Morine and Winter resurfaced and reached the breaking point. Morine was angry at the way the government was taking care of the defeated William Donnelly[72] and again suspected (with reason) that Winter would renege on their leadership agreement. Winter complained that Morine was persistently antagonistic and difficult and had allowed Board of Works money to be spent for "personal aggrandizement." He requested Morine's resignation. When Morine refused, Winter asked the governor to dismiss him. If the *Evening Telegram* is to be believed, McCallum had become close to Morine,[73] which may explain why Morine was persuaded to resign—although he claimed he had been the victim of "studied deceit and practiced treachery."[74] His supporters agreed.[75]

The government did not intend to open the legislature until April 1900. The temporary legislation enforcing the French Shore treaties and the modus vivendi, however, was set to expire on December 31, 1899. The British government was anxious that it should be re-enacted speedily and without a fuss—the Boer War in South Africa had started in October and diplomatic problems with France had to be avoided. So McCallum asked Winter to convene a special session to deal with the matter.[76] Winter

* K.D. MacKenzie to Bond, November 13, 1899 (RBP 3.18.004). Tait thought the member's behaviour was contemptible.

contacted Bond, who, after talking to his supporters, agreed that his party would support a renewal of the legislation. He pressed Winter to arrange a regular, not a special session, given that sessions early in the year were inconvenient.[77] There were, no doubt, also political reasons for the request, and Winter decided to ignore it.* That proved to be unfortunate.

Robert Bond, ca. 1900. (ASC, RBP 12.01.005)

The legislature met on February 19, 1900. The Throne Speech dealt only with treaty enforcement renewal, and a brief Address in Reply was introduced immediately. Bond then moved an amendment: after passing the treaties bill, the legislature should move on to regular business—and the present government did not have the confidence of the House.[78] He launched into a lengthy criticism of the Winter government, arguing that it had lost public support. Bond's motion was seconded by Morris, who alluded to constant crises, faction fighting, and misrule. Whether Bond and Morris had decided on this tactic before the session opened is unknown, but it is certainly conceivable, and is supported by the fact that three government supporters (including a minister) crossed the House,† an event that might imply some prior manoeuvring. On the other hand, Bond could have moved the amendment purely as a demonstration, not expecting it to pass. Whatever the case, the government was certainly taken by surprise. The amendment passed by fifteen votes to nine. It was a thin House: six members were absent (including Morine, who was in London with R.G. Reid) and there

* McCallum asked Winter why he had not told him that Bond wanted a regular session. Winter replied that the nature of the session was not Bond's business and remarked that when Bond was in government, he had treated the claims of the opposition with "lofty disregard" (McCallum to Winter, February 9, 1900, and reply of same date, PANL, GN 3/27).

† Woodford (Minister of Public Works), St. John, and Callahan. Cowan had defected to the Liberals earlier.

was one vacancy. Four erstwhile government supporters did not vote.* The Treaties bill passed the House unanimously the same evening and the legislature was prorogued the next day.

Morris's reasons for supporting the non-confidence motion are clear enough. He had supported the 1898 contract—his district stood to gain from it and he was friendly with the Reid family and did legal work for them. He was mistrusted by Bishop Howley and by Bond, and he had probably once expected to merge his faction with Winter's. But he could not have predicted the Tory party's severe unpopularity and disintegration. By early 1900, he was extremely exposed politically: Morine was widely disliked, Winter was weak and on the way out, and Bond was clearly in the ascendant and leading the anti-contract crusade. The safe and sensible move for him, then, was to return to the Liberal fold. He could then pressure Bond and his allies into preserving the essence of the railway contract from within the government.

Winter resigned on March 5 and Governor McCallum asked Bond to form a ministry.† Bond agreed to do so but wanted an immediate dissolution or, at the very least, a dissolution after his government had met the House. As in 1899, the governor refused, going so far as to tell Bond that he would do everything possible to prevent an election during the next two years. Bond protested: he would refuse to take office "if you are not prepared to consider the advice of your proposed Ministry upon the question of a dissolution, and have arrived at an unalterable determination that

* *Evening Herald*, February 20, 1900. The report of the debate appeared in the *Evening Herald*, February 22, 23, 26, 27, and 28, and March 1, 3, and 7, 1900. The four were Gibbs, Watson, Rogerson, and Blandford—all Morine supporters (McCallum to Chamberlain, February 22, 1900, CO 194/245, 67). Bond put the number at five, with somewhat different names: Watson, Rogerson, Blandford, Bremner, and Bradshaw (draft article, probably for the *Evening Telegram*, 1900, RBP 3.19.012).

† McCallum to Chamberlain, tgm., March 5, 1900 (CO 194/245, 93). Morine had advised Winter not to open the legislature until he got back, and cabled him not to resign but to hang on (draft history, Chapter 7, Morine fonds, PANL, MG 271.2).

the people shall be debarred for the next two years of that Constitutional privilege which the majority of their representatives are desirous that they shall exercise without unnecessary delay."[79] What happened next is unclear, but Bond did put together a government that was sworn in on March 15[*] and, at the end of the month, McCallum agreed to a fall election.[80]

Bond also had to deal with Morris. He wrote to him on March 7,[81] noting that Morris had "voluntarily" seconded and supported the non-confidence motion. He offered him a place in the new government on the understanding that the question of future policy would be held in abeyance until the dissolution (which, Bond hoped at the time, would be soon). At that point, he said, those who disagreed with him could "sever their connection." But Morris insisted on "a clear understanding of the terms upon which I enter your cabinet if I do so," and they met the next day. The result was a draft clause for inclusion in a future election manifesto; it stated, in summary, that since repealing the contract would be very difficult, the government would seek modifications. This was also (just) sufficient for Bishop Howley.[82] Morris joined the cabinet without portfolio. Bond was colonial secretary as well as premier.

Why Bond made the deal with Morris is another unknown. In essence, it was an agreement to negotiate a compromise on the railway contract, which neither of them wanted. However, an absolute repeal and the negotiation of a new contract would have been difficult, disruptive, very expensive, and the source of endless legal challenges. Indeed, Reid might well have refused to renegotiate and simply walked away with his extensive landholdings, which would have left the government in a very problematic situation. Perhaps it was to cover their chances that the Reids decided to back Morine and his troops in the approaching election—if they lost, they still had Morris.

The new Bond government met the House on March 29, 1900. The session lasted until May 4 and was concerned mainly with money bills.

---

* John Cook wrote from Heart's Content that "the news resuscitated old Charlie Rendell who was very sick indeed. I told him the other day, it was as good to him as a course of Dr. Williams Pink Pills" (Cook to Bond, March 26, 1900, RBP 3.19.002).

Given Tory defections, the uneasy alliance with the Morris faction, and the demoralization of Winter's group, Bond had a satisfactory majority. A noteworthy event was Morine's announcement (April 4) that he had been elected Leader of the Opposition. Winter appealed to the Speaker (who was a Morine sympathizer) to recognize him, instead—McCallum commented that this had to be "the first time . . . in constitutional history when any such appeal has been made." Predictably enough, the Speaker recognized Morine. Winter returned to the House only to move (successfully) that the ruling be expunged from the *Journal*, then he absented himself. It was, effectively, the end of his public career.*

Soon after the House opened, Reid asked for the government's permission to transfer the 1898 contract and other assets to a company composed of himself and his three sons. The company—rather than Reid personally—could then raise money for development purposes, an arrangement that had been worked out by Morine and Reid while they were in London.[83] Bond responded with stringent conditions: the necessary Order in Council would be issued only if Reid gave back the government telegraph system, accepted a fifty-year lease of the railway in place of the fee simple (the $1 million being returned), and agreed to adjust his land grants to an aggregate of 7,500 acres per mile and safeguard squatters' rights. Alternatively, the government would buy him out for what he had spent under the 1898 contract.[84] Acting on his father's behalf, William D. Reid angrily rejected the terms and let it be known that the Reids would only carry out work that was absolutely necessary. Then, according to Bond, "led away with the idea that Gold is all powerful, and that all public men may be bought into his service . . . he proceeded to try and buy up a sufficient number of my supporters to defeat the Govt. and carry his proposed [incorporation] Bill. On this occasion he counted badly, and . . . my friends

* *JHA* 1900, second session, April 9 and 15. The motion passed twenty-three to six (McCallum to Chamberlain, April 7, 1900, CO 194/245, 202–203; Assembly debates, April 4, and 6, 1900, in the *Evening Telegram* on April 6, 9, 17, and 23, 1900). Bond recommended against Winter's reappointment to the Supreme Court, and the Colonial Office refused to consider him for a colonial judgeship elsewhere.

were not amenable to his influence." No such bill was introduced and a party meeting approved Bond's position, Morris dissenting.[85]

When R.G. Reid arrived back in St. John's in May, he proved to be as inflexible as his son:

> The responsibility of operating nearly 650 miles of railway through a new and sparsely settled country was an undertaking of no small proportions, and, taken by itself involved a financial risk that no individual could with prudence assume . . . because it would be many years before the revenues of the line would be sufficient to meet the outlay. There was but one way in which the risk could be lessened, namely, by the expenditure of the capital necessary for the development of the enterprise wherever opportunity offered, along the line, thereby increasing the business and the earnings of the railway.[86]

However, financiers would never lend sufficient funds to an individual; the fee simple and the ancillary enterprises were necessary security and vital to the success of the operation. Bond, however, was equally inflexible. The Reids began to reduce staff and shut down work.[87] The future would be decided by the election, scheduled for November 8. The battle lines were drawn and the "Reid Deal" was the central issue.

Bond's fight with the Reid interest would continue throughout his term as premier, though it became less compelling to the electorate as the years passed. His position in 1900 was that the Reids should not be allowed to become a private corporation dominating Newfoundland transportation, communications, and interior development; they had to be kept in check if the government, representing the electorate, was to have any role at all. Newfoundland (in Bond's view) was not to become a company colony.

NOTES

1 Whiteway, *Duty's Call*, i.

2 Bond to Whiteway, January 25, 1898, *Duty's Call*, 3.

3 Whiteway to Bond, January 26, 1898, *Duty's Call*, 4–5.

4 *Evening Telegram*, January 28, 1898.

5 Murray to Chamberlain, October 13, 1897 (CO 194/238, 182–214).

6 Murray to Chamberlain, conf., January 11 and 13, 1898 (CO 194/240, 15 and 43).

7 On the talks with the Whiteway government, see Bond to M.F. Howley, June 13, 1899 (RBP 10.01.031).

8 *Evening Telegram*, January 8, 1898; Murray to Chamberlain, conf., January 11 and 31, 1898 (CO 194/240, 43 and 62).

9 The contract can be found in Murray to Chamberlain, February 25, 1898 (CO 194/240, 113–24).

10 Morine, *Railway Contract*, 9–17.

11 Rompkey, "Reid, Sir William Duff," *DCB* 15:865–67.

12 Winter in Assembly, February 22, 1898 (*Evening Herald*, February 25, 1898); Morine in Assembly, February 24, 1898 (*Evening*, March 3, 1898).

13 Morine, *Railway Contract*, 19; *Evening Herald*, July 21, 1898.

14 *Evening Telegram*, August 28, 1898.

15 Bond in Assembly, February 25, 1898 (*Evening Telegram*, March 1, 1898).

16 Murray to Chamberlain, tgm., February 28, 1898 (CO 194/240, 159).

17 Murray to Chamberlain, tgm., March 1, 1898 (CO 194/240, 164, 167–69). See also the M.F. Howley Collection, Roman Catholic Church Archives (RCA), Series 106, 29/6, which contains railway correspondence.

18 Murray to Chamberlain, conf., March 2, 1898 (CO 194/240, 195–201).

19 Bond to Coates, tgm., March 2, 1898 (RBP 10.01.027).

20 Chamberlain to Murray, tgms., March 2 and 7, 1898 (CO 194/240, 204, 210).

21 Council debates March 4 and 7, 1898 (*Daily News*, March 5 and 9, 1898).

22 Howley to Bond, March 7, 10, and 11, 1898, and Bond to Howley, March 7 and 10, 1898 (RBP 10.01.023). See also the *Evening Telegram*, October 29, 1898.

23 For a list of the 1898 legislation, see CO 194/241, 574–82.

24 Winter and Morine to Wingfield, July 7, 1898 (CO 194/242, 607–9).

25 See the Minutes on Murray to Chamberlain, March 16, 1898; Murray to Chamberlain March 26, 1898; and Chamberlain to Murray, April 15, 1898 (CO 194/240, 273–76, 298–99, 304–7).

26 Chamberlain to Murray, March 23, 1898 (CO 194/240, 130–33) and printed in Keith, *Selected Speeches*, 2:105.

27 Murray to Chamberlain, tgm. and secret, April 22, and conf., April 30, 1898; Chamberlain to Murray, tgm., April 25, 1898 (CO 194/240, 373, 393, 396, and 423–34).

28 Morine, *Railway Contract*, 23.

29 Murray to Chamberlain, June 11, 1898 (CO 194/240, 522); *The Times* (London), June 27, 1898 (CO 194/242, 497). See also *Daily News*, June 13, 1898.

30 The correspondence on these issues is in CO 194/242.

31 Bond to Murray, August 11, 1898, and Murray to Bond, August 12 and 15, 1898 (RBP 10.01.020).

32 Murray to Howley, conf., August 31, 1898 (RCA, Howley Collection, 106/29/7).

33 Bond to Murray, August 13, 1898 (RBP 10.01.020).

34 The constitution is in RBP 3.40.003.

35 *Daily News*, July 18, 1898.

36 Murray to Chamberlain, August 19, 1898 (CO 194/241, 57); *Evening Telegram*, August 18, 1898; Murray to Chamberlain, August 17, 1898, and Chamberlain to Murray, August 29, 1898 (Chamberlain papers, JC 9/4/1/29, 36).

37 Winter to Wingfield, tgm., August 19, 1898, and tgm., October 8, 1898 (CO 194/242, 648, 650).

38 Murray to Chamberlain, October 6, 1898 (CO 194/241, 339–43); *Evening Telegram*, October 5, 1898.

39 Murray to Chamberlain, October 20, 1898 (CO 194/241, 409).

40 Murray to Chamberlain, tgms., November 7 and 9, 1898, and conf., November 9, 1898 (CO 194/241, 563, 586, 592).

41 Murray to Chamberlain, February 27, 1898 (Chamberlain papers, JC 9/4/1/14).

42 *Daily News*, November 7 and 8, 1898.

43 Morine to Wingfield, conf., December 13, 1898 (CO 194/242, 561).

44 Murray to Howley, private, December 22, [1900?] (RCA, Howley Collection, 106/29/7).

45 Chamberlain to Murray, December 5, 1898 (CO 194/241, 347–62). Also printed in Chadwick, *Newfoundland*, 93–96.

46 Murray to Chamberlain, November 25, 1898 (CO 194/241, 809); Southey to Newfoundland Liberal Association, December 24, 1898 (PANL, GN 3/22).

47 Memorandum by Murray, December 29, 1898 (PANL, GN 3/22).

48 *ENL* 3:399.

49 Murray to Chamberlain, April 9, 1898 (CO 194/240, 329).

50 Morine to *Evening Herald*, April 19, 1900; Winter to *Evening Herald*, May 3, 1900.

51 Robinson to Winter, tgms., January 28 and February 9, 1899, and Winter to Robinson, tgm., February 10, 1899 (PANL, Winter fonds, MG 836.7). For Robinson, see *ENL* 4:612–13, and Baker, "William Ford Coaker," note 126, 263.

52 Bond to Parsons, February 16, 1899 (RBP 3.40.004).

53 F.C. le Berteau to Winter, March 3, 1899 (PANL, Winter fonds, 836.8).

54 See Callahan to Winter, March 6, 1899 (PANL, Winter fonds, 836.8).

55 "Meeting with Sir James Winter Re the Political Crisis," March 11, 1899 (RBP 3.18.005).

56 Bond to Winter, March 13, 1899 (RBP 3.18.005).

57 Howley to Bond, March 15, 1899 (RBP 3.18.005).

58 The correspondence is in RBP 3.18.005.

59 Winter to Bond, private and confidential, April 1, 1899 (RBP 3.18.005).

60 The correspondence is in PANL, GN 3/23.

61 *Evening Herald*, April 14 and 15, 1899; *Daily News*, March 14, 15, and 27, and April 14, 1899.

62 The April 1899 correspondence is in PANL, Winter fonds, 836.8.

63 *Evening Herald*, May 26, 29, 30, and 31, 1899; *Daily News*, May 31, 1899; McCallum to Chamberlain, May 31, 1899 (CO 194/243, 243–45).

64 McCallum to Robinson, May 1899, draft, (PANL, G3/23); McCallum to Chamberlain, June 2, 1899 (CO 194/243, 259–65).

65 Bond in Assembly, July 13, 1899 (*Evening Herald*, July 31, 1899, and offprint in RBP 3.18.002).

66 Deputation to Whiteway, October 11, 1899; Whiteway to deputation, October 13, 1899; Horwood to Bond, October 14, 1899 (RBP 3.40.004; see also *Evening Telegram*, October 21, 1899).

67 *ENL* 2:447

68 *Evening Telegram*, October 19 and November 9 and 14, 1899.

69 *Evening Herald*, November 13, 1899.

70 Tait to Bond, November 13, 1899 (RBP 3.18.004).

71 Edward English to Bond, November 15, 1899 (RBP 3.18.004).

72 See the November 1899 correspondence between McCallum and J.A. Robinson on this matter (PANL, GN 3/25).

73 See a lengthy letter from "Gaius," *Evening Telegram*, November 11 and 12, 1899.

74 Morine to McCallum, November 27, 1899 (PANL, GN 3/25).

75 McCallum to Chamberlain, November 28, 1899 (CO 194/243, 689–93); *Evening Herald*, November 27, 1899; *Daily News*, November 27 and 28, 1899. There is also correspondence in PANL, GN 3/25.

76 McCallum to Chamberlain, January 2, 1900; Chamberlain to McCallum, tgm., January 22, 1900 (CO 194/245, 7, 10); and McCallum to Chamberlain, conf., January 29, 30, 1900 (CO 194/245, 30, 35).

77 Bond to Winter, February 7, 1900 (RBP 3.19.001). Additional correspondence between Bond and Winter is also in this file.

78 *JHA*, 1900, 1–3.

79 Bond to McCallum, March 13, 1900 (RBP 3.19.005 and copy in PANL, GN 3/27).

80 McCallum to Chamberlain, March 16, April 2, 1900 (CO 194/245, 135–44, 177–83).

81 Bond to Morris and reply, March 7, 1900 (RBP 3.19.006).

82 Howley to Bond, March 6 and 7, 1900 (RBP 3.19.009).

83 Reid to Bond, April 7, 1900, encl. in McCallum to Chamberlain, October 10, 1900 (CO 194/246, 521); Morine, *Railway Contract*, 39.

84 Bond to Reid, April 14, 1900, encl. in McCallum to Chamberlain, October 10, 1900 (CO 194/245, 529).

85 Bond to McCallum, May 15, 1900 (RBP 3.19.005).

86 Reid to Bond, May 24, 1900, encl. in McCallum to Chamberlain, October 10, 1900 (CO 194/245, 533).

87 *Daily News* and *Evening Herald*, June 2, 1900; Reid to Bond, May 31, 1900 (PANL, G3/29).

CHAPTER EIGHT

Bond as Prime Minister: The First Term, 1900–1904

As the twentieth century opened, the Newfoundland economy was recovering (the bottom had been reached in 1898), but the political situation remained problematic. Premier Robert Bond—the term "prime minister" was starting to gain acceptance—held power because the Tory party had disintegrated and because Edward Morris, who had been the political guardian of the Reid interest in the railway and other enterprises and a supporter of the 1898 contract, was prepared to co-operate. Bond was never close to Morris and fundamentally mistrusted him. Without his support, however, Bond could not command a firm majority in the Assembly. Bond initially tried to separate himself from Morris, but Governor McCallum's refusal to allow a dissolution after the 1900 no-confidence vote meant that he had to seek allies in order to govern. Morris's support was essential. He was the political "boss" of Roman Catholic St. John's—which Bishop Howley did not like but had to accept—and he could attract Catholic voters throughout the island. Much as Bond loathed the Reid affiliation, he could not afford to alienate Morris and had to accommodate him. It was a key fault line in the new government.

THE 1900 ELECTION

Predictably enough, Morris did not play a prominent part in the 1900 election. The campaign was a heated contest between the Bond Liberals and the Reids, who funded and supported a Tory rump led by Morine, which many traditional Tories viewed not as the "real" Tory party but as a Reid-Morine operation. Winter (like Whiteway) took no part, and members of the mercantile community either stood aloof or quietly supported Bond. The Reids had bought partial ownership of the *Daily News*, which sang their praises. The other Tory paper, the *Evening Herald*, moved its support to the Liberals in early October—its editor, the mercenary but influential and energetic Patrick T. McGrath, was a Reid-Morris adherent who had clearly decided where the advantage lay.[1]

The Tories advanced a plausible case, which was that Reid should be allowed to fulfill the contract so that economic development—pulp mills, mines, lumbering—could become an actuality rather than a dream.[2] Tory handouts promised a reduction in the tariff and the expenditure of $5 million on resource development. The Reids' steamers and railway cars were plastered with Tory posters and flew campaign flags.[3] James Howley, on the west coast at Bond's behest, reported seeing Governor McCallum with R.G. Reid in the latter's private car. "It was said," he noted, that McCallum made speeches supporting the contract and the Reids.[4]

Bond's manifesto (October 1) attacked the contract and asked voters whether they wanted a Morine-Reid combination to control the government—as well as everything else in the colony. If elected, a Bond government would seek to modify the contract, promote economic development and land settlement, try once again to negotiate reciprocity with the United States, and reform the tariff. He emphasized that his was a national campaign that transcended political divisions: "The present situation does not present a contest between the Liberal and Tory parties. In the ranks of the Liberal party to-day are pronounced Tories, who, for public and patriotic reasons, have sunk their points of difference in order to combine against a common danger. Nobody who realizes what is at stake in this campaign can vote to abandon Government of the people, by the people and for the people, in favour of a Government otherwise constituted." The manifesto also deplored sectarian outbursts, a sentiment that may have been prompted by Bishop Howley's outspoken opposition to the contract.[5]

All this was very lofty and principled. But on the ground, as usual, the action was rough and tumble. There can be no doubt that some Liberals used scare tactics, particularly in relation to Reid's entitlement to four million acres (more than 1.6 million hectares) of land, and played on nationalistic sentiment. A vote for the "Bluenose" Morine would be a vote for the monopolist, the land grabber, the would-be "czar" of Newfoundland who, of course, was Canadian, while Bond was native-born. Verses circulated to this effect in Twillingate district, where Bond ran once again, this time with lawyer James A. Clift and George Roberts, editor and proprietor of the *Twillingate Sun.*[6]

He's Never Going To Fool Us Any More.[7]

[*sung to the tune of "Nelly Gray"*]

A peddling Nova Scotian came out here some years ago,
And very low and humble then was he
But now grown fat and saucy he would like to rule us all,
And deprive us of our homes and liberty.

CHORUS:

Oh! Blue nose Alfred B., what an ingrate you must be,
For you've found both wealth and comfort on our shore,
And you've sold our lands and railway for a paltry dirty fee;
But you're never going to fool us any more.

To Reid the "Czar," his countryman, he sold our mines and dock,
Of our railway and our timber we're bereft,
Hold fast to the remainder for the Czar is wanting all,
And Alfred would be pleased to sell what's left.

CHORUS:

Then vote for BOND, the native, boys, the loyal staunch and brave,
For ROBERTS and for CLIFT, good men and true,
And bury under ballots, fully fifty fathoms deep,
The tricky Nova Scotian and his crew.

The irrepressible William Coaker penned a vitriolic address on behalf of "The Liberals of Herring Neck and suburbs":

> We trust that Reid's avaricious schemes upon our rights and liberties are doomed. . . . This District will tolerate no Czar within its domain, and condemns in the strongest terms the master of White Slavery, now swaying in 'England's Oldest Colony.' . . . We denounce Alfred B. Morine of Queens County Nova Scotia, as the greatest enemy of dear old Terra Nova, and we appeal to every lover of Liberty and Our Country to stand firmly together and . . . hurl him and his squid-like party, where all enemies of Liberty, and unscrupulous tyrants should be.[8]

Morine later asserted that the electorate had been deceived. In his view—and he was there—most voters thought that Bond and the Liberals would cancel the 1898 contract and begin again. They did not understand what "modification" implied.[9] Whiteway also seems to have assumed that there would be a new start. Confusion there may well have been, but the result was a Liberal landslide—the Tories salvaged only four seats (in Bonavista and Port de Grave). After Bond and his colleagues won comfortably in Twillingate, letters of congratulation began to arrive. A supporter from Tilt Cove wrote: "We gives it to the torys here in Tilt cove, we tells them the four tory candidates that's returned will do to keep Sir Robert Bond and colleagues boots clean. . . . Now Sir there is fifteen of us clubed [*sic*] together we are going to have a ball (whirligig) some time in the Christmas and our request to you is that you will send us down two gallons of rum."[10] Bishop Howley was elated: "I feel deeply grateful to God for having saved our poor old country from what I deemed a dire and fatal calamity. And I had no scruple in having the prayers of the Church offered up in sincere thanksgiving."[11] Daniel Prowse chortled that "poor old Reid is very sore . . . I met him the other day and he was quite snappish with me and WD [Reid] looking as sulky as a bear."[12] Dr. Tait[13] reported that "The Reids . . . are still sullen and vindictive. They threaten to dismiss all the liberals in their employ, and in fact, they have done so already. They tell them to 'go to Bishop Howley and look for employment.'"[14]

Governor McCallum thought that the electorate had objected to Morine as a potential premier, and pointed out that Roman Catholics had been especially antagonistic to him since the 1883 Harbour Grace riot. However, clergy of all denominations had, he reported, supported the Liberals.* The abstention of Winter and his supporters had been damaging, as had the Tories' close identification with—and the involvement of—the Reids. Morine was on the Reid payroll, as were many of his candidates, which had raised a cry about a Morine-Reid combination taking over the colony.†

Despite having a clear majority, Bond had some difficulty in forming his government. He wanted an Executive Council of nine members. McCallum thought this too large and disliked the idea of department heads who did not sit on the Council.[15] But Bond had to juggle factional and denominational demands—Daniel Greene called the party "a curious political mosaic of strange and inconsistent contrasts."‡ He emerged with a nine-member cabinet, only three of whom held portfolios: Bond as colonial secretary, Horwood at Justice, and Edward Jackman§ at Finance. A.W. Harvey (now an MHA for Harbour Grace) was included, as well as

---

* But John Cowan (*ENL* 1:553) reported that in Bonavista Bay, a sectarian cry had been worked up by spreading the allegation that Bond would be controlled by the Roman Catholics, and that some members of the Church of England did not want a Methodist premier (Cowan to Bond, November 17, 1900, RBP 3.19.018; see also the *Daily News*, November 15, 1900). Bishop Howley claimed that clergy of all denominations had been "active against Reid" (letter to Sydney *Morning Post*, reprinted in the *Evening Telegram*, November 27, 1900).

† McCallum to Chamberlain, November 23, 1900 (CO 194/245, 627–30). McCallum described Morine as "masterful, impulsive and quarrelsome" but noted that in office he had been "earnest, hardworking, and willing to initiate reforms" (McCallum to Chamberlain, conf., October 11, 1900, CO 194/245, 541).

‡ Greene in Legislative Council, February 26, 1901 (*Evening Telegram*, March 2, 1901). Greene had been appointed to the Council in 1898.

§ Jackman, a tailor, was a prominent St. John's Roman Catholic (ENL 3:88).

Morris.* Bond had hoped that Horwood would become colonial secretary, not wanting the office himself—"it means slavery for me," he told McCallum.[16] Bishop Howley was unhappy at Morris's appointment, calling it "suicidal": "I cannot see how you can in justice or with safety admit Morris to your Executive Council." But Bond, most unwisely, thought there was no danger, "as I shall very effectively guard against that."[17]

MODIFYING THE RAILWAY CONTRACT

The first item on Bond's agenda was, obviously, modifying the railway contract, and he and R.G. Reid were soon in touch. Believing that they had reached a basis for negotiation, Bond formally laid out the government's position on December 13[18]: the colony would own and control the telegraph lines that were not the property of the Anglo-American Telegraph Company, but Reid could attach his own line to government poles along the railway; land grants that conflicted with "public interests" would be cancelled, but new grants would be issued for "such portions of the present grants as do not prejudice public or private rights" and Reid could select new areas to compensate for the land being taken back; and the government should be able to take back the reversionary interest of the railway at the end of the current leasehold, paying "reasonable compensation." If this was agreed to, Reid could transfer the "leasehold interest" to a limited liability company. Finally, there should be a guarantee that a "fair and equitable" amount of money would be spent on the development of Reid lands.

Reid found these terms "so unreasonable and so unjust, that I must express my unqualified dissent." The takeover of the telegraph lines amounted to confiscation without compensation and the other proposals were similarly objectionable. Reid felt he had fulfilled his contractual obligations to the letter only to be subjected to "misrepresentation and abuse." If the government was determined to oppose him, then it might be best that he should "retire, and the Government take over my properties and enterprises, on terms to be arranged between us." He emphasized the last point in a private letter.[19] Bond expressed surprise at the letter's

---

* Public Works (G.W. Gushue), Customs (E. Dawe), Fisheries (R.T. McGrath), and Agriculture and Mines (T.J. Murphy) were outside the cabinet.

"general tenor" and felt misunderstood. But if Reid really wanted to give up the contract, the government would consider "such terms as you may be prepared to submit."[20]

The discussions continued in Montreal early in 1901. Bond was there en route to London at the request of the Colonial Office. He had several lengthy meetings with Reid and his lawyers but no settlement was reached. Apparently advised by Sir Thomas Shaughnessy, Reid still seemed primarily interested at this stage in selling out to the colony. Bond was unsure about Reid's sincerity, and in any case the government did not, in truth, want to purchase unless it was on favourable terms.[21] Reluctantly, Bond continued on to London. New in office, it was a journey he did not want to make but could not refuse.[22] The French Shore question was always divisive and thorny, and this was the reason for the summons.

THE FRENCH SHORE YET AGAIN

Informal talks had taken place between the French ambassador in London, Paul Cambon, and Lord Lansdowne, the British Foreign Secretary, about the possibility of a final and comprehensive settlement—and for the first time the French government had indicated that it would consider abandoning the French Shore in return for adequate compensation. This was rightly considered a significant change of position, and the Foreign and Colonial offices decided to consult the colony. However, while the Newfoundland government readily agreed to renew the treaties legislation, there were objections to sending a delegation to London as requested—similar negotiations had failed in the past and could well be prejudicial to the party's popularity. In the end, it was decided that Bond and Morris (who was travelling to London anyway) would go. During their absence, Horwood would pilot a treaties bill through another special session of the legislature,* which opened on February 21 and closed a week later. The legislation passed, although Morine (unsuccessfully) tried Bond's tactic of the previous year by moving that the session should proceed to

* McCallum to Chamberlain, conf., January 9, 1901, and tgm., January 12, 1901 (CO 194/247, 24–28, 39–40). Anderson wrote, "Morris is a slippery gentleman. His presence is not likely to facilitate a result."

regular business. Some Legislative Councillors expressed unhappiness, however. "Is it possible," expostulated Edgar Bowring, "that Great Britain, so jealous of the rights and privileges of the Uitlanders in South Africa, and of the rights of the missionary in China, can be so utterly indifferent to the claims of Newfoundlanders on the Treaty Shore?"[23] Horwood reported to Bond that there was a great deal of friction within the party over appointments and the distribution of patronage, and that members were grumbling about Bond's absence; he recommended that regular business should not go ahead until Bond returned.[24]

The discussions in London got nowhere. The British government had no specific proposals to offer and Bond and Morris were understandably cautious. They insisted, among other things, that the French bounty system had to be adjusted. Colonial Office officials found the delegates' position unreasonable and inflexible—Chamberlain at one point used the word "ridiculous"—and showed little sympathy for the colony's position; nor did they appreciate the political minefield through which Bond was feeling his way. The French, too, were intransigent, insisting that bounties were non-negotiable and that there had to be free trade in bait. They also demanded territorial and financial compensation for abandoning the Shore. Bond failed to persuade the British government to allow clear land titles on the Shore and was warned off the idea of an arbitration.

Bond left London for Newfoundland in early May. He complained that the delegates' "relations to their Colleagues and Party had . . . been rendered exceedingly difficult and unpleasant by the secrecy that necessarily has to be maintained in relation to the negotiations, and by their inability to point to any material good having resulted from their prolonged visit to England."[25] It is no wonder that the colonial government followed up by refusing to issue a proclamation forbidding the use of cod traps on the French Shore, a move that the Colonial Office thought might ease matters with the French.[26] Officials were appalled.

The visit had not been a complete waste of time, however.* Bond had

---

* Bond visited the West Country, as he always did on visits to England, and opened a new gymnasium and chemistry laboratories at his old school, now named Queen's College, Taunton. A draft of his speech is in RBP 3.20.007.

been able to discuss several matters of concern to his government—the possibility of raising a loan, for instance, as well as the development of a Newfoundland branch of the Royal Naval Reserve[27] and the possibility of a separate reciprocity treaty with the United States. The latter was, of course, one of Bond's central ambitions. He had not been happy about Newfoundland participating in the Joint High Commission in 1898–99, which was still officially in existence. Bond approached Chamberlain on the matter, who noted that the colony had a strong case.[28] The Canadian government remained opposed, but was no doubt aware that Chamberlain was coming around to the view that Newfoundland could not be indefinitely denied the chance to negotiate. At the same time, Chamberlain knew that Sir Wilfrid Laurier would strenuously object.[29] The only way that Laurier could be sure of preventing a separate negotiation was by bringing Newfoundland into confederation, but he had always stipulated that settlement of the French Shore issue was an essential precondition and that did not seem likely—though he went so far as to write directly to Théophile Delcassé, the French Foreign Minister, to explain the situation.[30]

At Chamberlain's suggestion,[31] Bond returned to Newfoundland by way of Ottawa and Montreal so that he could meet Laurier and discuss reciprocity. Bond argued that if the Canadian government withdrew its protest against the 1890 draft convention, which he described as "offensive and unjust," the Newfoundland government would co-operate with Canada in renewed reciprocity negotiations. But if these talks did not result in free entry for fishery products into the US, then Newfoundland should be free to try and negotiate a separate agreement. Laurier would only say that if the Joint High Commission did not reassemble, or failed to obtain what Newfoundland wanted, his government would be "prepared to have the whole subject reconsidered." This was deliberately evasive. Bond did not retreat, and there the matter rested—for the moment.[32]

THE RAILWAY CONTRACT CONTINUED

The legislative session opened on May 23, much later than usual and still with no agreement concerning the railway contract. Since this was a central and difficult issue, business could only be routine while Bond continued to negotiate with Reid. The latter was willing to sell, but the former preferred revision and compromise. Bond also did not want to expropriate Reid by "forced legislation." By late June, Reid had agreed to return the telegraphs to the colony in return for compensation; concerning his land grants, he also promised, he would do what was needed to protect the rights of third parties.[33] But there were still many outstanding issues and Bishop Howley was becoming apprehensive. He wrote to the press warning that "the fruits of this tremendous struggle" might be lost.[34] He also assured Bond—who was offended by the letter—that he had "offered up most earnest prayers daily to the throne of God that you may be enlightened and strengthened to do right in spite of all influences to the contrary. It is indeed a desperate fight. The fight of a poor, small, humble people against the dreadful odds of power, influence, wealth, favour."[35]

Governor Sir Charles Cavendish Boyle (1849–1916), who wrote the "Ode to Newfoundland," undated. (ASC, RBP 12.14.001)

It was not until July 22 that McCallum's replacement as governor, the newly arrived Sir Cavendish Boyle,* signed a new agreement between the Reids and the Newfoundland government. Its main clauses provided that Reid would return to the government "all interest and property" in the railway system and the St. John's municipal basin, receiving $1 million with interest at 6 per cent. Adjustments would be made to Reid land grants, and the government would pay $850,000 for the lands to which Reid was entitled under the 1898 contract. The government telegraphs would be returned and, if either party claimed compensation, the sum would be settled by arbitration. Finally, the

* McCallum was transferred to Natal. I have not found any evidence that he was recalled from Newfoundland as some sources suggest (for example *ENL* 3:399 and Howley, *Reminiscences*, 1724). For Boyle, see Hiller, "Boyle, Sir Charles Cavendish," *DCB* 14:130 and *ENL* 1:237.

contracts as amended were to be assigned to the new Reid Newfoundland Company, which would absorb the Reid Railway Lands Co., the Reid Steamship Co. (both formed in 1900), and the St. John's Street Railway Co.[36] A separate and private agreement between Bond and Reid provided that the "additional rolling stock, equipment and accommodations . . . and the stations etc." provided or built by Reid under the two 1893 contracts would be paid for by the government, the amount being decided by arbitration if necessary.[37] The amended contract was very much Bond's work, and there seems to have been minimal consultation with his colleagues.

The revisions now had to go through the legislature. Bond was concerned that the government did not have a majority in the Legislative Council, where two members were Reid employees, and he asked the governor for the appointment of three new members.[38] Boyle fussed about the matter but eventually, at the end of July, two new members were allowed.[39] Bond had already brought the legislation to the Assembly on July 22:

> I believe . . . that if this Bill becomes law it will insure mutual confidence, cooperation and a blending of interests as between Government and Contractor. I look to this measure as removing all cause of friction between the people of this Colony and the Contractor, and as calculated to result in a steadier increase of prosperity, and a steadier wage for our working people.[40]

These were optimistic words. Morine accused Bond of behaving like "a mixture of Dick Turpin and Uriah Heep." He accurately predicted that the agreement would prove costly "now and in the future" and argued that Reid would now be unable to raise enough money for any ambitious development schemes. But since it was better than nothing, the opposition would not divide the House.* And, as it turned out, Bond's fears about the

---

* Morine in Assembly, July 28, in the *Evening Telegram*, August 1, 1901, and the *Daily News*, July 25, 26, and 27, 1901. He added: "I have always insisted . . . that the cost of operating that railroad would destroy the independence of this country."

Legislative Council proved exaggerated.[41]

So the 1901 contract became law. Governor Boyle thought the details bristled "with danger, difficulty and ambiguity, and . . . open[ed] doors which were better closed." It would also add at least $2 million to the public debt: "Remember, please, that when the debacle comes, as assuredly it will, I have ventured to differ with the policy of my present advisers."[42] Raising the money to pay Reid was an immediate priority. Bond was rapidly in touch with the financiers in London with whom he had dealt in 1895. He had been warned that, given the Boer War and other uncertainties, the markets were hardly buoyant. There was no alternative, however, and a loan was floated in London in September. Investors were not enthusiastic, leaving the underwriters with 75 per cent of the issue, but at least Reid got his million dollars.[43]

The highpoint of the 1901 social season, as far as St. John's was concerned, was a brief royal visit in October by the Duke and Duchess of Cornwall and York—the Duke being the future King George V. Local arrangements were the responsibility of a Citizens' Committee chaired by Whiteway. Thanks to Governor Boyle's lobbying, Bond was knighted immediately before a glittering dinner at Government House on October 23.* Whiteway absented himself. A Privy Councillor, he must have been invited, but his name does not appear in the press reports.

By this time, Bond had been in office for nineteen strenuous months. Outwardly his political position seemed impregnable—his popularity was high and his opponents were weakened and fractious. The colony was pulling out of the long, late nineteenth-century recession and a mood of optimism was taking hold. He seemed to have solved the railway controversy—he certainly thought so—and to have placed limits on the power and influence of the Reid family. He was moving toward reopening the

* Boyle to Chamberlain, tgm., August 25, 1901; secret, August 27, 1901, and September 30, 1901 (CO 447/67, n.p.). Boyle thought that a KCMG for Bond "would have an excellent effect" and argued against the grant of a CMG. He was also well aware that honours had to be distributed on a denominational basis, recognizing cabinet hierarchy. Bond was a new premier who had not accomplished anything especially worthy of imperial recognition, hence the hesitancy.

reciprocity question and there seemed to be a chance of progress on French Shore issues. But he had yet to clarify his domestic agenda beyond the railway contract. He must also have been aware that his party had some serious divisions. Morris was close to the Reids and had his own ambitions and supporters. Rumours were circulating that Whiteway was unhappy with Bond's behaviour—with his coldness and lack of gratitude, apparently—and that he intended to return to public life.[44] Whiteway also deplored the revised railway contract. He had disliked the 1898 contract, he wrote later, but the 1901 agreement was even worse—he could not see "one redeeming feature" in it.[45] Significantly, Whiteway's law partner, George Johnson, had begun picking holes in the revised contract during the railway debate.[46]

Recent commentators have suggested, with the benefit of hindsight, that sticking with the 1898 contract might have been a wise choice.[47] Morris, Morine, and others consistently defended their original position, and the argument became a fundamental cause of political division. The original contract had placed the responsibility for the railway and its allied enterprises entirely on the contractor and shifted the major onus for land-based development away from the government. The amended contract placed that onus on the Reid Newfoundland Company—not on an individual. It also proved to be very costly: the colony had to compensate Reid for what he had given up and take part in expensive arbitrations. In addition, in the 1920s, the colony had to take back the ownership of the railway system and that, in the long term, proved to be a very mixed blessing indeed. In the 1930s, Morine estimated that the cost of the 1901 changes had been about $33.5 million.[48]

These assessments make sense in many ways, but the position of Bond and his allies must be understood. Bond firmly believed that Newfoundland had immense economic potential—so if that was the case, why alienate control of the colony's resources to a private company whose principal members were Canadians? The power of the company needed to be contained. If it was not, it could (in theory) become sufficiently powerful to control both the government and the future of a small colony. As time went on, it would become clear that Bond had overestimated the value of the island's resources, and much else. But in 1900 and 1901, he spoke for the wide and genuine concern that the Reids represented a danger to an independent Newfoundland. Political realities meant that the 1898 contract could not be repealed and financial realities meant that Reid could not be bought out. The result was a costly compromise, unsatisfactory to both parties and the cause of much future difficulty.

IMPERIAL AFFAIRS, 1902–1904

The dominant imperial issues during these years were, as they had been for a long time, the French Treaty Shore and reciprocity with the United States, but there had been a significant background change. Between 1900 and 1907, British relations with Japan, France, the United States, and Russia were realigned. This has been called "a remarkable transformation of Britain's international situation. From near-isolation in 1900, the British had secured agreements that blunted challenges to their global position by the sacrifice of peripheral interests."[49] In this context, continued talks with France made sense, since it was clearly time to regroup and reassess. As far as the United States was concerned, Britain allowed a number of disputes to be settled in that country's favour and soon began to withdraw naval and military forces from North America and the Caribbean. Indeed, "by the end of 1903, by a series of concessions for which the United States made no return, Britain had acquiesced in American supremacy in the western hemisphere from Venezuela to Alaska."[50] This reality was to both help and hinder the Newfoundland government as it tried to deal with the fishing rights that both these powers possessed as a result of old treaties.

British officials were preoccupied with the stalemated French negotiations. They continued to press Newfoundland to give way on the bait question, even though the British government itself refused to cede territory as France demanded. If there was to be an agreement, officials insisted, Newfoundland had to concede bait. "It is all we ask them to do, and little enough, to enable us to get an arrangement," wrote John Anderson, "and if they will not do it, the only inference is that they do not regard the French rights as a serious burden, as they will do nothing to help themselves to get rid of it."[51] This was hardly fair comment, but nevertheless a strong dispatch followed; a second one specifically advised against an arbitration because the colony might well lose on the issues of exclusivity and "fixed establishments." It went on to state the old argument (which cut little ice in St. John's) that Britain could not make all the concessions: "The colony having come into existence subject to these burdens cannot claim relief solely at the expense of the rest of the Empire." More to the point, the dispatch argued, the colony had to accept a compromise that would necessarily involve bait. If the colonial government would not agree to some such deal, then "the entire responsibility for the continuance of the existing disabilities of the Colony must rest with them." Moreover, co-operation on the French question would be a condition for permission to begin separate reciprocity talks with the United States.[52]

This was imperial bullying. The government continued to argue that repealing the Bait Act would cause considerable loss to the Newfoundland economy and that France should at least stop paying bounties to the St. Pierre fleet.[53] Most members of the Executive Council, Bond and Horwood aside, opposed conceding bait to the French.[54] Bond had always been ambivalent about the Bait Act's value. It had been suspended in 1893, re-enforced by the Winter government in 1899, and enforcement continued after Bond became premier. But he seems to have concluded that the act was ineffective. Inspector of Customs Joseph O'Reilly reported that the French got all the bait they needed at Sydney and the Magdalen Islands, and that Canada allowed the export of bait to St. Pierre. Newfoundlanders with bait to sell but no buyers were harmed and a large trade was lost. The opinion on the south coast, O'Reilly said, was that, like the Americans, the French should be allowed to come inshore and purchase bait under licence.[55] Bond later told Morris that the Bait Act should be used to get rid of the Treaty Shore problem by allowing the French to purchase bait at a port of entry.[56]

Not surprisingly, though, the government took strong exception to the French question being linked to reciprocity negotiations. With Governor Boyle's support, it urged that the issues should be separated and that permission to negotiate reciprocity should be given.[57] The Colonial Office conceded the point. The Joint High Commission had died and further refusal seemed impossible—"and it is possible that though they won't bargain about it they may be less obstructive if we let them have their way about this."[58] The Foreign Office fell into line. Canada remained opposed (if unsurprised), and the possibility of confederation received another airing. Laurier was concerned about the prospect of a Newfoundland reciprocity treaty and dropped his insistence on a French Shore settlement as a precondition for confederation. He feared a loss of bargaining power with the US and the possible Americanization of Newfoundland.[59] Laurier's intermediary was a Canadian official helping to reorganize the Newfoundland Post Office department, who apparently obtained from Bond an outline of the terms that would be expected. But once again the matter went no further, although Laurier was urged on by his postmaster general and by Henry M. Whitney, the American industrialist who headed Dominion Iron and Steel Co. at Sydney, Nova Scotia, which relied on iron ore from Bell Island.[60] However, once it was clear that reciprocity negotiations could not start until later in the year, Bond agreed to a Canadian request to postpone further discussion until the 1902 Colonial Conference, which was to take place in London in July.[61]

THE 1902 COLONIAL CONFERENCE

Bond attended both the conference and the coronation of Edward VII, originally scheduled for June 26, as a guest of the British government. (Whiteway was upset because, although invited, he was not a guest.[62]) Bond arrived on June 17 and was escorted to the Hotel Cecil.[63] Other colonial representatives also there included Laurier and Sir William MacGregor, who would become the next governor of Newfoundland but was then representing the "West African Colonies and Protectorates." On June 19, Bond attended a giant reception laid on by Lord Salisbury (the prime minister) at Hatfield House, and the next day received word that he was to be made a Privy Councillor. He was sworn in on August 11. The festivities ground to a halt on June 24 when it became known that the king had to undergo surgery and the coronation would be postponed.

The delay did not affect the third Colonial Conference, however, which opened on June 30. It took place in the aftermath of the Boer War,

Participants in the 1902 Colonial Conference. Joseph Chamberlain (Colonial Secretary) is in the centre of the front row, flanked by Sir Wilfrid Laurier on his left and Sir Edmund Barton (Australia) on his right. Bond is at the left end of the row. Sir John Anderson of the Colonial Office, who had much to do with British policy towards Newfoundland, is in the second row, second from left. (Hocken Library, University of Otago)

which had been a sobering experience for Great Britain. There was concern about the country's international position, about the strength and efficiency of its armed forces, and—perhaps unnecessarily—about the economy.[64] Chamberlain stressed the need for closer relations between Britain and the Empire. In a frequently quoted passage, he told the conference: "We do require your assistance in the administration of the vast Empire which is yours as well as ours. The weary Titan staggers under the too vast orb of its fate. We have borne the burden for many years. We think it is time that our children should assist us to support it."[65] In particular he stressed—as he had before—the need for imperial co-operation in matters of defence and trade.

Bond did not submit any subjects or resolutions for debate; indeed, he initially thought that he might not be able to attend. Like the other first ministers (especially Laurier), he was opposed to closer political relations with Britain. But he was certainly interested in having Newfoundland play a role in imperial defence, hence his support for the Royal Naval Reserve.* As for trade relations, he opposed imperial preference, one of Chamberlain's flagship policies, and favoured the status quo.† In his reply to Chamberlain's opening speech—which began with "When I have regard to the numerical weakness of the Colony that I have the honour to represent, I am sometimes embarrassed"[66]—he stated that he was not much concerned "with the question of preferential trade." Most of Newfoundland's imports came from Britain or British possessions, and its revenues came from Customs duties: "It is a matter that involves very great consideration indeed as to how we can in any way deal with the question of preferential trade. Our policy is a free trade policy, essentially and necessarily so." He took no part in the debate on trade and tariffs held on July 18; when it was remarked that Newfoundland had made no proposals, Bond stated that "our tariff . . . has been framed solely for revenue purposes and I do not think it would be possible for us to make any preference. Further, I do not think it would be any advantage to the Mother Country for us to revise our tariff in any way."

The gathering in London provided another opportunity for discussions about French Shore matters, which again went nowhere. Under pressure from the Colonial Office, Bond consulted colleagues in St. John's once more on the bait issue. There was no change in position. Bond suggested that the problem should be put to the Colonial Conference, but John Anderson talked him out of it on the grounds that it could not be discussed intelligently.[67] The Colonial Office did not object to Bond obtaining an independent legal opinion on a French Shore arbitration, so he submitted the colony's case to R.B. Haldane and E.H. Coles. Like the Colonial Office, they advised against it: it would be impossible to predict the outcome and the dispute was best left to diplomats.[68] So ended Bond's efforts in that direction.

---

* Bond submitted a memorandum on the subject to the Colonial Office (Bond to Anderson, July 5, 1902, CO 194/251, 547).

† On the 1902 conference, see Kendle, *The Colonial and Imperial Conferences*, 39–54. Bond attended "more as an interested spectator than as an active participant," so Kendle thought (46).

It is unclear whether Bond had conversations with Laurier and other Canadians in London about reciprocity and confederation. In a press interview (copied into a notebook), he denied that he had discussed confederation with any member of the Canadian delegation.* When the matter was raised at a Canadian Club dinner on July 15, he said—as he always did in public—that confederation was a matter of terms, while also emphasizing the colony's strategic value, its "phenomenal recuperative powers," and its current prosperity. "We are not jealous of Canada," he said.[69] Bond's papers, however, contain an undated memorandum from this period—not necessarily a product of the London visit—outlining "the attitude of both the Government and the Opposition in the Canadian Parliament respecting any proposals for union of the Colony of Newfoundland with the Dominion of Canada." General in nature, it indicates that the initiative would have to come from Newfoundland, and suggests that the 1895 proposals might form a basis for negotiation "with such modifications as would be reasonable and necessary." The question would have to be put to the people of Newfoundland, and Canada would play no part in the ensuing debate.[70]

It is hard to escape the conclusion that Bond must have had discussions with the Canadians while in London. Later in the year, he received a letter from W.S. Fielding, Laurier's Finance minister, that strongly implies that this was the case. Fielding once again argued that Canada and Newfoundland should work together on fisheries questions, adding that the fisheries would be Newfoundland's most valuable bargaining chip in confederation negotiations—a chip that would be lost if Bond made a separate reciprocity treaty with the US. Fielding had heard that pro-confederation sentiment was growing in the colony and he suggested a conference on the issue.[71] Bond's response was unsympathetic and uncompromising. Public opinion was "strongly hostile to Confederation. No party would venture to go to the polls on the question." Moreover, he noted that "the attitude of your Government and the bitter and unjustifiable hostility of your press regarding the effort of Newfoundland to better her position is rendering the question of Confederation more hopeless

* RBP 3.22.003. The interview took place shortly before Bond left London.

than ever. . . . An AntiConfederate could desire [no] stronger weapons than have been placed in his hands by your government and press."[72] That put an end to Canadian overtures.*

RECIPROCITY DISCUSSIONS, 1902

Bond attended the postponed coronation on August 9 "in the full Court uniform of an Imperial Privy Councillor." With the conference finally closed (August 11), Bond set off for the United States to re-open reciprocity talks—taking with him the Coronation medal, the Freedom of the City of Edinburgh, and an honorary LL.D. from Edinburgh University.† Once again, August proved not to be a good month to arrive in Washington. John Hay, the Secretary of State in Theodore Roosevelt's Republican administration, was at his summer residence, as was the British ambassador, Sir Michael Herbert. However, Hay told his staff to receive Bond's proposals via the British Embassy. He was interested in a Newfoundland treaty because he saw potential economic and political advantages. It would formalize the colony's detachment from Canada, increase American influence in that region, and evade the imperial preference system (which Canada had adopted), while giving advantages to American fishermen and exporters. However, he was well aware that the Senate might not be as enthusiastic, and that outright hostility might well come from New England senators, especially from the influential Henry Cabot Lodge.[73] Lodge was a key person, given that he was closely allied to the fishing firms based in Gloucester, Massachusetts, and that his son-in-law, another federal politician, was facing re-election. Lodge was unlikely to do anything Gloucester did not want.

Bond understood the need for lobbying, which he did in both New York and Boston. He tried and failed to meet Lodge in person, and so wrote to him outlining the reasons why Newfoundland wanted an agreement and what it should contain. He concluded:

---

* Fielding to Bond, November 12, 1902 (LAC, Laurier fonds, 68094). Bond said much the same to the Lieutenant Governor of Nova Scotia (A.G. Jones to Laurier, November 3, 1902, LAC, Laurier fonds, 67983).

† He was unable to get to Cambridge to accept an Hon. LL.D. at that university.

> I have always advocated freer trade with the United States as against Confederation with Canada . . . [even though] I have no doubt that the Colony could now obtain very liberal terms. Under Confederation, Canada would monopolize the whole trade of the Colony and also command the North American fisheries through the bait supplies which would then vest in her. . . . I am opposed to Confederation with Canada, believing that reciprocity with this country [the USA] will be of far greater benefit to the people of the Colony, and until I am convinced that there is no prospect of this, I shall continue to oppose the movement.*

When Hay returned to Washington, he consulted Senators Lodge and Frye, the New England members on the Foreign Relations Committee. Apparently reassured by their replies, Hay began serious negotiations with Bond. A draft treaty, similar to that of 1890, was ready by mid-October, at which point Lodge began to backtrack. Mid-term elections were approaching; he now thought that the treaty would be unpopular in Gloucester and should be modified. It could certainly not be dealt with until after the elections. An annoyed and frustrated Hay agreed to the postponement but did not suggest any alterations. Herbert informed Bond, who immediately jumped to the conclusion that this was the result of another hostile Canadian move.[74] Nevertheless, the draft

Henry Cabot Lodge (1850–1924), a strong New England opponent of Robert Bond's attempt to negotiate reciprocity with the United States, undated. (Library of Congress, 72073)

* Bond to Lodge, September 11, 1902 (RBP 7.08.006). He enclosed a twenty-two-page memorandum on the history and advantages of reciprocity (RBP 7.08.011).

treaty was signed on November 8. It went to the Senate on December 3 where, predictably, Lodge and his allies buried it in the Foreign Relations Committee.[75]

The British signature had come with the condition (based on an assurance Bond had given in 1901) that "Great Britain and all British Colonies and all countries entitled to most-favoured-nation treatment in Newfoundland will receive the same treatment both as regards bait and import duties as [the] United States."[76] But there was an addition in the signed version of the treaty that had not been in the draft—"No heavier duty shall be imposed on articles coming from the US than is imposed on such articles coming from elsewhere"—language that seemed to give most-favoured-nation status to *all* US imports, not only those enumerated, and to prevent Newfoundland from implementing an imperial preference. A dispatch went to St. John's: "It is the declared policy of His Majesty's Government that the . . . relations of the different parts of the Empire *inter se* should not be hampered by any agreements with foreign countries requiring that such countries should receive the same treatment in tariff matters as may be accorded to other parts of the Empire." The British government had not fully understood, it seems, that Bond was opposed to imperial preference—though he had made his views clear enough at the Colonial Conference—nor that he might try to make agreements at variance with it.[77] But they took no further action, since there seemed little chance of the draft treaty being ratified. Had there been such a chance, there is no doubt that the British government would have intervened. For the same reason, no action was taken by the Canadian government, in spite of protests from Nova Scotia.[78]

So reciprocity was sidelined, lobbying efforts changed nothing, and Bond was angered by the hostility of Nova Scotian newspapers. He suspected that Nova Scotians had encouraged the New England opposition and he was outraged by the documents Lodge submitted on behalf of Gloucester: "One can scarcely imagine that an intelligent body of men could be influenced by them." Bond was also thinking about how to retaliate, should the treaty fail.* Nevertheless, he tabled the draft treaty in the Assembly. The negotiations showed, he said, that he had succeeded in securing "for this Colony that dignity, recognition and right that had been accorded to the other colonies of the Empire." If nothing else, "the Colony had established once and forever the right to direct negotiations with the United States and the recognition by His Majesty's Government of its equality with other colonies of the Empire as regards trade negotiations."[79] Though possibly overstating the case, Bond rightly thought this achievement significant; but there matters had to rest until the Americans officially reacted. Until then, it was a stalemate.

THE FRENCH SHORE SETTLEMENT, 1904

In contrast, the French Shore issue finally moved toward a conclusion. Serious Anglo-French talks resumed in July 1903. This time, negotiations were not focused only on the Newfoundland problem but also addressed several other important disputes in Africa and elsewhere. The Treaty Shore was now placed in diplomatic context as one of a range of issues that had to be settled if there was to be a genuine understanding between the two countries. This made trade-offs possible. In addition, since both parties refused to bargain about bait and bounties, John Anderson suggested that these issues should be avoided altogether. France would give up whatever territorial rights it possessed on the Treaty Shore, but retain a right to fish concurrently with British subjects within its former limits.[80] It was a neat compromise that was put to France in November. The talks remained fragile, but the Newfoundland government was informed of the new approach in January 1904 and asked to undertake to pass regulations governing a concurrent fishery.

To the Colonial Office's surprise and annoyance, Bond (and his government) was hesitant. This was not the full and final settlement that Newfoundlanders had always wanted—French bounties would remain in

---

* Bond to Herbert, January 1, 1903 (RBP 7.09.005). At the Colonial Office, Anderson thought "the pamphlet issued by the Gloucester people is the most extraordinary tissue of misstatement I have seen for a long time" (Anderson to Bond, private, January 10, 1903, RBP 7.09.005).

place, bait was available on the Treaty Shore where French fishermen and naval squadrons would still appear, and might not the French set up floating lobster canneries and bait depots? And how would such an agreement play politically? Moreover, Morris was away and Bond did not want to face problems from that quarter. Governor Boyle went to work and eventually, on January 26, the government passed the necessary Minute of Council. Bond explained to Anderson: "I have had to feel my way very carefully so as to be certain of a united Council and party in dealing with this matter later on."[81] There was no further consultation.

The Anglo-French Convention concerning Newfoundland was part of a package of agreements—the *Entente Cordiale*—that was signed on April 8. The final text, a *fait accompli*, did not reach St. John's until April 12, several days after it was tabled in the British Parliament. Rumours mounted and the opposition press began the attack: "SOLD TO FRANCE. THE BAIT ACT GONE. BOND BETRAYS US. FRENCH FISHERMEN GIVEN BAIT."[82] This did not prompt the government to publish or table the convention. Bond and Morris were troubled by the wording of Article 2, which provided that the French could fish on the Treaty Shore "during the usual fishing season closing for all persons on the 20th October of each year."[83] Taken literally, this could be read as applying to British subjects. Reassurance that it applied only to French subjects did not arrive until April 19. On that day, the *Daily News* printed the text of the convention; in the Assembly, Morine tackled Bond, noting that there was nothing in the text requiring ratification by the legislature. This was acutely embarrassing, since he had assured the Assembly on April 7 that a convention would have to be approved locally. He squirmed and, at his request, Governor Boyle informed London of the government's claim that "to be binding any convention must be subject to ratification by the Legislature of [the] Colony."[84] On April 21, Bond finally tabled the convention in the Assembly, endorsing it in a long speech. This island, he said, "may henceforth be hailed not only as our native land, but our own land, freed from every foreign claim and the blasting influence of foreign oppression—ours in entirety—solely ours."[85] There were government-organized celebrations in St. John's and elsewhere, with flags, processions, bonfires, and fireworks.[86]

There was no sympathy whatsoever in London with the idea that the convention should be confirmed locally. Officials rejected Bond's request that the British government should at least ask the legislature to formally express its concurrence. Bond thought, "There is a very great principle involved in the matter, the sacrifice of which might be very far-reaching, and materially affect this Colony in the future."[87] The Colonial Office, however, took the view that the undertaking given in the celebrated 1857 Labouchere Dispatch did not apply in this instance, since no rights were being ceded to France and all the proprieties had been observed: "We cannot have the fate of other parts of the Empire involved trembling in the balance, or hang up an integral part of the readjustment with France, until the Colony has been pleased to legislate."[88] Faced with this intransigence, the government apparently decided to do nothing and avoid debate. But on April 27, the penultimate day of the session, Morine introduced a series of highly critical resolutions accusing the imperial government of violating the colony's rights and giving away too much to France: nothing less than "the complete abolition" of all French rights would be acceptable. Bond eventually moved amendments approving the convention and his government's actions, which passed on a strict party vote.[89]

Whiteway published a spiteful and hostile letter,* but the general reaction seems to have been positive, even celebratory. Boyle reported that the convention had been received with enthusiasm, and told Bond that he appreciated how "your every action throughout the negotiations has been in defence of the Colony's interests."[90] Harvey and Co. told a London correspondent that the arrangement was thought to be "excellent," if not as sweeping as had been hoped.[91] And the following appeared in the *Newfoundland Quarterly:*

A Tribute to Sir Robert Bond

Cheer, for the reign of the Frenchman is ended
'Long the great coast from St. John to Cape Ray;
Cheer for the man who has rendered each bay to us

* *Free Press*, April 26, 1904. Prowse thought Whiteway's attitude "mean [and] pettifogging" (*Evening Telegram*, May 12, 1904).

Free and untrammeled, forever and aye.
BOND! Not a name in our colony's story,
Statesman or patriot, thine can eclipse:
Every flag raise to him,
Shout from the bays to him—
Thunder our praise to him—guns, hearts and lips.
Grand day of history, down thro' the years
Glad generations shall hail it with pride,
With this brave name placed in honour beside.
Full in the flame of it,
Bright with the fame of it,
ROBERT BOND, boast of his land and compeers.[92]

Morine and other critics were not altogether fair, but that was not their job. The British government had placed Bond in a very difficult situation. To his credit, he accepted (no doubt with Boyle's encouragement) that a compromise solution was the only way out, and also that ambiguity was an essential part of the deal. He and his government did not particularly like the convention, but there was nothing else on offer. The colony would be relieved of some serious if exaggerated disadvantages, while Britain paid the price in terms of West African territory ceded to France and financial compensation paid to French *armateurs* on the Treaty Shore. Above all, from Bond's perspective, the convention significantly enlarged the colonial government's sovereignty over its own territory. Future experience was to show that by abolishing French territorial rights the convention effectively terminated the French fishery on the Treaty Shore, apart from a few expeditions from St. Pierre and Miquelon. No concurrent fishery took place and the floating threats predicted by the convention's critics never appeared. That the agreement was to the colony's advantage cannot be disputed, but it also meant that subsequent governments and promoters could no longer blame the French Shore dispute for its domestic ills.

Bond and others seem to have genuinely believed that because the convention had been endorsed in the British Parliament and the Newfoundland legislature, it would come into force in the 1904 fishing season[93]—a mistaken assumption that crept into a speech on April 21, 1904. It is difficult to understand why. Clearly the convention could not be implemented until it had been ratified by Britain—and by France, where it was controversial and widely criticized. In addition, French establishments on the Treaty Shore had to be surveyed and valued, and regulations for the future concurrent fishery had to be agreed to. Problems immediately resulted on the Treaty Shore in 1904, which annoyed the British government and provided ammunition for the opposition parties gearing up for the election that year. Commodore Paget of the British naval squadron reported that several merchants sent vessels to fish on the Treaty Shore as a result of Bond's speech and enthusiastic press comments. A French captain arrived at Cap Rouge to find fifteen Newfoundland schooners in the harbour and the shore fringed with cod traps, the crews claiming to have government authority. The magistrate at St. Anthony produced a letter from the Minister of Fisheries to the effect that there were no exclusive rights. Land was being cleared on the west coast for whale factories, too. The situation was, at best, "confused." The government, said Paget accurately, "are chary of admitting that they have been rather previous in their admissions."[94]

DOMESTIC AFFAIRS, 1901–1904

Bond's adventures in external affairs won him great credit and to some extent overshadowed his government's domestic activities. These were very much influenced by Bond's belief in the colony's economic potential, its probable role in transatlantic communications, and his genuine concern about education—as well as his deep-rooted suspicion of both the Anglo-American Telegraph Company and the Reid family, and the need to win the election scheduled for 1904. As a result, his government's domestic record was mixed. It is arguable that not a great deal was achieved—other than the controversial 1901 railway contract and initial negotiations for a newsprint mill on the Exploits River.

On December 12, 1901, it had appeared as if the island's importance in transatlantic communications had been confirmed. On that date, Guglielmo Marconi received the first transatlantic wireless message at a makeshift station on Signal Hill in St. John's. There was great local excitement and

Sir Robert Bond and his ministers with Guglielmo Marconi at Signal Hill, December 1901. (PANL, B1-91)

immediate hopes and expectations that Marconi would build a permanent receiving station on Signal Hill or at Cape Spear. Bond sent his congratulations and visited Signal Hill with members of his government. But there was a problem. The Anglo-American Telegraph Company—A.M. Mackay, superintendent—served an injunction alleging that Marconi's activities breached its fifty-year monopoly on landing telegraph cables and receiving telegraph messages (due to expire in 1904)—even though Marconi's feat introduced an entirely new technology. Anglo-American enlisted Alfred Morine and Marconi turned to Sir James Winter. Bishop Howley urged Bond to buy out Anglo altogether.[95] In the end, rather than spend time and money on a court battle in Newfoundland, Marconi moved on to Canada. With the support of its federal government, he built a wireless station at Glace Bay, Nova Scotia, which opened in December 1902.[96] There was anger and disappointment in St. John's, which Bond must have shared.

Another cause of difficulty was the government's wish either to buy Anglo-American's telegraph line between St. John's and Whitbourne or to run its own wire—the idea being to link the government system, which existed outside the Avalon Peninsula, with the capital city. It proved impossible to do either[97]; Bond's aim from this point on was to follow Howley's advice and try to buy out Anglo and remove it from the colony.

The government's relations with Anglo were given a thorough airing when the legislature opened on February 20, 1902. The Throne Speech promised that government telegraphs would be placed under the control of the Post Office, as in the United Kingdom.[98] But the session did not see the passage of a great deal of significant legislation and much of the business was routine. Fully elected local government[99] was given to St. John's, however; thenceforward it had a mayor and council with no government appointees, although the colonial government still retained a significant degree of control.*

Outside the legislature, the city and the government had to deal with an unprecedented sealers' strike. The men demanded a better price for "fat" plus concessions on "coaling money" and "the crop." The strike began on the morning of Saturday, March 8; crews marched to Government House where a flummoxed Governor Boyle advised them to appoint delegates to meet the sealing shipowners. Bond had departed for Whitbourne† and did not think it necessary to return until March 11, by which time matters had come to a head. Bond presided over a final settlement that included a decision to send some men home at government expense. In effect, he had

* From 1888 to 1898, the St. John's council had consisted of five elected and two appointed members. In 1898, the Winter government replaced the council with a three-member appointed commission, to minimize problems with the implementation of the 1898 Reid contract (Baker, "A History of St. John's City Council," online).

† In 1898, Elizabeth Bond sold the house on Circular Road and the household moved out to Whitbourne. Robert Bond spent the week in a hotel in St. John's—though "American," writing to the *Evening Telegram*, stated that there was not even a "third-rate hotel" in town, "only two poorly-conducted third-rate boarding houses" (*Evening Telegram*, September 11, 1902).

left the crisis to the governor, the inspector-general of the undermanned Constabulary, the shipowners—and to Morine, who agreed to act for the sealers (at no cost), many of whom must have been his constituents.[100] There was justified criticism of Bond in the press.[101]

Domestic affairs dominated the 1903 Throne Speech, delivered on March 5, but the first piece of business—as had become usual—was the renewal of the French treaties legislation. It passed the Assembly without difficulty, but only squeaked through the Legislative Council with the casting vote of the President.[102] The first major piece of legislation was designed to encourage coal and iron mining and the manufacture of iron and steel. It was an ambitious but impractical scheme; Bond was obviously influenced by developments in Cape Breton. In a long speech, he dwelt first on the reasons for building the railway—noting that apart from lumbering, the line had so far done little to stimulate economic diversification. Thus mining and agriculture had to be encouraged and new industries had to be sought, if only to "hold our population." Coal from Grand Lake and St. George's Bay should therefore be used to fuel blast furnaces on Bell Island and elsewhere—an industry that he hoped would develop as a result of the bill's proposed bounty system.[103] Bond was particularly (but, as it proved, excessively) optimistic about three coal seams that James Howley had located at the east end of Grand Lake between 1891 and 1893, and there were other enthusiasts. The Reids mined some 8,000 tons there in 1898–99, but then they gave up and returned the coal area to the government, finding the seams fractured and expensive to mine.* Their experience did not change any minds in the government, it seems; the bill passed without difficulty and optimism and coal exploration persisted for some years.[104] Coal mines and blast furnaces never materialized, however, and Reid's efforts at Grand Lake marked the peak of coal production in Newfoundland.

As colonial secretary, Bond was responsible for education. The 1874 and 1876 Education Acts had finalized the transfer of the public education system to the three major denominations (Catholic, Anglican, Methodist) and their superintendents, who in effect managed three separate elementary

---

* Martin, *Once Upon a Mine*, 40–42. Reid built a branch line to Grand Lake and named the junction "Howley," after the geologist.

school systems and supervised the four denominational academies in St. John's.* The government provided basic (but inadequate) grants; it was expected that churches, communities, and parents would also contribute. There was no Ministry of Education until 1920; the single interdenominational body was the Council of Higher Education, established in 1893.

In 1887, Bond had seconded an amendment to an education bill, moved by Morine, that called for the introduction of free, public, non-sectarian education.† The explosion that had resulted had no effect on Morine's views on the subject—they remained consistent, politically incorrect, and possibly damaging. Bond, though, retreated. He would never again challenge the system, but he was fully alive to the educational deficiencies that existed. In 1901, the colony had 639 schools of all types and 29,554 pupils—only about half the school-age population. On average there were 46 pupils at each school, most of which were one-room buildings. Few pupils stayed on after age 15 and education was not compulsory. Teachers, many of them untrained and the majority female, were paid a miserable average salary of $160 a year. The government grant per pupil was about 76 cents annually. On almost all criteria, Newfoundland lagged far behind Canadian provinces and the United Kingdom in its delivery of education.[105]

Bond advanced a partial but arguably inadequate response to the situation in the 1903 Education Act. It consolidated existing legislation, increased the government subsidy by $10,000 a year (to $91,702)—most of the increase going to outport districts—and addressed teachers' qualifications, salaries, and pensions, all of which needed significant improvement. What caught public attention, however, was the provision for "amalgamated schools" in "sparsely settled areas." Bond pointed out that of the 1,372 settlements on the island, 893 (65 per cent) had populations below 100,

---

* There was a General Protestant academy in addition to those of the larger denominations. Though recognized as a denomination for educational purposes in 1892, the Salvation Army did not appoint a superintendent until 1910.

† The speech can be found in the *Evening Mercury*, March 29, 1887. Morris spoke at length against the amendment.

and that nearly 73,000 residents over the age of 5 could not read.* The amalgamated school proposal was an attempt to provide a remedy. But the legislation contained such elaborate safeguards for the denominational system that no amalgamated schools were ever established in "sparsely settled areas," as intended. A handful did appear eventually, but not as a result of the 1903 Act and in industrial towns such as Grand Falls and Corner Brook. Since Roman Catholics maintained their own institutions there, these schools became exclusively Protestant.

With an election approaching in 1904, political rumour and speculation increased in 1903, most of it concerning the government's opponents. The loss of two seats in a 1902 by-election showed that Bond was not impregnable†; he lost two more MHAs in March 1903 when William Howley (St. George's) and Richard McGrath (Placentia) decided to sit as independents. McGrath charged that Bond was arrogant and controlling and that many Liberals were rebellious and dissatisfied, but he was also a disappointed patronage claimant.[106] So change seemed to be in the air. In 1902, William Horwood had become Chief Justice on the death of Sir Joseph Little,‡ and when Donald Morison resigned from the Bench to return to active politics, George Johnson replaced him. Morris then became Minister of Justice.

Morine's future seemed uncertain. He dissolved his law partnership with Michael Gibbs and moved into the Reids' handsome new terminus building in the west end of St. John's to become the company's full-time lawyer. He absented himself from the 1903 legislative session (the opposition was officially led by Mackay) ostensibly for health reasons, and went to

---

* *Evening Telegram*, May 7 and 8, 1903. David Alexander estimated that in 1901, 27 per cent of the population over the age of 10 could not read (Alexander, "Literacy and Economic Development," Table 5).

† The by-election was in Trinity Bay, where Whiteway apparently used his influence against the government.

‡ Morine thought that this was Morris's doing. Bond was away and wanted the post left vacant until he got back; Morris claimed that he did not know of a tacit understanding to give it to Winter (Morine, draft history, PANL, MG 271.2, folder 8).

Europe.[107] Many assumed that Morine would be leaving public life, and he did not deny it until later in the year.[108] By that time others were manoeuvring. In April, Morison, once more the Grand Master of the Orange Association, strongly hinted that he would run to fill a vacancy at Harbour Grace,[109] but that by-election never happened.[110]

The other wild card was Whiteway, now 75 years old. In November 1903, he and Morison joined forces to form a "New Party"; it was to be quite distinct from the official Tory party led by Morine and would be backed by *The Free Press* newspaper, owned and edited by J.A. Robinson, a former member of Winter's government. In their view, the Tory group led by Morine was "the Reid party" and the government party was not genuinely Liberal, but an incompetent mixture of former Liberals and Conservatives. The New Party was presented as embodying the best of the old Liberal and Conservative traditions.[111]

BOND, THE REIDS, AND PULP AND PAPER

Another important factor was the attitude of the Reid family. At first, relations between the Bond government and the Reids had been relatively cordial. W.D. Reid had gone so far as to say in December 1902 that he was pleased with the government's attitude.[112] But relations soured rapidly in 1903. The fundamental reason seems to have been Bond's decision that, if there was to be a pulp and paper development in central or western Newfoundland, it would not be undertaken by the Reid Newfoundland Company. Bond was not willing to further enhance the company's power and influence and he remained hostile and suspicious. He was prepared to talk seriously with the English Harmsworth interests, however. The owner of several newspapers, Alfred Harmsworth (later Viscount Northcliffe) had concluded that he needed his own source of newsprint in British territory. Early in 1903, Harmsworth's agent arrived in Newfoundland. By late March, Mayson Beeton had decided that, subject to a satisfactory agreement with the government and other interested parties, a successful pulp and paper operation could be established either on the Exploits River watershed or on the Humber River in the Grand Lake/Deer Lake area. On March 28, by Minute of Council, the government agreed to issue a renewable ninety-nine-year lease of an unspecified amount of Crown land in the area chosen, which included timber, mineral, and water rights. There were other concessions as well, but there would be no direct financial assistance from the government.[113]

The Reids had been nursing a Grand Lake scheme for some time and had undertaken engineering studies. They had ambitious plans, viewed Beeton and the Harmsworths as unwelcome interlopers, and resented the encouragement they received from the government. In April, the Reid Company submitted a comprehensive proposal, but one that envisaged government assistance. The company would build a paper mill at Grand Lake (the government guaranteeing a $3 million bond issue) and a flour mill in St. John's. It would resume exploration of the Grand Lake coal deposits, sharing the cost with the government.* To assist the fishery, it would erect two cold-storage depots, build refrigeration cars for the railway, and ensure that its steamers also had cold-storage facilities. It would improve the cross-country train and Gulf ferry service, construct hotels in St. John's, Bay of Islands, and Notre Dame Bay, and build three branch lines for $15,600 per mile.† The government turned down the proposal on financial grounds,[114] leaving the Reids to swallow the fact that they would not be the founders of the colony's pulp and paper industry. They would have to come to terms—eventually—with the Harmsworths over their use of Reid land holdings and the railway. It was obvious to the Reids that Bond would fight any further concessions to them—if Reid interests were to prosper, Bond had to go.

As if to reprimand the government, in October 1903 the Reid Company filed a claim for $3,488,000 in compensation for improvements made to the government telegraph system and losses incurred when the

* During the 1904 session, questions were asked about a coal exploration agreement with Harmsworths (*JHA* 1904, 21 and 49).

† The proposal, dated April 28, 1903, is in RBP 10.01.059. See also *Evening Telegram* and the *Daily News*, March 21, 1904. The proposed branch lines were from Grand Lake to Green Bay, Clarenville to Trinity, and Come-by-Chance to Fortune.

government resumed control of it in 1901.* Bond was outraged—it was "a further index as to the kind of men we have to deal with," he told Boyle.[115] It was soon the Reids' turn to feel Bond's resentment. In addition to the Gulf ferry, the Reid Company operated steamer services around the island and to Labrador. The government now decided that these services were inadequate and should be supplemented. On a temporary basis, the government steamer *Fiona* was put on a run between St. John's and Placentia, and tenders were called for additional coastal services. In February 1904, Bowring Brothers agreed to run steamers between St. John's and the Northern Peninsula, and between St. John's and Bonne Bay.[116] The Reids thought this deal was a violation of the spirit, if not the letter, of their contract with the government, a breach of faith that could cost the Company a great deal of money. The Company should be compensated; Bond dismissed the idea out of hand.[117]

Though it was a pre-election session, there was little in the way of crowd-pleasing legislation in 1904, though flour, kerosene, and molasses were placed on the free list. The Bowring steamship contract was endorsed, as was a deal with the Newfoundland Cold Storage and Reduction Co. to promote the export of fresh fish and establish bait storage depots at five locations around the island. The telegraph system was placed under the control of the Post Office, a move in Bond's campaign to free the government from any reliance on the Anglo-American Telegraph Company, whose monopoly expired in April.† Otherwise, the government expressed not altogether quiet satisfaction at the sound state of the public finances and a prosperous economy. Average annual total trade had risen from $12 million in the late 1890s to about $17 million: exports from $5.9 million to $9.4 million, imports from $6 million to $8 million. The

* An arbitration relating to the 1893 contracts held during the autumn of 1902 had already awarded the Reids $853,500 (RBP 10.01.054 and Horwood to Chamberlain, November 18, 1902, CO 194/250, 674).

† The government also established five Marconi stations on the Labrador coast. A bill to outlaw Chinese immigration, introduced by an opposition member, passed the Assembly without difficulty but was thrown out by the Legislative Council.

average price of fish had risen by nearly 39 per cent. The forest sector was expanding and there was promise, at last, of a significant degree of economic diversification. All this boded well for the election.

In June 1904, Bond went to London to take part in discussions about the regulations governing the concurrent fishery on the French Shore.* Boyle was there for most of Bond's stay and arranged a dinner for him to meet the colonial secretary, Colonial Office officials and others, though "I know you hate dinners."† Boyle had left Newfoundland soon after the legislature closed and was preparing for his next posting in Mauritius. The two bachelors got on well—Boyle had presented Bond with a pair of red ibis for display at Whitbourne. Though Bond was "a sportsman and taxidermist," the gift was also intended as a reminder of "the past three years of very happy and undisturbed relations with a Premier who has been to him, alike, a wise counselor, a staunch supporter, and a very true friend."[118]

Bond was in London when he heard that Edward Morris was to be given a knighthood. Such distinctions were highly valued and sought after. It was accepted that premiers and chief justices would normally be knighted, but to honour a person such as Morris was unusual. Moreover, Boyle and Bond had apparently agreed that no honours would be awarded in Newfoundland until the 1904 election was over and the reciprocity treaty settled, and Boyle had so advised the Colonial Office. So the news of Morris's knighthood came as a shock to both of them, since neither had been consulted. Bond was furious. It would cause a great deal of trouble, he told Boyle. Other members of the government "will be disgusted that Morris has been singled out for as you are no doubt aware <u>not one</u> of them trusts him." Horwood would resent it, and others could well conclude that he (Bond) had not been honest. The Colonial Office had behaved despicably. "If we in the Colonies acted like that we should be

* The Permanent Undersecretary, Sir Montagu Ommanney, thought the invitation to Bond to assist "would be agreeable to his vanity and would probably disarm any tendency on his part to criticize hostiley the Convention" (Minute, April 9, 1904, CO 194/254, 161).

† Boyle to Bond, June 20, 22, 1904 (RBP 3.23.009). Alfred Harmsworth was also present.

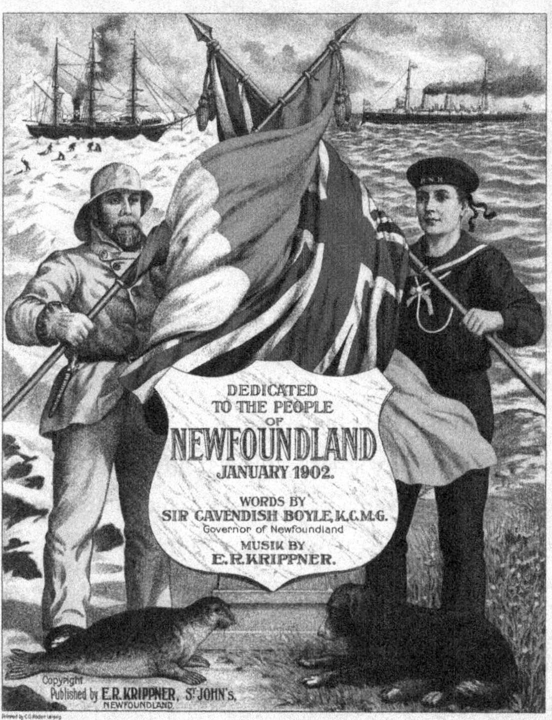

Governor Boyle was popular with the Newfoundland public. He supported the St. John's Regatta, liked hunting and fishing, and presented the Boyle Challenge Cup for hockey in 1904.[119] He also wrote verses, the most famous and long-lasting being "Newfoundland" (now known as the "Ode to Newfoundland"). The lines had been set to music by the German bandmaster and music teacher E.R. Krippner, who also obtained the copyright (how this happened is not known). The piece was performed for the first time in St. John's on January 21, 1902, and it was an immediate sensation. A Minute of Council later recorded that the piece should be "approved and officially recognized as the Colonial Anthem." Other musical settings soon appeared, however, and there were a number of other patriotic airs on offer, among them Bishop Howley's "Flag of Newfoundland" (also 1902). Boyle's niece, staying with him in 1903 and 1904, persuaded him that more appropriate music was needed for "Newfoundland." Boyle approached a childhood friend, the distinguished composer Sir Hubert Parry, who produced the tune used today. Krippner gave up his rights, but the government did not pass the legislation needed to make "Newfoundland" the colonial anthem. It was only during the 1920s that the piece became embedded as an unofficial anthem. It did not become fully authorized until 1975.[120]

regarded as rank amateurs and properly so."* It is possible that he saw and appreciated the "Ode to Sir Edward Morris" that appeared in the *Daily News* (June 28, 1904):

> **Ode to Sir Edward Morris**
> MY DEAR SIR EDWARD:
> I hasten to convey to you
> The news
> You have been knighted!
> Nay, hold up, hold up, my dear Sir Edward
> You have, really!
> I gather from our daily papers
> That you are a very smart politician indeed.
> Indeed, to give even a partial list of your achievements
> Would in itself fill a newspaper column.
> Some of your more important ones, however
> May perhaps be mentioned.
> For example, I read
> That "under your supervision
> The Southside hills have long been white with sheep;"
> And that you "solely inaugurated our very efficient jam factories."
> I am further informed
> That you "conferred a lasting book on the fishermen of the colony
> By taking a thousand dollars from the public treasury
> And paying it over to a certain Mr. Makinson
> For a recipe for cooking the gentle cod!"
> In short "largely owing to your individual efforts
> The land is flowing milk and honey
> And everything in the garden is lovely."

---

* Boyle to Bond, June 25, 1904, and Bond to Boyle, June 27, 1904 (RBP 3.23.009). But in 1901, Boyle had mentioned Morris as a possible candidate for recognition, in order to maintain denominational balance (Boyle to Chamberlain, September 30; tgm., October 14; secret, October 12; to Ommanney, private, October 11, 1901, CO 447/67, n.p.).

All of which is very excellent business.
My dear Sir Edward,
Comments such as I have quoted
Thrill the honest native heart of me
Like a blast of martial trumpets.
When one comes to think of your many achievements
One is overwhelmed.
Shake, my dear Sir Edward, shake!
This is no time for words.
Let us look into each other's eyes
In dumb sympathy.
You are, you are, you are, my dear Sir Edward,
The finest example of political humbug
That I ever did come across.

O.R.

THE 1904 ELECTION

Bond was back in Newfoundland by late July, a draft of the concurrent fishery regulations having been settled. After "Old Home Week," a project of the Cabot Club of Boston, finished on August 10,* the election campaign began to take shape. The Liberals faced two opposition parties. Morine had resigned as Tory leader and had been replaced in January by Goodridge, and it seemed clear that at that stage a coalition with Whiteway and his small band of followers was not possible. Apparently Whiteway was not prepared to lead a party in which Morine remained the most powerful force (despite his resignation as leader)—nor were his supporters, who were mostly Winterite Tories. Instead, Whiteway simply confirmed his intention to run in the election.[121] Between late February and late June, he published twelve long letters in the *Free Press* excoriating Bond's behaviour in the 1890–91 Treaty Shore crisis, his takeover of the Liberal party, his refusal to pay what Whiteway considered his just legal

* Morris was the local organizer; the government gave $1,000 toward expenses. There were fewer visitors than expected, according to the *Free Press*, August 9, 1904.

fees for handling government business, and—above all—Bond's management of the Reid railway contracts. Somewhat edited, the letters were later published in pamphlet form as *Duty's Call.*

Whiteway's manifesto appeared on August 23, 1904. This prompted another "Ode" in the *Daily News* (August 28), in which the writer described how, in a dream, he found Whiteway in his study:

Ode to Sir William Whiteway
"Sir William Whiteway, Sir," I said,
"Pardon this intrusion,
But I desire to put one question to you."
"Put it," quoth Sir William sepulchrally.
"Sir William Whiteway, Sir," I said,
"WHAT IS THE LIBERAL PARTY?"
Sir William regarded me blandly and answered
"I AM THE LIBERAL PARTY!"
I remarked that I was charmed to hear it,
Whereupon I woke up.
Well, Sir,
Since delivering yourself
Of that Manifesto
In the *Free Press* last week,
You will probably have come to the conclusion
That, taking it all for all,
The aforesaid noble utterance
Was just a trifle over-uttered;
Sir William,
You have once again
Made a mistake;
You have once again
Issued a Manifesto.
The writing of letters, as you are aware,
Is a much pleasanter business.
You are admirably cut out for the writing of letters,

And you never were cut out for compiling Manifestoes.
Take my advice, Sir William,
Stick to the writing of letters.

O.R.

Division among Bond's opponents continued until September 24, when Whiteway and Goodridge finally announced the creation of a United Opposition and the Tories produced their manifesto.[122] By this time, the government had scheduled the election for October 31, about a week earlier than usual. The opposition parties cried foul on the grounds that this would disenfranchise Labrador fishermen and speculated—with reason—that the real object was to free up politically active lawyers for the potentially lucrative telegraph arbitration hearings that were scheduled to start on October 27.

Bond's manifesto appeared in the *Evening Telegram* on September 28. He stood on his government's record, dilated on the prosperous condition of the country, and essentially promised to continue existing policies into the future.[123] The Liberals were in a strong position, given Bond's personal prestige, general economic prosperity and expansion, and the end of the Treaty Shore problem. Archbishop Howley (newly elevated in rank) endorsed the Liberal party, which gave it an advantage in Roman Catholic districts.* There was not much debate about issues. The Liberals painted their opponents as Reid-backed confederates and ridiculed the motley coalition—Goodridge, the bank crash premier; Whiteway, back in politics out of greed and personal spite; the shifty Morison; even Winter, dusted off to run in his old district of Burin. Electors should vote for "Bond, Prosperity, and Home Rule."[124] Bond himself faced an energetic challenge from Morison in Twillingate, where the election was hard fought. But a Liberal victory was never in doubt—the party was returned with a majority of twenty-four (thirty Liberals to six opposition members). Compared with the results of 1900, the Liberals had lost two seats and a very small

* *Daily News*, August 27, 1904. Howley was called Bond's "godfather." The *Trade Review* (November 10, 1904) thought that most clergy of all denominations were pro-Bond.

The Members of the House of Assembly elected in 1904. (PANL, C1-105)

percentage of the popular vote. The former premiers did badly: Goodridge lost in Placentia, Winter in Burin, and, in a sad end to a notable career, Whiteway was at the bottom of the poll at Harbour Grace. The old guard was finished.

There was general agreement, it seems, that the United Opposition would have done better had Morine not been part of it.[125] He was unpopular among Roman Catholics, a proponent of secular schooling, an avowed confederate, a Canadian, and a Reid employee. Though strongly entrenched politically in Bonavista Bay and both intelligent and articulate, these factors made him a political liability overall; he was certainly not the person to lead Bond's opponents—and an effective leader was needed. If there was a coming man, it seemed to be Sir Edward Morris. He was impregnable in St. John's, apparently close to the Reids, and unenthusiastic about Bond's leadership. But how his future would unfold was, as yet, unclear.

Bond's future very much depended on how he would fare in his second term, and whether his opponents could regroup into an effective party. Would his luck hold?

NOTES

1 Baker, "McGrath, Sir Patrick Thomas," *DCB* 15:643–44.
2 Speech by Morine, reported in the *Daily News*, October 4, 5, 6, 9, and 10, 1900.
3 P.T. McGrath in the Toronto *Globe*, reprinted in the *Evening Telegram*, November 21, 1900.
4 Howley, *Reminiscences*, 1722.
5 "Manifesto of the Hon'ble Robert Bond . . ." (RBP 3.19.014 and *Evening Telegram*, October 1, 1900).
6 *ENL* 1:451–52 and *ENL* 4:609.
7 The verses, signed "Pompho," are in RBP 3.20.005.
8 October 1900 (RBP 3.19.015).
9 Morine fonds, draft history, folder 12, PANL, MG 271.2.
10 Kenneth Boone to Bond, November 17, 1900 (RBP 3.19.018).
11 Howley to Bond, November 16, 1900 (RBP 3.19.009).
12 Prowse to Bond, November 15, 1900 (RBP 3.19.025).
13 *ENL* 5:336.
14 Tait to Bond, November 16, 1900 (RBP 3.19.008).
15 McCallum to Bond, December 1 and 7, 1900 (RBP 3.19.005).
16 Bond to McCallum, December 7, 1900 (RBP 3.19.005).
17 Howley to Bond, November 28, 1900, and memorandum of reply (RBP 3.19.009).
18 Bond to R.G. Reid, December 13, 1900 (RBP 10.01.036).
19 Reid to Bond, December 24, 1900, formal and private letters (RBP 10.01.036).

20 Bond to Reid, January 8, 1901 (RBP 10.01.036).

21 Bond to Horwood, February 19, 1901; memorandum by Reid, January 21, 1901, and by Bond, undated (RBP 10.01.041 and 10.01.049).

22 Hiller, "Bond, Bait and Bounties," in Hiller and English, eds., "Entente Cordiale," 81.

23 Legislative Council, February 27, 1901 (*Evening Telegram*, March 2, 1901) and *ENL* 1:233.

24 Horwood to Bond, February 28, 1901 (RBP 3.20.002) and *JHA* 1901, 5–15.

25 Bond to Ommanney, May 2, 1901 (RBP 6.07.012). See also Hiller, "Bond, Bait and Bounties," 81–82.

26 Little to Chamberlain, tgm., April 9, 1901 (CO 194/247, 360) and subsequent correspondence. See also CO 194/247, 383–86 and 388–90 and CO 194/248, 32–38.

27 Hunter, *To Employ and Uplift Them* and *ENL* 4:27–29.

28 Bond to Chamberlain, April 18, 1901, and Minute by Chamberlain, April 21, 1901 (CO 194/249, 577).

29 See for instance Laurier to Minto, conf., February 16, 1901 (LAC, Laurier fonds, 53458).

30 Laurier to Delcassé, December 20, 1900 (LAC, Laurier fonds, 51961).

31 Bond to Ommanney, April 25, 1901 (CO 194/249, 698).

32 Bond to Laurier, May 16, 1901; Laurier to Bond, tgm., May 21, 1901; Bond to Laurier, tgm., May 21, 1901; and Laurier to Bond, tgm., May 23, 1901 (RBP 7.07.004). Bond to Laurier, tgms., May 16 and 21, 1901 (LAC, Laurier fonds 56256, 56259) and Bond to Ommanney, June 7, 1901 (CO 194/249, 718).

33 Reid to Bond, June 26, 1901 (RBP 10.01.040).

34 *Evening Telegram*, June 5, 1901.

35 Howley to Bond, private, July 13, 1901 (RBP 10.01.042).

36 Contract encl. in Boyle to Chamberlain, conf., July 22, 1901 (CO 194/248, 105ff.).

37 Reid to Bond, July 20, 1901, and Bond to Reid, July 24, 1901 (RBP 10.01.040).

38 Little (Administrator) to Chamberlain, tgm., June 6, 1901 (CO 194/247, 442); memorandum by Bond, June 27, 1901 (RBP 3.20.010).

39 Chamberlain to Boyle, tgm., July 29, 1901 (CO 194/248, 26).

40 Speech offprint in RBP 10.01.048.

41 *Journal of the Legislative Council* (*JLC*) 1901, 58.

42 Boyle to Ommanney, private, July 23, 1901 (CO 194/248, 98). See also Boyle to Chamberlain, conf., July 22, 1901 (CO 194/248, 100).

43 The correspondence is in RBP 10.01.046 and 10.01.045.

44 *Daily News,* September 3 and November 23, 1901.

45 Whiteway, *Duty's Call*, 14.

46 Assembly debate, July 25, in the *Evening Telegram*, August 15, 1901.

47 O'Flaherty, *Lost Country*, 216, and Cadigan, *Newfoundland and Labrador*, 157.

48 Morine, draft history, folder 12 (PANL, Morine fonds, MG 271.2).

49 Reynolds, *Britannia Overruled*, 72.

50 Orde, *Eclipse of Great Britain*, 22.

51 Minute, January 3, 1902 (CO 194/249, 405). See also his Minute dated January 8 (CO 194/251, 504).

52 Chamberlain to Boyle, conf., January 22, 1902 (RBP 6.08.10).

53 Boyle to Chamberlain, secret, January 16 and 24, 1902 (CO 194/250, 21 and 57).

54 Boyle to Chamberlain, tgm., May 29, 1902, and secret, May 30, 1902 (CO 194/250, 414 and 422).

55 O'Reilly to E.M. Jackman, April 24, 1902 (RBP 6.08.007).

56 Bond to Morris, July 30, 1902 (RBP 6.08.003); William Smith to Laurier, June 9, 1902 (LAC, Laurier fonds, 65736).

57 Boyle to Chamberlain, tgm., April 4, 1902 (CO 194/250, 181).

58 Minute by Anderson, April 7, 1902 (CO 194/250, 179).

59 Campbell, *Anglo-American Understanding*, 260–64.

60 Whitney to Laurier, January 4 and 18, 1902; Laurier to Whitney, January 6, 1902; Mulock to Laurier, January 9, 1902 (LAC, Laurier fonds, 61279-80, 61385, and 61657).

61 Boyle to Chamberlain, tgms., May 7, 8, and 16, 1902 (CO 194/250, 299, 330, and 381).

62 The correspondence is in PANL, GN 1/3, 27.

63 Much of this detail is taken from "Memo. Respecting the Year 1902" (RBP 3.21.008).

64 Kennedy, *Britain and Empire*, 27–32.

65 Quoted in Mansergh, *The Commonwealth Experience*, 133–34.

66 This account is based on the October 1902 "Conference between the Secretary of State for the Colonies and the Premiers of Self-Governing Colonies. Minutes and Papers" (CO 885/8, No. 144).

67 Bond to Cox, July 11, 1902, and Minute by Anderson, August 5, 1902 (CO 194/251, 563–64 and RBP 6.08.011).

68 Opinion of Haldane and Coles, August 11, 1902 (RBP 6.08.006).

69 Wire reports in the *Daily News*, July 21 and 29, 1902. See also RBP 8.03.003.

70 RBP 8.03.024.

71 Fielding to Bond, September 15, 1902 (RBP 8.03.022).

72 Bond to Fielding, October 17, 1902 (RBP 7.08.006).

73 Dennett, *John Hay*, 423 and 425.

74 Bond to Herbert, October 17, 1902, with "Note of interview" (RBP 7.08.006).

75 Dennett, *John Hay*, 423–28; Campbell, *Anglo-American Understanding*, 265–67; and Tansill, *Canadian-American Relations*, 92–96.

76 Lansdowne to Raikes, tgm., October 18, 1902 (RBP 7.08.006).

77 FO to CO, December 29, 1902, and Ommanney to Horwood (OAG), January 9, 1903 (CO 194/251, 450–54).

78 Laurier to A.G. Jones, November 3 and 8, 1902 (LAC, Laurier fonds, 67857 and 67983).

79 Assembly debates, April 23, 24, 1903 (*Evening Telegram*, June 5 and 11, 1903).

80 Minutes of July 16, August 5, and undated, 1903 (CO 537/499, 1, 15–17, 26).

81 Bond to Anderson, January 26, 1904 (CO 194/254, 61A).

82 *Daily News*, April 11, 1904.

83 The text of the convention is printed in Hiller and English, eds., "Entente Cordiale," 125–34, and its essence is in Thompson, *French Shore*, 199.

84 Boyle to Lyttleton, tgm., April 20, 1904 (CO 194/254, 223).

85 *Evening Telegram*, April 22, 1904. Extracts in Hiller and English, eds., "Entente Cordiale,"135–38.

86 *Evening Telegram*, April 22 and 23, 1904, and *Daily News*, April 23, 1904.

87 Bond to Boyle, April 22, 1904 (PANL, GN 1/3/A, file 104).

88 Minute by Davis, April 23, 1904 (CO 194/254, 253).

89 The debate can be found in Hiller and English, eds., "Entente Cordiale," 147–59.

90 Boyle to Lyttleton, secret, April 25, 1904 (CO 194/254, 257) and Boyle to Bond, April 20, 1904 (PANL, GN 1/3/A, file 104).

91 Harvey and Co. to Morgan, Gellibrand and Co., May 8, 1904 (CO 194/255, 409) and *Trade Review*, April 23, 1904.

92 Dan Carroll, "A Tribute to Sir Robert Bond." *Newfoundland Quarterly* 4, no. 1 (1904): 8.

93 Boyle to Ommanney, conf., May 29, 1904, encl. in Bond to Boyle, May 9, 1904 (CO 194/254, 828–29).

94 Commodore A. Paget to the Admiralty, July 3, 1904, encl. in Admiralty to CO, conf., July 20, 1904 (CO 194/254, 610–16); *Daily News*, September 2 through 12, 1904; and *Evening Herald*, July 4, 1904.

95 Howley to Bond, December 21, 1901 (RBP 10.02.012)

96 Tarrant, *Marconi's Miracle*, 78, and James E. Candow, *Lookout*, 147–59.

97 Bond to Mackay, October 10, 1901, and Mackay to Bond, November 12, 1901 (RBP 10.02.010).

98 February 20, 1902 (*JHA* 1902, 3–6).

99 See *ENL* 5:547–48.

100 Busch, "The Newfoundland Sealers' Strike," 73–101; Candow, *Of Men and Seals*, 103–4; Boyle to Chamberlain, conf., March 12, 1902 (CO 194/250, 115).

101 *Daily News*, March 10 through 13, 1902.

102 Boyle to Chamberlain, secret, September 17, 1903 (CO 194/252, 551, and *JLC* 1903, 35–36).

103 Bond's speech was reported in the *Evening Telegram*, April 15, 1903. There is an offprint in RBP 4.07.004.

104 See J.P. Howley, "Report on Exploration and Boring . . . , 1904," in *JHA* 1905, Appendix, 139–47.

105 Rowe, *The Development of Education*, 91–92; McCann, *Schooling in a Fishing Society*, especially Table 23, 99; and McCann, "The Politics of Denominational Education " and "Denominational Education," in McKim, ed., *The Vexed Question*, 30–59, 60–79.

106 Assembly debates, March 24 and 25, 1903, in the *Evening Telegram*, April 3, 6, 8, and 9, 1903, the *Daily News*, January 22, 1903, and the *Free Press*, March 25, 1903.

107 *Evening Telegram*, February 4 and March 13, 1903.

108 *Daily News*, November 3, 1903.

109 *Free Press*, April 8, 1903.

110 *Free Press*, October 27, 1903.

111 *Free Press*, November 3 and 11, 1903. These developments were covered extensively in all the newspapers.

112 Horwood to Chamberlain, November 18, 1902 (CO 194/250, 674) and *Evening Telegram*, December 9, 1902.

113 This account is based on Hiller, "The Origins of the Pulp and Paper Industry in Newfoundland," 42–57.

114 Minute of Council, May 7, 1903 (PANL, GN 9, 15:123).

115 Bond to Boyle, October 23, 1903 (PANL, GN 1/3/A, file 255).

116 *JHA* 1904, Appendix, 203–10.

117 The correspondence is in PANL, GN 1/3/A, file 306. See also Boyle to Lyttleton, secret, February 9, 1904 (CO 194/254, 64).

118 Boyle to Bond, April 28, 1904 (RBP 3.23.009). See also Boyle to Bond, June 10, 1904 (RBP 3.23.009).

119 For details about Boyle's stay in Newfoundland, see Graham, *"We love thee Newfoundland,"* 81–87.

120 Graham, *Boyle*, 131–35, 159–75; Colton, "Imagining Nation," 27–38; *ENL* 4:150; and PANL, GN 1/3/A, file 42.

121 Letter to the *Free Press*, January 19, 1904, and *Daily News*, January 16, 1904.

122 *Free Press*, September 27, 1904, and *Daily News*, September 26, 1904.

123 *Evening Telegram*, September 28, 1904 (offprint in RBP 3.23.013).

124 *Evening Telegram*, September 14, 1904.

125 *Trade Review*, November 10, 1904.

CHAPTER NINE

The Second Term: External Affairs, 1905–1909

Outwardly it seemed that at the start of his second term as prime minister, Robert Bond and his Liberal party were in a very strong position. The government held a large majority in the House of Assembly and was supported by most of the electorate. Bond's faith in the colony's future and its resources was recognized and valued, as was his nationalism. The settlement of the French Shore issue was very much to his credit and, overall, voters seem to have favoured the general direction of his government's policies. By 1908, four years later, Bond was in serious political trouble, a direct result of two factors: his obsession with the US reciprocity issue and the hostility of the Reid Newfoundland Company. It is a complicated story in which Governor Boyle's successor, Sir William MacGregor, played an important part.

Like all his predecessors as governor, MacGregor was unused to the difficulties of responsible government. His previous experience had been in British New Guinea and West Africa, where he had been able to play a leading role, though not without some serious disputes locally and with the Colonial Office. A medical doctor from an underprivileged Scottish background—his father was a crofter—MacGregor was intelligent, talented, and energetic. But he tended (like Bond) to be obstinate and opinionated. He was unhappy with his transfer to Newfoundland, which he did not see as a promotion. He had been "pushed into a backwater," he complained. Ironically, Bond had suggested MacGregor's appointment, having met him in London in 1902. There was a smooth start, but MacGregor was discontented and somewhat embittered with his appointment.

He had wanted a posting in Australasia, for which he lobbied endlessly. He rapidly fell out of sympathy with Bond's agenda, with Bond personally, and with Newfoundland, which he described as "fossilised" and "moss-clad."[1] He was unlikely to displease the British government ever again.

THE FRENCH SHORE CONVENTION

Two prominent items were on the external affairs agenda in 1905: the 1904 French fisheries convention and the fate of the Bond-Hay draft reciprocity treaty. The former was of lesser importance (in retrospect anyway), but under pressure from fishing interests, especially over bait supply, the French government twisted and turned to try and interpret the convention's phraseology to its best advantage and thus influence the regulations that would govern the concurrent fishery.[2] Their efforts somewhat vindicated the critics who had thought the convention's wording ambiguous. The British government rejected the more preposterous French claims, but told Bond firmly that French fishermen on the Treaty Shore could obtain bait on the same conditions as Newfoundlanders, subject to local regulations—that is, they did not need licences under the Bait Act.

Governor Sir William MacGregor (1846–1919), undated. (PANL, VA 33-60)

The discussion then turned to whether French fishermen could set foot on Newfoundland soil. Bond argued that, while they could use the same fishing nets and "engines" as Newfoundlanders, they could not use the foreshore. The French government responded that the convention allowed fishing "on a footing of equality," so its fishermen should be able to haul their seines on shore. London decided to concede the point. The Newfoundland government adamantly and energetically refused its consent. To permit the French to land for any purpose would be the thin edge of another wedge, since the whole purpose of the compromise convention had been to deprive the French of all entitlements on land and confine them to territorial waters. There was considerable debate at the Colonial Office, where some officials thought Newfoundland had a point. But the Permanent Undersecretary, Sir Montagu Ommanney, who disliked Bond, thought the premier guilty of "hysterical exaggeration." The colony was directed, in effect, to toe the line,[3] and was also told that the French could land to haul seines.[4] In response, the colony banned the hauling of seines on land anywhere in Newfoundland, and this ended the argument.[5] Similar and increasingly complicated and sterile disputes with France continued until 1914. Joint regulations were never agreed to, and a regulated concurrent fishery never emerged. However, the discussion of French fishing rights did raise issues of principle that were also involved in how fishery privileges held by the United States in British North American waters were defined under Article 1 of the Anglo-American convention (or treaty) of 1818.[6] This subject was not new, but it came into focus once again in 1905.

THE US TREATY: BOND RETALIATES

In mid-October 1904, the British ambassador in Washington, Sir Mortimer Durand, misguidedly reported that there was a possibility that the Bond-Hay treaty, still buried in the Senate Committee on Foreign Relations, might get through. Should he take any action on Article 5, he asked?[*] The British government had never liked this article because it seemed to prevent Newfoundland from granting an imperial preference, and it now decided that ratification would be denied unless Newfoundland agreed to allow such a preference to be given.[7] As discussed previously, Bond opposed imperial preference; he summarized his arguments in a lengthy and combative Minute of Council, noting the imperial government's

* FO to CO, conf., November 8, 1904 (CO 194/255, 787). Durand was not a successful ambassador and was recalled late in 1905.

statements with "profound regret and astonishment" and protesting that its attitude constituted undue interference and a violation of responsible government.[8] Once again, opinion at the Colonial Office was divided over what one official called "an extraordinary production, even for Sir R. Bond." In the end, the colonial secretary, Alfred Lyttleton, who had succeeded Chamberlain in 1903, decided that ratification could not be refused. Newfoundland was informed that this was a divergence from imperial policy and a distinct concession.*

This discussion soon became irrelevant. In November 1904, President Theodore Roosevelt had suggested to Senator Lodge that action should be taken on the Newfoundland treaty. In February 1905, the Senate Committee attached amendments that severely reduced the concessions given to Newfoundland—free admission for salt cod and mineral ores was deleted, for instance—and increased American demands. Hay was furious, understanding that the treaty was dead, the victim of Massachusetts politics. He squarely blamed Lodge for the debacle.†

Bond had said in his 1904 election manifesto that if the American Senate rejected the treaty, his government would adopt another course of action. It took the form of retaliation. The first step, in March 1905, was to end the bait privileges enjoyed by American fishermen under the 1888 modus vivendi, and to enforce the Bait Act—suddenly useful once more—against the Americans as well as the French.[9] Newfoundland's resentment was understood in Washington and its actions were clearly within the colony's powers. Had Bond gone no further, it is unlikely that a serious crisis would have developed. But as H.B. Cox noted in London, anyone "who sups with Uncle Sam needs a long spoon, and I expect they will come off second best and give us no end of diplomatic trouble."[10] He was quite right.

---

* For the Minutes, CO 194/254, 488–92; Lyttleton to MacGregor, secret, February 9, 1905 (CO 194/254, 528). The colony's position was broadly supported by Governor MacGregor, but how far he influenced Lyttleton's thinking is unclear.

† Tansill, *Canadian-American Relations*, 95–96. Some thought that the tension between Hay and Lodge over the Newfoundland treaty contributed to the former's premature death on July 1, 1905.

Bond did go further, making the most controversial and mistaken decision of his political career. His policy of retaliation ran against the British government's intention to accommodate the United States as far as possible and against its insistence on upholding the treaty rights of foreign powers. It also was contrary to the readiness of most Newfoundlanders to trade with American fishing vessels. Bond might have had principle on his side, but he was stubborn and showed little willingness to be flexible.

The first piece of legislation considered by the legislature after it opened on March 30, 1905, was a new Foreign Fishing Vessels Act, replacing that of 1893. Its object, Bond said, was to "inform foreign fishermen that they are no longer entitled to enter within the three mile limit for any purpose whatever, except as provided for by treaty. . . . [The Newfoundland government's] policy is not to grant licences to such vessels, enabling them to enter any of the ports of this colony and purchase bait, ice, supplies and outfits for the fishery, and to ship crews, under existing circumstances."[11] Any government officer could search any foreign fishing vessel that was in a Newfoundland port or "hovering" within the three-mile limit, to ascertain whether the vessel had purchased bait or "outfits and supplies" within Newfoundland waters, or whether the master had hired or attempted to hire crew members locally—a now illegal practice. If bait and supplies were found on such a vessel, it was to be considered "*prima facie* evidence of the purchase of the said bait fishes and supplies and outfits within such port or waters."* The penalty was seizure of the vessel.

The legislation was based on a novel interpretation of the 1818 treaty. It was aimed not only at the American cod fishery, but also and particularly at the trade in frozen herring that took place on the south and west coasts. Herring was defined as a bait fish, but this trade had nothing to do with bait. American schooners arrived during the late fall and winter, often manned by expatriate Newfoundlanders, and purchased large amounts of frozen herring, paying in cash or goods. The fish then entered the United States duty free as a foodstuff. It had not been caught by American crews, but it was sufficient that it entered in American bottoms. Bond argued

---

* Once Royal assent was given (June 15), the bill became the Foreign Fishing Vessels Act, 5 Ed. VII, cap.4.

that the 1818 treaty did not give Americans any commercial privileges whatsoever on their treaty coast, where they were limited to fishing for themselves without setting foot on land. He then drew attention to the wording of Article 1. Americans had "the Liberty to take Fish of every kind" on the "Southern Coast of Newfoundland" and "on the Western and Northern Coast" between Ramea and Quirpon. In addition, they could fish "on the Coasts, Bays, Harbours, and Creeks" of Labrador, east and north of Mont Joli. Bond contended that the difference in wording was deliberate, and that Americans had no right to enter any "bay, harbour or creek" on the Newfoundland coast. They could only do so in Labrador. In short, by treaty the Americans had no right to participate in the frozen herring trade in any shape or form. The *Daily News* christened it "the Premier's bill to punish and pauperise the people of Newfoundland."[12]

Michael Cashin, never a loyal Bond supporter, left the Liberals to become an independent member so that he could speak and vote against the bill, which he said would damage his Ferryland constituents.[13] This lost Bond the support of an influential Catholic politician, which would be a long-term cost.[14] Morine ably and at length attacked both the bill and Bond's interpretation of the 1818 treaty, arguing that the whole policy was illegal, unenforceable, and based on the false premise that it was possible "to conquer the Senate by attacking the people." Newfoundland, he accurately predicted, would get the worst of it.[15]

Bond argued that the government had no quarrel with the American administration, but that it was absolutely necessary "to bring the fishing interests of Gloucester and New England to a realization of their dependence upon the bait supplies of this Colony." After all, Newfoundland was "mistress of the Northern Seas so far as the fisheries are concerned." In addition, he expected that by "standing upon our rights and exercising such powers as we possess in defence of those rights, we challenge the commendation and respect of all those within this Colony and beyond its borders, whose judgement is influenced by considerations of justice and patriotism." In the long term, Newfoundland fishermen would benefit from the legislation, and they would not aid and abet the Americans. These were serious misjudgments. Bond exaggerated the importance of the Newfoundland fisheries and while advancing patriotic, lofty, and principled arguments, he underestimated the fundamental pragmatism that governed international relations. In addition, working fishermen had to make a living and cared little about what were, to them, arcane arguments concerning treaty rights. His main supporters, it seems, were the fish exporters, who also wanted an export tax on herring.[16]

As previously noted, the policy of retaliation ignored the broad trend of British foreign policy in this period. British diplomatic support would obviously be needed if the policy was to succeed, and Bond's initiative was seen as troublesome and unwelcome. But there the matter rested until the herring fishery began in the fall. Bond was in London in September and early October, mainly to arrange a loan. He also had discussions with a Colonial Office that was becoming increasingly nervous about what might happen in Newfoundland when American vessels began to arrive for cargoes of herring.* There was concern in Washington, as well. The new Secretary of State, Elihu Root (appointed after Hay's death in July), visited Labrador and western Newfoundland in August to size up the situation for himself. It was a private trip, and he met neither Bond nor Governor MacGregor. He fished for salmon on the Codroy River, visited the Bay of Islands, and travelled as far north as Nain. Root concluded that colonial fishery regulations would inevitably clash with the treaty rights, and with the needs and priorities of New Englanders, and that Bond's legislation, which he thought was dictated by mercantile interests, would not be supported by local fishermen.[17] As the crisis developed, the response of the United States was largely governed by these assumptions. Root was also very careful to do nothing that would attract Senator Lodge's disapproval. All the same, neither

* Another topic was the Labrador boundary. The British and Canadian governments wanted the issue to go to the Privy Council. Bond was not convinced, apparently preferring arbitration. Officials at the Colonial Office thought Labrador should go to Canada in return for financial compensation to Newfoundland—paid, of course, by Canada (MacGregor to Lyttleton, September 18, 1905, and Minute by Davis, October 3, 1905, CO 194/257, 298–99; see also MacGregor to Lyttleton, November 17, 1905, CO 194/258, 79).

Elihu Root (1845–1937), US Secretary of State, 1905 to 1909, undated. (Library of Congress, 100792)

Root nor the President wanted to precipitate an unnecessary confrontation.

Root resisted Lodge's pressure to send an American naval vessel. Instead, the US Bureau of Fisheries schooner *Grampus* appeared in Newfoundland waters. The American government blandly said that the visit, which was under the direction of A.B. Alexander, Chief of the Fisheries Division, was "for the purpose of making observations on the movements of the schools of mackerel . . . and conducting other operations of a scientific and practical character." It was also expected that Alexander would "keep in touch" with American fishermen, "reporting upon their operations, assisting them with advice and counsel and using his good offices on their behalf upon occasion."[18] The *Grampus* visited St. John's in mid-August. Alexander paid friendly calls at the departments of Finance and Fisheries, and then departed for the west coast.* He left the impression that this was primarily a scientific cruise.[19] But with a senior US government official on board, its purpose was clearly more than that.

Early in October, the colonial government announced that it wanted to prevent Newfoundlanders from selling herring to American vessels and from hiring on as crew members.[20] This was obviously retaliatory, but there was another goal as well: to impose local control, both governmental and commercial, over the herring trade and build it up into a more valuable part of the economy. At the time, the herring fishery accounted for only about 4 per cent of total exports by value. Virtually all the herring pro-

* Jackman to Mews, September 20, 1905, and Watson to Mews, September 18, 1905 (PANL, GN 1/3/A, 152). At Finance, the minister was told that there was to be an investigation into "certain representations . . . [concerning] the carrying out of our Customs laws."

duced (frozen and pickled) went more or less equally to Canada and the United States.[21] "The past history of our local herring fishery," wrote the Department of Marine and Fisheries, "has been characterized as one of spasmodic enterprise, never on an extensive scale, nor as a distinct business worth cultivating on its own merits."[22]

The immediate task was enforcement of the government's policy, and this the Colonial Office did its best to impede. It belatedly referred the whole issue to the Law Officers, and applied strong pressure on the colony to delay or avoid strict enforcement. In the meantime, considerable uncertainty prevailed. There were indignation meetings in the Bay of Islands, with the *Daily News* referring to "solemn faces," "anxiety," and "excitement." Morine and William Howley gave advice about how to evade the Foreign Fishing Vessels Act.[23] The *Grampus* helped the approximately forty-five American schooners* involved in the herring trade to hire about six hundred Newfoundlanders outside the three-mile limit and at Sydney, Cape Breton. Alexander apparently encouraged his countrymen to ignore local laws and regulations.† HMS *Latona* looked on, consulting with the Newfoundland Commissioner of Fisheries, Joseph O'Reilly (who was also in the area, on board the *Fiona*). Its captain reported that enforcement of the locally unpopular Foreign Fishing Vessels Act had not been expected, and that the American visitors were well-liked. They had, he reported, "a reputation for liberality, they are noted for the way they feed their own crews, and whenever a fishing boat came alongside with fish they were sure

* Commodore Paget put the number at sixty in late October (Paget to Admiralty, January 16, 1906, encl. in Admiralty to CO, February 21, 1906, CO 194/264, 273). He may have included Canadian schooners. Inspector O'Reilly listed forty-six vessels from Gloucester, thirty-six from Lunenburg, and three from St. John's ("Report of the Fisheries Protection Service of Newfoundland for the Year 1905 . . . ," *JHA* 1906, Appendix, 188–90).

† MacGregor to Lyttleton, conf., November 21, 1905 (CO 194/258, 115). Inspector O'Reilly reported that Alexander "was active in advising the American captains to do things that were contrary to their right . . . under the Treaty of 1818" ("Report of the Fisheries Protection Service of Newfoundland for the Year 1905 . . . ," *JHA* 1906, Appendix, 186).

to be given a good square meal and a tot or two of grog. It was looked upon as a matter of business. . . . The Canadian vessels . . . were either unable or unwilling to pursue the same policy."[24] What the locals did find offensive was the American insistence on fishing on Sundays. MacGregor commented that "in no other country known to me is the Sabbath more strictly observed than in Newfoundland. . . . It is the one point with respect to which in this Colony there is no denominational difference."[25]

The behaviour of the American fleet reflected the position of the United States government. Having received erroneous reports early in October, Root lodged a formal protest with the British ambassador. Any American vessel, he argued, could fish on the treaty coast without a licence and, as long as it did not intend to trade, it did not have to enter at a Customs house. Such vessels should not violate local laws—but those laws had to be consistent with the 1818 treaty. The 1905 act was clearly inconsistent with that treaty. Since it violated American treaty rights, it should be repealed.[26] Durand rightly observed that the United States intended "to deal with the question in a very uncompromising not to say aggressive spirit."[27]

Although the British government rejected Bond's interpretation of the word "coast," it agreed that the colony had the power to prevent Americans from using the shoreline and to prevent Newfoundlanders from assisting them. It could also refuse foreign vessels permission to purchase fish for bait or export. The Law Officers added that parts of the Foreign Fishing Vessels Act did indeed violate American treaty rights, but they thought that Americans should pay light dues and observe "reasonable" local regulations. Nothing entitled Americans to hire Newfoundlanders to fish in territorial waters, and such crew members could be prosecuted. However, it was made very clear to the colony that American vessels should not be seized and that arrests of Newfoundland crew members would be regrettable, especially if it were done aboard American vessels.[28]

It was becoming obvious that the United States and Britain (let alone the Newfoundland government) had very different views about the definition of American fishing rights under the 1818 treaty. Moreover, since that treaty also applied to Canadian waters, Canada's government would have to be included in any resolution of the situation. Bond had precipitated a serious and difficult controversy that none of the other governments involved had wanted. As for the Newfoundland government, it found itself in the frustrating position of having announced an aggressive policy that it could not enforce. MacGregor reported that Bond wanted to take action against the American vessels that hired Newfoundland crews—and against transgressing Newfoundlanders, too. Morris, "moderate and more careful," thought the Americans were in breach of the treaty as well as local law, but with characteristic caution wanted to be sure of his ground.[29] By mid-December, Bond was understandably complaining that the wholesale evasion of the law on the west coast, aided and abetted by the *Grampus*, was a severe embarrassment. Even MacGregor showed some sympathy: the government had, under pressure, avoided prosecutions so as not to exacerbate the situation, but damage had been done to respect for the law and to the ministry's public standing.[30] In London there was simply relief that, by the time the fishery closed in January 1906, there had been no serious incidents—and there was praise for MacGregor. "He has stood up to his ministers well," wrote C.T. Davis at the Colonial Office, "and we are under a great obligation to him for preventing recourse to extreme matters."[31]

Meanwhile, the British political landscape was changing. A.J. Balfour's Conservative government resigned early in December 1905, handing over to the Liberals without an election (the last time in British political history that this occurred). Lord Elgin, a former viceroy of India, became colonial secretary, and his political undersecretary was Winston Churchill. More important, in relation to the North Atlantic fisheries, the Foreign Office went to the Liberal imperialist Sir Edward Grey, who was as supportive of a pro-American foreign policy as his predecessor, if not more so.[32] The previous year, another imperial enthusiast, Lord Albert Grey, had taken over as governor general of Canada (December 1904). He possessed "a restless and interfering nature,"[33] and was thought by some to be impetuous and lacking in judgment.[34] He was soon to interest himself in Newfoundland affairs.

At the end of 1906 legislative session, Bond introduced amendments to tighten up the 1905 Foreign Fishing Vessels Act. It was now compulsory for American vessels to pay light dues, enter at Customs, and obey local laws consistent with the 1818 treaty. They would be penalized if they hired local men, inside or outside the three-mile limit, as crew to fish in territorial waters.[35] The governor had referred the matter to London (where officials would have liked Bond to drop the legislation altogether), but MacGregor understood that Bond would never abandon it. It was therefore decided to press for changes that would minimize the objections that were sure to come from the United States.[36] A second secret telegram from the Colonial Office made it very clear that the British government refused to be identified with a policy that, in its opinion, was not in the colony's best interests and would invite American retaliation. Indeed, the legislation might well not be confirmed.[37] The government nevertheless incorporated the suggested changes.

The Colonial Office had to admit that the 1906 version of the legislation was an improvement over the previous year's, much as its purpose was deplored.[38] The bill went through the Assembly in a single day.* The suspending clause drew particular attention in London: it stated that the legislation was not to come into operation until the governor issued a proclamation "to the effect that the [Act] has been approved and confirmed by His Majesty in Council." This was unexpected; the usual clause (as in 1905) would have stated that the act was suspended pending a proclamation giving notice of enforcement. The new wording made the imperial government party to a policy of which it explicitly did not approve.[39] The genesis of the clause is not known, but Foreign Office officials thought the colonial government had been quite clever "in placing us on the horns of a dilemma," noting that "we must either formally approve a Bill which we have already practically condemned and privately disapproved or by disallowing it revive an earlier and in some respects more objectionable Act, which will encourage the U.S. to further encroachments and an expansion of their claims." There was nothing for it but to give approval[40]—but that never happened, as it turned out.

* There was no division in the Legislative Council (*JLC* 1906, 87).

INTERPRETING THE TREATY

These debates were taking place within the broader context of exchanges between the American and British governments over the interpretation of the 1818 treaty. It was known in Newfoundland that such discussions were occurring, but not their content or significance. Root had started the process with his uncompromising note of October 19, 1905,[41] to which the British government replied in early February 1906. There were several major points at issue. First, Root claimed that any American vessel could fish on the defined coasts; Grey argued that only American vessels with American crews could fish there. Second, Root claimed that an American vessel seeking to exercise the treaty right did not need a Newfoundland government licence and, if it did not intend to trade, did not have to enter at a Customs house. Grey conceded only the first point. Third, Root thought that the only concern of the Newfoundland government should be evidence of American registry. This Grey disputed, since proof of registry did not mean that the vessel was engaged only in fishing. American fishermen were bound to comply with colonial regulations as long as they were reasonable, did not interfere with American fishing rights, and applied "to all fishermen alike." On other points, Grey argued that American vessels should pay light dues, which they had recently refused to do. He also reminded Root that the Newfoundland government had had every right to stop foreign vessels from entering local ports to obtain bait, fishing supplies, and crews, as had been allowed under the 1893 act, repealed in 1905.[42]

Root's response was belligerent. His central argument—in many ways identical to that advanced by the French government before 1904—was that American fishermen were not subject to any colonial regulations whatsoever, whether reasonable or not. This was the long-established position of the State Department, relating to both the 1818 treaty and the Treaty of Washington (first articulated during the Fortune Bay dispute in the 1870s[43]). There was nothing in the 1818 treaty that gave any right "to makers of colonial law to interfere at all . . . with the exercise of the American rights of fishery." It was irrelevant that Newfoundland and Canadian fishermen in the same waters might be subject to colonial regulations—if the British colonies chose to regulate their own fishermen, so be it, but such regulations could not apply to American vessels, which were also free to ship crews of whatever nationalities they chose. Even further, the treaty granted "a perpetual right to the inhabitants of the United States which is beyond the sovereign power of England to destroy or change. . . . The existence of this right is a qualification of British sovereignty within that territory." Some mutually agreed upon regulations might well be necessary, but the US government "can not permit the exercise of these rights to be subject to the will of the colony of Newfoundland."[44]

By the time this note reached the Foreign Office, the United States had already protested Bond's criticism of the activities of the *Grampus* in 1905; Root had also told Gloucester that Newfoundland's action in forbidding the use of purse seines was unreasonable and his department would do what it could to help. No wonder that Grey feared "that things are going to be unpleasant between us and them as regards Newfoundland."[45] Faced with Root's implacability, Grey did not argue further, deciding that "the only course" was arbitration and the negotiation of a temporary agreement to govern the fishery in the meantime.[46]

Since arbitration meant that all parties concerned would have to agree on the terms of reference and other details, the immediate problem was a temporary arrangement. This was the only matter referred to St. John's. Elgin hoped that if a satisfactory deal could be worked out, arbitration might be avoided. But he accepted that a confrontation with the United States had to be avoided. Governor MacGregor, his imperial enthusiasms fortified by his recent association with Lord Grey, enthusiastically agreed. He assured Elgin that he would "not be forced into any act that would tend to precipitate a rupture, even should it mean the dismissal of ministers."* From this point on, MacGregor became more obviously hostile to Bond and his policies.

LORD GREY'S VISIT, 1906

Lord Grey was an imperial crusader determined to promote Anglo-American friendship by doing everything possible to solve outstanding

* The assurance came in August 1906 and is quoted in Hyam, *Elgin and Churchill*, 292.

issues between Canada, Newfoundland, and the United States, including the fisheries question. MacGregor had met him during a visit to Canada in May 1906 and invited him to come to Newfoundland.[47] Grey cleared the visit with Elgin and Laurier and, accompanied by five family members and an assistant, arrived at Port aux Basques on July 25, 1906. A special train laid on by the Reids took the party to St. John's, where they were greeted by MacGregor, the city's newly elected mayor (Michael Gibbs), and W.D. Reid, who also provided "grand illuminations" at the station. It was officially a private visit, as the Liberal press was at pains to emphasize. Bond explicitly said that he had no desire to talk about confederation, which was "neither in the interests of the Colony, nor of the Empire."[48] He was clearly unenthusiastic about the visit, wanting to distance himself and the government from it. Bond apparently blocked Morris's proposal to allocate public money for various festivities, and MacGregor advised Morris not to lay on a dinner for the visitors. However, Bond did attend a ball at Government House, took Lady Grey in to supper, and presided at the head of the table. Grey reported that people were surprised, since "Bond (like Pericles wasn't it?) never 'goes out.' He lives alone and works for The Commonwealth. No man enters his house to enjoy his hospitality and he never attends social functions." Grey and Bond met twice more, at an official Government House luncheon and at a private luncheon on August 3. When Bond suggested that Canada and Newfoundland should have a common fisheries policy, Grey mentioned confederation. Bond replied that confederation would injure Newfoundland by preventing industrial development, and the matter dropped.[49] Grey also told Bond that his anti-American policy was futile.[50]

Since Lord Grey spent most of his time in the company of MacGregor and the Reid clan, it is not surprising that he returned with favourable impressions of the governor and W.D. Reid and a negative one of Bond, whom he characterized as a crackpot. Further, he thought Bond was

> an ugly and formidable antagonist. He has the strength which a touch of madness brings (I understand there is madness in

> his family)* in addition to the strength which comes from position, patronage and prestige. He is like other madmen jealous, suspicious, avariciously tenacious of all patronage, a strong and unforgiving hater, and most vindictive, and consequently rules by fear. He is a good speaker and a ceaseless and [illeg.] worker, and he will fight hard to keep his position.[51]

Grey was apparently convinced that if Bond could be removed from power, then confederation might be possible. He must have discussed this idea with Reid and MacGregor, and he certainly made his views known to Elgin.† They were widely circulated. The alternative leader and a possible confederate seemed to be that good friend of the Reids, Sir Edward Morris. Lord Grey's visit did not achieve anything constructive in the way of settling either the fisheries crisis or the Labrador boundary dispute, but it did give Grey a distorted perspective that only intensified hostility toward Bond and his government in London and Ottawa.

THE MODUS VIVENDI

This attitude became even more firmly embedded when the Newfoundland government refused to co-operate over a modus vivendi. It first reminded the Colonial Office of the famous 1857 Labouchere Dispatch, and followed up with a lengthy Minute of Council, almost certainly drafted by Bond.[52] The colony's arguments were not unreasonable but they had no impact in London, where the Bond government was seen as stubborn, obstructive, and unco-operative. Sir Edward Grey's attitude—a row with Newfoundland was preferable to a row with the United States—was widely shared.[53] The unanimous decision was to refuse to sanction the 1906 act (the once-disputed suspending clause was suddenly very useful), negotiate a modus vivendi, and "then force the Colony to respect it."[54] Protests from St. John's became irrelevant; the British government went ahead on its own

---

* I discovered no evidence to support this allegation and I do not know where it came from.

† Grey to Elgin, private, September 8, 1906 (LAC, Grey fonds, 12:3655). Bond's attitude to the USA, Grey wrote, "is only to be explained by his madness."

and in early September proposed an agreement that included the continued suspension of the 1906 act. The 1905 act would remain in force but part of Section 1 and all of Section 3 would not apply to American vessels,* which would also be exempt from light dues. Otherwise, American vessels would report to Customs and obey local regulations.[55]

The United States government largely accepted this arrangement and even offered to pay light dues. However, it saw "very grave difficulties" with complying with local regulations because they banned Sunday fishing as well as the use of purse seines. It was decided, in the end, that Americans could use purse seines if they agreed not to fish on Sundays. The Foreign Office optimistically hoped that given this concession, the United States government would prevent the hiring of Newfoundland fishermen outside the three-mile limit, but failed to obtain a firm undertaking on this point. The agreement was settled on October 6.[56]

The Bond government was furious and refused its consent. The agreement was seen as interference in the colony's internal affairs—"subversive of the Colony's constitutional rights and calculated to work severe injury to the fisheries of the Colony." Moreover, it was "intended to override statutes that have received the Royal Assent."[57] The Colonial Office was unimpressed: this was a matter of international, not local, interest. It refused to accept that the colony's rights or laws had in any way been subverted or overridden.[58] Nor was it impressed by hostile resolutions passed at meetings of businessmen in St. John's and Harbour Grace. MacGregor played down their significance: "some important names" were missing and few of the signatories were involved in the west coast fishery.[59] If anything, the meetings probably confirmed the view held in Washington and London that the colonial government's policy was shaped by the merchant class in its own interest, and was profoundly unpopular among ordinary fishermen.[60] "The people," it was thought, were not on Bond's side.

Refusing to accept the legality of the temporary agreement, Bond and his government decided to test whether existing local legislation could be overridden in this way. Morris, as Minister of Justice, supported the move,

* These sections had to do with boarding and bringing foreign fishing vessels into port.

fortified by legal opinions that Bond had obtained from London[61] (although the Law Officers supported the Colonial Office[62]). It was therefore decided to prosecute two fishermen engaged by American vessels outside the three-mile limit.[63] (MacGregor was thankful that he had been able to persuade the government to limit the number of prosecutions,[64] but he feared that any at all "might seriously and prejudicially affect the foreign relations and interests of the empire."[65]) Instructed to take action,[66] Inspector O'Reilly arrested George Crane and Alexander Dubois of Woods Island for violating the Bait Act. The two men had shipped on an American schooner outside the three-mile limit on November 8 and loaded herring on November 12; they were duly convicted by the magistrate at Birchy Cove. They were represented by William Howley, who gave notice of appeal[67] and, through MacGregor, sought financial assistance. It was agreed at the Colonial Office that if the judgment was upheld on appeal (which it was), the British government would quietly pay the fines and costs.[68]

THE WEST COAST HERRING FISHERY, 1906–07

The west coast herring fishery was managed by Captain Anstruther (of HMS *Brilliant*) and A.B. Alexander, who had returned aboard USS *Potomac* (classed as a naval tug) to look after American interests as he and his government saw them.* The Newfoundland government insisted that the latter vessel had to pay light and harbour dues, which appalled officials in London and led to a US government protest.[69] Inspector O'Reilly found himself sidelined: "The Americans are doing just about as they like," he reported.[70]

Anstruther had arrived on October 15. Told by Magistrate March that there could well be trouble if the Americans used purse seines, he called a meeting of "the most influential fishermen in Birchy Cove," whom he described as "fine, stalwart, straightforward-looking men, whom one felt

* Bond alleged that Alexander and the ship's captain had failed to keep an appointment with the Minister of Marine and Fisheries in St. John's on September 19 (Bond to MacGregor, September 21, 1906, PANL, GN 1/4/2, box 2). Root had suggested sending two American cruisers to Newfoundland, but the Foreign Office thought not (Grey to Durand, November 6, 1906, FO 371/185, 408).

one could depend upon." Naturally enough, they opposed any attempt to interfere with their trade with American vessels and they appreciated the modus, though it meant that they would have to go out to sea to embark on American vessels. But they strongly opposed the use of purse seines, which they said would ruin the fishery. On October 22, Anstruther and Alexander (ignoring O'Reilly) drew up an agreement whereby no purse seines were to be used inside the Bay of Islands, and there would be no fishing at night or on Sundays.[71] Alexander had trouble obtaining the consent of all the American owners and captains, but purse seining did end. In addition, more than five hundred men shipped on American vessels without further incident—most of them boarding off the Newfoundland coast, some at Sydney, and some at St. Pierre. Between two hundred and three hundred men also shipped on Canadian vessels.*

Bond and the government were unhappy about Anstruther's actions, which they said were "calculated to inspire disrespect of and disregard for constituted authority in this Colony, occasioning embarrassment . . . and intensifying the unpleasantness of the present situation."[72] MacGregor thought that Bond wanted to find a way out, but would not abandon the draft 1902 reciprocity convention. He suggested taking soundings in Washington, but Elgin replied that nothing could be done given Canada's sensitivities on the question.† What preoccupied London was the possibility of further prosecutions and of colonial officials boarding American vessels to make arrests—even though MacGregor reported that this was highly unlikely.[73] All the same, the Colonial Office consulted the Law Officers again; discussion this time focused on the possibility of using an imperial Order in Council to

* Estimates of the numbers of men shipped vary considerably.

† MacGregor to Elgin, tgm., personal and private, November 18,1906 (CO 194/264, 58); Elgin to MacGregor, private and personal, December 21, 1906 (CO 194/266, 101). In fact, the US government had been told that if it approved the 1902 convention, it would be ratified in London. The Law Officers advised that this would have to be done by imperial legislation. Lord Grey lobbied against ratification and the matter was put off (Grey to Howard, February 11, 1907, FO 371/387, 126; Law Officers to CO, December 28, 1906, and internal Minutes, CO 194/266, 318).

enforce the modus under 59 Geo. III cap. 38 (1819), which empowered the British government to make regulations enforcing the 1818 treaty.[74] Winston Churchill aggressively wrote: "We must unhesitatingly enforce the modus vivendi by superior power." Bond should be so informed, and told that if there was any more "opposition of a mischievous and irresponsible character, we shall submit the whole question to arbitration—and enforce the decision of the tribunal."[75] The next stage of the crisis was being prepared.

THE MODUS PROTESTED

The winter herring fishery ended without incident in January 1907. It was a better fishery than those of the two preceding years, reported MacGregor, and employed over a thousand Newfoundlanders on 147 vessels—sixty-five from the USA, twenty-seven from Nova Scotia, and fifty-five local.[76] Satisfactory as this was in some respects, the Newfoundland government was smarting from the imposition of the temporary agreement. When the legislature convened on February 7—earlier than usual since Bond was going to the Colonial Conference in April—the first item of business was to debate an address to the British government protesting the modus. Local laws had been set aside, the colony's interests had been "made subservient to the purposes of foreigners" and its "rights under the Constitution" had been ignored. The agreement was unnecessary, unwarranted, and conferred privileges "upon American citizens in excess of those granted under the Treaty of 1818 [and] in excess of those enjoyed by British subjects in this Colony." It was a clear violation of the 1857 Labouchere Dispatch.[77]

Bond led off with a five-hour speech on February 12.* It was, he said, "a grave constitutional question" of imperial importance "how far, according to the principles of the Constitution, His Majesty's Ministers have the power to set aside or limit the operation of local laws which have received the Royal assent."[78] He was supported by other Liberals, including Morris. The opposition clearly missed Morine, currently exiled in Toronto;† it was led officially by the ailing Captain Charles Dawe. The most able opposition

---

* Dismissed by a Foreign Office official—"as usual, injudicious and wrong-headed" (FO 371/387, 384).

† There is more on this in Chapter 10.

speech came from Donald Morison, who had taken over Morine's seat in Bonavista.* He accepted Bond's views on responsible government and the importance of the Bait Act, and agreed that the colony's constitutional privileges had to be upheld. But he refused to accept that they had been infringed and questioned the relevance of the Labouchere Dispatch. The matter before the House, he said, "was one of policy rather than constitutional law or interference by the Home Authorities," and it was clear that the government's policy was widely unpopular.[79] This theme was underlined by Michael Cashin, still sitting as an independent, who presented a petition signed by a thousand of his Ferryland constituents that asked for the repeal of the Foreign Fishing Vessels Act.[80] The people who had been hurt were Newfoundlanders, not the Americans: "For the past thirty years they have fished in amity and good fellowship side by side with our own people, spending their money liberally and abiding by our laws and providing an enterprise for hundreds of our people . . . they have never injured our markets, nor interfered with the price of fish or unfairly competed with us." In addition, he made the fair point that if the government felt humiliated, why had it not resigned and forced a dissolution? The government of Natal had resigned *en bloc* in 1906 to protest British interference, withdrawing only when the Colonial Office gave way. The explanation, he thought, had to be fear that the Liberals might be defeated.†

The Address passed the Assembly on February 14. With procedural sleight of hand, Bond moved that since no division had been called for, the minutes should show that the Address had passed unanimously. Dawe and Morison registered vigorous protests; Cashin called the action "mean, low and contemptible."[81] But "unanimous" remained on the record.‡

---

* MacGregor called Morison "the ablest and most experienced member of the Opposition," with "a high character" in the community (MacGregor to Elgin, conf., March 16, 1907, CO 194/267, 382).

† Cashin in Assembly, February 14, 1907 (*Evening Telegram,* February 25, 1907); Hyam, *Elgin and Churchill,* 240–42. The issue in South Africa was the treatment of Africans by the Natal government.

‡ The Legislative Council later approved the Address (eleven to two), which was transmitted to MacGregor on February 22 (*JLC* 1907, 20–31).

The government might have had the best of the constitutional argument, but its opponents were right in saying that the enforcement of the Bait Act against American vessels was unpopular, particularly in districts where Americans had traded for bait or for pickled and frozen herring. Archbishop Howley wrote excited letters to the press in support of the government—"We are at the mercy of an insatiable American rapacity on the one hand, and a compromising British Diplomacy on the other"—and further backing came from D.W. Prowse and the *Evening Telegram*.[82] But there were no public meetings or petitions in favour of the government's stand. As Morison pointed out, their absence was in direct contrast to the events of 1857, to which the Liberals so often referred. The *Daily News* thought most people were uninterested and noted low attendance in the public galleries at the legislature.[83] Later in the year, Sir James Winter told the London *Morning Post* that "the feeling in the Colony is one either of indifference to and even ignorance of the whole question, or, among a very small fraction of the population, of strong antagonism."[84]

THE 1907 COLONIAL CONFERENCE

The legislature closed in late March. Bond now had to face the Colonial Conference in London, which was to begin on April 15, where he was sure to come under heavy pressure from the British government. He was followed by a series of derogatory and critical private letters from Government House to various people. MacGregor thought Bond was reluctant to leave Morris behind[85]—as well he might have been—and he later reported that Bond had arrived late at the conference because he wanted to avoid travelling on the same steamer as Laurier.* "Bond would not be a lesser sun; and perhaps he feared that might be said by some one that he

* Bond missed the first three sessions of the conference, April 15, 17, and 18. He was present on April 20 (*Minutes of Proceedings of the Colonial Conference, 1907*, Cd. 3523, May, 1907).

discussed Confederation with Laurier."* This was no more than spiteful gossip. MacGregor certainly had no interest in saying anything positive about Bond and he did not mention that heavy snowfalls had blocked the railway for several days, causing delays and forcing Bond to take the *Bruce* from Placentia to North Sydney and then catch a steamer from New York.[86] MacGregor glibly assured Elgin that he had "done what I could to try to break down the hermit character of this Government, which breeds suspicion and no good-will towards all our neighbours. My efforts have cost me money and some chagrin. Sir Robert Bond was bitterly opposed to the visit Lord Grey paid me here last year."

In a separate memorandum, MacGregor argued that neither Bond nor a majority of those involved in the fishery were any longer enthusiastic about the draft reciprocity treaty. Some, he thought, were ambivalent about the bait concessions offered the Americans, others advocated finding alternative markets for herring before interfering any further with the American trade. He did not explain Bond's supposed shift, instead strongly implying that the dispute had become a personal matter. It was the opinion of "at least some of Sir Robert Bond's colleagues, and certainly also of many others, that the question with the Prime Minister is more personal than political. It is, however, a question that can be readily exploited by an adroit use of the platitudes of patriotism, and, consequently, Sir Robert Bond will always have a large following in contesting and opposing the activities of the American."[87] The message was that Bond was not fully supported by other members of the government and that he was pursuing a personal obsession. There was some truth to this, but MacGregor exaggerated the amount of popular support for the anti-American policy. He also overstated Bond's personal dominance—people were afraid of him, he said, and feared being branded as unpatriotic: "Each one dreads the vindictive spirit of Sir Robert Bond. They allege that he is the most

* MacGregor to Grey, private, June 18, 1907 (LAC, Grey fonds, 5136). He added that Bond was a "hermit" who "will not appear unless he is to be the cynosure of the occasion. Morris is much broader." Grey passed all this on to Laurier, letter dated August 1, 1907 (LAC, Grey fonds, 2:452). See also MacGregor to Elgin, secret, July 18, 1907 (CO 194/268, 493).

vindictive of men; and they add that he has spies everywhere."[88] Such commentary was neither fair nor accurate.

The 1907 Colonial Conference was the last to use that name. In future, these meetings would be called "Imperial Conferences" and the self-governing colonies recognized as "dominions," whatever that might mean in practice. The changes represented a half-hearted recognition by British politicians and bureaucrats that emerging colonial nationalisms had to be acknowledged and accommodated. But the "official mind" still found it difficult to sympathize with colonial politicians and their aspirations, on both the political and personal levels. They were viewed as parochial and lacking a genuine understanding of imperial priorities. They would not necessarily toe the Whitehall line and, on the whole, were seen as tiresome. Bond was walking into difficult territory.

Like other Newfoundland premiers before and after, Bond played a relatively minor role at the conference. His government had not submitted any resolutions and he seldom intervened in debate. He joined Laurier and others in opposing the creation of an "Imperial Council," and indicated that his negative views on imperial preference were unchanged. When the subject of naval defence was raised, he offered an expansion of the Newfoundland Naval Reserve and echoed and reinforced an argument advanced by L.P. Brodeur, the Canadian Minister of Marine and Fisheries: the cost of policing the imperial treaties of 1818 (with the US) and 1713 (and after, with France) should be counted as important naval contributions.[89]

Predictably, Bond was preoccupied with the fisheries dispute, which was not on the original conference agenda. However, the presence of the other colonial premiers, the many social events, and the attention of the press all gave him opportunities to publicize Newfoundland's case and attempt to bring pressure to bear on the British government. He did so vigorously, specifically attacking the modus vivendi at a dinner hosted by the National Liberal Club, which the *Daily Mail* thought "a dramatic incident."[90] There was also the opportunity to discuss the issue with British politicians. How many meetings took place during the conference is unclear, but there was certainly a thorough discussion on May 11 attended by Bond, Elgin, Sir Edward Grey, Winston Churchill, and several officials. Bond was bluntly criticized by a clearly irritated Grey: "You are trying to settle a big question on small points," he said. "You take up a position which we could not take up on behalf of Cornwall. You have no sense of responsibility because you know *we* have to bear the brunt."[91]

Nothing was settled. Bond no doubt thought that his position had been strengthened by the decision of the Newfoundland Supreme Court concerning the Crane and Dubois appeal, which had been announced on May 7. The court upheld the original conviction on the grounds that, as British subjects resident in Newfoundland, the defendants were subject to local law. They had no treaty rights and were not part of the crew of the American vessel in question. Since they did not possess licences, their actions had been in violation of the Bait Act.* There was no appeal to the Privy Council.† Morris assured MacGregor that there would be no more prosecutions relating to the 1906 season.[92] But there could be more prosecutions in the future, and Bond told the press that the decision showed that neither the modus nor the British government could set aside local statutes.[93]

Bond wanted to bring the fisheries issue to the Conference and he drafted a resolution for discussion. Annotations on a copy of the draft show that Arthur Deakin (Australia), Sir Joseph Ward (New Zealand) and F.R. Moor (Natal) concurred with its sentiments—although the other premiers (including the ever-cautious Laurier) did not.[94] The latter agreed that Bond should bring the matter to the conference but thought it should

---

* O'Reilly vs. Crane et al, *Decisions of the Supreme Court of Newfoundland, 1904–1911*, 292–300. The defence had been handled by W.R. Howley and Sir James Winter. Legal fees, and eventually the fines, were discreetely paid by MacGregor, acting through the local manager of the Bank of Montreal. He was presumably reimbursed by the Colonial Office (CO 194/267, 51 and 387; CO 194/268, 4, 274, 284, and 294).

† The British government gave instructions that there should be no such appeal (Elgin to MacGregor, tgm., October 9, 1907; Howley to MacGregor, October 18, 1907, and January 27, 1908, PANL, GN 1/4/2, box 3).

be treated confidentially, adding ambiguously that "the resolution itself is one as to which you may have further discussion."[95] Laurier, in fact, told Bond privately "that he had brought himself to an impasse, and that he should retrace his steps, and that he never could get anything by forcing an issue with the U.S."[96] It made no difference. On May 13, Bond told Elgin that the premiers thought that the conference should not close "until an expression of opinion is recorded" on the question.[97] The next day Bond was allowed his moment and presented a resolution. The conference was asked to agree that the British government

> cannot possibly admit that the United States, under the Treaty of 1818, has any right to engage Newfoundland fishermen to fish for them within British jurisdiction in contravention of the Bait Act of 1887; and that when a common right of fishing is exercised within the jurisdiction of the Dominion of Canada or Newfoundland, those countries have absolute authority to make regulations . . . , and, provided there be no discrimination . . . to insist upon their observance by all parties concerned. . . . [And] if His Majesty's Government failed to support those Colonies in this position, it would constitute a serious infringement of the autonomous rights of the Colonies. Therefore any arrangement made with the United States Government in respect to the North American Fisheries should necessarily embrace a recognition of these principles.

After it had been agreed that the proceedings would be private "subject to any further decision," Bond outlined the history of American participation in the Newfoundland fisheries, the relevant treaties, the failed reciprocity deals of 1890 and 1902, and the development of the current dispute. He made clear his unhappiness with the 1906 agreement and the American claim that its citizens "can do as they please and violate our fishing and other laws with impunity." The colony had every right to legislate for its fisheries, and such laws also applied to foreign fishermen, even when exercising a treaty privilege. What he wanted from the British government was formal assent to Newfoundland's 1906 Foreign Fishing Vessels Act, permission to enforce colonial law, and a definition of American rights under the 1818 treaty. The colony

> asks for nothing but justice and responsibility sanctioned by the spirit and forms of the British constitution. We do not think it just that permission should be given by His Majesty's Government to a foreign power to override or contravene the laws of the Colony, or that an undertaking should be given to a foreign power by His Majesty's Government not to sanction certain Colonial legislation.

As for arbitration, "I cannot see what there is to arbitrate upon." The treaty was clear and unambiguous.*

Grey responded that "we have come to the point where argument is exhausted, and I do not think there is any more to be done . . . by argument." There were only three options: a semi-permanent agreement, arbitration at The Hague Tribunal, or an ultimatum to the United States that the British interpretation of the treaty would be enforced. Since the outcome of an arbitration would be uncertain, and an ultimatum was impossible, the best way forward was an agreement. Given that Canada was also affected by the 1818 treaty, Laurier's remarks were clearly important. He sympathized "very largely with Sir Robert Bond," he told the conference, "and to a large extent share his views." The Americans had "put up pretensions which . . . are absolutely untenable. . . . Their right to complain only commences with the allegation . . . that the regulations have been designed to harass them . . . and I never heard that there was such a contention." The Newfoundland legislature had every right to prohibit Sunday fishing and the use of purse seines. He thought, however, that preventing Newfoundlanders from engaging to fish on American schooners might

* There is a printed copy of the speech in RBP 7.13.002; the final text is in the *Proceedings of the Colonial Conference*, 587–600. The summary of the discussion is based on the confidential record in CO 885/18.

The participants in the 1907 Colonial Conference. Lord Elgin (Colonial Secretary) is in the centre of the front row, with Sir Wilfrid Laurier on his left. Bond is in the second row, far right. Also present are Winston Churchill, Herbert Asquith, and David Lloyd George.

be construed as an invasion of American treaty rights—"although, for my part, I feel altogether as Sir Robert Bond feels on this point."

Elgin sought to wind up the discussion soon after Laurier spoke, but Bond wanted to move the adoption of the resolution. Grey objected, in part because it did not contain any opinion or recommendation as to how the dispute was to be settled. Bond then stated that he would accept "a full submission of all questions at issue to arbitration." Grey repeated his reluctance to arbitrate and again urged an agreement with the United States that would allow the engagement of Newfoundlanders in return for recognition of local regulations. If Bond would not make this concession, then the regulations would have to be discussed with the Americans. Given that Canada had an informal agreement with the United States that seemed to be working, Laurier was reluctant to commit to an arbitration, but he stated that if Bond was to decide that was the best route, his government would consider it. After a few testy exchanges, Elgin and Grey agreed that Bond's statement could be published (but not the discussion) as long as the resolution was withdrawn. The conference agreed. Bond was not happy. "I was reluctantly compelled to become an unwilling party to that decision, in order to secure any mention whatsoever of the case of Newfoundland in the Conference proceedings."[98]

The next day, the *Daily Mail* printed a sensational report, alleging that Bond had pleaded with Elgin to save the fisheries, and when the latter demurred, had jumped to his feet saying, "This is a gross humiliation and neglect which you would not dare to offer to a Colony powerful enough to be able to give effect to its resentment. It is most unjust. I repeat again that you are deliberately neglecting us for the sake of American interests." He then was said to have walked out.[99] Churchill told the House of Commons that the report was "from beginning to end a baseless and impudent fabrication" and expressed surprise "that a person who has lately been created a Peer of the realm [Northcliffe] should be willing to allow newspapers under his control to employ, for political objects, methods of such transparent mendacity."[100] In response, the *Mail* claimed that Bond had confirmed the accuracy of the report, which Bond—hurrying between social events at Bristol and Rochester—firmly denied. He repeated the denial in an after-dinner speech at the West Indian Club, adding that Newfoundland should be treated "not as a 'spoilt child,' but as a colleague of the Mother Country in common with all the other Dependencies."* But he told Sir Francis Hopwood† at the Colonial Office that all "misunderstanding and misrepresentation" would have been avoided if the précis of the conference proceedings "had treated the Colony with more courtesy and had published what had really taken place instead of two or three lines which were calculated to utterly mislead the public."[101] Bond was assured that his "able and elaborate" statement—which did not lend itself to précis, said Hopwood—would be published in full in due course.[102] With that Bond had to be satisfied.

---

* *Free Press*, June 25, 1907. There is a typewritten draft of this very favourable report, amended in Bond's handwriting, in RBP 5.06.005. He may have written it himself.

† Hopwood had been permanent under-secretary since January 1907, following Sir Montagu Ommanney. He was a friend and supporter of Wilfred Grenfell.

A NEW MODUS AND IMPERIAL PRESSURE

The publicity that Bond gave to the fisheries dispute during the conference, and the sympathy he received in some quarters, did not change any minds in the Foreign or Colonial offices. On May 17, Bond met Elgin and for the first time made concessions. He agreed to submit the fishery regulations currently in force to the Colonial Office and to the United States government for comment. If agreement could be reached in this way, then another temporary agreement might not be needed—Elgin pointing out that if there was to be an arbitration, it could not take place for some time.[103] In a sense, Bond had been misled. Grey still wanted an agreement, there was no intention of assenting to the 1906 act, and officials were determined to prevent prosecutions of Newfoundlanders shipping aboard American fishing vessels. This became clear to Bond when he was consulted about a note to be sent to the American ambassador in London. It proposed, in effect, a continuance of the 1906 modus with the addition that officials would not be able to serve process on Newfoundlanders working on board American vessels contrary to local law. Bond (and the colonial government) strongly objected to the addition, which was eventually dropped, but other aspects of the draft remained unchanged.[104] It outlined the "points of divergence" between the British and American governments, agreed to submit local regulations for American comment, and conceded that American vessels need not necessarily pay light dues. It requested only that American ships report at Customs houses and abstain from both using purse seines and from fishing on Sundays. There was no reference to arbitration.[105]

Elihu Root thought the offer was "the coolest piece of cheek" he had ever seen,* in that Britain was in effect asking for concessions without making any in return. His reply was uncompromising: the Americans could not surrender their "rights" to hire local fishermen, use purse seines, and fish on Sundays. If they did so, the treaty would become useless to them. Since the two sides were so far apart, the best solution would be a renewal of the 1906 agreement pending a reference to The Hague Tribunal.

---

* Quoted in Tansill, *Canadian-American Relations*, 114. Tansill's summary of Grey's note is not fully accurate.

The only concession hinted at was an offer not to use purse seines—as long as Newfoundlanders could be hired as usual.[106]

Though Grey had hitherto opposed arbitration, he now saw no other option. Bond had already acquiesced at the Colonial Conference and the Canadian government also fell into line—although reluctantly, since (like Bond) it thought the treaty clear and unambiguous.* There remained, however, the contentious issue of negotiating and enforcing a temporary agreement. On August 10, the Newfoundland government was informed that the British government proposed a modus along the same lines as the previous year, except that it prohibited the use of purse seines. It could be confirmed and enforced by the colonial government and legislature, but if they refused to do so, the British government "must proceed to take whatever measures are necessary. . . . Imperial interests of great importance are involved."[107]

Before a local response was sent, MacGregor convened a special meeting of the Executive Council and read out a memorandum. He wanted, he told Elgin, to give the government "a solemn warning."[108] MacGregor's central theme was imperial loyalty and responsibility. The government should assist "the Ministers of the King in their present efforts to better our position in the manner that they deem most suitable and practicable in the general interests of the Empire." If they thought an agreement pending arbitration was a political necessity, then the colony should co-operate and try to obtain the best terms possible. If it refused, Newfoundland would be "regarded by some as intransigent, as intractable, and as forcing His Majesty's Ministers to proceed in this question without us; while others could hardly fail to think that we were withholding our advice and assistance where it was due to the King's Ministers." MacGregor went further. He expressed doubts about the value of the Bond-Hay draft

---

* Grey to Elgin, tgm., August 14, 1907 (*Further Correspondence,* Cd. 3765, 158); Laurier to Grey, August 10, 1907 (LAC, Grey fonds 2:461); Peter Neary, "Grey, Bryce, and the Settlement," 365–66; and Alvin C. Gluek, Jr., "Programmed Diplomacy," 53. Gluek argues that Grey manoeuvred the American government into making the first approach concerning arbitration, so as to ensure co-operation from Bond and Laurier.

convention, thought an agreement would have no appreciable economic impact, and saw "nothing derogatory to our constitutional rights in recognising the political necessities of the Empire, of which we constitute but a small minority." Newfoundland might possess responsible government, but that did not "relieve it from the constitutional obligation of giving recognition to, and of complying with, engagements deemed necessary by . . . His Majesty's Government with a foreign power."[109]

Bond was understandably angered by MacGregor's lecture. If important imperial interests were involved, why had the colony not been told earlier? Why had there been no assurance that all questions in dispute would go to arbitration? Why were the views of the colonial government discounted? He then went on to argue (less convincingly) that the colony had discouraged encroachments by foreigners since 1836, but that no sanctions had been imposed on American fishermen until after the failure of the 1902 draft agreement, which had been accepted by the British government. The Newfoundland government could not admit MacGregor's criticism. The United States was "the natural market for the products of this Colony, and is the cheapest and best market for such products and manufactures as the Colony requires." On the wider issues, Bond argued that the government had an inherent "constitutional and moral responsibility" to resist "by every constitutional means any action . . . that in their opinion is subversive of the rights of His Majesty's subjects in this Colony and destructive to their material interests." The colony was not pursuing an independent foreign policy any more than Canada was, and was enforcing its local laws in the same way. These laws had received Royal assent and to prevent their enforcement was a violation of the colony's constitutional rights. The difficulty resulted from the main difference of opinion: "the wisdom and expediency of giving way to the pretensions of the United States Government . . . as to the limitation and suspension of the statutes of this Colony in order to meet the unrighteous demands of that Government." In short, Newfoundland was required to relinquish what it perceived to be its rights "in order to prevent unpleasant relations between the United States and British Governments."[110]

Bond was quite right on the main point, though his version of history was obviously coloured by his own preoccupations and experience. He now clearly understood the realities of the situation. He could not beat the Colonial Office but he could put up a good fight. He must have suspected that his position was being persistently undermined by MacGregor, Lord Grey, and their allies, and common sense and the newspapers must have told him that he now faced an unprecedented political challenge at the popular level.

Not only was the British government determined to avoid trouble with the United States, but Bond now had an immediate political threat—Sir Edward Morris resigned from the government in July 1907 to become an independent.[111] Bond's primary aim, therefore, was to avoid the imposition of a new temporary agreement, which he saw as a humiliation for himself and the colony. The government protested British policy as "unprecedented and objectionable" and refused to pass legislation confirming the proposed agreement. However, if the temporary agreement was withdrawn, Americans would be allowed to purchase herring under special licences, paying $2 a barrel.[112]

This was, in effect, an offer to return to the situation as it had been in 1904, and was made on August 21. It was rejected by the British and American governments as being too late: Gloucester vessels had already set out, apparently, and the US revenue cutter *Gresham* (with A.B. Alexander once again on board) would sail on September 1.* Moreover, the proposal did not allow Americans to hire Newfoundlanders. So there would be an agreement—no matter what the colony's government thought or wanted[113]—and it was settled on September 7. As before, it overrode parts of the 1905 Foreign Fishing Vessels Act and stated that Royal assent would not be given to the 1906 Act. The American government waived the "right" of American fishermen to use purse seines and to fish on Sundays, but American vessels would be able to ship Newfoundlanders outside the three-mile limit. They were to pay light dues and to report at Customs. There could be local modifications if they were mutually agreed upon.[114] In some respects, this was a better arrangement than in 1906, but the Bond

* Elgin to MacGregor, tgms., August 21, 30, 1907 (*Further Correspondence,* Cd. 3765, 160–62). The first American vessel did not, in fact, arrive on the west coast until October 5.

government continued to insist (with reason) that given the "honourable compromise" that had been offered, it was unnecessary and insulting.

Worse was to come.

THE ORDER IN COUNCIL

On September 9, the government learned that, since there had been no formal acceptance of the modus by the colony, it would be enforced by an imperial Order in Council issued under 59 Geo. III, cap. 38 (1819).[115] This was done (admittedly with some reluctance) in order to avoid prosecutions similar to the Crane and Dubois case, the British having eventually decided against imperial legislation.[116] Colonial Office predictions of large-scale prosecutions in the future (and even the "risk of war with the United States") constituted exaggerated commentary, and the Order in Council was a very heavy-handed intervention.[117] Specifically, it provided that legal process could not be served against Newfoundland citizens on board American vessels, which were to be immune from seizure.

Predictably enough, Bond and his government were outraged. Quite justifiably, they were also unimpressed by the Colonial Office argument that given the "sacrifices" made by Britain in 1904 to obtain an end to the French Shore treaties and the impending arbitration, it was entitled to the colony's co-operation.[118] Bond was convinced (wrongly, as it turned out) that both the modus vivendi and the Order in Council would weaken the colony's case at The Hague. He also continued to claim that the Order, which he thought violated both international law and the colony's constitutional rights, could not suspend colonial laws that had already received Royal assent.[119] MacGregor published the Order on September 24 (a delay had been agreed to in the hope that the colony would come to terms).[120] At the same time, there were public meetings at several locations on the west coast where resolutions were passed supporting the colonial government in general terms, but asking that all restrictions on the sale of herring should be removed. Some also added that men did not want to have to ship outside the three-mile limit. The opposition press claimed, probably accurately, that the events had been arranged by the government, which agreed to the requests.[121] It was, in effect, proposing to put into force the "honourable compromise" that had been rejected in Washington and London, and to maintain at least theoretical control over the fishery and inshore waters.

At this point, Governor MacGregor discreetly intervened. He probably met A.B. Alexander when the *Gresham* called at St. John's in mid-September,[122] and later urged him to persuade the Americans to purchase herring rather than hire Newfoundlanders as crew, since this would avoid trouble and friction.[123] MacGregor also spoke to Inspector Joseph O'Reilly, emphasizing the need to be conciliatory,[124] and advised HMS *Brilliant* and Captain Anstruther to keep a distance.[125] His hope was that Alexander and O'Reilly could work out a local arrangement that suited all parties, and that is what happened.

When the season opened in mid-October, there was considerable uncertainty on the west coast. The Gloucester vessels expected, as before, to catch their cargoes with Newfoundland crews shipped outside the three-mile limit. Local fishermen were reluctant to go outside the bays in small boats, and wanted to sell directly to the Americans. The agents of some American owners considered taking on crews at Sydney. They were all unwilling to have their vessels enter at Customs and pay duty on the large amount of gear they had brought with them. O'Reilly let it be known that free licences would be available to allow American vessels to buy and sell herring. He talked to the agents, who in turn contacted the owners. On October 17, Gloucester vessels began entering at Customs. They paid duties on surplus nets and gear, which were then sold to local fishermen. The price for herring was set at $1.50 a barrel salted and $2 frozen. Only two American vessels actually fished under the modus—the other fifty-five in effect became trading vessels.* This arrangement seems

* O'Reilly to MacGregor, conf., October 22, 1907 (LAC, Elgin fonds, Newfoundland, 169–72). O'Reilly said the deal had needed "very delicate handling (Alexander to MacGregor, private, November 17, 1907, and encl. in MacGregor to Elgin, secret and personal, November 26, 1907, LAC, Elgin fonds, Newfoundland, 192). See also MacGregor to Elgin, tgms., October 18, 21, and 22, 1907 (CO 194/269, 346, 497, and 531); Macgregor to Elgin, conf., December 23, 1907 (CO 194/270, 229); and "Report of the Fishery Protection Service . . . 1907, by Joseph O'Reilly, Special Commissioner . . ." (*JHA* 1908, Appendix, 184–89).

to have satisfied everyone, though the US government was not happy that the fishery was effectively under local control. There was no British naval vessel present and the *Gresham* left early.[126] In all, eighty-nine vessels participated in the fishery. The catch, and its value, were lower than in the previous two years.[127]

CONSTITUTIONAL DISCUSSION

Bond now argued that since the temporary agreement and the Order in Council had become irrelevant, they should be withdrawn.[128] The British government, however, held that unilateral cancellation was impossible and that a formal agreement of some kind would have to be put in place.[129] Bond decided to appeal to the prime ministers of the other self-governing colonies. The most important of these, from Newfoundland's point of view, was Laurier, to whom Bond explained his views on the modus and the Order in Council.[130] Laurier referred the matter to his Minister of Justice, A.B. Aylesworth, who responded that, in his opinion, Newfoundland had "no constitutional ground of complaint" since the British government had the power to make the regulations in question as they applied to Newfoundland. But Aylesworth held that no such action could be taken in Canadian waters affected by the 1818 treaty, given the powers granted to the Canadian government by the British North America Act. Laurier passed on the opinion, urging Bond to concentrate on preparations for the arbitration.[131]

Bond and James M. Kent (who had become Minister of Justice after Morris's resignation) did not accept Aylesworth's reasoning, but there was nothing more to be done.[132] At the Foreign Office, Sir Louis Mallet chortled that "Sir R. Bond has been well snubbed."[133] From Australia, Arthur Deakin wrote that he was not sufficiently well informed to make a public statement, "though I strongly question the manner in which your Colony has been treated."[134] The other colonial premiers were similarly reluctant to become involved. Bond was on his own.

Neither the modus nor the Order in Council was lifted, and Bond remained angry and resentful. MacGregor reported, negatively as always, that "his present frame of mind is such that I am not sure that to damage the King's government would not give him greater pleasure than to secure the

Bond-Hay Convention." Probably to show his discontent, Bond boycotted a Government House levee and dinner held on November 9 to mark the King's birthday, leaving for Whitbourne by the morning train. It was an action that gave offence and was roundly criticized.[135] His "frame of mind" may also explain why the government seemed to be doing little or nothing to draw up draft terms of reference for the fisheries arbitration. This was causing frustration elsewhere, especially since officials in London wanted the arbitration to be a colonial enterprise.[136] Bond did not like working with Canada, however; Laurier regarded the fisheries question as primarily a Newfoundland dispute and thought that Bond—whom he did not want to offend—should take the lead. Thus Laurier was scrupulously polite; he offered assistance and waited to hear from St. John's.[137] The situation did not change until January 1908, when Bond finally sent Laurier draft terms of reference, the same month that the Americans began drafting their questions for the court. By the end of May, both drafts—American and British—were ready, after extensive correspondence. It then remained for the diplomats and politicians to reconcile the two documents, which diverged in some important respects.[138] A formal arbitration agreement was not arrived at until late January 1909, by which time Bond was no longer in office.

It was obvious that Bond had alienated official opinion in Ottawa and London and that there was no hope of his reciprocity treaty passing the US Senate. His attempt at retaliation had failed miserably, developing into a legalistic debate over the meaning of the 1818 treaty and the colony's constitutional rights. Bond had been forced to agree to arbitration and to allow the American herring fishery to carry on without disturbance, and he had been humiliated by the modus and the Order in Council. P.T. McGrath was not the only commentator to point out that the country was apathetic on the fisheries issue[139]—even Archbishop Howley lamented the absence of the "old time spirit of patriotism[140]—and that Bond was neglecting bread-and-butter issues. "Our noble Premier has been too busy ballyragging the Gloucester fishermen to give any time to producing any record for himself and party," wrote a correspondent to the *Daily News*.[141]

The last act came during the legislative session of 1908. Politically divided though it was, the Assembly showed a united front concerning the way the colony had been treated by the British government. Tabling the official correspondence, Bond explained why his government had refused to accept the modus and the Order in Council. Both were unnecessary, he said, and interfered with colonial legislation that had received Royal assent. As for the Order, it was invalid and ultra vires, since concessions made in the modus were new rights to which the 1819 statute (59 Geo. III cap. 38, 1819) did not apply. Had it been enforced, he would have taken legal action.[142] Bond did not speak in the debate on the resolutions, which asked the legislature to approve the government's refusal to consent and requested the cancellation of the modus and the Order. Instead, the debate was led by William F. Lloyd, an English-born lawyer and editor of the *Evening Telegram* who, though serving his first term in the Assembly, was emerging as a capable Liberal member.[143] Lloyd avoided partisan attacks and concentrated on issues of principle, echoing Bond's arguments. "Colonial home rule" had to be respected, and the Order represented "a species of martial law." The Crane and Dubois case had shown the weakness of the British position—why had there not been an appeal to the Privy Council?—and the Order was not only insulting and humiliating but prejudiced the colony's case at The Hague. Sir Edward Morris congratulated Lloyd, adding that he had never understood "why on every point the British government had made such a complete giveaway to the United States of the case of the colony." The resolutions passed unanimously.*

All the same, Bond and the Liberal party had been severely damaged by the confrontation over reciprocity. There is no question that the colony had been bullied—principally by the British government, but also by that of the United States. Bond's stubborn attempts to assert and uphold Newfoundland's right to regulate its fisheries were no doubt admirable, deriving from a fundamental belief that, within the British Empire, the

---

* Assembly debate, January 31, 1908 (*Evening Telegram*, February 14, 15, and 17, 1908, and *JHA* 1908, 40–41). It cannot be ascertained if any MHAs absented themselves. The Legislative Council passed the resolutions without a division (*JLC* 1908, 50–53).

colony should independently regulate all its internal affairs. But this was the era when the status of self-governing colonies was still emerging and their subordination to British foreign policy was widely assumed. For Bond and his government to question the general trend of imperial policy toward the United States was self-defeating and ultimately humiliating. It was also detrimental politically. Eyes were turning toward Sir Edward Morris, a moderate (backed by the governor), who might be able to lead the colony into safer and more co-operative pastures.

NOTES

1 Joyce, *Sir William MacGregor*, 300, 303, and 313.

2 See Hiller, "The 1904 Anglo-French Newfoundland Fisheries Convention," 82–98.

3 Minute by Ommanney, January 23, 1905 (CO 194/256, 84); Lyttleton to MacGregor, secret, February 23, 1905 (CO 194/256, 89).

4 MacGregor to Lyttleton, tgm., March 18, 1905, and reply, tgm., March 27, 1905 (CO 194/256, 311 and 343).

5 MacGregor to Lyttleton, April 29, 1904 (CO 194/256, 481).

6 The text can be found at http://en.wikisource.org/wiki/Treaty of 1818.

7 FO to CO, conf., December 2, 1904 (CO 194/255, 829).

8 Minute of Council, December 28, 1904; encl. in MacGregor to Lyttleton, secret, December 31, 1904 (CO 194/254, 521ff.).

9 *Evening Telegram*, March 23 and 24, 1905.

10 Minute by Cox, April 13, 1905 (CO 194/259, 564).

11 Speech on second reading, April 7, 1905 (offprint in RBP 7.11.019).

12 *Daily News*, April 11, 1905.

13 Cashin in Assembly, April 7, 1905 (*Evening Telegram*, April 12, 1905).

14 *Evening Telegram*, April 10, 1905, and *Daily News*, April 11, 1905.

15 Morine in Assembly, April 7 and 12, 1905 (*Evening Telegram*, April 11, 14, 15, and 17, 1905).

16 For example, Robert Thorburn to Bond, March 22 and 25, 1905 (RBP 7.11.010).

17 Jessup, *Elihu Root*, 2:84–85—an adulatory biography.

18 A.A. Adee to Durand, July 25, 1905, encl. in Durand to MacGregor, July 27, 1905 (PANL, GN 1/3/A, file 152).

19 MacGregor to Lyttleton, September 18, 1905, and a Minute by Davis, October 3, 1902 (CO 194/257, 294–95).

20 MacGregor to Lyttleton, tgm., October 5, 1905; MacGregor to Lyttleton, conf., October 7, 1905 (CO 194/257, 375 and 390).

21 MacGregor, *Report on the Trade and Commerce*, 185.

22 "Annual Report of the Department of Marine and Fisheries . . . 1905," *JHA* 1906, Appendix, 147.

23 *Evening Telegram*, October 13, 1905, and *Daily News*, October 18, 20, and 24, 1905; MacGregor to Lyttleton, conf., October 23, 1905 (CO 194/257, 459).

24 Capt. H.T. Hibbert to Paget, December 26, 1905, encl. in Admiralty to CO February 21, 1906 (CO 194/264, 278).

25 MacGregor to Elgin, conf., January 1, 1906 (CO 194/262, 6).

26 Root to Durand, October 19, 1905 (CO 194/260, 591); Tansill, *Canadian-American Relations*, 100–101.

27 Durand to Lansdowne, October 19, 1905, encl. in FO to CO, October 31, 1905 (CO 194/260, 588).

28 Law Officers to CO, October 24, 1905; Lyttleton to MacGregor, tgm., October 25, 1905; MacGregor to Lyttleton, tgm., October 26, 1905; Lyttleton to MacGregor, tgm., October 27, 1905; and Law Officers to CO, November 21, 1905 (CO 194/261, 134 and 138; 194/257, 498–500; 194/261, 140).

29 MacGregor to Lyttleton, tgm., secret and personal, October 30, 1905; tgm., October 30, 1905 (CO 194/257, 599 and 572).

30 MacGregor to Lyttleton, conf., December 4 and 13, 1905 (CO 194/258, 168 and 195).

31 Minute by Davis, February 8, 1906 (CO 194/262, 64); CO to FO, January 24, 1906 (FO 371/184, 60).

32 Hyam, *Elgin and Churchill*, 45.

33 Neary, "Grey, Bryce," 358.

34 Miller, "Grey, Albert Henry George, 4th Earl Grey," *DCB* 14:439–41.

35 MacGregor to Elgin, tgm., April 7, 1906 (CO 194/262, 263A).

36 Elgin to MacGregor, tgm., May 1, 1906 (CO 194/262, 270).

37 Elgin to MacGregor, tgm., May 1, 1906 (CO 194/262, 273; PANL GN 1/4/2, Box 2).

38 Minute by Davis, May 25, 1906 (CO 194/262, 419).

39 Minute by Davis, May 25, 1906 (CO 194/262, 419); CO to FO, June 8, 1906 (FO 371/184, 330).

40 Undated Minutes, June 1906, FO to CO, June 16, 1906 (FO 371/184, 324, and 349).

41 Tansill, *Canadian-American Relations*, 100–101.

42 Tansill, *Canadian-American Relations*, 104–5.

43 Reeves "The Fortune Bay Dispute," and Korneski, *Conflicted Colony*, 15–46.

44 Tansill, *Canadian-American Relations*, 105–8.

45 Tansill, *Canadian-American Relations*, 108; "Memorandum by Mr. Whitelaw Reid, July 11, 1906; Minute by Grey, July 12, 1906 (FO 371/184, 392 and 400).

46 Minutes by Grey and others; FO to CO, July 30, 1906 (FO 371/184, 458 and 486, and CO 194/265, 338).

47 MacGregor to Elgin, secret, July 9, 1906 (CO 194/263, 15).

48 *Evening Telegram*, July 23, 24, 25, and 27, 1906.

49 Grey to Laurier, August 8, 1906 (LAC, Grey fonds (MG 27), 12:3613).

50 Grey to Elgin, August 16, 1906 (LAC, Grey fonds, 12:3635).

51 Grey to Laurier, August 8, 1906 (LAC, Grey fonds, 12:3613).

52 MacGregor to Elgin, tgm., August 14, 1906 (*Foreign Relations of the United States* [*FRUS*], 1906, 1:719) and MacGregor to Elgin, tgm., August 19, 1906 (*FRUS*, 1906:1, 721–24, 725–29).

53 Minute by H.B. Cox, August 22, 1906 (CO 194/263, 77).

54 Minute by Gorst, August 21, 1906 (FO 371/184, 653).

55 Elgin to MacGregor, tgm., September 3, 1906 (CO 194/263, 80); Reid to Root, tgm., September 6, 1906 (*FRUS* 1906:1, 697); and FO to CO, September 7, 1906 (CO 194/265, 412).

56 Reid to Grey, October 6, 1906, and enclosures (*FRUS* 1906:1, 701).

57 MacGregor to Elgin, tgm.. September 15, 1906; tgm., October 12, 1906 (CO 194/263, 219 and 325).

58 Elgin to MacGregor, tgm., September 19, 1906, and tgm., October 16, 1906 (CO 194/263, 221 and 327. See the Minute by Davis, October 13, 1906, in CO 194/263, 323.

59 MacGregor to Elgin, conf., October 13, 1906 (CO 194/263, 330).

60 On the American view, see Tansill, *Canadian-American Relations*, 112, note 81.

61 MacGregor to Elgin, tgm., October 26, 1906 (CO 194/263, 387); Bond to E.H. Coles, tgm., October 19, 1906; Coles to Bond, tgm., October 24, 1906 (PANL, GN 1/4/2, box 2).

62 Law Officers to CO, October 20, 1906 (CO 194/266, 153).

63 MacGregor to Elgin, tgm., November 8, 1906 (CO 194/263, 587).

64 MacGregor to Elgin, secret, November 8, 1906 (CO 194/263, 591).

65 MacGregor to Bond, November 6, 1906 (PANL, GN 1/4/2, box 2).

66 Morris to MacGregor, November 6, 1906 (PANL, GN 1/4/2, box 2).

67 Howley to MacGregor, November 22, 1906 (PANL, GN 1/4/2, box 2); MacGregor to Elgin, tgm., November 17, 1906 (CO 194/264, 27).

68 MacGregor to Elgin, November 22, 1906, and internal Minutes (CO 194/264, 112).

69 MacGregor to Elgin, conf., November 3, 1906, and internal Minutes (CO 194/263, 535). See also FO 371/185, 362.

70 Morris to MacGregor, October 26, 1906, enclosing a report from O'Reilly, October 23, 1906 (PANL, GN 1/4/2, box 2, 1906).

71 Anstruther to Admiralty, October 24, 1906 (copy in PANL, GN 1/4/2, box 2).

72 Minute of Council, November 7, 1904 (PANL, GN 1/4/2, box 2); MacGregor to Elgin, secret, November 8, 1906 (CO 194/263, 591).

73 MacGregor to Elgin, tgm., November 19, 1906; tgm., November 23, 1906; and tgm., private and confidential, November 26, 1906 (CO 194/264, 62, 125, and 146).

74 Law Officers to CO, October 20, 1906; November 30, 1906 (CO 194/266, 153 and 266).

75 Minute by Churchill, November 22, 1906 (CO 194/264, 61).

76 MacGregor to Elgin, February 1, 1907 (CO 194/267, 7).

77 *JHA* 1907, 11–12.

78 *Evening Telegram*, February 13, 1907.

79 Morison in Assembly, February 13, 1907 (*Evening Telegram*, February 21, 1907).

80 Cashin in Assembly, February 13, 1907 (*Evening Telegram*, February 15, 1907).

81 *Evening Telegram*, February 26, 1907, and *JHA* 1907, 10–14.

82 Howley in the *Evening Telegram*, January 14, 1907; Prowse in the *Evening Telegram*, January 15 and 18, 1907; and MacGregor to Elgin, conf., January 21, 1907 (CO 194/267, 43). See also *Evening Telegram*, March 2, 1907.

83 *Daily News*, March 27, 1907.

84 Extract in *Free Press*, October 8, 1907.

85 MacGregor to Grey, private, April 2, 1907 (LAC, Grey fonds 50784).

86 *Evening Telegram*, April 4 and 10, 1907.

87 MacGregor to Elgin, secret and personal, April 2, 1907 (CO 194/268, 81 and 84).

88 MacGregor to Elgin, secret and personal, April 1, 1907 (CO 194/268, 4).

89 Minutes of Proceedings of the Colonial Conference, 1907, 143, 213, 304, 470; Kendle, *Colonial and Imperial Conferences*, 83–106; Hyam, *Elgin and Churchill*, 317–42; and Hyam, "The British Empire in the Edwardian Era," 55–57.

90 *Evening Telegram*, April 29 and May 17, 1907.

91 "Notes of Interview between Lord Elgin, Sir E. Grey, and Sir R. Bond. Also present, Mr. Churchill, Mr. Hurst, Mr. Cox, etc.," May 11, 1907 (CO 194/270, 569–75).
92 MacGregor to Elgin, tgm., May 8, 1907 (CO 194/268, 294).
93 Statement to Reuters, printed in the *Evening Telegram*, May 21, 1907.
94 Copy in RBP 7.13.006.
95 Bond to Laurier, May 11, 1907; E.J. Lucaire (PS) to Bond, May 13, 1907 (RBP 7.13.005).
96 Laurier to Grey, September 25, 1907 (LAC, Grey fonds, 2:532).
97 Bond to Elgin, May 13, 1907 (RBP 7.13.005).
98 Bond to Churchill, June 7, 1907 (RBP 7.13.007).
99 The report is printed in the *Evening Telegram*, May 17, 1907.
100 *Hansard* (online), May 15, 1907.
101 Bond to Hopwood, May 16, 1907 (RBP 7.13.007).
102 Hopwood to Bond, May 17 and 21, 1907; Churchill to Bond, June 6, 1907 (RBP 7.13.007).
103 Elgin to Grey, private, May 17, 1907 (CO 194/270, 579; FO 371/388, 74); Hyam, *Elgin and Churchill,* 296.
104 Bond to Elgin, June 10 and 15, 1907; Elgin to Bond, private, June 18, 1907 (CO 194/270, 600, 603, and 614; RBP 7.13.005).
105 Grey to Whitelaw Reid (US ambassador), June 20, 1907, encl. in Elgin to MacGregor, July 19, 1907 (*Further Correspondence,* Cd. 3765, 147–51; RBP 7.13.005).
106 Reid to Grey, July 12, 1907 (*Further Correspondence,* Cd. 3765, 151–53); Tansill, *Canadian-American Relations*, 115.
107 Elgin to MacGregor, tgm., August 10, 1907 (*Further Correspondence,* Cd. 3765, 157).
108 MacGregor to Elgin, personal, August 18, 1907 (LAC, Elgin fonds, Newfoundland, 142).
109 Memorandum to the Executive Council, August 13, 1907 (RBP 7.13.005).
110 Bond to MacGregor, August 14, 1907 (RBP 7.13.005).
111 See Chapter 10.
112 MacGregor to Elgin, tgms., August 14 and 21, 1907 (*Further Correspondence,* Cd. 3765, 157–59).
113 Minute by Keith, September 2, 1907 (CO 194/269, 136).
114 Elgin to MacGregor, tgm., September 7, 1907 (*Further Correspondence,* Cd. 3765, 165–66).

115 Elgin to MacGregor, tgms., [?] September 9 and 11, 1907 (*Further Correspondence,* Cd. 3765, 165–68).
116 Minute by Hopwood, August 15, 1907 (CO 194/266, 217).
117 H.B. Cox to the Lord Chancellor, June 21, 1907 (CO 194/270, 629).
118 Elgin to MacGregor, September 9, 1907 (*Further Correspondence,* Cd. 3765, 165–67).
119 MacGregor to Elgin, tgm., September 20, 1907 (CO 194/269, 262).
120 MacGregor to Elgin, tgms., September 22 and 24, 1907 (CO 194/269, 309 and 312).
121 MacGregor to Elgin, tgm., September 25, 1907 (CO 194/269, 362); *Evening Telegram*, September 25, 27, and 28, 1907; *Daily News*, September 25, 28, and 30, 1907.
122 Strongly hinted at in MacGregor to Elgin, personal, September 15, 1907 (LAC, Elgin fonds, Newfoundland, 153–54).
123 MacGregor to Alexander, private and personal, October 5, 1907 (PANL, GN 1/4/2, box 3).
124 MacGregor to Elgin, tgm., secret and personal, October 15, 1907; MacGregor to Elgin, personal, October 25, 1907 (LAC, Elgin fonds, Newfoundland, 82 and 164).
125 MacGregor to CO, personal, tgm., October 4, 1907 (PANL, GN 1/4/2, box 3).
126 Bryce to Grey, conf., November 1, 1907, encl. in FO to CO, November 14, 1907 (CO 194/271, 534).
127 MacGregor to Elgin, January 11, 1908 (CO 194/272, 7).
128 MacGregor to Elgin, tgm., November 1, 1907 (CO 194/270, 15).
129 Minutes by Davis, Cox, and Elgin, November 4 and 5, 1907 (CO 194/270, 11–14).
130 Bond to Laurier, September 26, 1907 (copy in LAC, Laurier fonds 129710–13).
131 Aylesworth to Laurier, October 14, 1907; Laurier to Bond, October 23, 1907 (LAC, Laurier fonds, 129737–45).
132 Kent to Bond, November 13, 1907, encl. in Bond to Laurier, November 15, 1907 (LAC, Laurier fonds, 132033–38). For Kent, see *ENL* 3:167.
133 FO 371/390, 300.
134 Deakin to Bond, November 26, 1907 (RBP 7.13.005).
135 MacGregor to Elgin, secret and personal, November 26, 1907 (LAC Elgin fonds, Newfoundland, 188–89); *Free Press*, November 12, 1907; *Daily News*, November 12, 1907.
136 Gluek, "Programmed Diplomacy," 53.

137 Grey to James Bryce, July 29, 1907 (FO 800/331 [Bryce papers], 60); Laurier to Bond, November 30, 1907 (LAC, Grey fonds, 2:617); MacGregor to Grey, private and confidential, October 12, 1907 (LAC, Grey fonds, 5143).

138 Gluek, "Programmed Diplomacy," 53–57.

139 Letter in *Evening Telegram*, October 29, 1907.

140 *Evening Telegram*, October 7, 1907.

141 "An Englishman" to the *Daily News*, October 31, 1907.

142 Bond in Assembly, January 30, 1908 (*Evening Telegram*, January 31, 1908).

143 *ENL* 3:350.

CHAPTER TEN

The Second Term: Domestic Issues, 1905–1908

Though the second Bond administration was necessarily preoccupied with the fisheries confrontation with the United States and Britain, domestic affairs were not altogether neglected. After all, this was the essential small change of local politics. Most voters were not interested in the international ramifications of bait politics and treaty interpretation, but they were concerned about how their households could survive. The St. John's of 1906, for instance, seemed more preoccupied by the temporary cancellation of the noonday gun fired from Signal Hill on Sundays, leading to some of M.A. Devine's most memorable verses.* Bond's main preoccupations were not widely shared overall. By 1908 (an election year), the hostility of the Reid Newfoundland Company and the British government toward Bond made regime change—to use a contemporary phrase—probable, if not definite.

The government's domestic policies showed no great divergence from those of its first term. The feuds with the Reid and the Anglo-American telegraph companies continued, as did encouragement to the nascent pulp and paper industry. But what came to be known as "Bond's fads" became more prominent, providing ammunition for a growing opposition that eventually centred on Sir Edward Morris. By 1908, the Bond government was no longer facing a disorganized and elderly group of opponents, as it had in 1904.

---

* They were entitled "The Sunday Gun." The ban was apparently requested by sermon-preaching clergy and did not last long.

THE GRAND FALLS DEAL

Probably the most important initiative of the Liberal government was the newsprint mill to be built on the Exploits River at Grand Falls. The deal had been largely settled before the 1904 election, but necessary legislation endorsing the government's contract with the Harmsworth brothers (through the Anglo-Newfoundland Development Company [AND], their subsidiary), was introduced in 1905.[1] Agreements with the government and various private parties, including the reluctant and hostile Reid Newfoundland Company, provided that AND would control 2,300 square miles (just under 6,000 square kilometres) of timber lands through a ninety-nine-year renewable lease that included mineral, water, and timber rights, at a rental of $2 per square mile. There was no royalty due on wood cut for pulp, and there were other tax concessions. For Bond and Morris, who saw eye to eye on this matter, it was a justifiably generous package. They felt the colony would be amply compensated by the opening of the interior to settlement and industry. Bond spoke of

> a forest wilderness transmuted into a thickly inhabited territory. The mineral deposits of the interior would be brought to light and applied to the purposes of the arts and services of men. . . . God and nature has richly endowed this land with resources of various kinds. We have vast stretches of agricultural land, forests and immense water powers. It was not intended by Providence that those lands should forever continue to bring forth nothing but rank and useless vegetation or those rivers . . . [to] flow through solitudes.[2]

The scheme also proved that the effort and expense of building the railway had been worthwhile. As Morris said, "It was really the first fruits and justification of the policy of building the railway."[3]

The opposition subjected the agreement to fierce criticism, arguing that it was too generous, too lavish, and created a huge monopoly. The area would be "kept under padlock as a howling wilderness forever," said Morine. "They could pay far too much for their development and were in too much of a hurry."[4] The government majority saw the bill through the Assembly but there was trouble in the Legislative Council, where there was some sympathy for the popular opposition that had emerged. There was surprise that Bond, the great foe of the Reids, would endorse a concession of such magnitude, and beyond that, fear of a crisis similar to that which had erupted over the Reid contracts and another legacy of expense and political bitterness. Unease was most prevalent among the mercantile and professional classes and, of course, Bond's political adversaries took advantage of it. They were probably behind the Citizen's Protective Association, formed to protest the agreement. Whiteway turned up and, predictably, condemned the deal as "a curse."* The Association petitioned the Legislative Council, but thanks to its Liberal majority—there had been four new appointments—the bill survived. There were plenty of amendments though, and third reading was delayed for over two weeks while changes were negotiated.

Grand Falls, ca. 1909. (Courtesy of Bryan Marsh and the History of Central Newfoundland website)

* *Daily News*, May 11 and 13, 1905. Another critic was William Coaker, who had campaigned against Bond in 1904. See his letter in the *Free Press*, June 20, 1905.

The agitation had its impact. When Bond began talks with the English papermaker Albert E. Reed about a development at Bishop's Falls (also on the Exploits River), the final terms were less generous than those awarded to AND. This proved to be a far smaller enterprise anyway, and Reed eventually undertook to build a pulp mill only. The deal was not completed until just before the 1908 election, thanks to the delaying tactics of the Reid Newfoundland Co., whose relations with the Bond government continued to deteriorate.*

ANGLO AND THE REIDS

Early in February 1905, the result of the arbitration regarding the Reid Company's telegraph claim became public. The government had been stung by the amount claimed and it was outraged by the award of $1,503,100 with interest at 3 per cent since October 31, 1903.[5] "There is a most intense feeling here against the Telegraph Award," Bond wrote, "and the bitterness against the Reid Company is rather increasing than otherwise. One cannot see any measure of justice in their receiving a million and a half of dollars for a property that they got for nothing and was paid $60,000 by the late Government to take over."[6] With the company pressing for payment, the government urgently cabled London for advice—was there any way that the award could be appealed or set aside? The Law Officers thought not,[7] so there was nothing for it but to pay. Morine had acted for the company; he was no doubt behind the statement in the *Daily News* that the colony's case had been badly handled by Morris (who appeared for the government) and the Executive—in fact, the case had been "given away."† (The *Free Press* claimed that Morris was attacked by some of his government colleagues but had soon climbed back "on top."[8])

A special loan act authorized the government to borrow £340,500, most of which was to pay the telegraph award, but approximately £68,000 of which was earmarked for the extension of the government's telegraph system. More explicitly, this would fund a government cable across the

---

* Hiller, "Origins," 60–64, and Philip Sykes, *Albert E. Reed*, 105–12, 149–51. The mill was sold to AND during the First World War.

† *Daily News*, February 22, 1905. I am not aware of any analysis of this arbitration.

Cabot Strait that would connect with the Commercial Cable Company's network on the mainland.[9] This was the latest move in Bond's campaign against Anglo. The government created a division of the Post Office specifically to handle all local telegraphs, bar the rights still held by Anglo and the Reid Company, but it was prepared to allow foreign business to be handled by a private company if fair terms could be arranged. Discussions with Anglo broke down. During the summer of 1905, the government built a competing line from St. John's to Whitbourne. In 1902 it had built one from Whitbourne to Port aux Basques that connected with the rest of the government network, which had reduced telegraph rates by 60 per cent. With the new cable across the Strait, the colony would be freed from reliance on Anglo, said Bond.* To remove any doubts about the government's power to purchase the Anglo lines, a further Telegraph Act provided the necessary authority.†

This was not all. The government decided to impose a special tax on coal used for non-domestic purposes, and placed taxes on telegraph, telephone, and express companies. Once again, complained Morine, Bond was going after the Anglo and Reid companies—"the continued object of the dishonesty and malice of the government."[10] Anglo protested to Governor MacGregor and to the Colonial Office, asking for disallowance.‡ Bond's counter-argument—that the legislation was non-discriminatory since it also applied to the Marconi Company of Canada, which had agreed to establish stations in southern Labrador—was accepted, and officials did not think it unreasonable that Anglo should contribute to the

* Bond in Assembly, May 18 and June 9, 1905 (*Evening Telegram*, May 23 and June 15, 1905); *Daily News*, February 4, 1905. Bond raised the question of imperial assistance for the Cabot Strait cable to no avail (MacGregor to Lyttleton, conf., January 9, 1905, CO 194/256, 30; *ENL* 5:346).

† Loan (Telegraph Services) Act, 5 Ed. VII c.2. The Commercial Cable Company diverted a transatlantic cable to Quidi Vidi in 1909.

‡ Anglo-American Telegraph Co. to CO, June 8, 1905, and MacGregor to Lyttleton, tgm., June 9, 1905 (CO 194/257, 137, and 194/261, 331). Anglo also protested the Cabot Strait cable.

revenue after a fifty-year monopoly.* The Reid Company petitioned the King and the Colonial Office about the coal and express company taxes, suspecting (with reason) that they were levied to help compensate the colony for the telegraph award, but again with no result.[11]

More immediately and locally, the Reids decided to challenge the existing status quo. In the wake of the telegraph award, and presumably with the consent of his sons, R.G. Reid offered to sell the railway and steamship operations to the colony for $3 million, retaining the company's other assets. The sale would remove friction, he said, and allow the company to concentrate on economic development. He wanted an answer in less than a month.[12] Bond refused to be rushed, insisted that the sale should include the dry dock, and reminded Reid of his perspective: Bond had thought that the 1901 contract would mark a new beginning—especially, he alleged, because Reid had said at the time that if the contract was satisfactory, he would not pursue a telegraph claim. The government had been conciliatory, but what had happened? It had received the "most insulting letters from your Firm" and faced a "studied effort" to resist reasonable requests.

Reid was not moved. He refused to transfer the dock and defended the arbitrations, but offered to sell all the company's "franchises and agreements" for $9 million. The government turned him down because of the expense.[13] This may have been prudent, since the railway alone was losing over $100,000 annually.[14] The Reids would be staying in Newfoundland, it seemed, but some accommodation would have to be found—and that was unlikely if Bond remained in charge.

THE REIDS AND ALFRED MORINE

If reciprocity with the United States was the first of Bond's obsessions, the second and third were the Anglo and Reid companies—and in all three cases he adopted confrontation as his modus operandi. He sidelined Anglo effectively, but the Reid Company remained an influential and powerful fixture. Given R.G. Reid's health problems, the firm was

* Bond to MacGregor, July 27, 1905, encl. in MacGregor to Lyttleton, conf. (CO 194/257, 223). It did not help the company's case locally that Morine was its solicitor.

controlled by its general manager, the eldest son, William D. Reid.[15] In 1905, W.D. began a campaign against Morine, the company's solicitor and long-time defender, and Morine's brother Horace, who had been general passenger agent since 1898. Whether W.D. Reid was working mainly on his own or in collaboration with his father and brothers cannot be ascertained; nor can it be proved conclusively that his moves were part of a long-term strategy to create a pro-Reid opposition party that could defeat Bond. Both suppositions seem likely, however. It must have been clear to the Reids that despite all his talents, Morine was in many ways a political liability. This was also obvious to the now-anti-Bond William Coaker, who argued both that Morine had to go and that there should be a new political party.*

Horace Morine was sacked for disobeying an order, though he claimed the real reason was his opposition to an increase in the railway tariff proposed by W.D. (who had allegedly said that if he was going to be soaked by the new coal duty, he would soak the passengers†). Getting rid of Alfred Morine was more problematic, since he had signed an agreement with R.G. Reid in 1899 to act as his solicitor for twelve years, with a generous salary. If Reid breached the agreement, he would have to pay Morine's salary to the end of the contract's specified term.‡ So Morine had to be forced or bullied into resignation. W.D. went about this so obviously that Morine complained it was "the town talk."[16]

---

* Letter to the *Free Press*, November 28, 1905. Coaker's letter foreshadowed future priorities—there should be prohibition, non-denominational schools, civil service reform, redistribution of seats, and single-member districts. And St. John's had to be taught that it contained only one-eighth of Newfoundland's population and depended entirely on the outports.

† *Daily News*, September 8 and November 4, 1905; *Evening Telegram*, December 13 through 24, 1905. Horace Morine's suit for a month's pay in lieu of notice failed.

‡ The agreement (November 14, 1899) is in PANL, RNCP, file 272. The salary was $8,000 for the first two years and $10,000 thereafter. Morine had acted for the Reids from at least early 1898, working on a retainer of $5,000 a year for five years (W.D. Reid evidence in the *Daily News* case, *Evening Telegram*, February 17, 1906).

Morine understood what was up, and told R.G. Reid that he wanted an amicable separation and would leave Newfoundland "if it be made worth my while."[17] Even so, W.D. made an extraordinary series of vicious attacks on Morine's legal work.[18] In a single memorandum (October 4, 1905) about a single case (Meaney vs. Reid Newfoundland Co.), Morine was accused of neglect of duty, absence from the office, undue devotion to "angling and driving," and sacrificing Reid interests in his "desire and eagerness for political fame." His payment was "far in excess of your actual worth," and he had used information obtained as Reid solicitor "in your unwise and nonsensical attacks upon the Government." He was "a man entirely void of gratitude." There can be no doubt that Morine was surprised, hurt, and offended by this onslaught, but knowing that his association with the Reids was at an end, he replied in kind. If there were bad relations with the government, it was due to W.D.'s hostility and his "notorious disregard of the rights of God and man." He had quite deliberately created problems as "the best way to get the Government to their knees." W.D. had set himself "to the task of annoying the Government, especially the Premier, attempting to bully him, as you attempt to bully everybody." Then he turned to the Bowring steamship contract: "Your obstinate stupidity . . . forced this disaster on the Company."* Charges against himself he rejected as "grossly defamatory." It is significant that the Reids' Montreal lawyer could not find any evidence of negligence on Morine's part, though he thought Morine could not sustain the argument that he was the lawyer for R.G. Reid personally, rather than for the company.[19]

Morine may possibly have held the high ground in these legal matters, but details of half-hidden political machinations could well emerge—good reason, he felt, for the Reids to back off. But they decided to brazen it out; hence the high-profile case of the Reid Newfoundland Company vs. Alfred Morine, Henry Y. Mott, and the News Publishing Company. This was a tangled affair. In 1898, Morine and Reid had concluded that J.A. Robinson, then the proprietor of the *Daily News* and a Winter supporter, might not be as faithful a friend as they needed. It was therefore

* The *Daily News* (April 20, 1906) estimated that the Bowring contract cost the company about $54,000 a year.

arranged that Robinson would sell the paper to Henry Mott* for $7,500—$3,500 down, the rest in annual instalments. W.D. provided the down payment. It was understood by all parties that the *News* would support the 1898 railway contract and Reid interests in general. When the case went to court, all this was agreed to—but almost everything else was disputed. W.D. claimed that the money paid in 1898 was a loan (not a political donation as the defence claimed), and that when Morine secured Mott's payment (by an unregistered mortgage in his own name), he was acting as a trustee for R.G. Reid, whose solicitor he was at the time. The Reid Company now claimed repayment both from Mott and Morine, even though the latter seems to have kept the newspaper going with his own money after 1901.[20]

The case came to trial in February 1906.[21] Morine and Mott lost, two of the three judges finding for the company.† Facing court orders to make substantial payments to the Reid firm, hard bargaining resumed. The Reids refused to pay Morine anything extra for handling the telegraph arbitration. Neither would they provide compensation for what he had spent on the *Daily News,* nor for the loss he might suffer when selling it. The final agreement (May 19, 1906) provided that Morine would move to Canada by the end of July that year, and not return to Newfoundland before the end of 1911. He was not to "advise, act or write" against R.G. Reid or the company, but must be "ready and willing" to provide advice if asked. He would be paid $5,000 on leaving Newfoundland, and a total of $40,000 in half-yearly amounts beginning in January 1907—large sums for the time.‡ Morine resigned his seat in the Assembly in June; Donald Morison took over both his vacant seat in Bonavista and his controlling interest in the

---

* A Nova Scotian, Mott (1855–1946) came to St. John's to work as a piano tuner before turning to politics and journalism. He was Speaker in 1898 (*ENL* 3:634).

† The judgments by Emerson and Horwood in favour of the company were reported in the *Evening Telegram*, March 1 and 15, 1906. Judge Johnson's decision in favour of the defendants is in the *Telegram,* March 16, 1906.

‡ The agreement and allied correspondence is in PANL, RNCP file 272. In early 2019 dollars, the settlement would amount to about $1.1 million, all in.

News[22] (Mott had already resigned as its editor[23]). Morine convened a farewell meeting at the British Hall on May 24. "I came here by accident," he said, "and leave it unwillingly."[24]

Earlier in the year, Morine had acted as Leader of the Opposition for the last time. The legislature had opened on March 1, 1906, and although Michael Cashin (still an independent) proved to be a highly aggressive questioner, the session was generally not acrimonious. On many issues—the fisheries question aside—there was an unusual degree of consensus. Perhaps Morine's feud with the Reids and his service with Bond (and James M. Kent) on a commission to investigate affairs at the General Hospital, had led to something of a rapprochement. Indeed, Morine went out of his way to praise Bond's handling of the commission.* MacGregor reported, with exaggeration, "the practical obliteration of the line that separates a party in power from the opposition."[25]

There was unanimity, for instance, on Morine's proposal that a commission should be established to investigate the payment of old age pensions.[26] The first such scheme in the British Empire had been introduced by New Zealand in 1898. Bond indicated that he was familiar with it and that he supported old age pensions in principle. There were two problems. First, it would be hard "to award and distribute the pension without disturbing the thriftiness of the people, or tending to pauperise them"—a condescending and revealing comment. The second was the cost. Applying the New Zealand scheme in Newfoundland would cost $250,000 a year—where would the money come from? The colony did not have a large moneyed class, so the fund would have to come from fishermen's earnings. This was not something to rush into.[27] Morine's proposal was accepted but there was no further action by the Bond government on the matter; a limited pension scheme was not introduced until 1911.

There was also strong support for a bill to restrict, but not prohibit, Chinese immigration, as William Howley had first proposed in 1904. His bill had failed, but it had focused attention on the small but slowly growing

* Morine in Assembly, April 11, 1906 (*Evening Telegram*, April 20, 1906). Bond's work "had been long and laborious. . . . His duties could not have been performed by any other man."

Chinese community. The press became increasingly excitable on the subject during 1905, when the arrival of seven Chinese in August coincided with a fire that destroyed the locally owned Globe Steam Laundry. The *Telegram* warned that "the yellow peril" threatened local jobs, and reports circulated alleging unsanitary and overcrowded conditions in the Chinese laundries. Morris stoked the growing racial paranoia when he introduced the 1906 bill, referring to the local Chinese as "a most undesirable class of people" who competed "with servant girls and washerwomen." He further warned of an "influx of coolie labour" and presented a petition supporting restriction from the Longshoremen's Protective Union.[28] Based on Canadian precedents, the legislation (6 Ed.VII c.2) imposed a $300 head tax and other restrictions on Chinese immigrants.*

The Assembly was also generally in favour of legislation, promoted by Morine, to restrict the use of steamers in the Labrador fishery, although there was a division between those who favoured a total ban and those prepared to allow steamers to take stationers to Labrador but not to fish there. The former argued that crews travelling by steamer would unfairly get the best trap berths, having arrived earlier in the season. The latter pointed to the widespread criticism of overcrowding and other problems on the schooners that took stationers to Labrador, and to the unfavourable publicity such conditions generated for the colony—Dr. Wilfred Grenfell had been particularly outspoken on the subject. Bond was in the second group, telling the House that he did not want to see steamers in the inshore fishery. "The rich man might profit by it, but the poor man would certainly lose. Monopoly might flourish, but individuality will decay."[29] A similar bill had been defeated in the Legislative Council in 1905; in spite of the formation of a Joint Select Committee to try and find common ground, the Council defeated the legislation,

* The Legislative Council reduced the tax to $300 from the original $500 (Hong, "Newfoundland's 1906 Chinese Head Tax," online; Morris in Assembly, April 17, 1906, *Evening Telegram*, April 21, 1906; *JHA* 1906, 57 and 60). The Chinese community numbered only about 130 at this time.

session after session.* Merchants active in the Labrador fishery did not welcome regulation, it seems.

BOND'S "FADS"

Some of the government's plans caused a great deal of controversy and became known as "Bond's fads." One of them, first announced in the 1904 election manifesto, was a plan to develop a pickled herring industry along Scottish lines, part of the government's goal of increasing fish sales in the American market. It was predicted that the superior "Scotch cure"† would find ready markets in North America and Europe. In the government's first term, it had tried (and failed) to promote cold-storage technology. The Scotch-cure initiative was part of its quite reasonable plan to develop the herring fishery, which, as the Fisheries Department said, "has been characterised as one of spasmodic enterprise, never on an extensive scale, nor as a distinct business worth cultivating on its own merits."[30]

The precedents were not encouraging. The Scotch-cure process had been tried in Placentia Bay, White Bay, and Bay of Islands without much success.[31] The Bond government was undeterred, however, and decided (like the Canadian government) to bring in a Scottish expert to mastermind an experiment. William Mair, about to retire as the Assistant Inspector of Sea Fisheries for Scotland, was hired in mid-1905. After visits to the west and northeast coasts, he recommended the adoption of drift-net fishing in the open sea, which would lengthen the herring season and supplement the fishery in the bays.[32] Legislation then provided for a bounty on Scotch-cured herring as well as financial encouragement for any Scottish concern that would begin drift-net fishing. Bond spoke at length, enthusiastically forecasting yet again another new industry.[33] In 1907, the legislature approved an agreement with the Scottish firm of George Flett and Company. Unable to bring a steam drifter across the

---

* *JLC,* May 4, 1906, 74–75. The vote was nine to five. The Labrador bill was discussed in the Assembly on March 16, 27, 28, and May 1, 1906 (*Evening Telegram,* March 22, April 4, 5, 6, and 7, May 31, 1906; *JLC* 1907, 62–63; *JLC* 1908, 57).

† "Scotch cure" herring was packed in barrels when fresh, with the gills and guts removed without splitting the belly. Less salt was used than in other cures.

Atlantic, the Fletts (father and son) modified two local schooners, brought out four experienced fishermen, four coopers, and nine women, and began operations at Twillingate (which, Governor MacGregor had to point out, was in Bond's district). The fishery was unsuccessful and the vessels were damaged in a September storm. The Fletts moved their operations to a curing station built for them by the government in the Bay of Islands. The results here were also disappointing. Flett decided to pull out, amid political controversy.[34]

Another "fad," in the opposition's view—and more justifiably—was Bond's perennial enthusiasm for a "Short Line" transatlantic transportation route across the island. In 1907 the legislature confirmed an agreement between the government and a syndicate that intended to provide "rapid transit between the Old World and the New, by way of and through this Island." The syndicate was created by Harry C. Thomson, a London-based barrister, traveller, and author, in alliance with the firm of Ochs Brothers of London and Paris, whose senior partner, Albert Ochs, was a diamond merchant and art collector. Thomson visited Newfoundland several times and ultimately decided that the necessary rail line should run between Green Bay and Bay of Islands. (He also proposed a line between Bay of Islands and the Strait of Belle Isle, where at some time in the future he envisaged a tunnel to the mainland—an idea that still has currency.) James Howley met Thomson in 1904 in the Grand Lake area and described him as "an exceedingly nice old gentleman," a wonderful raconteur who was quite obsessed by the scheme.[35]

Bond introduced the agreement to the Assembly in a lengthy speech on February 28, 1907.[36] Newfoundland, he said, seemed "to have been intended by the Great Creator as a stepping stone between the Old World and the New." Fast steamers would run from the west coast of Ireland to Green Bay, St. John's, and the Canadian mainland between May and January. (In winter, St. John's would be the terminal port.) Another steamer would connect Bay of Islands with the Canadian mainland. Bond (and Thomson) claimed that the route between Ireland and Green Bay was largely a safe, "fog-free zone," a phrase that would come back to haunt him. Bond emphasized the potential international and imperial importance of the scheme—and as for Newfoundland: "We can see in this project a great revolutionary force that will change the whole aspect of things in this Colony for the better." Morris supported the deal and, ever the populist, concentrated on the potential domestic economic benefits.*

Mariners in the opposition, such as Charles Dawe and William Winsor, thought that the idea of a "fog-free zone" was absurd and that navigation into Green Bay was too difficult. The idea was just another "fad," like the Bell Island smelter.[37] Bond, stung, replied to his critics with an aggressive speech defending his political record. It included a sustained personal attack on the rightly skeptical Charles Dawe.† A survey of a railway route between Green Bay and Bonne Bay was carried out later that year,‡ and a prospectus issued in London in 1908. Thomson was still corresponding with Bond in 1910,[38] but there was no further activity of any significance. During the election of 1908 and before, the scheme became a convenient target for Bond's political opponents.

Another target was the government's decision to build a museum, a move made in response to lobbying by James Howley, who had been looking after exhibits housed (unsatisfactorily) in the St. John's Post Office building.[39] The purpose-built museum (on Duckworth Street) was a distinguished Edwardian design by the prominent English architect Sir Aston Webb, with a frieze on the front that reflected the themes of Bond's 1897 postage stamp issue, celebrating the colony's economic potential. But it was expensive, and there were snide grumbles about the cost of a building to house the remains of "dead Beothuks."

---

* Morris in Assembly, March 1, 1907 (*Evening Telegram*, March 15, 1907). "Watchman" in the *Daily News* (March 5, 1907) thought that Morris treated the scheme as a joke and avoided the main issue, and this is perhaps accurate.

† The Colonial Office also thought the scheme impractical. See the Minutes on MacGregor to Elgin, March 13, 1907 (CO 194/267, 338).

‡ "Report of R. Elliott Cooper, Esq., . . . on the proposed Newfoundland 'Short Line' Railway," *JHA* 1908, Appendix, 128–35. The cost of a 92-mile line was estimated at approximately $2.07 million.

The Newfoundland Museum. Construction began in 1905; the design was by the prominent English architect Sir Aston Webb. (City of St. John's Archives, 02-07-006)

THE RESIGNATION OF EDWARD MORRIS

These attacks might have been survived had the Bond government not been mortally wounded by the resignation of Sir Edward Morris. The exact course of events is unclear, but it seems that in late June 1907, men employed on roadwork in Kilbride (just south of St. John's) went on strike for better pay. Bond was away at the time. On June 23, a deputation visited Morris in his capacity as the senior MHA for St. John's West (which included Kilbride). He told the men that an increase from $1 to $1.25 a day was reasonable, and wrote to the Minister of Public Works, George Gushue, asking him to order the change. Gushue, too, was out of town, but on July 10 he told Morris the increase would go ahead, and it would apply throughout the island. This was later confirmed by Bond (who had returned on July 8) and by the government. Morris then precipitated a dispute with Bond about who should take credit for the increase, and whether he had been misled by other government members and insulted in the press. On July 20, Morris submitted his resignation; it was formally accepted by MacGregor on July 26.[40]

Bond bluntly told Morris that he did not believe that the "frivolous" issue of the pay increase was the real reason for the resignation. Morris indignantly denied it, but Bond was almost certainly correct. The two men had always had a guarded relationship, and the rumour mill had been predicting a split for some time.[41] The resignation gave Morris and his allies (who included the Reids) time to prepare for the 1908 election. P.T. McGrath resigned as editor of the *Evening Herald* and as Clerk of the House of Assembly; in November, he started a pro-Morris newspaper, the *Evening Chronicle.*[*] Morris had obviously been waiting for a pretext to split with Bond and make a bid for the premiership.[42]

These events were watched with great interest by Lord Grey and Governor MacGregor, who had met up at Hawke's Bay on the northwest coast, intending to continue to Labrador to fish. MacGregor cut the trip short because of urgent cables from the Colonial Office, but Grey continued on. "Bond is killed," Grey reported to Laurier; W.D. Reid ("the Rhodes of the Island") heartily agreed.[43] MacGregor told Elgin that "a strong and growing feeling of jealousy and rivalry" between Bond and Morris had been evident for some time. He emphasized yet again how Bond was "of an exceedingly jealous and intolerant disposition, characteristics that with time are becoming more marked." He was (MacGregor wrote), "socially isolated, controlling, vindictive, and a splendid hater." On the other hand, Morris was "more a man of the world, much broader minded, and is held to be of a sympathetic disposition." Whether Morris would join the opposition or form a new party, he professed not to know. But Morris was certainly a man who could be sent for should a new ministry be needed.[44]

There was an additional complication—the revival of confederation as a possible solution to the "Newfoundland problem." In mid-1907, Lord Grey met Harry Crowe aboard a transatlantic steamer.[45] A Nova Scotian with extensive interests in the Newfoundland lumber industry, Crowe was a political busybody who enthusiastically promoted both Newfoundland

---

* *Daily News*, July 29, 1907, and *ENL* 1:783. The first edition appeared on November 20, 1907.

joining Canada and, more generally, Anglo-Saxon union. Crowe presented himself to Grey as a confidant of Bond, and they certainly did know each other. Grey said that, according to Crowe, Bond realized that it was "beyond his power to make Newfoundland into a 'Dominion' and that he has got himself politically into a rather tight place." The 1901 Reid contract was problematic and he wanted a way out. That seemed to be confederation with Canada, as long as Bond did not have to make the first move. Grey introduced Crowe to Sir Frederick Borden, also travelling on the ship, who was carefully noncommittal.* Laurier cautiously responded to Grey that he was "not so sanguine about Newfoundland as you seem to be."[46] Newfoundland had to take the initiative and, more immediately, he wanted to settle the terms of reference for the fisheries arbitration and the disposition of the Labrador boundary dispute.†

MacGregor thought confederation would happen eventually but he was not an enthusiast. Unlike Grey, he mistrusted (and misunderstood) Crowe, describing him as an "obscure individual in [Bond's] confidence" who was employed in "underground transactions . . . a kind of secret agent" or intermediary between Bond and members of the Canadian government. Crowe evidently showed him some of the correspondence. According to MacGregor, the idea was that Bond would meet Laurier in Montreal in November. The pretext would be to discuss the Labrador boundary; the real topic, confederation. Assuming that these talks were positive, Bond would seek a dissolution and an immediate election. With a renewed majority, he would stump the country and call for a referendum. A key point was what MacGregor would do if Bond resigned—would he grant a dissolution, or call for either Morris or the Official Opposition to form a ministry? Crowe tried to find out and MacGregor refused to be drawn. The governor was also unsure about the nature of Bond's involvement and rightly dubious about the scheme's practicality—assuming that a plan existed at all.[47]

---

* Borden was the Canadian Minister of Militia and Defence (Grey to Laurier, June 13 and 18, 1907, LAC, Grey fonds, 2:427, 431).

† Grey to MacGregor, October 25, 1907 (LAC, Grey fonds, 5155). Crowe had written to Laurier.

MacGregor's skepticism was justified, as was his refusal to become closely involved in such speculative schemes. Whatever the details, and whether or not confederation was ever a serious consideration, the evidence suggests that Bond was becoming concerned about his political future, especially after Morris's resignation. He may well have thought that a quick election in the fall of 1907—after the free sale of herring on the west coast had been allowed and before Morris and his allies had got fully organized—might gain him another term in office. There was certainly local gossip to this effect. But he had left such an initiative far too late, and Bond certainly could not assume that MacGregor would do what he was advised to do.[48] In any event, both MacGregor and Grey were increasingly confident that Bond would be defeated in 1908, and that the pliant and more "reasonable" Morris would take his place. Grey naively hoped that this would usher in confederation.

THE 1908 LEGISLATIVE SESSION

The legislature met unusually early in 1908, on January 9. The official reason, given in the Throne Speech, was that the government had to deal with two major issues—the Labrador boundary dispute, which was to be settled by the Judicial Committee of the Privy Council, and the fisheries arbitration. It was a short session, closing on February 18 without much in the way of vote-grabbing legislation. Charles Dawe resigned as Leader of the Opposition on opening day; illness had made it impossible for him to attend and he died in late March. That left the unremarkable Mark Chaplin as the senior opposition member.[49] Cashin and Morris sat as independents. Later in the month, Morris was asked by the other MHAs on the opposition side to lead and reorganize the Conservative party. He agreed only to act as Leader in the Assembly during the session.[50] Cashin and Morison—particularly the former—vigorously attacked the government. Morris was necessarily more subtle, given that he had been party to many of the decisions that his new colleagues found wanting. He criticized aspects of government policy, always taking care to position himself as a champion of the working classes. It was a clever performance and at times it put the government on the defensive, as during discussion of education policy.

After consulting the denominational superintendents,[51] the government had decided against introducing free elementary schools. Instead, the education grant would be increased by $11,000, which would be spent on providing schools where none existed. The decision was defensible; Bond pointed out that, since 1900, the education grant had increased by 66 per cent and that elementary education was "practically free." But if education was to be completely free, it would have to be compulsory, and this would be a very costly.[52] Morris supported the increase, but argued that school fees (which formed part of a teacher's income) should be abolished. It was, he said, "only the very well-to-do children—the child of the merchant, the child of the planter or well-to-do fisherman . . .—who were able to pay fees." He also proposed that teachers' salaries be increased. There was no need for compulsion to attend school. And, clearly, it was time for the creation of a proper Department of Education (which, when he was prime minister, Morris did not establish).* Morris was thus presenting himself as a reformer with fresh ideas, and with sympathy for the families who could afford neither fees nor to send their children to school. The stance made Bond appear to be the cautious defender of the status quo.

A similar situation developed over the government's agricultural policy, which envisaged the creation of a model farm and the encouragement of "practical farmers" to settle in the interior. Ever the agricultural enthusiast, Bond had been deeply impressed by a 1905 visit to the Agricultural College and Model Farm at Guelph, Ontario. He wanted something similar in Newfoundland, where well-qualified experts would train young men to become full-time farmers—fishing and farming, he said, did not mix. Morris was generally supportive, but thought the first step should be the establishment of a government department devoted solely to agriculture. He then moved resolutions calling on the government to consider the restoration of a land-clearing bonus, and the preparation of a primer on agriculture for use in schools. Something more "comprehensive" than a model farm was needed, he thought.[53]

---

* Morris in Assembly, January 16, 1908 (*Evening Telegram*, January 21, 1908). There was no department of education until 1920.

Some of Morris's other interventions were more blatantly political. An early example of such grandstanding was the introduction of resolutions that would require the government to talk to owners of sealing ships about looking after crews following their return from the ice, and making sure that they got safely home. There had been cases of severe hardship in 1907: several steamers had been lost or disabled, the railway line had been blockaded by snow, and stranded sealers had had to sleep in the railway station and elsewhere. Bond held that the previous year's situation had been exceptional, that governments always looked after the sealers if necessary, that his government was dealing with the issue—and if there was no agreement with the shipowners, there would be legislation. The resolution, he said, was therefore superfluous. The debate became rancorous; John Bennett (who sat with Morris for St. John's West) took the opportunity to cross the floor. The resolutions were defeated[54] and an agreement reached with the owners,[55] but the initiative once again underlined Morris's populist stance—as did his attempt to place tea and sugar on the free list.[56] It was also, in all probability, part of a strategy to raise his political profile in the Protestant districts of northeastern Newfoundland, where most sealers lived.

For the same reason, Morris and his allies pressed for the steamship service to the north to be continued all winter and, if necessary, for the government to build a special steamer that could negotiate the ice. Morris dwelt eloquently on the seasonal isolation of the north, "a Siberia." In fact, the government had already agreed to send Bowring's *Portia* to the northern districts for as long as the ice allowed, but it shied away from the cost of an icebreaker.[57] Nevertheless, Morris had touched on an issue that greatly concerned the northeast coast. He did it again when he reintroduced yet another bill to prohibit steamers from prosecuting the Labrador fishery. Such legislation had already been defeated three times in the Legislative Council and Bond predicted correctly that it would be defeated there again, but its reappearance was no doubt politically advantageous for Morris.[58] Still another move that no doubt appealed to the north was Morris's support for a petition that called for a branch railway between Bonavista and Clarenville.[59] (Morris could not escape, of course, that he had been a consenting party to Bond's policies on the United States' fishing rights, the Bait Act, and the development of the herring fishery.) Meanwhile, Cashin remained outspokenly critical, particularly of the Fletts and the Scotch cure experiment.

With the end of the session, the election campaign began in earnest. In the four years since the last contest, the political scene had changed significantly. Bond's preoccupation with reciprocity and the American fishery, as well as his antipathy to the Reid interest, had alienated a significant portion of the electorate and some important players, including Governor MacGregor. He had lost some active political supporters of whom the most important was Morris, now clearly at the centre of the anti-Liberal forces—as Archbishop Howley had feared from the outset. Bond could not expect a guaranteed victory in the approaching election. He could not mount a crusade as he had in 1900, since the American issue was foreign, seemed distant and abstract to most voters, and created problems for many of them. And this time he did not face a disorganized opposition.

NOTES

1 The following discussion is largely based on Hiller, "Origins of the Pulp and Paper Industry," 55–60.

2 Bond in Assembly, April 27, 1905 (*Evening Telegram*, May 1, 1905).

3 Morris in Assembly, April 27, 1905 (*Evening Telegram*, May 2, 1905).

4 Morine in Assembly, April 27, 1905 (*Evening Telegram*, May 1 and 2, 1905).

5 MacGregor to Lyttleton, tgm., February 3, 1905 (CO 194/256, 207); *Evening Telegram*, February 3 and 4, 1905.

6 Bond to D.W. Prowse, March 8, 1905 (RBP 7.11.012).

7 MacGregor to Lyttleton, tgm., March 3, 1905, and Lyttleton to MacGregor, tgm., March 6, 1905 (CO 194/256, 281–89).

8 *Free Press*, February 21 and March 28, 1905.

9 "An Act respecting the immigration of Chinese Persons" (5 Ed. 7 c.2).

10 Morine in Assembly, June 7, 1905 (*Evening Telegram*, June 12, 1905).

11 Horwood to Lyttleton, conf., August 24, 1905 (CO 194/257, 257ff.).

12 R.G. Reid to Bond, April 8, 1905 (PANL, Reid Newfoundland Company Papers [RNCP], file 357); Bond to MacGregor, May 3, 1905 (PANL, GN 1/3, 83; *Evening Telegram*, May 20, 1905; *Free Press*, May 2, 1905).

13 Bond to Reid, April 20, 1905; Reid to Bond, May 2, 1905; Bond to Reid, July 7, 1905 (PANL, RNCP, file 357 and GN 1/3/A, file 83).
14 PANL, RNCP, file 466.
15 Rompkey, "Reid, Sir William Duff," *DCB* 14:865–67.
16 Morine to R.G. Reid, conf., October 10, 1905 (PANL, RNCP file 272).
17 Morine to R.G. Reid, conf., October 19, 1905 (PANL, RNCP file 272).
18 Reid's attacks and Morine's replies are in PANL, RNCP files 272 and 273.
19 C.S. Campbell to W.D. Reid, November 6, 1905 (PANL, RNCP file 272).
20 *Daily News*, November 1, 1905. See also PANL, RNCP file 272.
21 *Evening Telegram*, February 16, 17, 19, and 20, 1906, and March 1, 15, and 16, 1906.
22 *Daily News*, May 22 and June 13, 1906; *Evening Telegram*, May 18, 1906.
23 *Daily News*, February 24, 1906.
24 *Evening Telegram*, May 25, 1906.
25 MacGregor to Elgin, secret, April 9, 1906 (CO 194/262, 288).
26 *JHA* 1906, 23-25.
27 Bond and Morris in Assembly, March 22, 1906 (*Evening Telegram*, March 28, 1906).
28 Assembly, April 27, 1906 (*Evening Telegram,* May 30, 1906).
29 Bond in Assembly, March 27, 1906 (*EveningTelegram*, April 7, 1906).
30 "Fisheries Report, 1905," *JHA* 1906, Appendix, 147.
31 See Reeves "Our Yankee cousins," 300–301, and Reeves, "Alexander's Conundrum Reconsidered," 15–16.
32 *Evening Telegram*, April 5, 1906; *JHA* 1906, Appendix, 200–201.
33 Bond in Assembly, April 25, 1906 (*Evening Telegram*, May 19, 1906).
34 MacGregor to Elgin, January 14, 1908 (CO 194/272, 32); "Annual Report of the Department of Marine and Fisheries . . . 1907" and "Report" by William Mair, nd. (*JHA* 1908, Appendix, 144, 193–97).
35 Howley, *Reminiscences,* 1818–21.
36 Offprint in RBP 11.01.021; *Evening Telegram*, March 1, 1907.
37 Dawe in Assembly, March 1, 1907 (*Evening Telegram*, March 12, 1907). See also *Free Press*, March 5, 1907.
38 Thomson to Bond, December 4, 1910 (RBP 11.01.028); the prospectus is in RBP 11.01.027.
39 Maunder, "The Newfoundland Museum," online; e-mail from John Maunder, November 10, 2017.

40 Morris to Bond, July 20, 25, and 27; Bond to Morris, July 24, 26, and 30, 1907 (RBP 3.26.002); *Free Press*, July 16, 1907.

41 *Evening Telegram*, August 9, 1907.

42 See also Foran, "Battle of the Giants," in Smallwood, ed., *The Book of Newfoundland,* 3:159–61; Noel, *Politics in Newfoundland,* 45–47.

43 Grey to Laurier, August 1, 1907 (LAC, Grey fonds, 2:451).

44 MacGregor to Elgin, private, August 1, 1907 (LAC, Elgin fonds, Newfoundland, 121).

45 Baker, "Crowe, Harry Judson," *DCB* 15:245–46.

46 Laurier to Grey, June 26, 1907 (LAC, Grey fonds, 2:441).

47 MacGregor to Elgin, November 26, 1907 (LAC, Elgin fonds, Newfoundland, 180–84).

48 MacGregor to Grey, private and conf., October 12 and November 11, 1907 (LAC, Grey fonds, 5143, 5409).

49 *Daily News*, January 9, 1908; *Free Press*, January 14, 1908.

50 *Daily News*, March 5, 1908.

51 "Substance of interview between Sir Robert Bond and Rev. Canon Pilot, Rev. Dr. Curtis and V.P. Burke . . . ," January 6, 1908 (RBP 5.02.010).

52 Bond in Assembly, January 16, 1908 (*Evening Telegram*, January 18, 1908).

53 Bond in Assembly, February 5, 1908 (*Evening Telegram*, February 18, 1908; a copy of his speech is in RBP 2.05.005); Morris in Assembly, February 5, 1908 (*Telegram*, February 20 and 21, 1908; *JHA* 1908, 47).

54 Assembly debates, January 22 and 24, 1908 (*Evening Telegram*, February 1, 3, 4, and 5, 1908, and *JHA* 1908, 25–26).

55 *Evening Telegram*, February 22, 1908.

56 Assembly debate, February 13, 1908 (*Evening Telegram*, March 3, 4, and 5, 1908; *JHA* 1908, 65–66).

57 Assembly debates, January 30 and February 7, 1908 (*Evening Telegram*, February 10, 11, and 26, 1908).

58 Assembly debates, February 4, 5, and 6, 1908 (*Evening Telegram*, February 18, 22, and 26; *JLC* 1908, 57–58).

59 Assembly debate, February 14, 1908 (*Evening Telegram*, March 7, 1908).

CHAPTER ELEVEN

The Tie Election and the Loss of Power, 1908–1909

The legislature closed on February 18, 1908. Nine days later, a requisition with more than two hundred signatures endorsed the January offer of the opposition leadership to Sir Edward Morris.[1] This time he accepted and, on March 5, a stormy night, he launched the "People's Party" at a large meeting crowded with sealers at the British Hall (a prudent choice—the British Society was exclusively Protestant). He had already published a list of thirty promises, all of which he claimed could be implemented without increasing taxation—indeed, taxes would be lowered. He went over many of them in a long speech, claiming they encapsulated "a policy which is broad enough . . . to take in every interest and meet the general requirements of the whole people of the country. . . . For the past eight years the present Government has not built a road to a cabbage garden," but under his leadership there would be branch railway lines, more steamer services, more telegraph and telephone lines, marine works, agricultural bounties, and the list went on. He made a special pitch to the apparently enthusiastic sealers present, claiming credit both for the government's agreement with the owners about looking after crews and for an increase in the price of seal fat. Morris was endorsed by other speakers, including Mayor Gibbs, Michael Cashin, and Sidney Blandford.*

The *Evening Telegram* thought that the People's Party was nothing more than the "Tory or Reid Party in a New Dress."[2] There was some truth

* The promises are listed in the *Daily News*, March 5, 1908. Reports of the meeting can be found in the *Evening Chronicle*, March 6, 1908, and the *Daily News*, March 6 and 7, 1908.

to this accusation. With the exception of Cashin, all who spoke at the meeting had established Tory or opposition backgrounds. The elected Tories had unanimously signed the January letter, and among the signatories of the requisition were such impeccably Tory names as James Baird and Augustus Goodridge. The new party was an alliance of those who, for whatever reason, opposed or were disillusioned with the Bond government and those who saw in Morris a better chance to get ahead. They included people new to public life, some of whom would become familiar figures in the years ahead—including Frederick Alderdice, John Crosbie, William Coaker, and Richard Squires.[3] Insofar as it had a programme, the People's Party happily absorbed policies that the Liberals had been advancing for years, added new, similar, and enhanced promises with a popular flavour, and signalled an end to Bond's financial conservatism. It also implicitly promised terminating the constant and expensive battles with the Reid Newfoundland Company. Altogether, it was an attractive package.

THE PEOPLE'S PARTY AND THE 1908 ELECTION

Toward the end of May, Morris toured the larger centres around Conception Bay with Donald Morison—a Roman Catholic with an Orangeman—to talk to the Labrador men before they left for the northern fishery.[4] Morison's wife was from Harbour Grace and he had many local contacts. Active campaigning then paused during a very dry summer; a correspondent to the *Evening Telegram* remarked in mid-July that it was unusually quiet politically for an election year.[5] Even so, newspapers supporting the People's Party were sent all over the country (including to Labrador). And, as usual, the Bond government did its best to ensure that money was spent to its advantage.[6] Candidates began canvassing their districts. Given the election, Bond had advised against a visit by the Prince of Wales. MacGregor had tentatively invited Lord Grey to come, but the latter wondered whether it would be appropriate. Remarkably, MacGregor did not consult Bond but did ask P.T. McGrath, who thought that a visit might damage Morris's chances. MacGregor, of course, took his advice.[7]

The political temperature rose in August, when the campaign resumed in earnest. Morris and Gibbs visited the west coast between Port aux Basques and Bay of Islands,* no doubt hoping to build on the herring fishermen's resentment at Bond's anti-American policies and to cement the support of the local newspaper, the *Western Star*.† The government, in fact, had decided to continue the herring fishery arrangement established in 1907, apparently at MacGregor's suggestion, and the British government agreed to revoke the Order in Council though not the modus,[8] but this did not mean that earlier difficulties would be forgotten. All the same, the fisheries dispute was not a major issue in the election.

Morris also toured Conception Bay again, visited Grand Falls, and travelled around Trinity and Bonavista bays in October.[9] In contrast, Bond did very little campaigning outside his own district. The newspapers traded insults, each party accusing the other of sectarian tactics and being soft on confederation. The People's Party paraded Bond's "fads" and alleged extravagance, and did its best to pin blame on the Liberals for a substantial drop in the price of fish (between 35 and 40 per cent).[10]

Despite the government having nothing whatsoever to do with the price of fish, the issue soon became an important factor in the election. The Labrador catch was down but the shore fishery was good—in Bond's district of Twillingate, "enormous."[11] The weather had been fine and it should have been an excellent year for the fishery. But international markets were glutted with fish from the previous season (some of it badly cured), and also with supplies from foreign competitors. New fish began to arrive before the old stock had been disposed of—and the resulting rush to get rid of the old fish drove prices down even further. Meanwhile, the cost of coal, flour, and imported provisions was rising. Merchants were cautious, having lost money in 1907–08, and disorganized marketing did not help.[12] The official Fisheries Report laconically remarked that "the usual over-production has had the usual effect on the fish markets of keeping them glutted."[13] It was no coincidence that William Coaker launched the Fishermen's Protective Union (FPU) at Herring Neck in the midst of this crunch (although after the

* *Daily News*, August 12, 13, and 20, 1908, and *Telegram*, August 20 and 24, 1908. Gibbs had contested the district in 1904.

† The *Free Press* (September 29, 1908) claimed unconvincingly that the *Western Star* was non-partisan.

William F. Coaker (1871–1938) aged 30. (*History of the Fishermen's Protective Union of Newfoundland*)

voting was over). The price collapse certainly caused hardship; in such circumstances, it was difficult for the Liberals to claim that everything had gone well under their stewardship.

Bond nevertheless ran on his government's record since 1900. He refused to bid against Morris, promise for promise. In his manifesto, published at the end of September, he asked electors to judge him and his government on their record and to ignore "that huge parasite, a venal press" that was "threatening to degrade the public life of the country," as well as the "attempt by unscrupulous demagogues to tempt the people to their ruin." He went over the deeds of the previous Tory government and his efforts to put right what it had done wrong—especially the 1898 railway contract—pointing out that "the leading men in the combination that now flaunts itself before the country as 'the People's Party' were the perpetrators of that crime." His government had given "all classes in the community . . . due and proper consideration." The French Shore difficulty had been solved, and the government had defended the colony's constitutional rights in the disputes over the fisheries and the Labrador boundary. Morris had deserted the government "under cover of a puerile excuse that cannot be regarded by any sensible man as aught else but a mere pretext" and he could not be trusted. As for Morris's promises, for the most part they represented Liberal policy and were so expensive that they pointed to bankruptcy, confederation, and "the domination of the Reid Newfoundland Company over this country." Bond promised only reduced taxes and the introduction of old age pensions.[14]

A second Morris manifesto followed on October 3.[15] It was largely a repetition of the many promises contained in the "preliminary Manifesto" of the previous March, but he added sections attacking the Bond government's record, proclaiming that "I am, and have been all my life, a staunch,

A political cartoon from the 1908 election campaign. Bond's "fads" are ridiculed, as well as his domestic record. (Courtesy of Robert Hong)

unwavering opponent of Confederation on any terms." Newfoundland could and should maintain its independence and become "one of the more flourishing colonies of the Empire." He would, he repeated, accomplish everything on his long list "without imposing additional burdens on our people or increasing taxation." MacGregor reported that Morris promised "great activity and betterment in practically every branch of administration."[16] He sent both manifestos to Lord Grey who—surprisingly—thought Bond's document was the more statesmanlike. Grey even told James Bryce (the British ambassador in Washington since early 1907) that if he himself were a Newfoundlander, he would vote for Bond.[17] MacGregor, predictably enough, thought that the ablest men were with Morris and that they would handle the fisheries arbitration better: "They

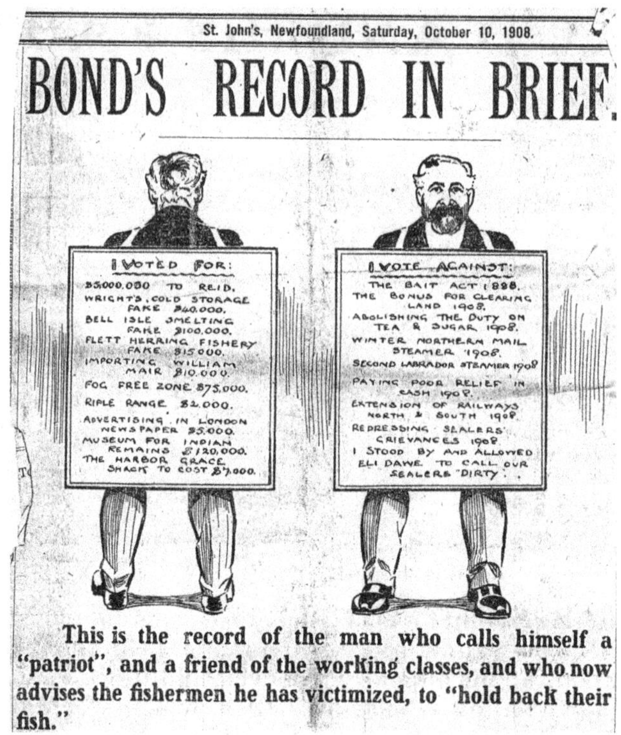

In this political cartoon from the 1908 election campaign, Bond's record is mocked. (Courtesy of Robert Hong)

are more talented by nature; and they are free from personal feeling on the question, and could thus handle it to better advantage."[18]

The nature of Bond's manifesto and his decision to stay in his district throughout October—he hired the government vessel *Fiona* for $1,350—caused comment and speculation. His seat was safe (though possibly not as safe as Morris's) and he could certainly have visited the Conception Bay districts where the People's Party was gaining ground. In addition, the tone and content of his manifesto allowed the opposition press to claim that he was arrogant and had no "future policy." Morris, on the other hand, offered a programme that was "strongly constructive."[19] There are two possible explanations for Bond's choices. One is that he genuinely thought that his government was secure, that its record spoke for itself, and that the electorate would reject Morris and all his works. The more likely is that Bond could not bring himself to compete with Morris in terms of promises and campaigning—to do Morris the compliment of taking him seriously. He clearly found the tone of the People's Party newspapers and of its campaign deeply offensive, and he despised the party's close association with the Reids. This was his eighth general election, and he may well have sensed that times were changing and the threat of being voted out was real. At anchor in Green Bay on October 24, he wrote out in his notebook the words of "A Prayer," which begins "Heavenly Father, guide, protect us/As we sail life's troubled sea." The notebook also contains a few quotations—"Failures are but pillars of success" and "What is defeat? Nothing but education."* Bond's refusal to fight was a significant factor in what was to come, however, and it helps explain the outcome.

Polling day was Monday, November 2. It was clear soon enough that the parties were neck and neck, with the People's Party edging ahead. But when the last result arrived from St. Barbe, probably on November 10, it established that the parties were equal, with eighteen seats each. There was a recount at Harbour Grace later in the month, but nothing changed.[20] The Liberals had lost twelve seats compared to 1904 and in terms of the total popular vote the People's Party was fewer than 1,000 votes behind.† If the result was a shock to Bond, Morris expressed outrage that he had not won outright. Speaking to his district party workers, he said that the government's conduct had been "the story of a crime." The electoral machinery had been stacked with Liberal partisans, government money had been splashed about, and there had been "false cries" about confederation

* The notebook is in RBP 3.27.009. The first quotation is from the Buddha; the second from Wendell Phillips.

† Liberal seats lost compared to 1904: one in Bay de Verde; one in Ferryland; one in Fortune Bay; two in Harbour Grace; two in Harbour Main; one in St. George's; one in Trinity Bay; three in St. John's West. The total vote was: Liberal 48,270, and People's Party 47,485 (my calculation, based on figures in *ENL* 1:705–6). But see the *Daily News*, December 11, 1908, and MacGregor to Crewe, conf., November 25, 1908 (CO 194/273, 319), in which he gave the People's Party seventy-one more votes than the Liberals.

and sectarianism.[21] As the *Daily News* put it, Bond's supporters had been returned "by bribery, government patronage, clerical influences, sectarianism with a double edge, false cries . . . and a campaign of falsehood and malice."[22]

It is certainly true that the Liberals had the advantage of being in power, and had the backing of Archbishop Howley and most of his priests.[23] It was alleged, probably accurately, that Liberal candidates (including Bond) reminded Protestant audiences that the opposing party included a significant number of Roman Catholics, and told Catholic audiences that Morris was "at war" with Archbishop Howley.* On the other hand, the People's Party apparently reminded Catholic voters that Morris could be the first Catholic premier since 1861, while telling Protestants that Morris was only a nominal Catholic—it was Bond who did Howley's bidding.† And where Liberal candidates may have had some discretionary government funds at their disposal, the People's Party enjoyed the financial and logistical support of the Reid Newfoundland Company, used its telegraph network for political purposes[24] (which was illegal), and was supported by most of the St. John's newspapers.

GOVERNOR MACGREGOR AND THE TIED VOTE

No matter what had been said or done during the campaign, Governor MacGregor was now the umpire in a tied contest. He had suspected that this outcome was possible, and understood that in such a situation his position would be "all but untenable."[25] He was "between Scylla and

---

* *Free Press*, December 8, 1908. It was said that during his canvass, Bond always referred to "Edward *Patrick* Morris," "Michael *Patrick* Cashin," and Michael *Patrick* Gibbs."

† *Evening Telegram*, November 30, 1908. Though MacGregor and others liked to assert that Bond had been "saved" by Howley's influence, Noel (*Politics in Newfoundland*, 65–67) has pointed out that the Liberals lost six Catholic seats and six more in "mixed" constituencies. The Liberal vote fell by 16 per cent in Catholic districts, against 6.2 per cent in Protestant districts. The swing "may be explained by the understandable inclination of Catholic voters to favour the party with a Catholic leader."

Charybdis," he told Lord Grey after the result, since whatever he did he could be seen as either "a blind partisan" or as "a devotee of the other side."[26] Umpires are supposed to be neutral, and MacGregor knew he had to tread very carefully in this truly extraordinary situation—and also act within the limits prescribed by constitutional precedent.* He also knew that he was well thought of at the Colonial Office, which Bond certainly was not, and that he possessed a certain amount of discretion. MacGregor was not neutral; he thought it would best for all concerned if Morris took over the government. He carefully never said as much, and he tried not to egregiously violate any constitutional norms or precedents. But it is quite clear that he was on Morris's side, as he had been for some time.

On November 11, after the St. Barbe result was known, Morris called on MacGregor and presented him with a letter (dated November 12), which he had signed as "Leader of His Majesty's Opposition in this Colony." He claimed—with considerable nerve—that since Bond had not obtained a majority, he should be asked to resign and, pending the formation of a new government, the current administration "should be limited entirely to the transaction of ordinary routine business." MacGregor read it in Morris's presence and told him to expect no reply before he, MacGregor, had talked to James Kent, the Minister of Justice, and to Bond, who was at Whitbourne.[27] MacGregor also consulted the Colonial Office, where the consensus was that Bond should not be asked to resign, but that the governor should exercise discretion concerning appointments and related matters until the situation became clear.†

Bond had telegraphed his government's law firm in London (Burn and Berridge) asking for advice about the constitutional position, posing two questions. Did not the government retain office with full authority until defeated in the legislature? And, since it was unlikely that either side would be able to elect a Speaker, would it not be the correct procedure for

* Ties, or near ties, had occurred in individual English constituencies. The casting vote was given by the returning officer.

† Crewe to MacGregor, tgm., November 16, 1908 (CO 194/273, 286). The telegram was drafted by the future constitutional expert, A.B. Keith.

the governor to convene the legislature and immediately dissolve it?[28] T.H.D. Berridge, who was also a member of Parliament, talked to Sir Courtenay Ilbert, the Clerk of the House of Commons, and Raymond Asquith, a young and reputedly brilliant lawyer (and the son of the prime minister). Their view was that the Bond government could retain office with full authority until it was either dismissed by the governor or defeated in the legislature, which had to meet in the regular way. The governor would use his discretion concerning a dissolution.[29]

Bond discussed the situation with MacGregor on November 14, but delayed his official response to Morris's letter until November 17, after he had heard back from Berridge. His response was scathing and, given the governor's bias, ill-judged. Morris, he said, was not yet "Leader of the Opposition" but the leader of a political party, and thus had no standing to offer advice to the Crown. If he did not understand this, Morris was either ignorant or confused, "and I, therefore, dismiss any thought of selfish ambition, morbid cupidity, or vanity." His "advice" was unethical, unprecedented, and displayed "a disregard for local precedents, to which he himself has been a contributor." His memory had clearly "lapsed." All the members of the Executive Council had been returned, and it was not yet known whether the legislature would sustain them. The governor should follow Ilbert's advice.[30] MacGregor told Morris that he would co-operate with the ministry as long as they acted "in good faith, legally and constitutionally."[31] Lord Grey wrote that Morris's letter confirmed "my feeling of disappointment in him" and that Bond "is an abler man." Bond had had the pleasure of "eating him up."[32] It was a very different and more accurate assessment of Bond than Grey had formed in 1906.

MacGregor's views, however, were quite fixed. He took no exception to Morris's intervention, and pointed out to Bond that Ilbert had not said that the legislature should be dissolved when it convened, but had left the question of a dissolution "entirely at the discretion of the Governor." Furthermore, Ilbert was not the only expert on such matters and he had little or no knowledge of local circumstances. "I do not think that I should be justified in allowing myself to be guided to a decision on such questions by the opinion of any expert, however experienced. . . . I am inclined to think that the Governor should retain and exercise full freedom to act as he deems best in the public interest. . . . I am not able to say when or under what circumstances the Legislature may or should be dissolved." It should meet, he suggested, early in 1909, taking the average of the last three years.[33] Bond responded, accurately, that he had not officially given MacGregor an opinion about a dissolution, though he was quite prepared to discuss the matter, and suggested the average of the last ten years.[34]

Both men had their eye on timing because of the implications for whether a Bond government might be defeated in the House. Bond's timing did not suit MacGregor because he had been informed that at least one People's Party member would be away at the seal fishery in March. MacGregor wanted to ensure that neither party had an unfair advantage.[35] So he asked why the legislature could not meet during the first week of February 1909. Bond thought it would be difficult to get government business and the public accounts in order that soon, but agreed to February 7 or 8. MacGregor insisted on February 4.[36] The date was later moved to February 25 to allow J.M. Kent to participate in the final negotiation of the fisheries arbitration reference in Washington, which was signed on January 27.* In the event, the legislature did not convene until March 30. So much for MacGregor's insistence on an early date.

Bond sent off another letter to Berridge in mid-December that reviewed possible scenarios when the House met. His questions naturally revolved around a dissolution. If it proved impossible to elect a Speaker on a government motion, even if amended by the opposition, would it be improper for the governor to refuse a dissolution and ask the opposition to form a ministry, even if this "could hardly [not] be regarded as other than a partisan act"? Should not the governor dissolve the legislature when it met? Or should the governor insist on the legislature trying to proceed with business, even if it meant calling on the opposition to form

* The text of the "Special Agreement for the Submission of Questions relating to Fisheries on the North Atlantic Coast" is in *JHA* 1909, Appendix, 442–49. The summons was unexpected. Bond had at first wanted to go himself, but no doubt thought it safer to stay in Newfoundland (the correspondence is in CO 194/275, 35, 42, 49, and 135).

a ministry? And if he did, and the new ministry failed, who would get the dissolution? Bond's view, of course, was that the governor should dissolve the legislature when it convened; he had arrived at this conclusion soon after the tie was established and he did not change his mind.[37] This rigidity would prove to be unfortunate.

MacGregor did his own research, both independently and in consultation with the Colonial Office. He allegedly refused to talk politics with Morris,[38] at least temporarily, and also to speak with Bond about the dissolution.[39] He understood, of course, that if there was a deadlock over the election of a Speaker, Bond would probably ask for dissolution. But should it be granted? A spring election would be a calamity, he thought. If Bond could engineer a Speaker and six months' supply, however, then he could stay in office until the fall, when an election would have to take place. If Bond could not do this, should not Morris be sent for and asked whether he could form a ministry and get supply?[40] (Supply had not been a serious issue in 1894, but that precedent seems to have been generally ignored during these discussions.) Given that the two parties had an equal number of seats, and given that governments had a decided advantage in any election, the 1908 result "can only be regarded as a moral, though not a numerical, victory for the opposition," whose members would think that another election "in fairness to them" should be "held under their auspices." He would, however, try all constitutional expedients before allowing a spring election.[41]

Early in January 1909, MacGregor told the Colonial Office that if Bond was unable to proceed with business, he would not grant him a dissolution. Instead, he would consult Morris and, if he "undertakes to form a Ministry, with a prospect of passing Supply," give him the task. If he failed, then he would ask Bond and Morris to co-operate to pass six months' supply. If they refused, he would call on a respected MHA with "few enemies" to appeal to the patriotism of the members.[42] This was a very strange proposal indeed, but the Colonial Office by and large agreed that MacGregor had to try and find ways to get supply through the legislature. But if it was impossible to find a ministry that could undertake to vote supply "with a reasonable prospect of success," the dissolution should be given to Bond—which, of course, was not MacGregor's intention.

If there was no Speaker elected, he was told, MacGregor himself should open the legislature, prorogue, and then dissolve it.[43]

In summary, at this stage of the crisis Bond held that the legislature should be dissolved when it convened and a new election arranged. He no doubt assumed that his government would remain in charge, and that uncertainties relating to supply could be fixed retroactively, as they had been in 1895. However, MacGregor had decided that Morris should be given the chance to form a government and vote supply, since he had allegedly won a moral victory in the 1908 election. Opinion at the Colonial Office was mixed, but in general supported the view that supply should be voted punctually, not retroactively (in spite of the 1895 precedent), and that this was the governor's primary responsibility. Officials were also prepared to give a trusted governor a considerable amount of discretion, given a shared bias against the Bond government.

Both political parties attempted unsuccessfully to induce members-elect to change sides.[44] The governor reported these overtures, remarking that doing so "is necessarily attended by great notoriety, which in the present intense state of party feeling could hardly fail to assume such a bitter personal character as would go a long way to act as a deterrent."[*] For example, George Roberts, one of the Liberal members-elect for Twillingate (and editor of the *Twillingate Sun*) was approached early in March by a People's Party intermediary who made several offers, starting with the magistracy at Twillingate and ending with $25,000 in cash.[45] James Davis (Liberal member-elect, Placentia-St. Mary's) asserted that Morris offered him $2,000 immediately, $800 a year for four years, and then the position of Superintendent of the Penitentiary. This was indignantly denied by both Morris and Cashin, who in turn claimed that it was Davis who had taken the initiative, that he was a spy, and that he had turned up drunk.[46] George Gushue (Liberal-elect, Trinity) similarly told Bond that he had been approached on several occasions.[47]

Also plotting in the background was Harry Crowe, who believed that

---

* MacGregor to Crewe, secret, January 7, 1909, and to Crewe, tgm., February 15, 1909 (CO 194/275, 10 and 152). Two election petitions were filed against People's Party candidates—and one in return—but they were not proceeded with.

if Bond could hold on to power, he would explore—or could be persuaded to explore—the possibility of confederation.[48] He intervened at two levels. Locally, in December 1908, he told Bond about a conversation on the train in Grand Falls with Joseph Downey (People's Party-elect, St. George's), a former Crowe employee.[49] Downey had said, Crowe reported, that he was disillusioned with politics and was not convinced that it would be in the country's best interest for Morris to form a government. Crowe went on his way to Canada, persuaded that Downey was sincere and would change sides in return for being made Deputy Minister of Fisheries.[50] Bond was cautious yet co-operative, proposing that Downey should first be elected as Speaker for the next session of the Assembly and then get his permanent job—but Downey would have to approach him directly and in writing, via Crowe. Downey then demanded $2,000, so Crowe said,[51] and the required letter was never written. Bond came to think that Downey "was playing a game all through. . . . That he thought to entrap me . . . and failing to entrap me, he hoped with the assistance of his guide and friend Sir E.P. Morris to weave a web out of such material he possessed."[52]

Crowe knew that the Downey manoeuvre was over by the time he reached Ottawa, but it had been part of a far larger and more ambitious scheme, which he put to Lord Grey in late January 1909. It should be possible, Crowe thought, to engineer a Bond-Morris coalition to carry confederation. Bond could be influenced by Archbishop Howley, by the prospect of a seat in the House of Lords, and by the knowledge that he had saved Newfoundland from a Morris government. Morris could be brought into line by the Reids and by the Canadian business interests that had helped fund the People's Party. Morris would persuade his anti-confederate supporters to absent themselves, their expenses presumably to be looked after. The remainder would be told to support Bond as premier until confederation was a fact, at which point Bond would retire, Morris would become either provincial premier or a member of the federal cabinet, and the Reids would get rid of the railway. This was an amazingly cynical proposal. It was based on the proposition that bringing Newfoundland into confederation was a great imperial good, even if its achievement meant accommodating greed, ambition, self-interest, and dubious personal morality. More fairly perhaps, the plan was also based on a genuine fear of what a Reid-allied Morris government might mean for Newfoundland and its future. Bond, Crowe, Howley, and their allies genuinely believed that it might be disastrous.

Grey was intrigued by Crowe's scheme and called in the Chief Justice, Sir Charles Fitzpatrick, who was a relative of Archbishop Howley and so could take soundings in Newfoundland—though Howley's views were hardly objective. Grey also talked to Laurier, who was characteristically cautious, and sent off private letters to MacGregor, Lord Crewe—colonial secretary since April, 1908—and James Bryce.[53] In late January 1909, he went himself to Montreal to speak to Edward Clouston[54] and Thomas Shaughnessy (preceded by Crowe) and found them co-operative.[55] Some days later, Fitzpatrick went to New York to see James Kent and get his assessment of the situation. Kent, who was in the US for the fisheries negotiations, in turn contacted Bond, who claimed to be unaware of what was going on.* Kent urged that the meeting of the legislature should be postponed until he returned, "so that I may deliver message to you verbally." Grey—who had asked Bryce to delay Kent if he could, to buy more time†—would contact MacGregor if necessary.[56]

Grey also spoke to William Goode, a Newfoundland-born, British-based journalist who was in Toronto acting as Canadian manager for *The Standard of Empire*, a British weekly.[57] Grey had known Goode for some time and, since the latter knew Bond, recruited him as an intermediary. Goode then wrote to Bond at considerable length.[58] He argued that Bond was seen as the only Newfoundland politician who had a chance of carrying confederation, but there was a real danger that Morris would be confirmed in power. Within three or four years that would mean colonial bankruptcy, social discontent, and increasing American influence "detrimental to the Empire and most dangerous to Canada." It might also mean, owing to the influence of the Reid interests, a demand for confederation

* Bond knew what Crowe had in mind in general terms, but did not know about the Ottawa and Montreal visits.

† Hallett, "Grey," 208. Howley said the same to Bond, without explaining why (Howley to Bond, January 26, 1909, RBP 7.15.003).

with Canada on Canada's terms—and, given the increasing influence of the western provinces within Canada, these terms might not be generous. Now was the time to act: Morris should be "forced," via the Reids, Shaughnessy, and Clouston, to support a Bond government committed to confederation. Lord Grey broadly shared this view, Goode wrote, but understood that Bond's attitude was critical. If Bond did not think that confederation was advisable "under the present circumstances," and if he did not think that even with Morris's support, the Newfoundland people would support negotiations, then "Fitzpatrick's enthusiasm or rather pessimism was useless." He added:

> Still, if a man who loved his country and had sacrificed so much for it as you have done honestly believed that Confederation was unwise from the present point of view he would loyally accept your opinion, although he would still think you were mistaken from the point of view of Empire. He believed that Confederation was inevitable and he thought that under your auspices it could be accomplished better than [by] any other—at least for years to come. . . . The present situation presented possibilities which might lead to Confederation on terms more favourable to Newfoundland and more equitable to all parties than at any subsequent time.

But what about Laurier? Grey agreed that Quebec issues (such as the Labrador boundary) tended to make Laurier cautious. Goode noted, however: "I have discussed Newfoundland with him many times and have always found him genuinely anxious to support that Colony in every way. He is, of course, anxious for Confederation, but feels that anything done by him or from him might embarrass Bond, of whom he has the very highest opinion. He feels that the initiative must come from the people of Newfoundland." Goode told both Grey and Laurier that Bond "would not advocate it, at any price, if [he] believed that Newfoundland would not get a fair deal or if she would not benefit by the change."

Crowe was in St. John's at about the same time, where he saw both Bond and Morris. The latter was—according to MacGregor[59]—unprepared and surprised, but was nevertheless pleasant, cordial, and made some polite remarks about Bond. He refused to commit himself to the scheme, however, "until he heard directly or indirectly from you [Bond]. . . . In the event of a mutual agreement all he would ask was your word. If no understanding was reached he would pledge his word that nothing more would be heard of it directly or indirectly from him." Crowe thought Morris was sincere and that there was a real chance that his scheme could succeed.[60] Crowe also saw Archbishop Howley and at least three members of the Executive, so that his "secret" became known more widely than it should have been. He was an indiscreet and somewhat naive plotter, which did Bond no good. In addition, Howley tried to put pressure on Bond through Jackman—one of his usual intermediaries—and through Kent, after he returned from Washington.[61]

The central figures remained MacGregor and Bond, who disliked and mistrusted each other but who shared a deep skepticism about Crowe's manoeuvrings. Confederation, wrote MacGregor, "will not come in my day. Nor could Bond or Morris, or both combined, bring it about at present." Giving Bond a peerage, he felt, could only be regarded as a joke.[62] Bond made his opposition to a deal with Morris clear to Crowe, and on February 10 told MacGregor that he repudiated the confederation manoeuvrings of "a busy body and an adventurer," who had acted without his authorization. Furthermore, Bond would not hold office by Morris's permission.[63] Writing to Goode, Bond expressed surprise that Grey and Fitzpatrick should have listened to and confided in Crowe, who had been extraordinarily indiscreet. "The Reids through O'Shaughnessy [*sic*] and Morris are unquestionably in possession of the proposal, and so far as Morris and the Reids are concerned, a more thoroughly unscrupulous lot could not have been consulted." He went on: "The proposal is so amazing, especially when emanating from such a distinguished source, that it staggers me every time I think of it. . . . If I were to entertain for one moment the proposal . . . I would despise myself so long as I drew breath."[64]

Kent reported to Howley and Fitzpatrick a week later. He said that Bond was reluctant to introduce confederation as a live political question and that to hold office in the way suggested would be humiliating and dangerous. Bond did agree, though, that confederation on good terms would be preferable to "temporary independence under the rule of the Reids and their tools." Thus the role of the Canadian government, if it wanted confederation, should be to help Bond and his government stay in power. Specifically, Grey should pressure the Colonial Office to order MacGregor to follow Bond's advice concerning a dissolution, allowing the Liberals to fight the election holding the government.[65] These exchanges all took place on the assumption that the legislature would open on February 25.

Bond knew about Kent's letter to Fitzpatrick (dated February 16).* Why neither Kent nor Bond telegraphed a summary to Fitzpatrick in code is not known. In any event, once Grey and Fitzpatrick understood Bond's reaction to Crowe's proposal, they gave up the attempt to manoeuvre confederation by influencing events in Newfoundland (Fitzpatrick with some reluctance[66]). The Colonial Office also adopted a hands-off stance, leaving MacGregor free to make his own decisions. Bond was well aware that the governor

> appeared to be in sympathy with this Reid combination. The Reids simply live and move and have their being there. If the Governor goes out of town fishing or shooting his companion is W.D. Reid. He has long since given up his carriage and horses, and when he goes out Reid's automobile conveys him. His two A.D.C.'s are members of the Morris-Reid party and one of them was my opponent in the District I represent; the other was returned as a Morris-Reid candidate.†

* Bond to Goode, private and confidential, February 26, 1909 (RBP 8.03.025). The evidence is inconsistent about the dates of some of this correspondence.

† Bond to Goode, private and confidential, February 26, 1909 (RBP 8.03.025) The ADCs were Alan Goodridge, who had run against Bond in Twillingate, and William Warren, the People's Party member-elect for Port de Grave.

This makes it difficult to understand why Bond, with the knowledge of other senior Liberals and presumably their support, offered formal advice to MacGregor concerning a dissolution on February 18—before Kent's letter arrived in Ottawa. It was a very risky strategy and, in retrospect, extremely ill-judged.

When the legislature met, Bond told MacGregor, it should be immediately dissolved and an election held as soon as possible, "so as to establish the Government of the Colony upon a firm and proper basis." There was no point in trying to elect a Speaker since a deadlock would be inevitable. British precedents showed that the Crown always granted a dissolution when it was requested by a prime minister. True, colonial precedents were less consistent—some governors had refused requests for dissolution, but in all such cases another party in the legislature had held a majority. The current Newfoundland situation was unique. Thus the governor had to follow the underlying principle and ask whether or not the House of Assembly "is likely to be able to carry on effectively the public business of the country. When the Representative of the Crown is satisfied that it cannot do so, it has been the invariable practice for him to accede to the advice of his Prime Minister and at once grant a dissolution." If MacGregor were instead to form a new ministry, this "would only result in your transferring to others the duties and responsibilities that the electors confided to your present ministry three months ago, and in your accepting the advice of others, who have not been approved as ministers by the people, that you decline when proffered by your present constitutional advisers." In summary, an immediate dissolution was desirable because deadlock was inevitable, there was no prospect of any ministry carrying on public business, the supply bill would expire on June 30, and the country needed political stability. In addition, dissolution would avoid the expense of a second session of the legislature in the current year.[67] The wording of the letter and other evidence suggests that Bond understood that the advice might well be rejected and, if so, that his government would have to resign. The *Evening Telegram* published a pledge of loyalty to Bond signed by all the elected Liberals; it included the undertaking that, "Should you regard it as necessary to resign the government to further this end [an immediate election], we shall stand firm."[68] The People's Party published its own loyalty pledge the next day.

Like Bond, MacGregor had not changed his mind on the question of dissolution of the House. He was determined to follow the process he had already outlined and he officially ignored the loyalty pledges (which, of course, underlined the probability of a deadlock). The Colonial Office approved, on the grounds that he had to try to avoid a dissolution.[69] Thus encouraged, MacGregor drafted his reply to Bond, which—as he spitefully put it—"I caused to be delivered to that gentleman at his country seat at Whitbourne on the evening of the 20th."[70] It had to have been long in gestation and it rejected Bond's advice. First, a spring election had to be avoided if at all possible, as had been the practice since 1861. Second, the legislature had to be allowed to meet and attempt to function—as Bond had suggested in his letter of November 13, 1908—and it could not be assumed that it would neglect to grant supply. Other factors were also mentioned: a general election had recently taken place; there had not been then, "and there is not now, any great specific political question at issue before the country, the dividing line between the parties being in fact more personal, or party, than political." Elections were expensive and the Audit Act provided that elections could not be paid for on Executive responsibility. In addition, there was no guarantee that an election would be a "certain remedy" for the current situation. Finally, Bond's advice would "introduce a somewhat novel procedure in British parliamentary practice, for the only modern instance . . . in which a chamber of elected representatives has been dissolved without being allowed to proceed to business is a foreign one and that example had a very unfavourable sequel." MacGregor appended documents from 1854 and 1861, and an extract from Bond's speech moving a vote of no confidence in February 1900, all of which dealt with the undesirability of a spring election.[71]

In response, Bond repeated that a deadlock was inevitable and that in this instance a spring election, though unusual and unfortunate, was both necessary and practicable. However, if MacGregor wanted "to test the possibility of securing a ministry 'which can induce Parliament to vote supply and which will carry on the business of the country,' I place . . . my resignation in your hands to facilitate your attempt to do so." He thought, though, that MacGregor should inform him whether, in the event of a deadlock, he would grant a dissolution to Morris or himself, arguing that he had the better case.* MacGregor received the letter at 7 p.m. the next day, February 23. Annoyed by what he saw as brinksmanship,[72] he would not be drawn on the question of a dissolution, refused to acknowledge the loyalty pledges, and accepted Bond's resignation pending his attempt to find a new ministry. He suggested that the meeting of the legislature should be postponed for a week, to March 4. Bond agreed, while expressing regret that MacGregor refused to discuss the dissolution question and reminding him that the loyalty pledges had been officially brought to his notice.[73]

THE PEOPLE'S PARTY GOVERNMENT, 1909

MacGregor then wrote to Morris (February 25). A spring general election was "so undesirable in the interests of the country as a whole that it should be avoided if any ministry can be formed with a reasonable prospect of being able to induce Parliament to grant Supply and to carry on the business of the country." Morris was asked whether he could form such a ministry.[74] He lost no time, replying immediately that he was prepared "to undertake the formation of a ministry to meet the House at an early date and with a reasonable prospect of passing supply and carrying on the business of the country."[75] He met MacGregor later in the day. The governor chose not "to make detailed inquiry as to how Sir Edward Morris expects to be able to induce Parliament to grant supply, but [I] have thought that I was bound to accept his written assurance that he has a reasonable prospect of being able to do so."[76] He sent Morris a memorandum, though, stating that he wanted a ministry that could get at least six months' supply. It stipulated that if the new ministry failed, MacGregor was at liberty to call on any member of the legislature to form a coalition; and that he would give no undertakings about a dissolution. But he conceded that Morris needed time to prepare to meet the legislature and that

* Bond to MacGregor, February 22, 1909 (*JHA* 1909, Appendix, 368–74). The letter also argued against most of MacGregor's contentions.

he should have the chance, if necessary, to form a coalition. The two men also discussed the possibility of an election being held "about May 10."[77] Both must have known that a spring election was almost certain and that they were acting out a piece of political theatre—one that was very much to Morris's political advantage.

The official changeover took place on March 3. Morris became prime minister, the other senior ministers being Michael Cashin (Finance), Donald Morison (Justice), and Robert Watson (Colonial Secretary).* Morris wanted Michael Gibbs appointed to the Executive Council (without portfolio), even though he had been defeated in the election, and MacGregor agreed without much argument.[78] The opening of the legislature was again postponed, this time to an unspecified date later in the month. Bond had expected that the legislature would open rapidly after the change of government but, having got what he wanted, MacGregor lost his earlier sense of urgency. He had pressured Bond to convene the legislature as soon as practicable and he could very well have insisted that Morris do the same—test the House, and then decide about the future. But Morris and his ministers were given almost a month to go through the files and extract what was politically useful to them—which they did.[79] Morris also immediately squashed any idea of Kent continuing as the Newfoundland agent at the North Atlantic Fisheries Arbitration, though he would probably have performed much more creditably than Morris's candidate, Sir James Winter, who was described at the Colonial Office as "a pleasant if dull old man."[80]

MacGregor had nothing but unqualified and exaggerated praise for the new ministry. "They are men of unexceptionable character and some of them of considerable business experience."[81] The governor had also made up his mind about who should get the dissolution, assuming that Bond would not give Morris "a fair trial." Bond had resigned voluntarily, he had indicated that MacGregor should approach Morris, and had said that he would obstruct the new government in the House. Thus Morris would get the nod if he advised a dissolution.[82] Bond's perspective was

---

* The other members were Blandford, Woodford, and Piccott (MacGregor to Crewe, tgm., March 3, 1909, CO 194/275, 261). For Watson, see *ENL* 5:522.

very different: Morris would inevitably fail even to elect a Speaker. Discredited by this defeat, he would either have to resign or be dismissed, and MacGregor would have to recall Bond and grant him the dissolution he had originally recommended. In those circumstances, the Liberals could win the election. "I do not fear the result of the General Election," he told Goode. "Reid's money bribed and debauched a section of the people last election, but they will hardly attempt it on the same scale again. In any case we shall know what to expect, and shall guard against it."[83] Bond was badly mistaken.

Officials in London were less impressed than the governor with the Morris government's behaviour.[84] MacGregor was told not to allow the release of the correspondence between himself and Bond relating to the crisis without Bond's permission—as Morris requested and MacGregor apparently thought proper, saying he did not want Morris to be at a possible disadvantage.* But A.B. Keith, soon to become a constitutional expert, was alone in questioning MacGregor's views on the dissolution. "Sir Robert Bond's resignation was only offered as giving the Governor a chance of obtaining a stable Government successfully. From the point of view of fairness, I find some difficulty in seeing why Sir Edward Morris should be granted a dissolution which was denied to Sir Robert Bond." His colleagues at the Colonial Office, however, thought that to recall Bond to give him the dissolution would be "absurd."[85]

When the legislature finally met on March 30, the political atmosphere was bitter and tense. The governor directed the Assembly to choose a Speaker. Morris, seconded by Morison, moved that William Warren should take the chair. Bond, seconded by Kent, proposed William Ellis.[86] Following accepted usage, the Clerk (the ubiquitous and slippery P.T. McGrath) put the first motion, which was defeated eighteen to seventeen.

* MacGregor to Crewe, tgm., March 6, 1909; Minutes by Dale and Crewe; Crewe to MacGregor, tgm., March 8, 1909 (CO 194/275, 293–94); MacGregor to Crewe, conf., March 6, 1909 (CO 14/275, 296). Bond was understandably outraged by the situation and accused the government of using secret correspondence for partisan purposes and also of pressuring the postmaster general to hand over private telegrams (correspondence in RBP 3.28.006).

The Clerk then put the second motion, which resulted in a tie vote, all the Liberals, Ellis included, voting against their own candidate. "So the Clerk declared this motion also negatived." For Ellis to vote against himself was a deviation from usage, in that each candidate should have voted for the other.[87] After a recess, MacGregor prorogued the legislature for a week.[88] The sitting had lasted two hours. Keith thought that Bond should have accepted Warren and later had "a real victory."[89]

Morris sent MacGregor an official report the next day, noting that "the policy and understanding of the Opposition was to prevent the election of a Speaker."[90] A second letter made the case for a dissolution and a general election. He had agreed to form a government, he said, because, unlike Bond, he believed "that if the Legislature were asked for supplies they would be granted." He had faced the House, Bond had not, and Bond had been deliberately obstructive. A coalition was not possible, nor was any other ministerial alternative, and an election would give him a substantial majority. Bond had really been defeated in 1908—he had gone to the country after eight years in power and with "the immense advantage which the possession of the Government always affords a party in appealing to the electorate." Furthermore, he had held onto office when he ought to have resigned as soon as the election results were known.[91]

But MacGregor had laid out his course. So he now had to ask both leaders to consider co-operating in the public interest to pass supply so that an election could be postponed until the fall. In the meantime, the current government would remain in power.[92] Morris replied that he would "consider and adopt any reasonable proposal" as long as the negotiations took place "upon neutral territory," inappropriately naming Government House. Bond's view was that, after an unnecessary delay, the Morris government had been defeated on March 30. He would, therefore, not express any opinion on "the present political situation while your [MacGregor's] present advisers continue in the conduct of public affairs."[93] He later told the governor that the government's behaviour since it took office "has rendered it impossible for any political opponent possessing self-respect to have any association whatever with them."[94]

As he had said he would do, MacGregor then approached Sir James

Winter and Daniel Greene (with Morris's consent), both of whom had been premiers; they both thought attempting to form a coalition would be unwise[95] (Bond was offended that he had not been consulted, as well). The *Evening Telegram* noted that both men were opposed to Bond, and that W.D. Reid had also had a long interview.[96] MacGregor defended himself unconvincingly,* but he had nothing to lose. He had been promoted to the governorship of Queensland and would soon be leaving.[97] But first, the governor had to decide about a dissolution.

Keith remained Bond's only supporter at the Colonial Office. The assurance that Morris had given on February 25, he argued, "may have been given in good faith (I confess I trust Sir E. Morris as little as I do Sir R. Bond: the only difference is that we know Sir R. better than Sir E.) but it was based on nothing and turned out worthless. It therefore comes to this: Sir E. Morris by an assurance which had no foundation in fact even if honest gets into office and asks for a dissolution, which was refused to Sir R. Bond who gave an assurance which was true. Frankly that seems to me unfair." Other officials thought that the "governing fact" was that there had to be a dissolution so that government could be carried on and that questions of fairness—or the advantage of being in power at dissolution—were not relevant.[98] A few days later, Keith noted, "I understand that it is held that a victory for Sir E. Morris is preferable to one for Sir R. Bond, and the victory of the latter is practically certain if he gets a dissolution in office."[99] MacGregor was notified accordingly—he was not bound to recall Bond and although the dissolution would be at his discretion, it might be preferable to retain Morris.[100] On April 10, Morris got his dissolution. Polling would take place on Saturday, May 8, Morris's 50th birthday. Because of the timing of the seal fishery and winter work in the woods, it was the earliest date practicable, Morris said; a later date would interfere with preparations for the cod fishery.†

* MacGregor to Crewe, conf., April 12, 1909 (CO 194/276, 84). MacGregor claimed that he never talked politics with Reid.

† MacGregor to Bond, April 14, 1909, and encl. in Morris to MacGregor, same date (RBP 3.28.006). Bond had complained that ice would make campaigning in the north very difficult and that it would be impossible to canvass some districts properly within the time allowed.

Bond fruitlessly tried to convince MacGregor that Morris had been defeated on March 30. Their lengthy (and detailed) correspondence continued into the campaign. In summary, Bond insisted that Morris had been defeated on the motion to appoint Warren as Speaker and so should then have resigned or been dismissed. He (Bond) should have been recalled, especially as his original advice had proved to be "absolutely sound." Instead, MacGregor had accepted the same advice from Bond's opponents. The governor responded that the original advice envisaged an "extraordinary course," while that of Morris did not. The vote had taken place in a House that was not yet properly constituted and so it was therefore not decisive. Finally, the vote had not followed proper usage, since Ellis should never have voted against himself.[101] At MacGregor's request, the Colonial Office later sent a public dispatch approving his actions during the crisis, specifically his decision to grant Morris the dissolution, which the latter later tabled in the House.[102]

Commentators have agreed that, biased as he was, MacGregor acted both legally and constitutionally and that Bond made errors of judgment.[103] It has to be appreciated, however, that the tie had put Bond in a very difficult position. Even though all his ministers had been returned in 1908—a point to which Bond repeatedly returned—it was, in fact, a technical defeat. There would have to be another general election sooner rather than later, and to have a chance of winning he had to control the government. This was why he adamantly advised MacGregor that the House should be immediately dissolved when it convened. Bond anticipated that his advice might be rejected, but apparently thought (mistakenly) that Morris would be required to meet the House without delay and if he, too, failed to carry on business, Bond would be recalled—hence his resignation and his obstructionism over the election of a Speaker. Although Bond would have been well-advised to have met the House instead of letting the political initiative pass to his opponents, in the event of deadlock MacGregor still would have called on Morris to try his hand, and he might well have given him a dissolution if he failed to carry on business. So even if Bond had allowed the election of Warren as Speaker and defeated Morris in a properly constituted House, MacGregor would probably have done the same thing. Bond really could not win. His only chance to regain power was at the polls, and that was slim.

THE 1909 ELECTION

Bond and the Liberals thus went into the 1909 election as the underdogs. The People's Party forces were buoyed by their success the previous November. Their weeks in office had enabled them to extract potentially damaging material from government files. They had control of government money and patronage, and the financial and other resources of the Reid Newfoundland Company were at their disposal. Morris published a hard-hitting manifesto that repeated the promises of the 1908 campaign, adding an attack on Bond for irresponsible handling of public finances, campaign irregularities, hanging on to office when he should have resigned, and a lack of tangible achievements.[104]

Bond's manifesto followed on April 17.[105] Once again, it was an unusual document. He made no promises. The party stood on its record since 1900, and voters should judge between Bond and the Liberals, and Morris and the People's Party. If the latter won, Bond warned, the affairs of the country would be shaped by the Reids and the future would bring financial ruin and confederation. "Should you [be] misled by delusive promises and false representations [to] give them a majority, be not surprised if public spirit dies out in the hearts of public men; and if some of them retire in disgust from a service which entails upon them incessant labor and responsibility, and but little gratitude and reward." Bond himself might well be among them. "Having toiled continuously for nearly thirty years to improve the condition of the Colony and its people . . . if by your votes you show yourselves indifferent to these services, I shall not waste what may remain to me of life in unavailing opposition to the deliberate decision of the people." He hoped and expected otherwise. What was needed was industrial development and lower taxes; given the problems in the fisheries, it was no time to undertake large railway expenditures. "Unsound finance spells ruin . . . AND CONFEDERATION WILL BE INEVITABLE." For an election manifesto, it was a decidedly personal document, replete with complaints about how he had been treated by Governor MacGregor and warnings about the future, and infused with disillusion and mistrust. It was hardly a stirring call to arms.

It was a short and nasty four-week campaign. The press was full of sensational accusations and counter-accusations, many of them concerning confederation and who had tried to bribe whom to cross the floor of the House. The Liberals complained bitterly about the "Prostitution of the Telegraph Service," by which they meant the use of newly instituted daily news and fisheries messages for party political purposes.* Morris raised the temperature by launching a libel action against the *Evening Telegram* for stating that he was in the Reids' pocket and would sell the country to Canada,† and he had the prominent businessman Walter Baine Grieve arrested for criminal libel. Grieve, the manager of Baine, Johnston and Co., had written to a dealer in Placentia Bay to the effect that he would only issue supplies if Bond was victorious, since Morris was in the pay of the Canadian government and working for confederation. Morris swore on oath that "I am and have been all my life opposed to Confederation. . . . I have never received one cent in my life from any Canadian Government or any person outside this Colony in connection with my Election Fund or Party Fund or Personal Fund." The cost of the last and current election was paid for by party members, "and by permanent residents of Newfoundland. . . . No persons outside of this Colony, directly or indirectly, have subscribed to our Party Fund." Whether or not this was true, Grieve apologized and withdrew his statements.[106]

While he was fending off allegations that he was soft on confederation, Morris was able to turn the tables on Bond, thanks to Harry Crowe's indiscretions. In his manifesto, Bond pointed out that he had rejected proposals emanating from "men in high positions in Canada," and that as far as he was concerned, confederation could only take place "with the free

* *Evening Telegram*, April 28, 1909. The news messages were compiled by the partisan and apparently tireless P.T. McGrath.

† *Evening Telegram*, April 24, 1909. Morris complained about the April 23 edition. The *Telegram* published a grovelling apology on June 7, 1909.

will and consent of the electors of this country." But courtesy of Joseph Downey, the Morris side had access to some potentially damaging correspondence. People's Party newspapers made great play with the letters that had passed between Crowe, Downey, and Bond. Most harmful of all were some 1907 letters between Crowe and Sir Frederick Borden, discussing possible terms of union. Incredibly, Crowe had given copies to Downey.[107] On the face of it, the correspondence could be used as the basis for accusations, which stuck, that Bond had been dallying with the possibility of confederation.

The Liberals made attempts at damage control in the *Evening Telegram.* Both Crowe and Borden issued statements to the effect that Bond had not been involved in what had been an entirely private exchange of views. Crowe also emphasized that he had never been Bond's agent, and provided his own version of the unfortunate encounter with Downey.[108] Fighting a difficult election in Placentia-St. Mary's, Edward Jackman (Bond's Finance minister) stated that he had been told in London the previous December that Morris's campaign funds had been subscribed in Montreal by financial men hoping to bring about confederation, and that he had been approached in St. John's about a party coalition, with Morris's knowledge. Challenged by an opponent to swear an oath that this was true, Jackman did so.[109] Nevertheless, Bond's credibility was severely damaged.

The correspondence first appeared in the *Daily News* on April 27, just as Bond was starting an election tour in Conception Bay (this time he spent little or no time in his own district). Bond thought the timing was deliberate. There was a Liberal meeting that evening in Clarke's Beach, which William Warren, the People's Party candidate for the district (Port de Grave), also attended. If Warren had expected to speak—and if the *Evening Telegram*'s report is remotely accurate—he was disappointed. Bond spoke for three hours, ending after midnight.[110] The *News* article, said Bond, had improperly published private correspondence between Crowe and Downey, and Crowe and Borden, about quite different matters. "However, they are blended together with Machiavellian ingenuity for the purpose of deceiving the public."

Before leaving St. John's, he had

> heard of Downey's letter to Morris and was quite prepared for the assault. I cabled Crowe of the plot and requested him to forward Downey's letters to me. . . . I also fortified myself with Crowe's letters to me and my replies. In the whole range of history there has never been disclosed a more diabolical plot to deceive than that which Morris has attempted to hatch out of this correspondence. The whole thing is worthy of a Tammany Shark or Bowery confidence man and it is difficult to conceive that a man who has had bestowed upon him the honour of knighthood could . . . stoop to such low villainy. . . . It shows that even the King's favour cannot create a gentleman out of such common clay.[111]

Bond went on to Harbour Grace (where he spoke for just under three hours) and Carbonear (three hours, twenty minutes).[112] Early in the afternoon of April 30, the steamer on which he was travelling anchored off Western Bay, in Bay de Verde district. Bond, the captain, and two crew members, got into a boat and rowed to the wharf so that Bond could land and send some telegrams. A crowd gathered on the wharf—men, women, and children. Among them, prominently, was one of the People's Party candidates, John C. Crosbie (a minister without portfolio).[113] It was not a friendly gathering. There was shouting, the chanting of slogans such as "Bond's Day Is Done," and warnings that the boat should not land. A crewman later testified that the crowd was "all in an uproar" and one of Crosbie's supporters, A.W. Bishop, shouted that "he would throw me [Bond] over the wharf if I tried to land." Bond called out to Crosbie that he would hold him responsible "for anything that occurs here" and began to climb up the ladder. According to Bond's account, Bishop and the men around him then became "violent in language and gesture." Bishop warned Bond that if he came any higher he would "kick [him] overboard," stepped down to the second rail and gave Bond "a violent kick in the chest leaving me breathless and insensible and I fell backward into the sea." If the boat had not swung away from the wharf, Bond would have landed across it and could have been seriously injured. He did hit an oar, hurting his back, before landing in the sea. Bond could not swim and there was an undertow, but the crew managed to pull him out of the water. When sufficiently recovered, Bond called Crosbie a scoundrel and told him again that he would hold him responsible and get a warrant issued for his arrest. "It was your own fault," Crosbie replied, "and you deserved it." Bond retreated to the steamer and the next day charged Bishop, Crosbie, and others with aggravated assault. On May 3, Bishop appeared before Magistrate Tuff in Western Bay, who sentenced him to six months imprisonment. Bond intervened, describing Bishop as "the tool of others," and the sentence was reduced by half.* Crosbie's day in court was delayed until May 28, when he appeared before Magistrate Penney in Carbonear. The case was dismissed.[114]

Bond continued his tour, speaking at Bay de Verde, Old Perlican—where Crosbie and his "roughs" tried to break up the meeting—Lower Island Cove, Northern Bay, Trinity, and Catalina.[115] He presumably made it to Twillingate for election day. Because of severe ice conditions in St. Barbe, the last result did not arrive until June 8, but it soon became clear that Morris had a comfortable majority. The Liberals lost eight seats,† reducing the party to ten members in the House. Every district with a Roman Catholic majority except St. John's East went to the People's Party, and many others as well. Bond and his colleagues were elected without difficulty in Twillingate.‡

One of the government's first acts was to consider the case of A.W. Bishop. This was prompted by a petition from Western Bay complaining

* This account is based on Bond's deposition of May 1 and the evidence of Bond and the boat crew on May 3 (printed in *Evening Telegram*, June 9, 1909; also *Evening Telegram*, May 1 and 4, 1909). The *Telegram* reported that the District Judge, George Penney from Carbonear, sat with Tuff.

† They lost one in Carbonear; one in Ferryland; one in Harbour Grace; three in Placentia-St. Mary's; and two in Trinity Bay.

‡ The total Liberal vote held up well compared to 1908. But more people came out to vote, and most of them favoured the People's Party.

that Bishop had not been represented by counsel. The assault had been caused by political excitement, Bond had not been injured, and if Bishop (who was married with six young children) served the full term, he might miss the Labrador fishery. The *Free Press*—which thought the incident merely "unfortunate"—added that Bishop could not appeal a three-month sentence and this was unfair. Magistrate Tuff saw no reason to change his mind. It had been an assault "of brutal violence," he wrote, and could have resulted in serious injury or death. But Morison, who for obvious reasons had no interest in pursuing the charges against either Crosbie or Bishop, disagreed. Bishop had been convicted on the unquestioned evidence of prosecution witnesses. Tuff had exaggerated the whole incident and a sentence of $10 or 30 days would have been more than adequate. He recommended, and the Executive agreed, that Bishop should be pardoned and released. MacGregor speedily did what was wanted, and Bishop was released.[116]

The legislature opened on June 1 for a short session. Bond attended only one sitting, on June 8. Kent had pleaded with him to be present on opening day and "take charge of the Opposition forces and guide their action in the House":

> It would be a fatal mistake, in my opinion, for us to remain passive during the opening sittings of this Parliament. . . . Great disappointment amongst our friends inside and outside the House will result from any failure on our part to act vigorously. It will be a serious blow to their hopes if you are not present. . . . It is most important that you should attend the House. Your absence will materially affect our supporters outside particularly in view of the report so diligently circulated by your opponents that you intend to be absolutely passive.[117]

It made no difference, and "the report so diligently circulated" was no doubt accurate, though it may not have told the whole story. Bond, unconvincingly, told the *Evening Telegram* that he had had "a very bad cold" and that there was not much for the opposition to do in the current session. He needed a holiday, he said, and he "would like to take a leaf out of Roosevelt's book and ditch the whole political business, at any rate for a time. I desire—what I have long desired—rest. I feel that I am entitled to it." He was staying on only because the party and his constituents wanted him to.[118] Kent therefore had to lead the opposition and there were no fireworks. MacGregor commented that the session was "remarkable for its harmoniousness and speedy dispatch of business," but he was upset by one incident. On June 10, Morris moved the adoption of a glowing and adulatory address to be presented to the departing governor. The opposition forced a division, over Morris's objections, and the five Liberals present voted against it.[119]

The outlook for the Liberal party was grim. It was reduced to ten seats and some key figures had been defeated. It was also effectively leaderless. Bond was utterly disillusioned. The events of 1907–09 had destroyed his idealism and made him deeply pessimistic about the future of his country and his countrymen. That the electorate could choose Morris and the People's Party over himself and the Liberals was a rejection that he could not easily accept. It was, in his view, a victory for the Reid interest and its allies, which would in turn lead to a compromised political future for the country based on irresponsibility and extravagance. His enemies had won, reciprocity had failed, and the colony's political scene had become debased and corrupted. He had lost the will to fight and, at the relatively young age of 52, wanted to leave public life. He asked the Liberal papers to keep his name out of the news, he did not write for them, and outside the legislature he took little (if any) part in active politics. He secluded himself at his Whitbourne property, squire of the small town, carefully keeping himself at a distance from the everyday gossip of St. John's.

Where was a new leader to be found? The Liberal party had become the Bond party under his remote and imperious leadership, the malcontents following Morris. There was no obvious successor, no one willing to take on the admittedly difficult job of changing, refocusing, and rejuvenating the Liberal party and leading the attack on the People's Party. It was the first time that such a hiatus had occurred in the Conservative/Liberal lineage. Carter had been the obvious successor to Hoyles, Whiteway to Carter, and Bond to Whiteway—though the latter had turned, snarling, against his erstwhile protégé. Able though he was, James Kent was reluctant, relatively inexperienced, and far less aggressive that Robert Bond could be. None of the other senior Liberals had Bond's experience, reputation, or standing, and none of them wanted the leadership. Not surprisingly, the Liberal party became paralyzed. Morris and his party, therefore, enjoyed an extended time in power—and the door was open for William Coaker's Fishermen's Protective Union, very soon to become a major political force. It was a significant turning point in Newfoundland's political history.

NOTES

1 *Evening Chronicle* and *Daily News*, March 5, 1908.

2 *Evening Telegram*, March 6, 1908.

3 Hiller, "Squires, Sir Richard Anderson," *DCB* 16 (online).

4 *Daily News*, May 23 and 25, 1908, and *Evening Telegram*, May 22, 23, 25, and 26, 1908.

5 *Evening Telegram*, July 15, 1908.

6 *Evening Telegram*, July 10, 1908; *Daily News*, August 15, 1908.

7 MacGregor to Grey, personal, April 11, 1908 (LAC, Grey fonds, 5244).

8 MacGregor to Lucas, personal, May 18, 1908; MacGregor to Crewe, tgm., July 2, 1908 (CO 194/273, 57, 115).

9 *Daily News*, September 5 and October 10, 1908.

10 For examples, see the *Daily News*, September 3, 1908, *Free Press*, October 13, 1908, and W.G. Gosling in the *Evening Telegram*, November 30, 1908.

11 "Fisheries report, 1908," *JHA* 1909, Appendix, 228.

12 Speech by John Anderson, reported in the *Evening Telegram*, October 13, 1908; letters from W.G. Gosling in the *Evening Telegram*, November 30 and December 1 and 2, 1908.

13 "Fisheries report, 1908," *JHA* 1909, Appendix, 228.

14 *Evening Telegram*, September 29, 1908 (RBP 2.27.011).

15 *Free Press*, October 13, 1909.

16 MacGregor to Crewe, conf., November 25, 1908 (CO 194/273, 319).

17 Grey to MacGregor, November 2, 1908 (LAC, Grey fonds, 5257); Grey to Bryce, November 2, 1908 (FO 800/331, 257).

18 MacGregor to Bryce, private, September 27, 1908 (FO 800/331, 347).

19 *Daily News*, September 30, 1908; *Free Press*, October 6, 1908.
20 *Evening Telegram*, November 11, 1908.
21 *Free Press*, December 1, 1908; *Daily News*, November 26, 1908.
22 *Daily News*, December 12, 1908.
23 Cashin, *My Life and Times*, 76.
24 D.W. Bradley (Lewisporte) to Bond, November 2, 1908 (RBP 3.27.007); *Evening Telegram*, December 19, 1908.
25 MacGregor to Grey, private, October 8, 1908 (LAC, Grey fonds, 5252).
26 MacGregor to Grey, private, December 27, 1908 (LAC, Grey fonds, 5264).
27 Morris to MacGregor, November 12, 1908 (*JHA* 1909, Appendix, 342); encl. in MacGregor to Bond, private, November 12, 1908 (RBP 3.27.007); MacGregor to Crewe, secret, November 13, 1908, and to Crewe, tgm., November 13, 1908 (CO 194/273, 291 and 285).
28 Bond to Burn and Berridge, tgm., November 12, 1908 (RBP 3.27.007).
29 Berridge to Bond, tgms., November 16 and 18, 1908, and Berridge to Bond, November 18, 1908 (RBP 3.27.007).
30 Bond to MacGregor, November 17, 1908 (*JHA* 1909, Appendix, 343–48; RBP 3.27.007).
31 MacGregor to Morris, November 19, 1908 (*JHA* 1909, Appendix, 348–49; RBP 3.27.007).
32 Grey to MacGregor, December 27, 1908 (LAC, Grey fonds, 5264).
33 MacGregor to Bond, November 24, 1908 (*JHA* 1909, Appendix, 349–51; RBP 3.27.007).
34 Bond to MacGregor, November 25, 1908 (*JHA* 1909, Appendix, 351–52; RBP 3.27.007).
35 MacGregor to Bryce, personal and confidential, December 3, 1908 (FO 800/331, 371); MacGregor to Crewe, conf., December 2, 1908 (CO 194/273, 360).
36 MacGregor to Bond, November 27, 1908; Bond to MacGregor, December 3, 1908; and MacGregor to Bond, December 9, 1908 (*JHA* 1909, Appendix, 353–55; RBP 3.27.007).
37 Bond to Berridge, December 15, 1908 (RBP 3.27.008).
38 MacGregor to Crewe, tgm., November 30, 1908 (CO 194/273, 357).
39 MacGregor to Crewe, conf., December 17, 1908 (CO 194/273, 391).
40 MacGregor to Crewe, secret, November 25, 1908 (CO 194/273, 350).
41 MacGregor to Crewe, conf., December 24, 1908 (CO 194/273, 412).
42 MacGregor to Crewe, secret, January 7, 1909 (CO 194/275, 10).
43 Minute by Lucas, December 8, 1908, and Crewe to MacGregor, secret,

December 17, 1908 (CO 194/273, 369–73); Crewe to MacGregor, secret, January 28, 1909 (CO 194/275, 78).

44 Cashin, *My Life and Times*, 72.

45 Roberts to Bond, April 18, 1909 (RBP 3.28.007).

46 The correspondence is in RBP 3.28.005.

47 Gushue to Bond, April 15, 1909 (RBP 3.28.007).

48 The account here is based in part on Hiller, "The Constitutional Crisis of 1908–09: A Sub-Plot," and Hallett "The 4th Earl Grey," 205–13.

49 *ENL* 1:640.

50 Crowe to Bond, January 6, 1909 (RBP 2.27.16). See also Bond's account of the Downey affair, after it became public in April 1909 (RBP 3.28.009).

51 Draft of a newspaper article, 1909 (RBP 7.15.006).

52 Notes for campaign speech, 1909 (RBP 3.28.009).

53 Grey to MacGregor, private and confidential, January 25, 1909, to Crewe, January 25, 1909 (two letters); and to Bryce, January 26, 1909 (LAC, Grey fonds, 22: 5518, 5530, 5534, and 5553).

54 For Clouston, see Miller, "Clouston, Sir Edward Seaborne," *DCB* 14:219–22.

55 Grey to MacGregor, private and confidential, January 27, 1909, (LAC, Grey fonds, 22:5561, 5559). See also Crowe to Fitzpatrick, January 26, 1909 (LAC, Grey fonds, 22:5561, 5559) and Grey to Crewe, very secret, January 28, 1909 (LAC, Grey fonds, 22:5563).

56 Kent to Bond, tgm., February 3, 1909, and Bond to Kent, tgm., February 4, 1909 (RBP 7.15.006).

57 Leith-Ross and Brodie, "Goode," *Oxford Dictionary of National Biography*, online.

58 Goode to Bond, private and confidential, February 7, 1909 (RBP 7.15.006).

59 MacGregor to Grey, private and confidential, February 8, 1909 (LAC, Grey fonds, 22:5599).

60 Crowe to Bond, February 12, 1909 (RBP 8.03.025).

61 Fitzpatrick to Grey, February 26, 1909, and encl. in Howley to Fitzpatrick, private and confidential, February 17, 1909 (LAC, Grey fonds, 22:5630 and 5636).

62 MacGregor to Grey, private and confidential, February 2, 1909 (LAC, Grey fonds, 22:5591).

63 MacGregor to Grey, private and confidential, February 11, 1909 (LAC, Grey fonds, 22:5606).

64 Bond to Goode, private and confidential, February 26, 1909 (RBP 8.03.025).

65 Howley to Fitzpatrick, private and confidential, February 17, 1909, and Kent to Fitzpatrick, conf., February 16, 1909 (LAC, Grey fonds, 22:5615 and 5636).
66 Goode to Bond, private and confidential, March 8, 1909 (RBP 8.03.025).
67 Bond to MacGregor, February 18, 1909 (*JHA* 1909, Appendix, 355–58).
68 *Evening Telegram*, February 18, 1909.
69 MacGregor to Crewe, tgm., February 19 and 22, 1909; Minute by Dale; Crewe to MacGregor, tgm., February 20, 1909; and MacGregor to Crewe, conf., February 25, 1909 (CO 194/275, 154–57 and 166).
70 MacGregor to Crewe, conf., February 25, 1909 (CO 194/275, 166).
71 MacGregor to Bond, February 20, 1909 (*JHA* 1909, Appendix, 359–67).
72 MacGregor to Crewe, conf., February 24, 1909 (CO 194/275, 290).
73 MacGregor to Bond, February 24, 1909, and Bond to MacGregor, February 24, 1909 (JHA 1909, Appendix, 375–79); MacGregor to Crewe, conf., February 24, 1909 (CO 194/275, 290).
74 MacGregor to Morris, February 25, 1909 (*JHA* 1909, Appendix, 382; CO 194/275, 233).
75 Morris to MacGregor, February 25, 1909 (*JHA* 1909, Appendix, 383).
76 MacGregor to Crewe, conf., February 26, 1909 (CO 194/275, 241).
77 MacGregor to Morris, February 26, 1909 (*JHA* 1909, Appendix, 383–84).
78 MacGregor to Crewe, conf., March 4, 1909 (CO 194/275, 275); MacGregor to Morris, March 1, 1909, and Morris to MacGregor, March 1, 1909 (*JHA* 1909, Appendix, 385–89).
79 See *Daily News,* March 18, 1909, for telegrams between Bond and the Colonial Secretary office during the 1908 campaign.
80 MacGregor to Crewe, tgm., March 3, 1909 (CO 194/275, 254); MacGregor to Crewe, tgm., April 8, 1909, and a Minute by Keith, April 12, 1909 (CO 194/276, 63).
81 MacGregor to Crewe, secret, March 6, 1909 (CO 194/275, 302).
82 MacGregor to Crewe, secret, March 6, 1909 (CO 194/275, 302).
83 Bond to Goode, February 26, 1909 (RBP 8.03.025).
84 See the Minutes on MacGregor to Crewe, conf., March 1, 1909, and on MacGregor to Crewe, tgm., March 6, 1909 (CO 194/275, 293–94, 321).
85 Minutes by Keith and Johnson, March 25, 1909 (CO 194/275, 295).
86 *ENL* 1:772, and 5:511–12.
87 May, *A Treatise on the Law,* 145. The copy in the Memorial University library was once owned by P.T. McGrath.
88 *Proceedings of the House of Assembly* (*PHA*), March 30, 1909, 5–7.

89 MacGregor to Crewe, March 31, 1909, and Minute by Keith, April 21, 1909 (CO 194/275, 405).

90 Morris to MacGregor, March 31, 1909 (*JHA* 1909, Appendix, 398).

91 Morris to MacGregor, March 31, 1909 (*JHA* 1909, Appendix, 401–6).

92 MacGregor to Morris, March 31, 1909; to Bond, March 31, 1909 (*JHA* 1909, Appendix, 405–7).

93 Morris to MacGregor, April 1, 1909, and Bond to MacGregor, April 1, 1909 (*JHA* 1909, Appendix, 407–9).

94 Bond to MacGregor, April 6, 1909 (RBP 3.28.007).

95 MacGregor to Crewe, secret, April 5, 1909 (CO 194/276, 57).

96 *Evening Telegram*, April 10, 1909.

97 *Evening Telegram*, March 27, 1909.

98 Minutes by Keith, Dale, Johnson, Just, and Hopwood, April 1, 1909 (CO 194/275, 398–99).

99 Minute by Keith, April 5, 1909 (CO 194/276, 34).

100 Crewe to MacGregor, tgm., April 5, 1909 (CO 194/276, 38). See also Crewe to MacGregor, tgm., April 3, 1909 (CO 194/275, 401).

101 The correspondence between April 5 and April 24, 1909, is in RBP 3.28.007. MacGregor to Crewe, conf., April 9, 12, and 24, 1909 (CO 194/276, 72, 91, and 227).

102 MacGregor to Crewe, tgm., May 12, 1909, and Crewe to MacGregor, May 14, 1909 (CO 194/276, 374–75); *JHA* 1909 (second session), 13–14; *Free Press*, June 8, 1909.

103 Keith, *Responsible Government*, 209–11; Forsey, *Royal Power*, 59–64; Noel, "Politics and the Crown," 285–91.

104 "Manifesto of Hon. Sir E.P. Morris," April 10, 1909, in the *Daily News*, April 12, 1909 (RBP 3.28.012).

105 RBP 3.28.008; *Evening Telegram*, April 17, 1909; MacGregor to Crewe, April 20, 1909 (CO 194/276, 106, enclosed both manifestos).

106 *Daily News*, April 16 and 29, 1909, and May 18, 1909; *Evening Telegram*, April 23, 1909; *Free Press*, April 27 and May 4 and 25, 1909; MacGregor to Crewe, April 27, 1909 (CO 194/276, 251).

107 *Daily News*, April 27, 1909; *Free Press*, May 4, 1909.

108 *Evening Telegram*, April 28 and 29, and May 6 and 7, 1909.

109 *Evening Telegram*, April 28 and May 8, 1909.

110 *Evening Telegram*, April 28, 1909.

111 Incomplete notes for the speech are in RBP 3.28.009.

112 *Evening Telegram*, April 29 and 30, 1909.

113 See Harris, *Rare Ambition*, 58–68 and *ENL* 1:563.

114 *Free Press*, June1, 1908; *Daily News* and *Evening Telegram*, June 29, 1909.

115 *Evening Telegram*, May 4, 5, 6, and 8, 1909.

116 Petition of Joseph Coish and others, May 19, 1909, Magistrate's report, May 26, 1909, Morison to MacGregor, May 29, 1909, and Minute of Council, June 4, 1909 (PANL, GN 1/3/A, file 150). See also *Evening Telegram*, June 9, 1909; *Free Press*, May 18, 1909.

117 Kent to Bond, May 28, 1909 (RBP 3.28.011).

118 *Evening Telegram*, June 8, 1909.

119 *JHA* 1909, second session, 42–43; MacGregor to Crewe, conf., June 18, 1909 (CO 194/276, 460); *Evening Telegram*, June 11, 1909.

CHAPTER TWELVE

In Opposition, 1910–1914

Robert Bond was a reluctant Leader of the Opposition. He played a minor role in the 1910 session, threatening to resign nine days before legislature convened on January 26. He told James Kent that the electors had left him "utterly powerless . . . to cope with the grave situation that now confronts the Country." He could not "prevent the inevitable, . . . the mortgaging of the future of our Country beyond repair."[1] A number of supporters tried to persuade him to reverse this decision and on January 24 he finally agreed to stay on. He thought there was little use in fighting "a venal and disproportionate majority." But his supporters had remained loyal in the face of temptations to desert the party, so he would do his best "to ward off the disaster that I feel threatens our Country. . . . Although my very soul revolts against association with those who constitute the dominant party in the Legislature."*

He also refused to take part in ordinary social events. In 1912, he told MacGregor's successor as governor, Sir Ralph Williams, that all he had done since 1909 was to attend legislative sessions. Opposition newspapers had kept his name out of the news, and he had "not made any attempt, apart from my utterances in the House of Assembly, to influence public opinion." He read the *Evening Telegram* but had written nothing for it. "I have sometimes thought that my oftentimes absence from official and social functions when I would have met you may have been misunderstood. . . . Let me say then that I risked this rather than the risk of coming into contact with those

---

* Eight Liberals to Bond—Kent, Shea, Clift, Gear, Dawe, Jackman, Pitts, and Knowling—January 19, 1910 (RBP 3.29.002.); Bond to Kent, January 24, 1910 (RBP 3.29.002).

who as disgraced parties [were] placed in position as Ministers of the Crown, and for whom I can have no other feeling but contempt."[2]

Governor Williams—not highly regarded at the Colonial Office, perhaps unfairly—thought that Bond was "full of bitter personal mortification at his complete downfall" and that this now motivated his political actions.* He was largely correct, as he was in thinking that the two political parties were similar in many ways. When Bond responded to the Throne Speech on January 26, 1910, he claimed with reason that "its principal contents are endorsements of the policies which I have been advocating for thirty years."† Bond and Morris were of the same political generation, had served in the same governments, and they were both colonial nationalists. It would have been surprising if there had not been a considerable degree of continuity. Where they fundamentally diverged, Williams thought, was over the Reid Newfoundland Company and its influence and interests. He was correct once again, but it was not quite that straightforward. Morris was less conservative than Bond, more flexible, and much more willing to spend money and play to the gallery. He was also less authoritarian.

Though Edward Morris and many of his supporters had been in public life for years, the People's Party seemed to represent a new beginning, new political leadership, and a focus once again on domestic issues and priorities. This government was not very much interested in external or imperial affairs until the Great War intervened. The Liberals, on the other hand, seemed to represent a discredited past; they were unable to reconstitute the party as long as Bond remained influential. His sense that he should resign was, in fact, sound: if the party was to rebuild, then it had to find a new leader. But it might not be the same party, and potential candidates may well have feared Bond's disapproval. It is hard to escape the

* Williams to Crewe, secret, February 15, 1910 (CO 194/280, 31–32). Williams's previous posting was the Windward Islands

† Bond in Assembly, *Proceedings of the House of Assembly* (*PHA*) January 26, 1910, 23–32. The Morris government made a long-needed change in 1910 by instituting an official "Hansard," though debates were still reported in the newspapers in some detail.

conclusion that although Bond fundamentally wanted to leave politics, he was jealous of his legacy (possibly like Whiteway) and saw himself as the embodiment of a Liberal tradition. So the new force in Newfoundland political life proved to be William Coaker's outport-based Fishermen's Protective Union, of which both Bond and Morris were instinctively wary.

The People's Party's approach to governing was displayed in the 1910 Throne Speech. It was expansive and optimistic, reflecting its manifestos of 1908 and 1909.[3] The branch railway programme was central, but there were many other proposals. As the session continued, the government unfolded ambitious plans for extended coal and oil exploration (in collaboration with English companies), agricultural development, the export of beach pebbles, a copper smelter on the west coast, the promotion of wool manufacturing, and cold-storage facilities for fish and farm produce. There would be more money for education, lighthouses, the telegraph system, dredging projects, and a new poor asylum would be built. All of this and more, the government claimed, was easily affordable without tax increases, given the country's prosperity and the diversification of its economy: "This Island," boasted Michael Cashin, the Minister of Finance, "is one of the richest and most productive of the overseas possessions of the British Empire."[4]

For all its talk and promises, the People's Party did not achieve a great deal that was long-lasting, other than its branch line railway programme and old age pensions, and its more fanciful "fads" deserved as much ridicule as some of Bond's. But for a few years it did spend more on essential services while managing to run a small surplus on current account. In 1913–14, it slipped into deficit until the Great War temporarily rectified matters. More notably, however, the public debt increased by 38 per cent between 1908–09 and 1914–15, mainly because of the additional railway mileage. The Liberals had to be careful in their criticism of this, though, since during their term the debt had increased by about 30 per cent (albeit over a longer period).

Bond made only two major interventions during the 1910 session, both of which sparked sharp exchanges with Morris over their respective roles in the political history they had shared since the 1880s. The first was his response to the Throne Speech, which he called "a balloon full of gas."

The second, and more important, was his reply to the branch railway proposals. The government planned five branch lines: from Shoal Harbour (near Clarenville) to Bonavista; from St. John's to Trepassey; from a point near Whitbourne to Heart's Content and Grate's Cove; from Goobies to Terrenceville (Fortune Bay)*; and from Deer Lake to Bonne Bay. There would be no tenders. Instead, the Reid Newfoundland Company would build the branch lines for $15,000 per mile, paid in cash (not bonds this time), and would operate them for forty years in return for land grants of 4,000 acres per mile. Labourers would be paid $1.50 a day.

Work had started on the Bonavista branch the previous October without legislative authorization, because the Labrador fishery had failed. About 2,500 men were employed in its construction by mid-November 1909.† Morris estimated that building about 250 miles (about 400 kilometres) of railway would cost $4 million—there had been no surveys except on part of the Bonavista branch—and argued that the government had made an excellent deal. It was based on earlier railway contracts, but the colony was paying less per mile in both money and land, and the workers' pay was higher. The project "will do great things . . . by [its] effect on the whole trade and revenue of the country. . . . It is not a question of whether it will pay. It is a question of whether it is necessary. We do not ask whether lighthouses will pay. We do not ask whether roads will pay. . . . I say we shall have more money than we require to meet the interest on this outlay." He went on to stress the income that would be derived from a royalty agreement with the companies mining on Bell Island.‡ Even less convincingly, he claimed that the government would stimulate farming and settle families along the railway lines.[5]

---

* Originally known as Head of Fortune Bay, the name was changed in 1905.

† Clarke, "Railway Branch Line Construction," 12. When criticized for this expenditure, Morris said he did not "care for the Audit Act when there are people in need of bread. . . . It is all very well to preach political economy and morality when you have a good dinner inside you. Talk is cheap but action speaks louder than talk" (*PHA*, February 8, 1910, 159).

‡ The companies agreed to pay 7.5 cents per ton for ten years (Morris, *PHA*, March 4, 1910, 432).

Morris presented the branch railway scheme as a continuation of Whiteway's "policy of progress." The former premier had died in 1908 and the People's Party now claimed it was his true successor. Bond would have none of this. The Whiteway policy, of which he had been a part, was "a developing and colonizing policy; this is mere pandering to local clamour in certain settlements for more rapid transit than is now available." He could agree to the lines to Fortune Bay and Bonne Bay, since they would go through areas that seemed to have some economic potential. But the other lines did not—and the whole purpose of the original policy had been to encourage settlement and a domestic market. Beyond that, the contract was biased in the Reids' favour. The Newfoundland government would carry the costs and risks of loan flotations, the public debt would increase, and yet more Crown lands would be alienated. The whole scheme was a giant speculation. Given the government's other expensive promises, the scheme meant "the mortgaging of the future of this country beyond repair, and when it is too late, the people of this country will awake to the realization of the fact." He also attacked Morris for supporting the 1898 Reid contract, which had "blasted as with a whirlwind the ripening hopes of those who saw in [Whiteway's policy] the opening of a great industrial future for this country, and the unreasonable antagonism of the Reid Newfoundland Company has converted a railway policy designed as a blessing to the people of this country into little short of a curse."[6] Supporting Bond, Kent argued—correctly as it turned out—that Morris had underestimated both the mileage and the cost, and that the only people to profit from the deal would be lawyers and the Reids.[7]

Morris, of course, argued that he had been as much a part of the history of railway development as Bond, which was true, and he defended his support for the 1898 deal. "I am satisfied to leave the judgement of my actions to some future Pedley or Prowse, absolutely certain as to what the verdict will be." He had prevented Bond from repealing a contract that converted liabilities into assets, agreeing only to "reasonable and justifiable amendments." He went on: "Does any man expect that that railway will be operating fifty years from now? It will be old iron by that time, and we shall probably be travelling by airships or some equally new method."* People's Party members lined up to support Morris and the branch lines, to praise Whiteway, and to pour scorn on Bond and his record. The lines would mean both employment and prosperity for the outports, which had been neglected long enough; Trepassey would become an important winter port; there would be colonization and the exploitation of "dormant resources." R.J. Devereux went as far as to say that the policy "would make us almost independent of the failure or partial failure of our staple industry" and he compared Whiteway to Cecil Rhodes.[8] Richard Squires, a Morris protégé and a future prime minister, unjustifiably accused Bond of betraying Whiteway and his policies. The legislation went through the Assembly; even in the Legislative Council there was little active criticism

THE HAGUE TRIBUNAL AWARD

There is no record of Bond's activities for the rest of 1910, but he must have been following the proceedings of the North Atlantic Fisheries Arbitration at The Hague, which began on June 1. A "Special Agreement" had been signed in Washington on January 27, 1909, while Bond was still in office. It set out the tribunal's terms of reference and defined the seven questions it was to decide. It has been convincingly argued that the Americans skilfully managed to shape the wording to be advantageous to themselves.[9] Root had foreseen that the tribunal would require a regulated fishery, no matter what the United States might argue, and wanted to be assured that a neutral process would be created to assess both existing and future regulations, and to decide controversies. The American team had clear objectives.

The other side had to accommodate strains between the Canadian, Newfoundland, and British governments, a situation that was not helped by the political turmoil in Newfoundland. Even after that crisis had subsided, the British were disunited, in part because the official leader of the "British" team, A.B. Aylesworth, was in some respects ineffective.[10] It was the Canadians who did the bulk of the background work; Newfoundland's

---

* Morris, *PHA*, February 8, 1910, 153–61. The railway finally closed in 1988. The branch lines had disappeared long before.

contribution to the preparation of the case seems to have been minimal. Both Morris and Morison went to The Hague but left the colony's oral argument to Sir James Winter—who, says Gluek, "cut a sorry figure"*—and to Sir Robert Finlay, a former British attorney general.† The other leading British counsel was the current attorney general, Sir William Robson.

The award came down on September 7. The main question was whether Britain had the right, without the consent of the United States, to regulate the joint fishery in a reasonable manner. The court held that Britain had such a right, which was inherent in British sovereignty. However, the regulations had to be both reasonable and consistent with the 1818 treaty. Following the direction in the Special Agreement, the tribunal ruled that the reasonableness of existing regulations should be decided by an arbitral process, as should future regulations, if they were disputed. The remaining questions addressed subsidiary yet important issues that had arisen during the dispute. The court ruled, somewhat ambiguously, that American vessels exercising treaty privileges could employ crew members who were not American citizens, that but these crew members would derive "no benefit or immunity from the treaty." American vessels should enter at Customs and pay the same dues as Newfoundlanders; they could enter any bay or harbour, on or off the treaty coasts, for shelter or repairs, but should report at Customs if the stay was prolonged; and they could fish in any bay, creek, or harbour on the treaty coasts—a defeat for the position originally advanced by Bond. They could not combine trading and fishing.

The final issue was how to define the three-mile marine limit. The court decided that it should generally follow the sinuosities of the coast; in a bay, a baseline should be drawn where it ceased to be a bay and became open sea (the tribunal recommended that this be defined as a width

* Gluek, "Programmed Diplomacy," 60. Finlay and Robson were very uneasy about Winter speaking at the hearings, which he did on July 4 and 5 at the Newfoundland government's insistence. George Buchanan, a British diplomat stationed at The Hague, reported that Winter "is a wretched creature, who has not properly studied the case" (Buchanan to Mallet, July 2, 1910, FO 371/1038, 401).

† Finlay was on a retainer from both Newfoundland and Canada.

of ten miles). It further suggested specific baselines for several Canadian bays, and for Placentia and Fortune bays in Newfoundland.*

The award was well-received by all parties. The British, Canadian, and Newfoundland governments all thought that the essential points had been decided in their favour, though they all had reservations about the external review of fisheries laws and regulations (despite it having been foreshadowed in the Special Agreement). Robson observed that "we have saved our sovereignty but we can't exercise it."[11] Elihu Root, who had spoken for six days, wrote that "we practically got substantially all that we were entitled to."[12] The Gloucester interest was satisfied. In his much later analysis, Tansill describes the result as a compromise,[13] and he is right. The more extreme American claims were dismissed, but Canada and Newfoundland had to accept that their fishery regulations could not be unilaterally defined and enforced. British legalities were preserved, but the Americans got the practicalities that they had sought. The final agreements were not concluded until July 1912.

There was no immediate comment from Bond. The reference to the matter in the 1911 Throne Speech was brief and neutral. It praised the use of arbitration but indicated that there were issues still to be resolved.[14] Such comments as there were from government speakers were unenthusiastic; the party line was clearly that what had been gained, if anything, had probably not been worth the expense.[15] The government was certainly not prepared to give any credit to Bond, who alone spoke at length on the matter, calling the decision a victory since it upheld Newfoundland on the fundamental issue. "I am content the honour and dignity of Newfoundland as a self-governing state of the Empire has been upheld, the jurisdiction and sovereignty of Great Britain and over this Island and its territorial waters has been confirmed, and a way has been made plain

* Fraser, "The Hague Arbitration," in MacKay, ed., *Newfoundland*, 400–410; Callahan, *American Foreign Policy*, 521–23; Tansill, *Canadian-American Relations*, 118–20. With reference to the three-mile limit, the US Senate had insisted on the exclusion of the Bay of Fundy and the Gut of Canso from the terms of reference. Conception Bay was also excluded. The full text is available at www.arbitrationlaw.com.

whereby the people of Newfoundland may enjoy to a fuller extent than heretofore the riches that lie at their very feet." But he objected strongly to the review of existing regulations, thought that American vessels should pay light dues, and disputed the decision about "bays and creeks," though he thought it understandable. As for the three-mile limit, that had been Canada's question. Pointedly, he acknowledged the role of British counsel and blamed what had been the opposition press before 1908—and Winter himself—for providing the Americans with valuable ammunition. He urged the government to do what it could to encourage herring export to the United States market, rather than letting the Americans catch or buy all they wanted.[16]

POLITICS IN 1911

In contrast to the previous and subsequent years, Bond attended the House regularly during the 1911 session, being absent only when snow blocked the railway line and he could not get into St. John's from Whitbourne. He spoke at length and aggressively on some issues, often accusing the government of giving too many inducements and concessions to outside businesses. He was a much more effective opposition spokesman than any other Liberal. Bond well understood that flexibility was needed to attract and encourage investment in the colony, as his administration's record showed, but he clearly felt that the Morris government was going too far. But he was on thin ice, because any criticism of Morris's plans could be met by reminders of his own failures. The first instance of this was cold storage in the fishery.

Cold-storage bait depots had been on the political agenda since at least the mid-1890s. Governments of all stripes had passed legislation to encourage such facilities—Winter in 1898, Bond in 1904, and Morris in 1910—all done in the hopes of stimulating fresh fish exports to North American markets.[17] In 1911, Morris introduced legislation to confirm a contract with two Maine businessmen who undertook, with subsidies, to build five cold-storage plants, smokehouses, and fish-packing establishments, as well as glue factories and fertilizer plants. Morris hoped the deal would lead to the exploitation of more fish species, more home processing, more jobs, and more exports to "the neighbouring continent," since new markets for fish were urgently needed.[18] Bond supported the principle of cold storage, of course, but thought the contract was loosely worded and too generous. In his view, the government was subsidizing an American firm to engage in the general fish trade, which constituted unfair competition with local businesses. And since it would be able to export any kind of fish, including bait fishes, the deal nullified the Bait Act.* The government (supported by the recently established Board of Trade) denied that there was any threat to the Bait Act. Tempers flared. Attacking Bond on February 22, Crosbie asked:

> What has he ever done for the fishermen, I should like to know. If I remember rightly, he was born with a silver spoon in his mouth and left a fortune. Has he ever had the pluck to put one dollar of it in the fisheries of the Colony[?] Not likely. He never did and he never will. He lives at Whitbourne and the best I have known him do is to sell his milk to the Butterine Factory† and take away business from the farmers.

Bond lost his temper, which prompted further abusive remarks from Crosbie and Cashin.[19] This turned out to be a fuss about nothing, since the project fell apart in 1912 and cold-storage depots remained a dream, certainly before 1914.

There were similar debates over the government's plans to encourage peat cutting and a proposal to build an explosives factory at Cape Broyle. Both schemes involved British firms, and the opposition thought the government granted too many concessions and did not sufficiently safeguard

---

* Bond, *PHA*, February 14, 16, and 22, 1911, 71–75, 113–15, 149–55. The governor thought it a good bill (Williams to Harcourt, conf., March 16, 1911, CO 194/283, 60).

† Owned by Bond's friend Robert Brehm (Sexty, "The Brehms," 30–33, 45–49).

the colony's interests.* There was also a significant divergence of opinion over agriculture. The Bond government had adopted a policy of encouraging full-time professional farmers and had started a model farm to provide training and to experiment with suitable crops. From 1910, the Morris government took a different and more traditional approach, which was probably more realistic. It rejuvenated the Board of Agriculture (originally established in 1889) and promoted the establishment of local agricultural societies (there were sixty-six in 1911) through which improved seed and livestock were to be distributed, for the most part to fishermen who were also subsistence farmers. There would be additional encouragement for sheep,† pig, and poultry farming. Bond strongly opposed an increase to the Board's funding. He thought that the policy was misguided, that the Board existed primarily to provide jobs for government supporters who knew little about agriculture, and that the societies were a waste of time.‡ The government responded that its policy would help ordinary people and that the model farm, which it abolished, had been a waste of money. "We do not want half a dozen scientific professors out at a model farm, training a number of boys who will then go to Canada and practice there."[20] Once again, tempers became frayed. R.J. Devereux, a member of the Board, attacked Bond for allegedly sneering at fishermen, and Cashin—over the top as always—called Bond "the greatest political hypocrite that ever had a seat in this House, and the greatest bloodsucker."[21] In truth, Bond's agricultural policy had been fully established only in 1908; Morris was—as he

---

* Bond and Morris, *PHA,* February 15, 1911, 82–97. There is relevant correspondence in PANL, GN 8/1, 42. On the explosives company, see *PHA,* February 15, 1911, 97–100. Bond did support a copper smelter deal with a British company, however (*PHA,* February 16, 1911, 103–5).

† A problem here was what to do about the dogs used for hauling wood, which sometimes attacked sheep. The Morris government proposed to replace dogs with Sable Island ponies.

‡ Bond, *PHA,* March 8, 1911, 349–54, 383–88. The opposition persistently attacked the appointment of three government MHAs to the Board—Devereux, Downey, and Seymour. William Coaker was also critical (Williams to Harcourt, February 13, 1911, CO 194/283, 15).

said—in effect systematizing and trying to improve practices that had gone on for years. The approach was also politically advantageous for the People's Party.

On other social issues, Bond supported legislation to prevent using Inuit people for exhibition purposes, and persuaded the government to include the Innu, as well.* With respect to education, he supported a grant to build schools in communities where there were none, and to extend the school year in others. He argued strongly in favour of more technical education, and for amalgamated schools in small places. "It is disgraceful that there should be . . . a large number of children without education simply because the people are divided as to which altar to kneel at."[22] But he clashed with the government about old age pensions. Morris and his supporters accused Bond of having done nothing about pensions except to appoint a useless commission of investigation composed of upper class people who knew little, if anything, about "the poor and lowly." The government proposed granting, as a start, four hundred pensions of $50 per annum to men over 75 years of age who could prove that they needed the support and had lived in Newfoundland for twenty years. Bond defended his government's record, argued that the pension should be universal for both men and women over the age of 65,† and asked how the four hundred were to be selected—would they be the government's "chosen favorites"? In essence, the opposition argued, these payments were a form of poor relief. Not unreasonably, Morris held that this was a moderate and affordable scheme, and that half a loaf was better than no bread at all.[23] The last subject of dispute was the country's finances. The government was, of course, exuberant about the Newfoundland's relative prosperity. The opposition alleged extravagance and jobbery. Pointing to the largest revenue ever, Cashin claimed that the factors behind the current boom gave "promise of maintaining themselves on a still expanding scale in the years

---

* *PHA,* February 23 and 27, 1911, 206, 215. Bond described the Innu ("Mountaineer Indians") as "a noble race . . . a superior race to the Esquimaux, but almost as innocent." He did not know Labrador.

† Although he thought that a minimum income of $2 a week should be a disqualification.

to come." Newfoundland was "assured of a permanence of prosperity and advancement which few countries can excel." He went out of his way to criticize the Bond government, and once again praised Whiteway's legacy.[24] Bond called attention to a history of economic uncertainty, an increase in the public debt of almost $5 million since 1909, and $300,000 assigned to public service expenditures, alleging serious financial irresponsibility and irregularities. In return, Morris dismissed Bond as "a Cassandra, a prophet of evil, a Jeremiah pouring out his lamentations, complaining of everything in which for eight years he himself excelled." His was "a creative policy" where Bond had been "content to allow things to drift along as they were."[25] Bond was, in fact, sounding necessary notes of caution, which neither Morris nor Cashin seemed willing to notice.

Once again, Bond's activities after the session ended are not documented. Morris departed for a three-month trip to Britain to attend the coronation of George V, an imperial conference, and the Festival of Empire at the Crystal Palace—where Newfoundland's exhibit was housed in a downsized replica of the Colonial Building—and, of course, to meet Colonial Office officials. According to the government newspapers, it was all a great success. As far as domestic politics were concerned, Morris obviously knew that the Liberal party was in trouble and that he faced no serious challenge from that quarter. Nevertheless he took no chances, especially since the 1913 election was now on the horizon. In a 1911 Burin by-election, Morris toured the district twice.[26] Significantly no Liberal candidate ran, Bond was nowhere to be seen, and the People's Party won by default.

The political scene was soon fundamentally changed, however, by the arrival of William Coaker's Fishermen's Protective Union.[27] By November 1911, three years after the FPU's formation at Herring Neck, it had more than 12,500 members and 106 locals located from St. Anthony to the north shore of Conception Bay. It had established the Fishermen's Union Trading Company and published a weekly newspaper, the *Fishermen's Advocate*. The union's motto—*suum cuique* (to each his own)—was seen by some as both secular and subversive. Coaker wanted the FPU to be a non-sectarian movement of outport workers who had long been exploited by an allegedly unfair mercantile system. It was an outport rebellion against the dominance of the power brokers in St. John's. Coaker was not a revolutionary, but the FPU was determined that there must be fundamental reform. This meant that it had to do more than lobby St. John's politicians; it had to enter politics and contest elections.

The FPU could never hope to sweep the country, however, because it remained largely confined to its original heartland, the east and northeast coasts of the island. It never firmly established itself on the west and south coasts, perhaps because of the difficulties of distance, or because the seasonal rounds and local economies were different in these regions. But its most important obstacle was the unbending hostility of Archbishop Howley—and by extension that of the Roman Catholic Church as a whole. Because the FPU's original constitution required a membership oath, Howley condemned it as a "secret society" and thus it was forbidden by canon law. When Coaker later changed the constitution, the prohibition was lifted. Howley was given assurances regarding the preservation of denominational schools, as well, but the hostility remained. Howley was a social conservative who (like Bond) saw the union as a threat to social order and the authority of his Church. The union's aims, he wrote, would cause "an upheaval of our whole social fabric: . . . set class against class and . . . end in the ruin and destruction of our commercial and business system." Priests were asked to "stamp out this Society at once."[28] Union locals that had spontaneously appeared in Roman Catholic districts

Sir William F. Coaker in later life. (*History of the Fishermen's Protective Union of Newfoundland*)

The flag of the Fishermen's Protective Union. Originally printed in Richard Hibbs, *Who's Who in and from Newfoundland 1930*, 2nd ed. (St. John's; R. Hibbs, 1930)

closed down. In effect, the FPU was permanently frozen out of Catholic Newfoundland.*

For many years Coaker had been a Liberal supporter and worker—but he was a Whiteway Liberal and his relations with Bond were uneasy. By 1904, the two men had parted political company, Coaker telling his brother that Bond was "despictable" [*sic*]. Coaker supported Whiteway and the United Opposition in that year's election.[29] Thereafter, he supported Morris, whose populism he found attractive. After the 1909 election, Coaker sent congratulations along with a list of actions that the new government should take.[30] He continued to badger Morris on a wide range of issues until October 1910, when he accused the government of treating the FPU "with silent contempt."[31] Morris responded at length, protesting that the government was doing all it reasonably could. It did not prevent Coaker from telling the FPU Convention in December that the union should "place all the members we possibly can in the House of Assembly and do for ourselves what the existing political parties will not do." A "Union Party" should therefore "take the field in 1913."† Probably Coaker had always intended to do this, but the preliminaries had to be observed. He hoped that the future Union Party would hold the balance of power in the Assembly, and thus be able to obtain the legislation that it wanted.

Relations between Coaker and Morris continued to sour in 1911. The *Fishermen's Advocate*, increasingly critical of the government, lost the privilege of publishing legislative debates and Morris consistently refused to do what Coaker demanded.[32] In November, that tireless busybody Harry Crowe decided to take a hand, having met Coaker to discuss conditions in the logging camps. He told Bond that Coaker personally favoured "an

* There were a few FPU locals in Roman Catholic settlements on the Northern Peninsula and Notre Dame Bay from the start. After the ban was lifted, a few more appeared in Ferryland district and St. Mary's Bay. See Fitzpatrick, "Archbishop M.F. Howley."

† Coaker (compiler), *Twenty Years*, 17. Governor Williams reported that Morris thought Coaker to be "a dangerous and mischievous lunatic and [he] ignores him in all public affairs" (Williams to Harcourt, conf., May 7, 1912, CO 194/285, 370–72). Williams endorsed Morris's view of Coaker.

understanding" that would lead to a political alliance of his union and the Liberal party. He thought that Morris feared the growth of the FPU and would probably take steps either to destroy it or get its support.[33] On Crowe's advice, Coaker wrote to Bond in November suggesting an alliance provided that, if the Liberals won the next election, the new government would bring in twenty-one pieces of legislation "which the F.P.U is pledged to secure."[34] Bond told Coaker in his reply (November 17) that he did not object to the proposed legislation, which he thought was in line with Liberal party ideals, nor to the existence of the FPU as a union—he had noted its growth "with much interest and pleasure." But he did object to the emergence of a third political party. This he regarded as a mistake, and the FPU should back the Liberal party under Bond's leadership, thus uniting Morris's opponents. Perhaps unwisely, he went on to criticize Coaker's "balance of power" strategy as an unacceptable attempt to coerce the legislature. There was no reply.[35]

Bond's letter was polite but uncompromising. Coaker had been a political enemy since 1904 and, until recently, connected to Bond's opponents. A social conservative, Bond was allied to Archbishop Howley. Many businessmen and clergy were uneasy about the FPU, if not downright hostile to it, and Bond would have shared many of their concerns. Morine later wrote that Coaker and Bond were "diametrical opposites in temperament and ideology." He thought Bond "was born to be a Tory," while Coaker was "a Liberal by heredity and a Radical by nature."[36] The negotiation of any kind of alliance between these two men would prove to be very difficult indeed.

The exchange with Coaker did not mean that Bond had abandoned his decision to retire, however. Early in January 1912, his friend Robert Brehm told William Lloyd, editor of the *Evening Telegram*, that Bond had "pretty well made up [his] mind to go to Europe for the winter" and leave politics: "He has never fully recovered from the brutal treatment of the Crosbie gang of scoundrels at Western Bay." Lloyd had apparently persuaded himself that there was no substance to the "persistent rumours" about Bond's retirement and was disturbed by Brehm's letter.[37] Eventually Bond once again gave in. He had intended to go to Europe because his rheumatism ("the Western Bay legacy") was "exceedingly troublesome."

He changed his mind, not wanting to give his "old political friends disappointment and embarrassment" and "in order to prevent the old Liberal party going to pieces I must hold on to my seat this Session, if I have a leg to stand on." But he wanted to leave public life:

> It has become so debased, so low, so dishonest that there is not a fraction of any man of self-respect to have anything to do with it. We have arrived at a stage when graft is regarded as shrewdness and blackguardism as a quality to be dubbed "honourable." If I was ten years younger I would stump this Country from one end to the other, as I did in 1898 on the Railway swindle, and expose this present condition of things and try and end it. Or, if I could recognize any determination on the part of the public to return to the past and to rid the Country of the present disgraceful state of affairs, I would throw every personal consideration to the winds and fight as I have fought before. But there is no encouragement to do that. "Israel is bound to its idols, let it alone." When the Country comes to its senses, when it is done with humbugs and charlatans, it may desire my help. If it does, it shall have it.[38]

THE 1912 LEGISLATIVE SESSION AND AFTER

Bond attended the early part of the 1912 session but did not appear after March 21. He left much of the work to James Kent, who had to face serial insults from Cashin, Crosbie, and Morris. As in former years, the opposition criticized the government for extravagance, broken promises, and the branch line programme, which Bond called "a huge piece of electoral bribery undertaken without regard to either cost or utility."[39] He was on less certain ground, however, when attacking the government for accepting a gift of $100,000 from the Reids to build tuberculosis sanatoriums in St. John's and in each electoral district.* Bond thought the legislature

* Half the money, given by W.D. Reid, was earmarked for the St. John's sanatorium. The balance, from H.D. and R.G. Reid, Jr., was to fund the outport hospitals (*Evening Chronicle*, January 25, 1912).

should have been consulted and that there was an inherent conflict of interest. The sanatoriums would be expensive to staff and maintain. In addition, he questioned whether they were actually needed; he thought the best way to combat tuberculosis was to improve living conditions—especially in St. John's, where "our nostrils are filled with villainous odours arising from the gutters, the sidewalks, and the houses in the prevailing slums."[40] The government responded that the Bond administration had done next to nothing about the tuberculosis epidemic, there was nothing unconstitutional about accepting the gift, it did not matter where the money came from, and the sanatoriums were badly needed. There were heated exchanges between Bond, Morris, and Cashin, much like the following sample:

> RT. HON. SIR R. BOND – The Rt. hon. leader of the Government is getting very excited over the matter. And yet I am merely taking up his own words, that 50,000 of our people have gone down to their graves through neglect. These exaggerated statements are not proper to be made to an intelligent committee. We are not appealing to the galleries.
>
> RT. HON. THE PREMIER – I have been appealing to heads, not to heels.
>
> RT. HON. SIR R. BOND – You would appeal to any part of the human body that would respond to you.
>
> RT. HON. THE PREMIER – Now what does that mean? You do not know what it means.
>
> RT. HON SIR ROBERT BOND – . . . . I got up to point out a most important fact. . . . I only say that if a doctor diagnoses a case as consumption and the man is forcibly removed to a sanatorium his family should be supported by the State, and for this I am violently assailed.
>
> RT. HON. THE PREMIER – I did not attack the Rt. Hon. gentleman. I merely replied when he made a charge against myself.

RT. HON. SIR ROBERT BOND – You said that 50,000 people had gone down into their graves through neglect. Whose was the responsibility? It was either the Poor Commissioners or on the Executive Government's if these 50,000 people were paupers and the leader of the Government must bear his share of the blame. From time to time I am told by him that he courts criticism, and yet every time I criticise him he becomes heated, or if he does not, his followers do and I am subjected to any amount of personal vilification and abuse.

HON. MR. CASHIN – If you mean me, what I said was true.

RT. HON. SIR ROBERT BOND – You are insignificant, utterly insignificant.

HON. MR. CASHIN – You are a political hypocrite.

RT. HON. SIR ROBERT BOND – Mr. Chairman, I appeal to you to make the hon. member take his seat. He does not know the rules.

HON. MR. CASHIN – I am not to be taught by you.

RT. HON. SIR ROBERT BOND – Mr. Chairman, do you intend to permit this rowdyism here?

HON. MINISTER OF FINANCE AND CUSTOMS [Cashin] – You are the greatest political hypocrite that ever stood on the floors of this House.

RT. HON. SIR ROBERT BOND – I move that these words be taken down.

HON. MR. CASHIN – . . . . The Hon. gentleman seems to be too large for this Assembly or perhaps thinks it is not good enough for him. . . . As I said, he comes back here after sulking in his tent at Whitbourne for two years. He should have been here at this House the past two sessions instead of imitating Cincinnatus at the plough. . . . He will plead . . . that he has changed his mind, for he told us this evening during the debate that a man who could not change his mind was a fool. He changed his mind and what are we to think of him? Only a fool he says does not change his mind.

RT. HON. SIR ROBERT BOND – Mr Chairman, I rise to a point of order. The hon. member's remarks certainly have no relation to the matter before the Chair.

HON. MIN. OF FINANCE AND CUSTOMS – The Rt. Hon. gentleman is not going to bulldoze me; I do not intend to be stopped by him.

THE CHAIRMAN – The Hon. Minister of Finance and Customs is quite in order.

RT. HON. SIR ROBERT BOND – Sir, calling me a fool, is that in order?

RT. HON THE PRIME MINISTER – . . . . It is not fair to allege that the Minister referred to him as a fool.

RT. HON. SIR ROBERT BOND – I do not expect any fairness in this House to-night.

RT. HON. THE PRIME MINISTER – I submit that this charge is equally unfair . . . .

HON. MINISTER OF FINANCE AND CUSTOMS – . . . . He is not going to bulldoze me. I was a member of his party for several years, I know its inside workings, and I speak with authority when I say that he is the greatest party autocrat that ever occupied a place in this House.

RT. HON. SIR ROBERT BOND – I again object to this unseemly conduct.

HON. MINISTER OF FINANCE AND CUSTOMS – The hon. member can object as much as he likes. . . . I am not going to be dictated to by him as to what I may say or what I may not say. I will go further and assert here that the Government of which he was the head was a one-man Government. The public know that it was never a Government of the people,

> but a Government with Robert Bond as absolute dictator. . . . He is like a horse that when it falls breaks its knees and is never the same after. . . . For myself I care as little for him as I do for the meanest worm that crawls the earth.[41]

While it was an exaggeration to say that the Liberal government had done nothing to combat tuberculosis, the lead had been taken by the Association for the Prevention of Consumption, founded in 1908 with the encouragement of Governor MacGregor. The Morris administration certainly did much more, though the Reid-sponsored sanatoriums never materialized.* Bond underestimated the prevalence of the disease and unnecessarily discounted the value of sanatorium treatment. It is hard to escape the conclusion that his thinking was influenced by his dislike of the Reids and the government. It should be noted, though, that the FPU was also highly critical of the anti-tuberculosis campaign, seeing it as condescension to outport Newfoundland by St. John's aristocrats, who should first clean up their own backyard. If local capitalists such as the Reids and John Harvey (the merchant and Legislative Councillor who chaired the Association) paid better wages and improved working conditions, then perhaps there would be no need for sanatoriums.†

Another slanging match occurred during the debate on the Estimates[42]; Bond did not address the Budget, leaving the criticism to Kent.[43] Nor did Bond speak during the debate on raising a further loan of $2 million for the branch railways, and another (local) loan to fund expansion of the telephone system and building more lighthouses.[44] On March 21, 1912, his final day in the House as it turned out, Bond presented a batch of FPU petitions asking for an election in November.‡ While expressing

---

* There was a small sanatorium on Signal Hill from 1910 until 1917. The main St. John's sanatorium was built in 1916 (*ENL* 5:430–31; Candow, *Lookout* 125–26).

† See Knowling, "'Ignorant, Dirty and Poor'," 98–101. Bond also criticized unsatisfactory conditions on sealing steamers.

‡ This demand was based on the assertion that Morris's term ended in June 1913. Spring elections were avoided , thus there should be an election in November 1912.

concern over excessive government expenditures, he also asked for a branch line to Grates Cove. The legislature had been swamped with FPU petitions throughout the session and the campaign clearly annoyed the government. Morris was combative and unapologetic. Grates Cove would get its railway and, if it was re-elected, the government would further expand the railway system.* The election would take place in November 1913, he said, adding there was no "reckless expenditure" and the petitions were unfair and based on deception and inaccurate information.[45] In characteristic fashion, Cashin dismissed the petitions as bogus and a clear justification for the increase in the education grant. Morris thought them a product of "two or three agitators" who were "trying to make trouble in this country today," who were "either men who have been dismissed from the positions which they held or men trying to get in here. I know every one of them."[46]

Relations between the Morris government and the FPU had by this time completely broken down and the *Chronicle* was ruthlessly attacking Coaker.† In January 1912, nine Executive Council members had issued libel writs against Coaker and the *Fishermen's Advocate* for accusing them of graft. An apology had to be published.[47] In March, Coaker organized a mass meeting and parade of sealers in St. John's, while Morris addressed a sparsely filled hall—a telling contrast to what had occurred in 1908. In early April, Coaker sent a memorial to the governor demanding the dismissal of Morison as Minister of Justice because of a conflict of interest. Morison was a director and shareholder of the Anglo-American Development Company, which had been awarded, by the government of which he was a member, a licence to cut timber over a huge area of Labrador (13,853 square miles or almost 36,000 square kilometres). A subsidiary accusation was that Morison had given improper advice concerning a timber licence on the island to a financier who was also involved in the Labrador

* Morris had already promised to extend the Fortune Bay branch line to Grand Bank and Fortune.

† On May 20, 1912, for example, the *Chronicle* called Coaker (among other things) a blasphemer, a "sectarian firebug," a wife beater, and a deceiver (Baker, "'Coaker Week'," 53–57).

scheme.[48] Morris, who himself owned shares in a timber business and had been involved in speculation,[49] refused to sacrifice Morison. He was a prominent Orangeman with considerable influence in Conception Bay and on the northeast coast—and, in any case, an admission of sharp practice would damage the government as a whole. Governor Williams refused to intervene, calling Morison "a man of honour and integrity," if somewhat indiscreet.*

THE LIBERAL–FPU "ALLIANCE"

In November 1912, Dr. Wilfred Grenfell wrote to Bond criticizing the current state of affairs and asking whether he would be leading a party in 1913.[50] Bond treated him to another jeremiad.[51] His life's work, he said, had been destroyed by his successors:

> The whole future of the Colony has been mortgaged in order to buy up the Constituencies by wild cat Railway schemes involving an addition to the Public Debt of eight or ten million dollars, and by other liabilities, that . . . will leave us stranded financially, and our people crushed under the weight of increased taxation to meet the interest on Loans. Today the Revenue is swelled by reason of the circulation of millions of borrowed money. When the Railway work ceases, then look out for the debacle. We cannot hope to be able to borrow more money because the Colony's assets . . . have all been appropriated by the Reids, and their tools in the Government. The credit of the Colony has been ruined by the dishonourable conduct of Members of the Government. . . . So the outlook is not such as to induce one to again sacrifice comfort and health in guiding the public affairs of the Colony. . . . I regret to say that many of my Countrymen have a peculiar liking for Charlatans and Humbugs. I feel like letting them alone.

* Williams to Harcourt, May 6, 1912 (CO 194/285, 246). Colonial Office officials were somewhat critical (Minutes by Keith and C.P. Lucas, 242; *Chronicle*, June 28, 1912).

The approaching election was also of concern to William Coaker and, of course, to the Liberal party. In September, Coaker had again approached Bond, asking whether he would co-operate with the FPU. Unless he was assured of this, the FPU would form a separate party at its December convention in Bonavista and "contest the whole country." Bond simply pointed Coaker to his letter of November 17, 1911, which had not been acknowledged.[52] Coaker then approached William Lloyd, whom he had known since the 1890s. He proposed a new Liberal-Union party led by Bond, its platform incorporating FPU policies. There followed some more specific proposals about candidates, districts, and local affairs, which seemed on the surface to favour the FPU—it had already selected twelve candidates and had no intention of asking any of them to step down.[53] Lloyd immediately wrote to Bond, urging that an amalgamation should be negotiated. The FPU convention was approaching and—ominously—Alfred Morine had reappeared and seemed to be in Coaker's camp.[54]

There were consultations between Lloyd, Kent, Henry Gear,* and (presumably) Bond, and a counter-proposal went to Coaker on November 21.† There were two main problems with the FPU proposal, from the Liberal standpoint. Coaker wanted the FPU to be regarded "as a distinct entity—a party within a party"—while Bond stood for "a thoroughly united Liberal party with common aims and objects, and he [Bond] points to the fact that your Union is very largely composed of Liberals . . . who could have no reason to break away from their allegiance, provided the reasonable demands of the Union are honestly met." There had to be "undivided leadership" and, if victory ensued, all party members would have to support Bond, giving "due deference . . . to the prerogatives of the office of Prime Minister." Second, the name "Liberal-Union party" was unacceptable. This objection had to do with rival claims to the Liberal label and succession, a point on which Bond was sensitive. If the name changed,

* Gear, a former Liberal cabinet minister, was now an MHA for Burin (*ENL* 2:492).

† Lloyd to Coaker, November 21, 1912 (RBP 3.31.004; ASC Coll 009, 10.03.06). A slightly different proposal had been sent on November 19, 1912 (Lloyd to Coaker, November 19, 1912, RBP 3.31.004).

former Liberals who had joined Morris could "raise the Liberal standard," Morris could accuse Bond of abandoning the Liberals to form a new party, and it would "give him the opportunity he desires to jump back into the ranks of the Liberals and to throw over the most objectionable elements of his present following." However, the party manifesto would be submitted to the FPU for approval, and the Minister of Fisheries would be an FPU member. Coaker rejected the reply as insulting and negotiations collapsed.[55] "He prefers that each party shall paddle its own canoe," wrote Lloyd, "and that the F.P.U. shall be represented in opposition to Morris rather than the acceptance of the terms I placed before him."[56]

Lloyd, Kent, and other senior Liberals clearly believed that a deal of some sort with Coaker was necessary. Even Bond had moved some way toward an agreement, but he insisted on leading a single party. Harry Crowe urged Coaker to be flexible. Bond's great objection, he said, was that the FPU candidates had sworn allegiance to Coaker, "and it would be very embarrassing and humiliating for him to have a power within the party that would not recognize him as the only leader. . . . Do not allow any trifling technicality of the constitution of the Fishermen's Protective Union to stand in the way of your uniting with Sir Robert Bond and the Liberal Party."[57] Coaker remained firm about the need for separate FPU representation. He seems to have recognized, however—possibly influenced by Lloyd and Crowe—that the FPU needed Bond's reputation and the Liberals' political experience, and that the union would not be able to field credible candidates in all sixteen districts. It was clear that the FPU would face strong opposition in Roman Catholic areas and in St. John's. Governor Williams, about to retire on a pension that he thought inadequate, remarked that Bond was "a man of dominant and masterful personality. Mr. Coaker is equally dictatorial." If there was an alliance it could not hold, because Bond would never agree to hold power by Coaker's permission.[58] He was, once again, correct.

The FPU convened at Bonavista in mid-December 1912 as planned. It ratified a manifesto that had been in development for some time and which became known as the "Bonavista Platform." It has rightly been called "the most radical political programme ever placed before a Newfoundland electorate" to that time.[59] Its thirty-one clauses together demanded government regulation and reform of the fishery, administrative and constitutional changes, the extension of education, and greater attention to social welfare.[60] It was an ambitious and direct challenge to the other parties.

Whether or not he perceived the FPU as a challenge—and even though it was the last sitting before an election—Bond did not attend the 1913 session of the legislature. Instead, he went to England. Lloyd thought his absence would be politically disastrous, but Bond refused to reconsider. His health was bad, the "apathy of the public" was appalling, and the FPU's efforts to gain control of the government were not in the country's interest. If Coaker's attitude did not change, Morris would win the election and "misrule" would continue. If Bond were to attend the session, he would have to condemn Coaker's "iconoclastic announcements." It was better to stay away.[61] He departed on February 11. The new governor, Walter Davidson, arrived a few days later and complained to Kent that Bond should not have left "without some form of civility."*

Kent had no choice but to lead the opposition during a session that lasted from March 5 to April 16—shorter than usual. The FPU again sent in volleys of petitions. Given the approaching election, the government decided to appropriate some of the union's promises and provide some good things for the voters. The old age pension scheme was expanded. There was an increase in the education grant and the promise of adult night schools. A marine disaster fund was set up and the budget put sugar, tea, salt beef, and pork on the free list—a loss of some $385,000, estimated at about a tenth of total revenue. In addition, telegraphs would be extended and steamer service improved. Capitalists undertook to manufacture fish offal and other refuse into glue and fertilizer, and to build a railway from Quebec City to Cape Charles or the coast near Battle Harbour, with a link to Bonne Bay.[62] Bond's "fads" had returned in a new guise. Davidson quite rightly refused to allow the closing speech to be turned into an electioneering manifesto.[63]

---

* Davidson diary, March 1, 1913 (PANL, Davidson fonds, MG 136, Box 1). Davidson was another governor not well regarded at the snobbish Colonial Office. His previous posting was Governor of the Seychelles (*ENL* 1:595).

When Bond came back to Newfoundland in mid-April, St. John's was bubbling with political gossip and speculation. Would he lead a party in the November election? Would the Liberals make a pact with the FPU or would there be a split over the issue? Would Morris outbid the Liberals? Or would the FPU fight the election independently? Coaker once again approached Bond through Lloyd, proposing twelve Union candidates, the right to name two members of the Executive, approval of the Minister of Fisheries, and the incorporation of the Bonavista Platform into the party manifesto. Bond remained inflexible. He would meet Coaker only on the basis of his letter of November 17, 1911.[64]

Senior Liberals tried to persuade Bond otherwise. Kent urged him to come to town to meet potential supporters,[65] who in turn wrote to Bond, pointing out that the Liberal silence worked greatly to Morris's advantage.[66] Dr. James Tait, who had met Coaker, thought that he would negotiate fair terms and show some flexibility. There was no chance of winning without the help of the FPU and Bond should not be "too exact"—the important thing was to "Clean out Morris."* Crowe had been in London at the same time as Bond; they had met several times and Crowe had urged the alliance (and no doubt confederation, as well). He, too, returned to Newfoundland in April and urged Bond to meet Coaker. The FPU was getting stronger and more independent, so Morris might well be open to an alliance, too. Crowe also met with Archbishop Howley who, he said, supported a Liberal-Union agreement "to save the Country."[67] Given Howley's feelings about the FPU, this was a remarkable piece of news. Bond simply replied that he was doubtful that a satisfactory arrangement could be made—and especially as it seemed that Morine was behind Coaker, who had promised him one of the Bonavista seats. "The man múst be mad."[68]

The long-suffering Kent and others† continued to work on Bond's behalf and talk to Coaker. By late June, some form of understanding seems to have been reached, then Bond threw up another obstacle. He

* Tait to Bond, private and confidential, May 14, 1913 (RBP 3.32.003). Tait mentioned that George Knowling and others had also talked to Coaker.

† Coaker mentions a committee consisting of Kent, Clift, Lloyd, and Gear (Coaker, *Past, Present and Future,* Article 6).

would discuss policy—but "the selection of men as my supporters I cannot leave to Mr. Coaker. If I venture to assume the responsibility of conducting the public affairs of the Country I must demand the right to select the material to carry out that work. This has been my position from first to last." He had not known about Coaker's "ultimatum in respect to Candidates" and needed that information. He would then decide "whether I will lead the Party at the General Election or drop out. My reply will be final."[69] Coaker sent word that he wanted ten of the candidates to be approved by the FPU.[70] Bond objected, since the ten were "pledged by an oath of allegiance to the [FPU] Supreme Council in respect to political questions and issues," and if they were all returned, they would effectively hold the balance of power. Bond optimistically calculated that Morris would win at least eleven seats, Coaker would have ten, and Liberals at most fifteen. Thus if he formed a government, he would have to rely on one of the other factions—possibly even the People's Party, and "Nothing would induce me to risk such humiliation and degradation."[71]

There were more discussions with Coaker, who said, in effect, that if the joint party manifesto covered the principles laid down in the Bonavista Platform "as may be agreed upon," there should be no problem, since FPU members would necessarily support it. Kent added that Bond's attitude, and his refusal to enter into direct negotiations himself, was endangering the future of the party and encouraging its enemies:

> The Country today regards you as the leader of the Liberal Party and it would come as a stunning surprise to the electors if they learn you have retired at the present critical moment and on the eve of a general election. Such retirement would . . . lead to the breaking up of the party and the return to power of the Morris party not because of its strength but because of the disorganization created by your retirement from the leadership.[72]

Harry Crowe also talked to Coaker and tried to change Bond's mind, but without success.[73] It was now early July, about four months away from the election, and negotiations had effectively broken down. Coaker felt he could make no more concessions. Bond remained at Whitbourne, aloof, difficult, and intransigent. It looked as though Morris could count on a second term in office.

There was no movement until August 12, when Lloyd told Bond that Coaker was willing to meet him and discuss the letter of November 17, 1911.[74] If this was to happen, Bond replied, he had to be sure where Coaker stood. He posed five questions: Had Coaker discussed the terms of an alliance with the FPU councils? Did they know of Bond's reluctance to participate in the election and of his decision concerning candidates? Was the FPU prepared to give Bond "a unanimous call" and "to pledge me loyal and undivided support"? And had the Supreme Council given Coaker full power to pledge the union's support? If Coaker answered each question in the affirmative, then he should write. Bond added: "If you and the other members of the Party can arrange for some other Leader I shall be greatly relieved and everlastingly thankful."[75] Coaker answered "yes" to all of the questions,[76] wrote to Bond, and was invited to lunch at Whitbourne.[77]

They met on August 18.* This first step did not settle the alliance, however, and there were problems yet to come. Bond agreed in principle to lead the "Opposition Party" in November, but he wanted further undertakings from the FPU concerning party unity and loyalty. Beyond that, there had to be agreement about which candidates would run in which districts, and about the manifesto. Bond said he (not Coaker) would select six FPU candidates, which he thought fair, and that he would include fifteen items from the Bonavista Platform. Any more would involve large expenditures, and he was not prepared to make more pledges until he had seen the colony's books. His final point was that, if the party did not win, he would immediately resign.[78] Coaker was unimpressed. The manifesto had to include more from the Bonavista Platform and he stood firm on the choice of certain candidates.[79]

Bond also refused to budge. The opposition had to appeal to the public in general not just the members of the FPU, and that public would find

* In *Past, Present and Future*, Article 6, Coaker wrote, erroneously, that the meeting was in early September.

it difficult to reconcile condemnation of Morris's extravagance with potentially expensive promises. With reference to candidates, he could not simply abandon certain "old and faithful friends for mere party expediency. I would prove myself entirely unworthy of any man's respect." Given the apparent impossibility of reconciling the demands of the FPU with his obligations "to my numerous old supporters," he would abandon the negotiations and pull out of public life.[80] He conveyed this to Lloyd,[81] and also told Kent that since he (Bond) was obviously the stumbling block to an alliance, he would get out of the way. Kent advised him to reconsider and delay any public announcement.[82]

Coaker responded immediately and hastily to Bond's letter.[83] Bond refused to bargain— he could not promise anything more. "With me it is not a question of holding back from the fishermen and labouring classes all or anything they may reasonably desire, but rather, how much can I promise to undertake without risk of disappointing them." In any case, the crucial point was representation. He estimated that Union members constituted about a sixth of the electorate, so he had offered a sixth of the seats in the Assembly. This was fair, even generous, since most fishermen were not FPU members. The union had to be content "with a fair and reasonable recognition in the party"; if not, hostility from "merchants, planters, importers and shop keepers" might "assume formidable proportions at the polls."[84]

Coaker stopped bargaining. In view of the undertakings in Bond's recent letters, he wrote guardedly:

> I on behalf of the F.P.U. offer you our loyal support as Leader of the Liberal Party in the coming election, and while you endeavour to do all possible to perform the policy enumerated you can depend on the hearty support of the Union Candidates. I believe you will do your utmost to meet the wishes of the Fishermen's Protective Union, as they from time to time see fit to bring matters to the notice of the Government.[85]

Bond, Lloyd, and Kent were pleased. They obviously thought that the long period of political manoeuvring was over and that the campaign could now begin in earnest.[86]

But there was yet another crisis. Bond thought that if Henry Earle, who had represented the single-member district of Fogo since 1900, wanted to run there again, he should be allowed to do so, and he should receive the support of the FPU. Earle was an important merchant there but the FPU was also influential. Coaker predicted that Earle could never win. If Earle ran as a Liberal, wrote Coaker on September 6, he would field an FPU candidate against him.[87] Bond exploded. This was a duplicitous breach of the agreement and "a gratuitous insult. . . . If Mr. Coaker imagines he can play with me, there is a rude awakening for him. . . . This is one of the most dishonourable acts that I have ever experienced." He was pulling out.[88] In the end, he did not—and Lloyd's influence may have been an important factor. Lloyd pointed out to Bond that the Earles, father and son, were anti-FPU; he had spotted the son (William Earle)

A political cartoon from the 1913 election campaign that focuses on the difficulties Bond experienced with William Coaker. (Courtesy of Robert Hong)

lunching with Morris at the City Club. In addition, William Earle was reported to have said, "We'll bust up the combine, rather than give in."[89] Coaker also blamed William Earle, emphasizing that the FPU local in Fogo had come out against an Earle candidacy.[90]

Bond was not easily placated, however. He wrote an angry letter to Coaker on September 18 insisting that Earle, George Roberts, and Arthur Miller should be candidates if they wished, and that Bond should decide "both platform and representation." Unless Coaker withdrew his letter of September 6, he would retire from politics and publish the correspondence.[91] Coaker was apologetic. The letter was written hastily, he said, and was not intended to breach the agreement. He fully believed that Earle would retire.[92] The affair was not mentioned in the *Evening Telegram* but it did receive attention in the *Evening Herald*, now the main People's Party newspaper.* In the end Earle did not run, though it was rumoured that he was furious, protested to Bond, and threatened to work against his replacement, William Halfyard, a former teacher and the FPU's secretary-treasurer.[93] In Twillingate, Bond's old ally George Roberts also retired in favour of an FPU candidate, and Arthur Miller did not contest Trinity,† where Lloyd ran with two Unionists. The *Herald* calculated that fourteen former Liberal candidates were left out.[94] In terms of candidates, Coaker did better than had been agreed.

So it was an uneasy alliance that finally began its election campaign in late September (voting day was October 30). The FPU was ebullient, confident, perhaps cocksure; traditional Liberals were unhappy, given Coaker's attacks on St. John's and the mercantile elite, and his demands for potentially expensive expenditures on social services and rural infrastructure. They disliked what they saw as an emphasis on class. Roman

* At the end of 1912, the Evening Chronicle Co. bought the *Evening Herald*, turned it into a government mouthpiece, and closed down the *Evening Chronicle*. This reduced the Liberals to a single daily, the *Evening Telegram*, while the government had two—the *Evening Herald* and the *Daily News* ("The Transfer of the *Evening Herald*," 20).

† Miller had been elected for Trinity in 1904 and 1908. He was defeated in 1909. Roberts had represented Twillingate since 1900 (*ENL* 3:550 and 4:609).

Catholics were especially sensitive to the strident accusations in the government press that the FPU was both socialist and secularist. Governor Davidson noted that St. John's merchants seemed to share these views and took little interest in the election. Bond and Coaker were seen as merely using each other in an attempt to defeat Morris. In any case, Bond's contribution to the country—mainly in external affairs—was thought to be over.[95] P.T. McGrath thought—probably accurately—that Bond's former followers would divide into three groups: diehard loyalists, those who disliked the alliance and would not vote, and those who would vote for the government.[96]

Bond's manifesto appeared on October 4.[97] He did not hide his reluctance to lead the party, which he was doing, he said, only out of a sense of public duty. There was a need "to put an end to the present riot of political crime" that was "sapping our existence as an independent State of the Empire." He attacked the government's cozy and expensive relationship with the Reids, which was driving up the public debt and imperilling the colony's credit, and railed against irresponsible increases in expenditures generally, as well as against the politicization of the civil service. The manifesto also alleged that the loyalty of each and every member on the government side of the House had been purchased with public money. "This idea that the public Treasury is legitimate spoil must be weeded out." He listed a series of broken promises, then cautiously approached the issue of the FPU. For the first time, Newfoundland had

> felt the touch of one of the "irresistible tendencies of the modern State," namely the disposition among its citizens themselves to form "groups" for the advancement or defence of particular interests. In the world around us these "groups" have realized that . . . the Government does not represent them. **The formation of the Labor Party in England is to be interpreted in that way, as must also be the formation of the FISHERMEN'S PROTECTIVE UNION in Newfoundland.** . . . The largest "group" of Electors in the Island demand a representative voice in the legislation by which

> their interests are controlled. **They have united with thousands of others outside the Union in calling me to their service [and] their interests will be most carefully advanced and protected.**

The promises followed, many of them derived from FPU demands—but "the serious financial embarrassment brought about by the waste and extravagance of the present Government renders it impossible for the finances of the Colony to respond to further demands at this time."

Coaker also issued a manifesto aimed at his own district (Bonavista) that repeated much of Bond's document, but added the caution that FPU support was contingent on the Liberals keeping their promises. It also had an explanation for the alliance:

> Had we not cooperated with the Liberal party, the Union would have had to face the Government single-handed and if successful form a Government to rule the land. That was too great an undertaking for us at this time. . . . By cooperating with the Liberal party . . . we will secure reforms and legislation that the Union desires and we will possess an influential and very important voice in the conduct of public affairs, while in no way will our union suffer or my work in building it up be interfered with.[98]

By the time the manifestos appeared, the Liberal-FPU campaign had begun, certainly in St. John's and the north, and Bond was on his way to his district. He stayed there for the rest of the campaign, giving no assistance to Liberals fighting marginal seats, particularly in Conception Bay and elsewhere on the Avalon Peninsula. Given that the FPU vote would ensure his victory in Twillingate, his decision is in some ways difficult to understand—it has been called "folly."[99] But by this time Bond was an unenthusiastic party leader who had been signalling for some years that he wanted to leave public life; he shied away from direct confrontations with People's Party candidates. He had been scarred by the 1909 campaign and seems to have lost faith in the good sense of the electorate. He may also have been unwilling to allow the FPU to present itself as totally dominant in his own district. The leaders of the Liberal/Union party remained in the east and northeast, leaving the People's Party leadership largely unchallenged elsewhere.*

A political cartoon from the 1913 election campaign that focuses on Coaker's alleged "socialism." (Courtesy of Robert Hong)

* Bond was offended by the FPU supporters' habit of cheering for Coaker first and himself second. "He was a proud man," Coaker later commented, "and it was not discreet on the part of F.P.U. friends to annoy Sir Robert in this manner, but they had no intention of annoying him by so doing. Nevertheless, it left a certain sting that he could not forget" (Coaker, *Past, Present and Future*, Article 6).

If the Liberal/Union strategy (such as it was) aimed to discredit the Morris government and all its works, McGrath and the People's Party went after Coaker and the Union, smearing Bond by association. The *Evening Herald* wrote in early September that Coaker preached "rabid socialism, denouncing merchants and businessmen, vilifying clergymen and religious leaders, inveighing against all social institutions, and advocating policies that if put into effect must ruin the Colony's solvent existence." Bond-Coakerism would break the banks—Savings Bank deposits would be squandered, the Canadian banks would withdraw, and trade and industry would be paralyzed. "Do the people want another bank crash in 1914?"[100] Bond and Coaker would "CLEAN OUT THE SAVINGS BANK . . . IN ORDER TO PROVIDE THE MOTOR BOATS AND THE FARMS IN THE INTERIOR."[101] These apocalyptic and highly irresponsible prophecies had a serious impact; the bank's newly appointed Cashier, Robert Watson (a former member of the Morris government), asked Governor Davidson to speak to McGrath.[102] Whether he did so or not, a run on the Savings Bank developed and lasted into December, at which point government newspapers published a reassuring statement from the directors, and Bond and Clift visited the bank and ostentatiously made deposits.*

On October 19, the mentally ill James Hare made an attempt on the life of Bishop John March in his cathedral at Harbour Grace. The government press immediately used the incident to stir up even more anti-socialist paranoia. The *Evening Herald* said that Hare was a socialist and had "anarchistic ideas" picked up while he was working in Sydney, Nova Scotia. His actions made clear "what socialism and anarchism represent." He was obviously "of the incendiary class who in the guise of anarchism, socialism and nihilism are preaching destruction to law and order and the overthrow of all constituted authority." Furthermore, "anarchist papers"

---

* McDonald, *"To Each His Own,"* 43; *Evening Telegram*, December 17, 1913; and Davidson diary, December 2, 1913 (PANL, Davidson fonds, MG 136, Box 1). Davidson wrote that Bond "in his somewhat resonant and impressive manner paid in money." He thought the run was caused by FPU supporters withdrawing money to help prop up the Trading Company.

were being circulated in the colony, and the doctrines of "red revolutionists" obviously inspired the FPU and the *Fishermen's Advocate.*[103] Liberal Union candidates were now routinely referred to as "socialist." (McGrath later had the gall to deny that he had used the Hare case for political purposes.[104]) The incident encouraged a flight of Roman Catholic FPU voters to the People's Party. Though Archbishop Howley had withdrawn his ban on Catholics joining the Union, and reiterated the point at Kent's request in late September, his and the church's hostility to the FPU was well-known. The government also used the Union's support for elected school boards and non-denominational night schools to raise a "godless schools" cry; it, too, had a considerable impact in Catholic districts.[105]

Polling day (October 30) passed without incident except at Bonavista, where People's Party candidate Sidney Blandford was roughed up by some FPU supporters, who then tried to find and do the same to Donald Morison.[106] The voter turnout was (according to Davidson) the largest ever known. The Liberal/Union party won the popular vote, but it took only fifteen seats to the People's Party's twenty-one.* Morris's net loss was seven seats, his sole gain being a seat in St. John's East. The biggest upsets were in Trinity Bay and Bonavista Bay, where the FPU ensured large majorities for its candidates. Indeed, the FPU's electoral performance was impressive. The Roman Catholic districts on the Avalon Peninsula went to the People's Party, predictably enough, which also held onto its seats on the south and west coasts. The hardest fought districts were in Conception Bay (north), where the government took five out of seven seats (though with thin majorities)—some said thanks to Reid influence.[107]

The result showed that the FPU was in the ascendant. This put Morris on the defensive—for if the Union could expand geographically, as Coaker intended, it might win the next election. The Liberals, however, were reduced to seven seats, five of which were dependent on FPU support—the party was weaker than its numbers seemed to show. But on the surface, at least, it looked as if the alliance was holding.

---

* On November 13, 1913, the *Evening Telegram* reported 61,615 votes for the Liberal/Union party and 51,402 for the People's Party. See also Davidson to Harcourt, November 11, 1913 (CO 194/287, 406).

Members of the House of Assembly elected in 1913, outside the Colonial Building. Edward Morris is fourth from the left in the front row. (PANL, C1-201)

That year, the FPU convention opened in St. John's on December 2. Bond was invited to speak, but pleaded rheumatism. Kent, Lloyd, and two other Liberals appeared on the platform.[108] In his address, Coaker congratulated himself and the Union on the election result, referred to the Liberals only in passing, and did not mention Bond. Nevertheless, the Liberals cannot have been altogether displeased by the resolutions (presented to Davidson), which opposed Morris's intention to keep the defeated Sidney Blandford and Donald Morison in the Executive and give them seats in an enlarged Legislative Council.[109] Morris told the governor that he thought ministers could stay on as long as they found seats in "a reasonable time," which Davidson defined as sixty days. The question of the Legislative Council he referred to London.[110] In the event, both ministers resigned on January 2, 1914. It was the end of Morison's political career. Blandford was eventually appointed to the Council and resumed his portfolio.

Bond's papers contain an undated draft of a reply to a Throne Speech, clearly intended for the 1914 session.* Its existence demonstrates his initial intention to lead the opposition, and its contents say a great deal about his state of mind late in 1913. Addressing the election campaign, he bitterly condemned the *Evening Herald*'s attacks on the Savings Bank—there should be legislation to "render such [a] base political tactic . . . a criminal offence"—and the People's Party's use of sectarian tactics in Roman Catholic areas. In Harbour Grace district, he alleged, "it was declared that . . . the Nuns would be driven from the Convents and the Priests from the Sanctuary and every School would be closed within six months. . . . The people were told that there was a connection between certain members of the Opposition and the demented creature who attempted . . . to murder the R.C. Bishop of that place." In Placentia district there had been a deliberate stoking of prejudice against the FPU, and sectarianism had crept into St. John's from neighbouring districts. Such tactics had diverted attention from what should have been the central election issues—the railway policy, waste, and extravagance—with the anomalous and improper result of a government returning to power with a minority of votes cast. Then there was the Morison and Blandford affair: "In this Country men can be found so lost to all self-respect as to cling to office after the public have declared them unworthy of public trust." Looking to the future, how would the government find the money to pay for its railway policy? It would have to raise a loan "no matter what the cost, or the Colony will default in its obligations and become bankrupt. That is the outcome of the suicidal railway policy of the Gvt." His warnings had been disregarded and the decision to pay the Reids in gold "sealed the doom of this Country. The debacle may be postponed for a time, but the time is not far distant when its autonomy will be laid at the feet of the Money Changers." The government had to attend to the "conditions of life" in Newfoundland by reducing public expenditure and lowering the tariff. "It is impossible to view without grave anxiety the condition of things

* RBP 3.28.016. It is possible that Bond had been sent an advance copy of the Throne Speech.

in this Colony. But, 'Hope like a poising Eagle burns above the unrisen morrow.'* May hope not turn to despair."

Over the Christmas period, Bond changed his mind about leading the opposition. On January 2, 1914, he wrote to James Clift, a fellow member for Twillingate. He could not continue as leader, he said, because he could not expect "loyalty and support from the Opposition Party as at present constituted." He had made an agreement with Coaker in good faith, but the latter had made it very clear, most recently in his address to the FPU Convention, that the Union's aim was to control the government and "its energies shall be directed to that end irrespective of the written pledge given by him to me." This was humiliating to the Liberal party and destructive "to that unity which I had re-entered public life to establish

The House of Assembly in 1914. The government sat on the Speaker's left, a placement that was unique among British Parliaments and Assemblies and has been attributed to the location of the fireplace. (PANL, B14-21)

* The quotation is from Alfred Tennyson, "The Princess," Part IV: ". . . and Hope, a poising eagle, burns/Above the unrisen morrow."

and maintain." It put him in an impossible position, since he was not prepared to support Coaker's ambitions. The FPU was "only incidentally a political entity"; he was no more prepared to tolerate that corporate business taking over the government than he had been prepared to allow the Reids to take control in 1900. He also accused Coaker of irresponsibly spreading distrust in the Savings Bank in order to embarrass the government.[111] In a letter to the moribund Northern Liberal Association in Twillingate, Bond explained why he was also resigning his seat:

> In the first place, the country is in a state of wretched distraction, and the establishment of a third political party in the House of Assembly could have served no purpose other than to intensify its unhappy divisions. In the next place, having resigned the Leadership on a question of principle, I could not retain my seat as a member of that party under another leader. The position would have been absurd, and my attachment to the party only nominal. The time calls for service that is not nominal but real, and there was no honourable course for me but to resign both the Leadership and my seat.[112]

Since the legislature was scheduled to open unusually early, on January 15, the party had to act swiftly. Clift responded: "Your retirement would mean the end of the Liberal Party and would leave political matters as between the F.P.U. and the party led by Morris." Bond should therefore come to town and meet the Liberal committee.[113] Bond refused, so the party met on January 8 and 9 and decided to wait for Coaker's response.

This appeared on January 12.[114] Davidson thought it was probably composed by Morine.[115] Coaker denied any disloyalty and argued that Bond had understood from the outset that their agreement only applied to the 1913 election and the legislative sessions that followed—it was not "binding for a lifetime." Moreover, the FPU had never made any secret of its desire to control the government. "Is not Sir Robert's real grievance this, that he sees no prospect whatever that he would ever again be permitted to be the unquestioned and unquestionable Dictator of the Colony?"

As for the FPU's criticisms of the Savings Bank, they were entirely valid and had done no damage. Finally, Bond was letting down not only the Union, but his colleagues and everyone who had voted for him. He was needed in the legislature, "and he is no more justified in resigning now than he was in absenting himself during the 1913 session. . . . Battles are won by those who remain in the front ranks, not by absence and resignation." His attack on the Union was neither necessary nor excusable, and he was making an ungraceful exit.

Another meeting followed on January 13. The Liberals decided that, since they could not agree with all that Coaker had said and "particularly on the principle of F.P.U. control, they were unwilling and unable to unite with the Union members except for the purposes of opposition." Coaker wanted both wings of the opposition to sit as one party with all its members choosing the leader, but he eventually accepted the Liberal position. Each wing of the opposition would have its leader and they would sit separately, but they would co-operate and Kent would act as the official Leader of the Opposition.[116] There would be three parties after all.

When the House met for business on January 15, Morris made a graceful statement regretting Bond's resignation. He possessed "fine talents" and had always displayed "high attainments and splendid industry" as well as "splendid parliamentary courage . . . always ready to fight when fighting was necessary and always ready to be fair and reasonable when it was proper he should be so." For Kent, the retirement was a calamity. Bond had great experience, integrity, and ability: "He stands in my opinion above all our statesmen and to my mind he has no peer in the Colony." Both men hoped his absence was temporary.[117] There was a livelier exchange on January 19, when Coaker challenged Bond to face him in a by-election in Twillingate to decide "whether the fishermen have the right to control the Government of Newfoundland" and Halfyard questioned Morris's sincerity. Morris denied hypocrisy, emphasizing his personal regard for Bond. "I did not turn him out. I am a mourner at the funeral, but it is my hon. friends on the other side of the House who committed the execution that led to the funeral."[118]

Two days earlier, the *Fishermen's Advocate* had published a bitter and vitriolic attack on Bond, no doubt written by Coaker, under the headline "Sir Robert Bond Forsakes the Cause of the Thousands of Toilers who Nobly Rallied to his Support. . . . Threw the Union Overboard as Soon as he Discovered its Independence of Spirit."[119] Bond's resignation was characterized as a vindictive and base betrayal that deserved only contempt. "Coaker the backwoods farmer has in four years made himself a mightier man than Sir Robert as well as a far greater Party organizer and campaigner. . . . What will fishermen now think of their once ideal statesman . . . who dares to insult their intelligence by his aristocratic pretensions and utterances? . . . May he spend a happy winter at his castle and in the end find a blest abode in eternal life." Looking back nearly twenty years later, Coaker delivered a more measured verdict. Bond had made "a mistake, a costly mistake for the country. . . . The whole political complexion of the country and parties was changed by the resignation of Sir Robert Bond in 1914."[120]

NOTES

1 Bond to Kent, January 17, 1910 (RBP 3.29.002).
2 Bond to Williams, August 30, 1912 (RBP 3.31.003).
3 *PHA,* January 26, 1910, 3–7.
4 Cashin, *PHA,* March 8, 1910, 448.
5 Morris, *PHA,* February 3, 1910, 100–113.
6 Bond, *PHA,* February 8, 1910, 142–52.
7 Kent, *PHA,* February 9, 1910, 169–80.
8 Devereux, *PHA,* February 10, 1910, 209; *ENL* 1:614.
9 Gluek, "Programmed Diplomacy," 55–57; Tansill, *Canadian-American Relations,* 116.
10 See George Young to Mallet, June 17, 1910 (FO 371/1038, 355).
11 Quoted in Gluek, "Programmed Diplomacy," 68.
12 Quoted in Jessup, *Elihu Root,* 2:95.
13 Tansill, *Canadian-American Relations,* 119.
14 *PHA,* February 8, 1911, 4.
15 For example, Goodison, *PHA,* February 8, 1911, 18.
16 *PHA,* February 8, 1911, 29–38. There is an offprint in RBP 3.30.001.
17 For the general background, see Hewitt, "Exploring Uncharted Waters," 191–214.

18 Morris, *PHA*, February 14, 1911, 61–70; Hong, "'An Agency for the Common Weal'," 109–13; and Reeves, "Alexander's Conundrum," 15.

19 *PHA,* February 22, 1911, 138–86.

20 Morris, *PHA*, March 8, 1911, 377.

21 Devereux and Cashin, *PHA*, March 8, 1911, 388–94.

22 *PHA*, March 3, 1919, 311.

23 Morris, *PHA*, March 14, 1911, 447–86.

24 Cashin, *PHA*, March 21, 1911, 512–40.

25 Bond, Morris, and Cashin, *PHA*, February 28, March 1, 21, and 23, 1911, 221–41, 250–63, 512–40, 555–76.

26 *Chronicle*, April 3 through 15, May 2, and October 12, 1911.

27 The standard source is McDonald, "*To Each His Own*," based on the author's PhD thesis. See also Noel, *Politics in Newfoundland*, 77ff.; *ENL* 2:180–86; and Baker,"William Ford Coaker."

28 Circular letters, March 31, 1909, and March 16, 1909 (RCA, Howley Collection, 106/19/1, 106/19/2).

29 Coaker to John Coaker, November 14, 1904 (MUN, ASC, Coaker Collection, 009, 1.01.012).

30 Coaker to Morris, May 20, 1909 (PANL, GN 8/1, 20[i]).

31 Coaker to Morris, private, October 13, 1910 (PANL, GN 8/1, 20[i]).

32 McDonald, "*To Each His Own*," 35–36,

33 Crowe to Bond, private, November 12, 1911 (RBP 3.30.003).

34 Coaker to Bond, November 16, 1911 (RBP 3.30.003).

35 Bond to Coaker, November 17, 1911 (RBP 3.30.003). There is a copy in MUN, ASC, Coll. 009 (Coaker), 1911, 2.01.

36 Baker, "William Ford Coaker," 245–47.

37 Brehm to Lloyd, January 3, 1912, encl. in Lloyd to Bond, January 10, 1912 (RBP 3.31.007).

38 Bond to Lloyd, January 12, 1912 (RBP 3.31.007).

39 Bond, *PHA*, February 22, 1912, 37.

40 Bond, *PHA*, February 27, 1912, 109.

41 *PHA,* February 29, 1912, 189–95. The tuberculosis resolutions and bill were debated (*PHA)* on February 27, 28, and 29, and March 4, 1912, 82–112, 115–46, 147–95, 217–20.

42 *PHA,* March 4 and 7, 1912, 203–9, 234–51. On supplementary supply, see *PHA,* March 20, 1912, 332–44.

43 *PHA*, March 25, 1912, 392–432.

44 *PHA*, March 26 and 28, 1912, 433–60, 473.

45 Morris, *PHA*, March 21, 1912, 347–53.

46 Morris, Cashin, *PHA*, March 22, 1912, 423–30.

47 Noel, *Politics*, 109; *Chronicle*, January 27, 1912.

48 *Fishermen's Advocate*, April 6 and 27, June 15, and August 10 and 17, 1912; Williams to Harcourt, May 6, 1912 (CO 194/285, 246); and Noel, *Politics*, 108–10.

49 *Fishermen's Advocate*, October 26, 1912; McDonald, *"To Each His Own,"* 36.

50 Grenfell to Bond, November 5, 1912 (RBP 3.31.005).

51 Bond to Grenfell, November 9, 1912 (RBP 3.31.005).

52 Coaker to Bond, September 2 and 31, 1912, and Bond to Coaker, September 23, 1912 (RBP 30.21.003).

53 Coaker to Lloyd, November 15, 1912 (RBP 3.31.004 and ASC Coll.009, 10.03.06).

54 Lloyd to Bond, private and confidential, November 16, 1912 (RBP 3.31.004).

55 Coaker to Lloyd, November 21, 1912, and to Bond, November 22, 1912 (ASC Coll 009, 10.03.06).

56 Lloyd to Bond, November 22, 1912 (RBP 3.31.004).

57 Crowe to Coaker, private and confidential, November 27, 1912 (copy in RBP 3.31.004).

58 Williams to Harcourt, conf., December 19, 1912 (CO 194/285, 529–30). See also Williams to Harcourt, conf., May 7, 1912 (CO 194/285, 371).

59 Noel, *Politics*, 100.

60 Noel, *Politics*, 98–100; Coaker, *Twenty Years*, 50.

61 Lloyd to Bond and Bond to Lloyd, February 6, 1913 (RBP 3.32.006).

62 Davidson to Harcourt, conf., April 17, 1913 (CO 194/287, 188–95); Noel, *Politics*, 100.

63 Davidson to Lambert, April 14, 1913 (CO 194/287, 238).

64 Coaker to Lloyd, April 16, 1913, Lloyd to Bond, April 17, 1913, and Bond to Lloyd, May 2, 1913 (RBP 3.32.006).

65 Kent to Bond, private, May 6, 1913 (RBP 3.32.005).

66 Twenty-five St. John's Liberals to Bond, May 28, 1913 (RBP 3.32.003).

67 Crowe to Bond, May 29, 1913 (RBP 3.32.007).

68 Bond to Crowe, n.d. (RBP 3.32.007). Though undated, this letter seems to be a reply to Crowe's letter of May 29.

69 Bond to Kent, June 23, 1913 (RBP 3.32.005). Kent's letter to Bond of June 22 is not extant.

70 Kent to Bond, June 25, 1913 (RBP 3.32.005).

71 Bond to Kent, June 27, 1913 (RBP 3.32.005).

72 Kent to Bond, July 1, 1913 (RBP 3.32.005). See also Kent to Bond, July 4, 1913 (RBP 3.32.005).

73 Crowe to Bond, July 3 and 8, 1913 (RBP 3.32.007).

74 Lloyd to Bond, August 12, 1913 (RBP 3.32.006).

75 Bond to Lloyd, personal and private, August 13, 1913 (RBP 3.32.006).

76 Lloyd to Bond, August 14, 1913 (RBP 3.32.006).

77 Coaker to Bond, August 14, 1913, and Bond to Coaker, August 15, 1913 (RBP 3.32.004 and ASC, Coll 009, 10.03.06).

78 Bond to Kent, private and confidential, August 19, 1913 (RBP 3.32.005).

79 Coaker to Bond, August 23, 1913 (RBP 3.32.004 and ASC Coll 009, 10.03.06).

80 Bond to Coaker, August 25, 1913 (RBP 3.32.004 and ASC Col 009, 10.03.06).

81 Bond to Lloyd, August 25, 1913 (RBP 3.32.008).

82 Kent to Bond, August 27, 1913 (RBP 3.32.005).

83 Coaker to Bond, August 25, 1913 (RBP 3.32.004).

84 Bond to Coaker, August 26, 1913 (RBP 3.32.004 and ASC Col 009, 10.03.06).

85 Coaker to Bond, August 28, 1913 (RBP 3.32.004).

86 Bond to Coaker, Lloyd to Bond, and Kent to Bond, August 28, 1913 (RBP 3.32.004, .006, and .005).

87 Coaker to Kent and Kent to Bond, September 6, 1913 (RBP 3.32.004).

88 Bond to Lloyd and Bond to Kent, September 8, 1913 (RBP 3.32.006, 005).

89 Lloyd to Bond, confidential, September 6 and 8, 1913 (RBP 3.23.006).

90 Kent to Bond, September 8, 1913 (RBP 3.32.005).

91 Bond to Coaker, September 18, 1913 (RBP 3.32.004).

92 Coaker to Bond, September 19, 1913 (RBP 3.32.004).

93 *Evening Herald*, October 10 and 18, 1913; *ENL* 2:779.

94 *Evening Herald*, October 14, 1913.

95 Davidson diary, October 1, 1913 (PANL, MG 136, Box 1).

96 *Evening Herald*, October 14, 1913.

97 "Manifesto of Right Honourable Sir Robert Bond . . . [1913]" (RBP 3.32.001).

98 *Fishermen's Advocate*, October 6, 1913.

99 Noel, *Politics*, 112.

100 *Evening Herald*, September 4, 1913.

101 *Evening Herald*, September 6, 1913.

102 Davidson diary, October 11, 1913 (PANL, MG 136, Box 1); *ENL* 5:522.

103 For a response and additional details, see *Evening Herald*, October 20 and 22, 1913, and *Evening Telegram*, October 24 and November 4, 1913; O'Flaherty, *Lost Country*, 263.

104 *Evening Herald*, November 4, 1913.

105 McDonald, *"To Each His Own,"* 43; O'Flaherty, *Lost Country*, 262.

106 Press clipping in PANL, Coaker fonds, 2.01.001. For Blandford, see *ENL* 1:207.

107 Noel, *Politics*, 114; *Evening Telegram*, November 11, 1913.

108 *Evening Telegram*, December 6, 1913.

109 Coaker's address and the resolutions are in the "Journal of Proceedings . . . 1913," Coaker, ed., *Twenty Years*, 64–78.

110 Davidson to Harcourt, December 15, 1913, and conf. of same date (CO 194/287, 442–68).

111 Bond to Clift, January 2, 1914 (*Evening Telegram*, January 10, 1914).

112 Bond to Stephen Loveridge, January 3, 1914 (*Evening Telegram*, January 13, 1914).

113 Clift to Bond, January 5, 1914 (RBP 3.33.001).

114 *Evening Telegram*, January 12, 1914.

115 Davidson diary, January 18, 1914 (PANL, MG 36, Box 1).

116 Clift to Bond, January 14, 1914 (RBP 3.33.004); *Evening Telegram*, January 13 and 14, 1914.

117 *PHA*, January 19, 1914, 7–8.

118 Morris, *PHA*, January 19, 1914, 37–48.

119 *Fishermen's Advocate*, January 17, 1914.

120 Coaker, *Past, Present and Future* (1932), Article 6.

CHAPTER THIRTEEN

The War Years, 1914–1919

With Bond in self-imposed political exile—his resignation was an "act of despair," he said later[1]— the People's Party appeared to be riding high. The opposition was divided and had lost its most experienced and able member, while Edward Morris had a solid majority. The party did contain some difficult and at times intractable members, such as Michael Cashin, and Morris was also well aware of the potential threat posed by William Coaker's FPU, which had done extraordinarily well in the 1913 election. If it continued to expand and prosper, there seemed to be a real possibility it could form a government after the next election, scheduled for 1917, in spite of the hostility of the business class and the Roman Catholic Church. Though still in existence, the Liberal Party no longer seemed a political threat.

Union Party members, and Coaker himself, were energetic and vocal during the 1914 legislative session, applying pressure on the government for a variety of reforms. Morris responded cautiously but positively, even at the cost of confrontations with the Legislative Council. The financial situation was becoming difficult and the government could afford neither further tax concessions—indeed, there was a tax increase in the 1914 budget —nor large expenditures beyond those to which it was already committed. Political concessions favoured by the Union might be a viable way to maintain popularity.[2]

Such calculations became to some extent irrelevant in August 1914, when war in Europe broke out. Like the rest of the British empire, Newfoundland was automatically at war, and its response was very much shaped by Governor Davidson, with Morris's acquiescence. It was rapidly decided that the colony would raise a regiment and increase the strength of its Naval Reserve, this effort to be administered by a politically neutral citizens' organization that became known as the Newfoundland Patriotic Association (NPA), chaired by Davidson himself.* This was a unique and not uncontroversial response to the war—Coaker, for one, was unhappy about it—and the undertakings put further strain on the country's already troubled finances. Nevertheless, most people rallied to the flag, usually with enthusiasm.

Bond's views on the war and Newfoundland's response are not known. He took no part in the NPA's activities and was uninvolved in the war effort—his war was spent, it seems, in seclusion at Whitbourne. He refused to provide a signed appeal for recruits in 1916, writing that he agreed with Rudyard Kipling that "the most useful thing a Civilian can do in these days is to speak as little as possible, and if he feels moved to write, to confine his efforts to his cheque-book. . . . I feel that I could not exhort a man to go where, unfortunately, I cannot accompany him."[3] Similarly, he refused in 1917 to join a recruiting tour of the south coast.† Writing in 1918, Governor Sir Charles Harris (Davidson's successor) noted that Bond "is said to have done positively nothing to show his patriotism and public spirit since the outbreak of war."[4] Likewise, Alfred Morine later remarked that Bond "took no part during the Great War, perhaps because he was in indifferent health for a portion of the time at least."[5] Bond provided the press with year-end messages in 1915 and 1916,[6] but that was all.

He kept an eye on the political scene, though, and stayed in touch with Kent, fearing that the Liberal party might be swallowed up in a coalition government. But Kent continued to see himself as Bond's lieutenant—there was little chance of the party losing its separate identity while he was in charge.[7] Nevertheless, the political scene was shifting and coalition was being talked about. There were two reasons for this and they were connected. The country's financial condition was causing concern,

---

* The standard work is Patricia O'Brien, "The Newfoundland Patriotic Association." Davidson was appointed a KCMG in 1914.

† Bond to W.W. Blackall, February 3, 1917 (RBP 3.36.001). He reiterated: "I cannot exhort my young countrymen to go where I cannot follow them."

and confederation with Canada was re-emerging as an issue for debate. Morine gave a lengthy speech on the subject in February 1915, arguing that the "critical condition of our public affairs" made the subject "more acute"*; there was also discussion around St. John's. The Methodist College Literary Institute invited Bond to speak on the subject. He refused, but said that if confederation ever became an election issue, he would state his views.[8]

Morine was not the only person involved in raising the issue. Harry Crowe had never stopped lobbying in favour of confederation and, like Morine, was in touch with the Canadian prime minister at the time, Sir Robert Borden. Morris also proved willing to explore the matter; in the fall of 1914, he sent E.M. Jackman (Bond's former Finance minister) to Ottawa as his emissary. Also in favour of confederation were the Reid brothers, who wanted to unload their railway and steamship operations onto the Canadian government—especially now that the war had stopped branch line construction, taking with it some useful profits.

Matters necessarily unfolded slowly since, if confederation was to be carried in Newfoundland where it was generally unpopular, all political parties had to be brought on board. Of the senior Liberals, William Lloyd and James Clift were open to confederation but Kent was not. Coaker and the Unionists were skeptical, needing to be persuaded. Then there was the question of Morine, whose continued presence in Newfoundland was thought by some to be doing the cause more harm than good. Manoeuvring continued in 1915, with Kent refusing to take any part in it. At the end of March that year, Morris stated in conversation with Davidson that his own views on confederation were not "clearly defined." But he went on to say that the arguments in favour were stronger than those against, and that the Reids were losing so much money they had to sell the railway to Canada.[9]

The ground shifted again in 1916. Morine left the colony for a government job in Ottawa, obtained no doubt through Borden's influence (it proved to be short-lived). In March, Kent was appointed to the Supreme

* Morine, "Confederation," February 1915, typescript in RBP 8.03.026. Morine was one of the members for Bonavista Bay; Coaker took over Bond's seat in Twillingate.

Court and Lloyd took over as Leader of the Opposition. It was then announced that the two opposition parties had decided to merge and officially form the Liberal-Union Party. Bond wrote a warm letter of congratulation to Kent; his letter to Lloyd was angry and bitter.[10] What had occurred was "a political crime, namely, the obliteration of the Liberal Party as a distinct entity, and the establishment in its place of a political monstrosity." He contined:

> I cannot congratulate you on accepting the leadership of that party, because, in my opinion, it dishonours you, and blights your political future. . . . I believe you have made a mistake. I believe that those Liberals who voted with the "Coakerites" to accomplish the end which they have long had in view have betrayed a trust reposed in them by the Great Liberal party scattered throughout . . . this Colony. And I further believe that this betrayal will be [reflected] at the polls at the next General Election. Liberal-Unionism means Coakerism, and what that means . . . is recognized by the Liberal electors.

Bond (correctly) disputed Lloyd's statement in the *Evening Telegram* that the party name had been settled in 1913. He, Bond, had specifically rejected the name "Liberal-Union" when Coaker suggested it at that time, as Lloyd well knew. "Your statement places me in a false, and to my mind a most contemptible position before the Country; it charges my political friends and old supporters with disloyalty to the Liberal cause and to me as its leader." There is no record of a response.

So Bond's Liberal Party was gone, and the merger with the FPU that he and Kent had always resisted had finally occurred. As Bond saw it, it was a takeover by Coaker and Coaker's solicitor—now William Lloyd. It was a parting of the ways, after which Bond became even more politically isolated. He thought himself betrayed, but by resigning the leadership and his seat in 1914 and by remaining distant and inflexible, he had forfeited his ability to influence public affairs. He still commanded respect in some quarters, but many aspiring politicians saw him as increasingly irrelevant.

A pessimistic and gloomy Bond told a correspondent in October that he was not in touch with either of the political parties and "I have no more faith in one than in the other."[11]

Unlike Kent or Bond, Lloyd and Coaker were prepared to consider a wartime coalition with the People's Party. They met Morris at his suggestion after the 1916 legislative session and worked out a draft agreement, which collapsed because of Michael Cashin's objections.[12] There matters rested until 1917, when the political temperature again began to rise. This was partly because, under normal circumstances, 1917 would have been an election year. But there was also increasing public dissatisfaction with the state of the country and the war effort—thanks to profiteering, the steeply rising cost of living, higher taxation, the actions of the governor and the NPA, declining enlistments, and the prospect of conscription. Morris was spending more time in England and the Liberal-Union Opposition was widely mistrusted, mainly because it was dominated by the Unionists. There were also signs of friction between the party's two leaders, Coaker apparently complaining that Lloyd had no vision or energy—a man in the trench who could not see over the parapet.[13]

Sir Robert Bond in later life. (National Portrait Gallery, London, NPG X197721)

Not surprisingly, Bond began to receive requests to return to politics and lead a newly constituted Liberal party. "[A] state of chaos reigns," claimed a correspondent from Channel; there had to be an end to "the present orgies of corruption and dishonesty," wrote his old ally George Shea.[14] Even Coaker (it was said) wondered whether Bond would agree to take over from Lloyd.[15] Bond's response to those who inquired about his intentions was, as usual, ambivalent and evasive. Circumstances might arise that would persuade him to return to politics as "a public duty," but it would be with the greatest reluctance. In any event, did the country deserve a better government? And where would support for a new Liberal Party come from? The public had acquiesced in all that had been done by the Morris government since 1909, the press and the business community were effectively silent, and though the FPU represented "the greatest menace to the welfare of the Colony that it has ever had to face," it received widespread support, even from businessmen. Further, where was the outcry against Lloyd's betrayal of the party? "They have been as silent as the dead from first to last." Were Liberals "satisfied to become a mere appendage of the Coaker outfit?" It seemed that they were. There had to be signs of real change before he could be expected to make a move.[16]

While there were those who persisted in seeing Bond as a future political leader and a real and positive alternative to Morris and the governments that came after him, it is hard to escape the conclusion that Bond had no intention of returning to political life and that his decision in 1914 had been final. He made supportive statements, but always hedged about with impossible conditions. Those who inquired about his political future were assured of his patriotism and support, his willingness to assist, his loathing of their opponents, his fear for the country's future. But he took very little action. Proposals advocating his political reappearance continued for some time, but there can be no doubt that Bond had decided to leave not only politics but Whitbourne, if he could find a buyer for the estate. By 1914–15, Bond was a spent force, though many did not recognize it. He was a presence but not an effective player.

The Liberal-Union party expected to do well in the anticipated 1917 election, a contest that Morris wanted to avoid. Backed by Governor Davidson, who did not want to risk a change of government, the prime minister announced on June 15 that the life of the Assembly would be extended for one year. Morris then re-opened negotiations for a coalition, promising numerical equality in the government and an election in 1918. He was also prepared to create a militia department, regularize the position of the NPA, and impose a profits tax, actions that the opposition had been demanding. The arrangement also included a secret deal between the three leaders that Morris would resign in Lloyd's favour before the end of the year. Promises of knighthoods helped square key players in the People's Party. Thus the National Government was announced on July 17.[17] Confederation was not part of the agreement; it was effectively a dead issue, though Bond continued to think that it was the basis of what he saw as a Morris-Coaker alliance.

In a letter to one correspondent, Bond described the coalition as "a high political crime for it robs the people of Responsible Government. The people no longer govern, under Coalition and an extension of parliament, they have nothing to do with the whip and reins, nor have they any constitutional way of changing the Coachman."[18] To another, he wrote: "It has robbed the Country of the protection which rests in parliamentary criticism; it has facilitated the cloaking of the graft that has been rampant for eight years; it has enabled both parties to accomplish their respective personal aims and ends by compromise; it has opened the door to political corruption, and worst of all, it has, I fear, struck a fatal blow at Responsible Government in this Country."[19] As he assessed it in that letter, Morris represented the Roman Catholic interest, which controlled up to fourteen seats, and Coaker the FPU, which controlled at least six. If they stuck together they could control the government indefinitely, something that Coaker had been working toward for some time and that only Kent had resisted.

Letters urging Bond to return to public life continued to arrive. He was also approached indirectly by the new editor of the *Evening Telegram*, Harry Winter,[20] and asked to help form a new party and write for the paper.[21] He was alerted to the unhappiness of the Roman Catholic hierarchy with the coalition government—Archbishop E.P. Roche, Howley's successor, was concerned about "the Coaker menace,"[22] and the Church would never support the Liberal-Union party. "I may truthfully state," wrote J.J. St. John (a local retailer and long-time Liberal), "that everyone around town and in the more important outports as well, are asking what of the future? I give it as my humble opinion that the Liberal Party if they line up against the present unpopular combination would have another 1900 victory. Everywhere you go you can hear Merchant, Mechanic and laborer ask if there is any chance of Sir Robert Bond coming as Leader of the Liberal Party."[23] Bond was unmoved:

> I deeply regret the lack of honest, patriotic principles on the part of those of my Countrymen who are responsible for the present condition of the Colony. I fear that its true condition is not appreciated by the mass of our people. . . . But, I am sure that the future of our Country has been mortgaged beyond redemption; that we have been robbed of our independence, and that neither I nor any other man can now restore the old Country to the proud position that it occupied when I was forced to hand over the Government in 1909.[24]

Late in December 1917, rumours began to circulate that Morris (who was in England) had resigned. These proved to be true, which took everyone except Lloyd and Coaker by surprise, since Morris had not informed members of his own party. Soon after came the news that Morris had been elevated to the peerage on the recommendation of Governor Davidson, who had recently left the country. The political class was shocked, enraged, and derisive. Morris seemed to have ignominiously and deceitfully scuttled away from Newfoundland and its many problems to enjoy London and the House of Lords. Any chance of his becoming High Commissioner, which had also been rumoured, disappeared. Lloyd became prime minister and began to reconstruct the government—a necessary move because three ministers (Richard Squires, Michael Gibbs, and John Bennett) decided to take advantage of the situation by resigning, hoping that Lloyd would be forced to take them back on their own terms. Instead, Lloyd reduced the cabinet from twelve to nine, and allowed only Bennett back, as Minister of Militia.[25] The few members who disliked these developments, who were mainly from the People's Party, formed an unofficial opposition group; its main spokesman was John S. Currie, editor of the *Daily News*.[26] The group included Morine, who was now sitting as an independent after a brief time in Ottawa. The plan for an election in February 1918 was abandoned.[27]

Archbishop Roche was unhappy with the new government since, in his view, it contained too many Unionists and too few Roman Catholics, and he would have welcomed Bond's return to politics.[28] The Legislative Council was largely hostile, having had its powers over money bills trimmed. "Water Street," too, was uneasy. The second National Government hung together, however, bracing for a fight over conscription. But there were many who felt that a new political party was needed to contest a general election and, before that, the by-elections to fill eight vacancies. In the event, the life of the legislature was extended to April 30, 1919, a compromise forced by the Legislative Council, and there were no by-elections.

The newly formed opposition group was heterogeneous. Its members had various political backgrounds and histories, some in the legislature, some not, sharing little more than a dislike of Coaker and the Lloyd government. Some of them were more ambitious than others.* What it needed was a central figure to provide leadership and impose a semblance of unity. Eyes turned to Bond once again, and Squires tried to organize a deputation to visit him at Whitbourne.[29] Bond, as ever, remained reluctant to commit himself. It was not that he disliked politics *per se*, he told Harry Winter at the *Evening Telegram*, but "they have got down so low, have become so dirty, and the elements that now enter into them are so uncongenial." He was also slowing down. "Old slippers come to feel easier, old habits the more comfortable, and one's home and books the best of all." But—there was always a "but"—he would step forward if he was convinced that he was really needed, "provided always . . . that a clean, honourable, and congenial lot of men are forthcoming to form a team."[30] In addition, he had to be convinced that "the public realize the true position of affairs, and that they really desire my services."[31]

Quite what evidence was needed to change his mind, Bond did not say. He refused to meet members of the opposition group, recommended against fighting by-elections, were any to be held, and advised opponents

---

* The names mentioned in RBP are Henry Cowan, George Shea, C.T. James, H.A. Winter, W.J. Walsh, R.A. Squires, H. Gear, J. Puddester, J.C. Currie, and M.P. Gibbs.

of the government to concentrate on the election to be held in 1919.[32] When Henry Cowan, a prominent businessman, asked him directly in October 1918 whether he would lead a party, Bond simply replied that he had not decided, adding that the people seemed to be in "a state of political coma, or, are perfectly indifferent as to the conduct of public affairs. . . . There is no such thing today in this Country as a healthy public opinion." He saw no evidence whatever that the country wanted to be rid of the present government and looked to him to take over; his "old political supporters" should understand that they were under no obligation to him, and should take whatever political actions seemed most advisable to them.[33] Not surprisingly, the "opposition committee" disbanded soon after.[34] Extracts from Bond's letter to Cowan found their way into an editorial in the *Evening Telegram* in mid-November,* which Bond saw as "a gratuitous attack," strongly insinuating that the article had been written by someone close to Squires "for the purpose of bringing about an estrangement between myself and the *Evening Telegram*."[35] He was furious. "I have had a surfeit of Newfoundland politics lately," he told Shea, "and I turn from the dirty business with contempt and loathing."[36]

On November 11, 1918, the war unexpectedly ended and renewed political speculation soon erupted. It was too late in the year for an election, but there would have to be one in 1919. Attempts to draw Bond out of retirement continued. Lloyd was in Europe during the winter, attending meetings of the Imperial War Cabinet and the early stages of the Versailles peace conference. He arrived back in mid-March 1919, assuming that there would be a spring election, as had been decided the previous year. The government was not widely popular and there were internal difficulties. Lloyd wanted to leave public life if possible, the People's Party wing of the government disliked the alliance with the Unionists, and Coaker was restless and difficult, apparently undecided whether or not to declare political independence. Nevertheless, the National Government decided to enter a spring election as a unit, with polling to happen in early May. The legislature convened on April 2, in order to make the

* Now edited by Charles James (*ENL* 3:94).

necessary arrangements* and allocate funds to cover the expense of an election. The Assembly acted within a few days, but the Legislative Council took its time.

There was mounting opposition in St. John's to an early election. On the evening of April 2, a "public committee meeting of over two hundred persons" took place at the Casino Theatre that protested the government's plans; another, even larger, meeting was held on April 4. The main organizer seems to have been John J. St. John, who saw to it that active politicians were excluded.[37] On Monday, April 7, a large crowd† paraded to Government House, where a deputation went in to meet the governor, now Sir Charles Harris. The organizers wanted the election postponed long enough to allow the creation of a strong opposition party, with nominations no earlier than May 16. Many wanted Bond to lead this new party, and he was pressed once more to come out of political retirement.[38] Harris told the deputation that he had to act on the advice of his ministers, whom he immediately consulted. Their consensus, with which he agreed, was that the election should go ahead as planned.[39] Lloyd said as much in the Assembly on April 9, in response to John Currie's tabling of the Casino Theatre resolutions. Lloyd pointed out that the government had been forced in 1918 to accept a spring election.‡

Remembering 1909, Bond was appalled by the prospect of a spring election and the timing was a factor in his decision not to lead a new party. His official reply to the committee appeared in the *Evening Telegram* on April 7. He appreciated the committee's "gracious invitation" as evidence that his past services had been appreciated by "the patriotic and thinking portion of my countrymen." However, "in justice to the public, as well as to myself, I could not undertake a 'whirlwind' campaign such as is now

---

* The franchise was extended to Newfoundland servicemen under the age of 21 who had served overseas (Harris to Milner, April 19, 1919, CO 194/296, 51; *JHA* 1919, 14–17).

† Its size was estimated at three thousand people by the *Evening Telegram* (April 8, 1919).

‡ *PHA,* April 9, 1919, 75–77. The resolutions were tabled in the Legislative Council.

about to be forced upon this Country."[40] In a second, private letter to St. John, he pleaded his "state of health." Now 62, he said he no longer possessed "the physical energy and force necessary," especially for a spring campaign. He went on:

> I have no sympathy whatever with the present Coalition Government. I believe that a party government is best for this and for every Country; that its interests would be best advanced by means of a well-organized party, founded upon well recognized liberal principles, able and willing to deal with the grave difficulties that, for a certainty, now confront us; and my whole heart is with the popular movement working towards that end. But the occasion requires that the whole Electorate should have an opportunity of expressing themselves in a free and entirely untrammeled manner at the polls. . . . The decision announced by the Government in respect to the date of the Election necessarily prevents that. To overcome . . . this deplorable circumstance great energy and rapid organization is essential, and for the reason I have frankly stated I must now leave that work to younger and more robust men.[41]

Others continued to press the case. Currie argued that the outports would give support if it was known that Bond was running as a committed political leader who would help drive "the present, corrupt administration" from power, snap election or no. Campaign funds would be forthcoming from most Water Street firms, Archbishop Roche would be supportive, and "a strongly organized opposition" could find good candidates and win. Currie warned that Squires intended to lead "some sort of a party in case there is no other leader."[42] Bond replied that, while there was clear evidence of support in St. John's, he was struck by "the absence of any sympathetic expressions [?] or wired approval from the extern districts." This meant there would have to be outport meetings and "strenuous work." It was unlikely that "a suitable steamer" could be hired, "and suffering as I do from . . . acute rheumatism, I feel that I cannot . . . undertake the organization and leadership of a party."[43]

Immediately after this exchange, on April 10, the government suddenly and unexpectedly announced that the election would be postponed to the fall. Lloyd stated simply that the government had to show that it did not want "a snap verdict."[44] The decision was prompted, apparently, by Coaker's unilateral claim to nine districts, for which he also announced candidates. His ambitions caused widespread alarm—particularly in St. John's, where two pro-government members got cold feet and decided they could not face an early election. A contentious Liberal-Union party meeting then decided on the postponement—Unionists opposing, with one exception. Governor Harris and Lloyd were disappointed and "Coaker was furious."[45] He immediately gave notice that his party would withdraw its support once the legislature closed, if not before.[46] The political situation was becoming ever more unstable and uncertain, the major players watching and waiting, speculating how each of the others would act. The National Government was clearly falling apart. Ever the string-puller, P.T. McGrath began to look for a replacement for Lloyd. Currie described the government as "thoroughly demoralized and would go to pieces at the appearance of a new party"—which, of course, Bond should lead.[47]

More political news followed a few days later. Coaker was about to bolt, so Currie was informed, and this would put the government in a minority. But Lloyd could reconstruct the administration at least temporarily, and create "an amalgamation of all parties against Coaker." This, Currie thought, would be supported by the governor, with whom he had had a guarded and inconclusive conversation. Currie wanted Bond to lead that party, which he felt sure would get support in the outports. "The merchant and the workman are equally looking for your leadership" and "the opportunity offers of getting around you a government of energetic young men who will take the burden of detail off your shoulders and leave you free to dictate and direct the policy." Imperial affairs were likely to become increasingly important, he went on, and this required a Newfoundland representative "of whom the country will not have reason to be ashamed." He should not delay, or Squires might move in.[48]

Bond replied at length.[49] The step he was asked to take was "a very serious one for me, when I view it from the standpoint of health or the standpoint of home." He had worked so hard when in public life that he had injured his health; were he to return, "a break would come, for 'I am not so young as I used to be.'" His house was distant from St. John's, "and my engagements in public affairs would mean, practically, the abandonment of all home comforts and pleasures, and the sacrifice of financial interests here." He had ignored such considerations earlier in his career, but was not sure that he should do so again. There was

> no great issue before the Country. It is only a question as to who shall be the taxgatherers [*sic*] to pay the interest on the borrowed millions, and to defray the cost of the Civil Service. There is no great policy possible so far as development is concerned, for the whole future of the Country has been mortgaged. That mortgage has to be met, and to meet it the cost of the Civil Service must be reduced, and expenditure must needs be brought within our means, or we shall pass into the hands of a receiver—the Dominion of Canada. A bad fishery or two and the debacle must come. . . . What is there to induce one to sacrifice health, home, and happiness to engage in a struggle with such a declining [*sic*]? . . . There is just one question that constantly presents itself, and holds my decision in abeyance. It is this—if a debacle seems to be inevitable, is it wise or patriotic to permit those who have brought it about to profit by it? In other words, if terms must necessarily be made with Canada before very long, can the Colony's case be safely left to those who have demonstrated by their public life that self-aggrandisement is with them the first consideration? Of course there can be only one answer to such a question.

But, Bond went on, he was surely not the only person who could prevent the country's collapse. He was not going to make an immediate decision, which in his opinion was not necessary, but would "'wait and see' if 'a Saviour of his Country' is not brought to the front by the present political upheaval."

The upheaval reached the crisis point later in the month. On May 19, Lloyd was approached by People's Party emissaries who suggested that he stay on as prime minister but ditch Coaker and the Unionists.[50] Lloyd saw no reason for this. He and Coaker were long-time allies and the Unionists had consistently supported the National Government. So he tried to reach an interim settlement, suggesting that the government should carry on at least to the end of the session, when the future could be reassessed. He went as far as to offer to step down. But Cashin and his supporters were determined to break away.

Whether Lloyd talked to Coaker is not known, but he had clearly lost control of a government that was imploding. On May 20, he submitted his resignation as prime minister to Governor Harris, seeing no alternative. This was not made public, and it must have been assumed that Lloyd would stick with Coaker and patch up a government that could last until the election. Later the same day, Cashin handed his resignation as Minister of Finance to Lloyd. When the House convened shortly afterward, Cashin moved an adjournment to May 23, with the addition that the House should "place on record its opinion that the Government as presently constituted does not possess the confidence of the House."[51]

Currie had been asked to second the motion, but he did not. Lloyd rose, agreed that the parties composing the government could no longer work together, and informed the House that since he had resigned—the news came as a surprise to those present—and would willingly step down, the non-confidence vote was unnecessary. The Speaker insisted on a seconder before discussion could continue. After an awkward pause, Lloyd himself seconded the motion, which carried unanimously—amid laughter, for this was an unprecedented scene. Lloyd told Harris that he had done so because, if he had not, the motion would have failed and he would have been at the mercy of the Cashin faction, which could have withdrawn support at any time on any issue and blamed him for the result. He refused to withdraw his resignation, which Harris formally accepted the next day.

Lloyd recommended Cashin as his successor (Bond thought it should have been Currie), and the new government was sworn in on May 22.* It was composed mainly of former members of the People's Party, but also included two former Liberals, a former Unionist—and Morine.† Governor Harris thought that the collapse of the National Government was the result of Roman Catholic hostility to the FPU combined with mercantile jealousy of the Union's apparent commercial success.

Currie had kept Bond informed about political events, and floated the unlikely possibility that the governor might call on Bond to form a ministry. Bond had replied that he could not say what he would do in this eventuality, due to "a very important consideration apart from the personal one." Currie and his allies quickly decided that this meant that Bond would not re-enter public life and the correspondence ended.[52] Some had hoped that Currie would take an independent stand and might possibly become prime minister if Bond did not return to politics, supported by the *Daily News* and *Evening Telegram*. Bond himself seems to have been sympathetic to this possibility. However, both Cashin and Coaker made offers to him, and Currie—whom Bond suspected of closet dealings with Morine—decided to join Cashin, even though he had said that he would not. A correspondent told Bond that Currie, a Methodist, thought "he hadn't a ghost of a chance if Cashin's church supported Cashin, and 'as a practical politician of many years' experience' he [Currie] knew the present government had everything in their favour. First they had the Govt. & a surplus (?) of Two Million. They were going to spend $500,000.00 on public works. Cashin was a wealthy man & would get influence."[53] What finished this initiative was

---

* Lloyd left politics and became Registrar of the Supreme Court. His appointment needed legislation, since the Registrar had to be a qualified barrister of ten years standing; Lloyd had half that and insufficient experience. The *Daily Star* (June 5, 1919) remarked that the government could now "pay Dr. Lloyd the price of his treachery to Coaker."

† Currie to Bond, May 20, 21, 1919 (RBP 3.38.005). A final touch was that the Cashin government had to further amend the Election Act to allow Morine to run in the November election, since he had not been continuously resident in the colony for the required two years prior to nomination.

the *Telegram*'s decision to endorse the Cashin government.[54]

Bond had not intended his letter to Currie to be taken as an announcement that he was finished with public life, and he was angry that it had been so interpreted. He was also annoyed that Currie had circulated the letter to others, though he had not marked it as "private."[55] Bond had indeed left open the possibility that he might at some stage return to politics, but he must have understood that his missives from Whitbourne would be carefully scrutinized. Why had he prevaricated? Why had he not adopted a more prominent role?

Bond's explanation was that he needed to keep a geographical and personal distance from the heated, introverted political manoeuvrings in St. John's. Had he "gone to town" to join and advise Currie and his supporters, as he had been urged, he would have had to support their actions and he would have become identified with a particular faction. Although he did not say this explicitly, such a move might not have gone down well with "old Liberal" supporters. With Bond in the wings as the future party leader, Currie and his colleagues would have had "to make terms with Morine and Cashin, or Morine and Coaker, and I would have found myself saddled with one or the other party when I went to the Election, for I could not throw them over if I had been a party to advising the compact. As I regard the Cashin party [as] equally objectionable as the Coaker party there was no other course for me to adopt than to decline to advise Currie as to what action he should take in the premises." At that point, as it turned out, Currie had sold out. "[T]he Morris Government was bad, the Coaker-Lloyd Government was worse, but the Cashin-Morine combination caps the climax."[56]

Fruitless speculation about Bond's political future revived as the fall election approached. There were those who genuinely wanted him to return to public life, possibly at the head of a new party, others wanted to know his intentions, so that they could make their own arrangements. Among the latter was the ambitious Richard Squires. He called on Bond in mid-August and offered his support, adding that Coaker would join the coalition and only insist on naming candidates in Bonavista and Trinity. Bond was frank: Coaker was not to be trusted and had the support of every shareholder in the FPU Trading Company. Roman Catholics would vote for Cashin's candidates. That being the case, a new party and a three-cornered contest would hand the balance of power to either Cashin or Coaker. Bond told Henry Cowan that he did not want to be once again "deceived and betrayed by those two political factions," and would only re-enter political life when "I am convinced that I can render good service to my Country."[57] He later elaborated: "When the Electors throughout the Country evince a genuine desire for clean, honest Government, and a willingness to lend their aid in establishing such a Government in this Country they would find me quite ready to place my services at their disposal."[58] Once again, these were impossible conditions.

Bond's reluctance to become engaged cleared the way for Squires, who outmanoeuvred William Warren—another former People's Party member with independent ambitions—and announced the formation of the "Liberal Reform Party" on August 21. It absorbed many former Bondites, such as George Shea. An alliance with Coaker and the Unionists was announced on September 22. It would not be a three-cornered fight after all.

Coaker would have preferred an alliance with Warren—he and Squires had been hurling insults at each other for years—but many Unionists favoured Squires, who proved willing to negotiate a favourable deal. The Union would run twelve candidates and, assuming victory for the alliance, would receive four cabinet seats. Squires would be party leader, Coaker his deputy with a free hand in fishery matters. In the November 3 election, the Squires-Coaker alliance won twenty-four seats to the twelve won by the Cashin party, which had hastily renamed itself "Liberal Progressive."* The result introduced the general character of postwar politics. For all the factionalism and fluidity that persisted throughout the period, and the existence of exceptions, two broad groupings emerged—one was St. John's-based and largely Roman Catholic, the other was outport-oriented and largely Protestant.

As for Bond, there were many who regretted his decision to stay in retirement. The political confusion that followed the end of the war had

* See Noel, *Politics*, 140–44, and McDonald, "*To Each His Own*," 79–85. Morine came bottom of the poll in Bonavista.

provided him with an opportunity for a comeback. There was widespread disenchantment with the existing political class, and a realization that, for all its temporary wartime prosperity, the colony faced financial and economic problems and its future was at best uncertain. Out of this atmosphere emerged an inchoate craving for strong and honest government, and Bond was widely regarded as the man who could best provide it—who could, in fact, be the country's saviour. Those who thought this way tended to gloss over the defects in his political record and accentuate—if not exaggerate—his probity, fiscal prudence, and patriotism, contrasting them with the supposed failings of those who had followed him. There was a gathering consensus that, by defeating him in 1908–09, electors had made a bad mistake.

If Bond had returned to public life in 1919, there is no doubt that he would have received widespread, though not universal, support and an endorsement from Archbishop Roche. It is possible, in theory, that he could have won an election. But Bond was not a man to forgive and forget. Constructing a new party would have been fraught with problems, even though Morris and Lloyd were gone. He would never again bargain with Coaker, and the prominent contemporary names in colonial politics had been his sworn enemies: Cashin, Crosbie, and Morine among them. Though they might have been willing (again, in theory) to work with him, Bond mistrusted them all—and he had an imperious nature. So he would have had to find new candidates and new allies, as well as the financial backing to carry it off.

There can be no doubt, as well, that Bond simply did not want to re-emerge from Whitbourne. He was something of a hypochondriac, and he enjoyed both regular domesticity and his role as the local patriarch. He appreciated being treated as a political sage—the "once and future king"—and often let the press know what he thought. But after 1919, Bond was in practical terms irrelevant. It was his choice.

NOTES

1 Bond to Brehm, August 14, 1917 (RBP 3.36.002).

2 This analysis largely follows McDonald, *"To Each His Own,"* 44–47; see also Noel, *Politics,* 115–20.

3 Bond to P.T. McGrath, March 4, 1916 (RBP 3.35.001).

4 Harris to Long, secret, March 23, 1918 (CO 537/1167).

5 Morine, draft history (PANL, MG 271.2, folder 11).

6 *Daily News*, December 31, 1915, and December 30, 1916.

7 Kent to Bond, February 1, 1915 (RBP 3.35.001).

8 W.J. Ellis to Bond, February 26, 1915, and Bond to J.S. Currie, March 2, 1915 (RBP 8.03.027).

9 Davidson diary, March 31, 1915 (PANL, MG 36, Box 1).

10 Bond to Lloyd, March 28, 1916 (RBP 3.35.001).

11 Bond to English, October 2, 1916 (RBP 3.35.001).

12 O'Brien, "Patriotic Association," 130; McDonald, *"To Each His Own,"* 57–58; and *Fishermen's Advocate*, December 22, 1916 (clipping in RBP 3.34.002).

13 H. Gear to Bond, June 16, 1917 (RBP 3.36.002); O'Brien, "Patriotic Association," 277.

14 P. James to Bond, February 7, 1917 (RBP 3.36.002); G. Shea to Bond, February 5, 1917 (RBP 3.36.004). See also J.J. St. John to Bond, January 3, 1917 (RBP 3.36.003).

15 H. Gear to Bond, June 16, 1917 (RBP 3.36.002).

16 Bond to James, February 12, 1917, and Bond to Shea, February 9, 1917 (RBP 3.36.002, .004).

17 McDonald, *"To Each His Own,"* 60–63; O'Brien, "Patriotic Association," 280–81.

18 Bond to Gear, July 13, 1917 (RBP 3.36.003).

19 Bond to Brehm, August 14, 1917 (RBP 3.36.002).

20 *ENL* 5:589–90.

21 Brehm to Bond, August 2, 1917 (RBP 3.36.002).

22 Shea to Bond, August 19, 1917 (RBP 3.36.003); *ENL* 4:614.

23 St. John to Bond, September 21, 1917 (RBP 3.36.003).

24 Bond to T. Keats (Merasheen), November 19, 1917 (RBP 3.36.002).

25 McDonald, *"To Each His Own,"* 65–68; George Shea to Bond, January 5, 1918 (RBP 3.37.001).

26 *ENL* 1:578.

27 *Daily Star*, April 26, 1919 (cutting in RBP 3.38.007).

28 See the correspondence between Roche and Cashin, January, 1918 (RCA, Roche Collection, 107/23/4).

29 *Daily Star*, April 26, 1919 (cutting in RBP 3.38.007).

30 Bond to Winter, February 5, 1918 (RBP 3.37.001).

31 Bond to W.J. Walsh, February 12, 1918 (RBP 3.37.001).

32 Bond to James, July 23, 1918, and H.E. Cowan to Bond, October 2, 1918 (RBP 3.37.001).

33 Bond to Cowan, October 4, 1918 (RBP 3.37.001). For Cowan, see *ENL* 1:553.

34 James to Bond, November 17, 1918 (RBP 3.37.001).

35 Bond to James, November 19, 1918, James to Bond, November 21, 1918, and Bond to James, November 22, 1918 (RBP 3.37.001).

36 Bond to Shea, November 29, 1918 (RBP 3.37.001).

37 St. John to Bond, April 30, 1919 (RBP 3.38.003).

38 St. John to Bond, tgms., April 3 and 8, 1919 (RBP 3.38.003).

39 Harris to Milner, April 19, 1919 (CO 194/296, 52–54).

40 Bond to St. John, April 3, 1919 (RBP 3.38.003); *Evening Telegram*, April 7, 1919.

41 Bond to St. John, April 9, 1919 (RBP 3.38.003).

42 Currie to Bond, April 8, 1919 (RBP 3.38.005).

43 Bond to Currie, April 9, 1919 (RBP 3.38.005).

44 Lloyd, *PHA,* April 10, 1919, 84.

45 Harris to Milner, conf., April 21, 1919 (CO 194/296, 61–63).

46 Currie to Bond, May 7, 1919 (RBP 3.38.005).

47 Currie to Bond, May 7, 1919 (RBP 3.38.005).

48 Currie to Bond, May 10, 1919 (RBP 3.38.005).

49 Bond to Currie, May 12, 1919 (RBP 3.38.005).

50 Much of this account is based on Harris to Milner, conf., May 22, 1919 (CO 194/296, 90–92).

51 *JHA* 1919, 77.

52 Bond to Currie, May 21, 1919, and Currie to Bond, May 22, 1919 (RBP 3.38.005).

53 K.M. Blair to Bond, private, June 5, 1919 (RBP 3.38.006).

54 *Evening Telegram*, May 27, 1919.

55 Draft letter to Currie, May 24, 1919, marked "Not Sent" (RBP 3.38.005).

56 Bond to K.M. Blair, personal and private, June 3, 1919 (RBP 3.38.006).

57 Bond to Cowan, August 21, 1919 (RBP 3.38.004).

58 Bond to Cowan, September 1, 1919 (RBP 3.38.004).

CHAPTER FOURTEEN

The Twenties and the Final Years, 1920–1927

Although Robert Bond was not involved in active politics in the 1920s, he remained closely interested in public affairs and was quite prepared to let his views be known on what he considered the important issues. Calls for him to resurface and lead a new political party persisted after 1919, as the future of the colony became ever more problematic, and many people saw him as its potential saviour. But he always refused. He pleaded health issues, telling J.A. Robinson (publisher of the *Daily News* and a former political antagonist) in 1922 that he had "indifferent health—for I have never recovered from the Western Bay brutality" that had "set up a rheumatic ailment that has been I regret to say progressive."[1] In 1913, a London physician had reported that Bond was, on the whole, in good shape—though he should, if possible, retire—and that mentally he was "as bright and vigorous and keen as ever."[2] But it seems clear that Bond's health was deteriorating in the 1920s, perhaps earlier, and it obviously affected him. Apart from rheumatism, he had arthritis and other ailments.[3]

Bond was also fundamentally opposed to making the political compromises with old opponents that would have been necessary for a comeback. The political scene had changed since 1914 and become more fluid. Former certainties had disappeared, and in this landscape Bond was an outsider. He was a genuine patriot, wanting to preserve his country's political independence. But any return to politics had to be on his terms, which were demanding if not impractical—and not acceptable to other politicians.

Moreover, Bond had become deeply disillusioned. He told his brother George early in 1921 that he was "determined to leave this Country just as soon as I can conveniently depart." For where he did not say, but probably England. He had no personal connections locally, and "conditions here are not congenial. The people are painfully narrow, uncultured, unreliable, dictatorial, and quarrelsome. A peculiar people, of which it would be difficult to find a duplicate." He added that the Methodists were the most peculiar of all.* Clearly, Bond was deeply disturbed by his rejection by the electorate in 1908–09 and in 1913—decisions that he thought irresponsible and disheartening. How could voters have preferred Morris and his crew over himself and the Liberals? This attitude displayed a certain conceit (possibly understandable in the circumstances), even arrogance; both tendencies were probably exaggerated by his solitary and secluded lifestyle. But looking at the political scene after the Great War, Bond could not find a glimmer of hope. His country, he thought—and rightly, as it turned out—was lost.

Bond therefore decided to sell his estate. He produced an elaborate album for potential private buyers, with photographs taken by the Holloway Studios.† He also offered to sell it to the colony. The minimum price was $60,000.‡ The property included eight square miles of land (just over 20 square kilometres) plus unsold lots in the small town of Whitbourne as well as The Grange. Built in the style of an "Old English Country Mansion," it was a large house with seven bedrooms, a library, dining, drawing, and billiard rooms, a conservatory, and a glassed verandah, all furnished by Maple and Company of London. Bond thought that it would be more than adequate for the "Superintendent of an Agricultural Establishment and his Staff," should the government buy it. The estate would also be an ideal place for a "Reformatory for Juvenile Offenders, and also for a Poor

---

* Robert Bond to George Bond, January 14, 1921 (RBP 1.02.025). Though raised as a Methodist, Robert Bond was one of nature's Anglicans. He gave a bell to the Anglican church in Whitbourne in 1889, and after his political retirement any pretence that he was a Methodist ended. The 1921 *Nominal Census for Trinity Bay* (421–22) lists him as "Church of England" (PANL, GN 2/39A).

† The album is in RBP 12.04.001–006; "Extracts from a letter of Sir Robert Bond . . . in October 1920," PANL, GN 8/211.

‡ Bond to Dowden and Edwards (St. John's), August 28, 1922 (RBP 2.05.010). This is about $860,000 in 2019 dollars.

House"; the inmates could work on the farm, clear land for settlers, and make "boxes, barrels and baskets." The outbuildings included two barns, a caretaker's lodge, and a boathouse. For the government it was a ready-made model farm or reformatory; for the private buyer it was "A Sportsman's Paradise. A Delightful Retreat for a Summer Holiday, 'Far From the Madding Crowd.'" For either buyer, the estate had immense potential—that was the pitch. An essential precondition to a sale, however, was the settlement of a long-standing dispute with the government.

During the 1890s, Whitbourne had become a major base for railway expansion. Bond's Townships Company gave the government land for machine and engineering shops, seeing an opportunity to create employment and enlarge the settlement. But when the 1898 Reid contract stipulated that the shops be moved to St. John's, the population of the settlement began to decline. The Townships Company was wound up in 1903–04 with Bond as assignee. He bought the company's land in the Whitbourne area, then lodged a claim for damages against his own government, asserting that taking down the machine shops and moving the equipment was illegal.[4] There the matter rested until 1920, when Bond demanded action because of the possible sale of the estate.

Bond held that there had been an understanding that the railway would establish a permanent industry at Whitbourne in return for the free land. When that industry—the machine shops—was taken away, the land and the buildings on it should have reverted to the assignee of the Townships Company. If the government wanted to retain the land, it should pay for it; if it did not, the government should return the land, first clearing up the remaining debris. In any event, Bond thought that he (as assignee) was entitled to damages for the buildings destroyed by the Reid Newfoundland Company, for the continued use of his property, and for the loss of what had been assumed to be a "permanent business."[5] In 1921, the Justice Department decided that these claims had no merit.[6] For some reason Bond was not informed. In 1924 he revived the issue,[7] the department did not change its mind, and there the matter ended.[8]

Bond's cousin and housekeeper, Sarah Roberts, died in April 1924. By that time Bond was having second thoughts about moving away. As far as is known, there had been no serious offers for the estate. Bond's brother suggested that he might move to Nova Scotia, but Bond responded that he had no friends in Canada and did not like Canadians, anyway. At least he knew Newfoundland and was known there.[9] In a separate letter to George, he wrote that "my love of country life and its pursuits . . . has enabled me to escape a tragedy and to convert my retirement from active politics into a pleasure."[10] And to another correspondent: "I am happy with the simple pleasures of my country life, and of my library, and the fresh breezes of many active interests."[11] At this stage in his life, given the lack of interest in his property and the failure of his dispute with the government, Bond was not moving anywhere.

The Reverend George (left) and Sir Robert Bond at The Grange, possibly during the 1920s. (ASC, RBP 12.01.009)

His presence in Newfoundland, however, led to continued attempts to bring him back into public life. In 1921 a member of the Cashin party suggested that Bond should run in a Harbour Main by-election,* a course supported by the local priest, Father Whelan, who thought it was the only way to recruit a "real leader." There was another plan, it seems, to have Bond "called out" at mass meetings in St. John's and the district.[12] Similar letters urging his return came from James Kent[13] and also from Harry Crowe, who claimed that Lord Morris (whom he had met in London) would join Bond in establishing "a sound Government for the Island."[14]

Bond told Father Whelan that while he agreed about "the deplorable condition of our public affairs, and the absolute necessity for a radical change in the management of the same if the Country is to be saved from

* W.J. Walsh to Bond, January 11, 1921 (RBP 3.39.002). Walsh claimed that Cashin, Crosbie, and Higgins would all support him, as well as Archbishop Roche.

bankruptcy and ruin," running in a by-election would not change anything. If elected, he would have to have "an understanding" with one of the party leaders, a prospect he found repugnant. He would only consider re-entering public life at a general election, and then in association with "very different men from the majority of those who at present sit [in the House]." They had to be people who would

> overhaul our financial chaos and replace it by justice and order. For the high-road of financial honesty was forsaken in 1909, and since then our Governments have floundered in bye-paths and ditches of improper legislation, which have finally placed them in a financial morass. . . . Changes must come, or we shall have to face ruin. . . . If a grave crisis should come in which I can render the Colony some material assistance, my services shall not be withheld.*

It is noticeable that few (if any) of these letters, in 1921 or later, came from leading politicians, who had obviously decided that Bond was no longer important. He had been consulted in 1919, had refused to return to politics, and that was enough. Coaker certainly believed that Bond was never going to resurface. For the most part, the letters and appeals came from the older generation or from members of the general public, battered and bewildered by the vicissitudes of the postwar world. The former political parties had dissolved into factions and an unstable Squires-Coaker government seemed incapable of handling the serious and growing economic and financial crisis.

The war had increased the public debt from $30.5 million in 1913–14 to $43.5 million in 1919–20 and easy borrowing continued, sending the debt to

---

* Bond to Whelan, January 10, 1921 (RBP 2.02.011). He wrote less carefully to his nephew Fraser Bond: "An evil fate has just sent me an urgent appeal to accept a seat . . . by <u>acclamation</u>. Imagine such a thing! I would as soon, I really think sooner, proceed to Sing Sing . . . as to enter an institution [?] identified with meaner spirits" (Bond to Fraser Bond, January 10, 1921, RBP 1.02.024).

The Grange in summer, undated. (ASC, RBP 12.03.003)

$60.5 million in 1923–24.* The Bell Island mines were in difficulty and fish exporters faced serious market problems, especially in southern Europe. The all-important export price of fish, which had climbed during the war to a record peak in 1918, began to fall. From 1919–20 onward, there was a trade deficit and the value of total trade and government revenue both declined; from 1920–21, the government ran significant deficits. Had the cost of living also declined, adjustment could possibly have been easier. But in the early 1920s, the cost of provisions was almost double what it had been in 1914. Small wonder that the government worried about unrest in St. John's.

Another significant and expensive factor was the Newfoundland railway, which by the end of the war was dilapidated and in need of repairs (estimated at over $5 million). The Reid Newfoundland Company owed the Bank of Montreal about $1 million and was no longer interested in operating an unprofitable railway business in spite of its contractual obligations. Instead, it wanted to focus on its extensive land holdings, where it hoped to make some money. Under pressure from the Bank of Montreal,

* The numbers are rounded and approximate. The debt in 1909–10 was $27 million.

the company told the government in June 1920 that it could not carry on without financial assistance. The government was not unco-operative, although Squires himself was ambivalent. In 1920–21, a joint railway commission was established to run the railway; it was given a loan of $1.5 million and its losses were capped.* In addition, the government decided to seek help from the management of the Canadian Pacific Railway. In 1921, one of its senior officials, R.C. Morgan, became general manager. It was a cozy arrangement, given that the Reids, the Bank of Montreal, and the CPR were all intertwined.[15] In the Newfoundland context, the Reid company was "too big to fail."

One reason for the concordat with a company that both Squires and Coaker had vilified in the past was a justified fear of claims, counter-claims, and lengthy and expensive lawsuits. Another was the "Humber proposition," a scheme that originated with the Reid company. It wanted to develop a newsprint mill in western Newfoundland using the hydro-electric potential of the Humber River and timber from its extensive landholdings in the region.[16] An even more ambitious proposal had been approved by the legislature in 1915, but collapsed soon after. The Reids persisted, however, and once the war was over they resumed negotiations with the government and potential partners. By early 1922, the Reid company was proposing going ahead with the project in partnership with the giant British engineering firm Sir W.G. Armstrong, Whitworth and Co., as long as the Newfoundland government agreed to guarantee a $15 million bond issue. This proved to be highly controversial. Squires was dubious, though some of his ministers—Coaker and Warren, for example—were enthusiastic. Governor Harris was opposed to government guarantees in principle, and there was criticism from the Board of Trade, the press, and the public. Was this to be another "Reid deal"? Bond decided to speak out, his first public intervention for some time.

He did so in a letter published in the *Daily News* on March 8, 1922. In essence, it was a lengthy dissertation about responsible government. His main point was that if the administration was divided on a proposal of

* The Reids were also allowed to spin off their various enterprises into subsidiary companies.

this importance, it should not be submitted to the legislature: "That a measure of such magnitude, and grave financial importance can come before the Legislature if the Government is not united in the merits of the measure is, to me, unthinkable for it would be a violation of the fundamental principles of Responsible Government, as we know it to-day." Moreover, such a measure could not be introduced by a private member. He cited a range of constitutional authorities and appealed to the government to "pause before they pass a measure which may strike a fatal blow at the independence and autonomy of our country. Already the weary Titan staggers under the too vast orb of its fate. Any additional burden will, in my opinion, bring about a speedy collapse."

The reaction was immediate. The *Evening Telegram* noted many positive comments but cautioned that outside the government, no one had actually seen the proposed deal.[17] William Walsh, a Cashin supporter, wrote that the letter had caused a "sensation" and renewed his efforts to persuade Bond to return to active politics,[18] as did J.A. Robinson, who remarked that the letter had been received "with marked approval" and "very apparent and very real gratitude." He went on:

> The outlook is gloomy indeed. Unless a strong fearless man, of marked ability, unimpeachable integrity and admitted patriotism, appears on the scene, the end of Newfoundland's credit and autonomy is within measurable distance. . . . Only one man in Newfoundland can fill the requirements. . . . The hope is everywhere, a hope earnest and intense, that [the letter] may foreshadow that salvation which only Sir Robert Bond's active leadership can assure.[19]

Bond replied at length. Like Robinson, he was deeply troubled by the existing situation, but after serious thought he had concluded that there would be "no public advantage to accrue by my returning to public life."[20] Like Bond, Robinson was an admirer of W.E. Gladstone and reminded him of the great man's return to public life at an advanced age.[21] Bond rejected the comparison. Gladstone had "a constitution like steel," but he

Sir Robert Bond's desk at The Grange, undated. (ASC, RBP 12.03.078)

did not. He remained keenly interested in public life, but "the flesh is weaker, very much weaker." The Western Bay plunge had been "a very severe shock to my nervous system, and set up a rheumatic ailment that has been I regret to say progressive"—so much so that he had been thinking of moving to a kinder climate.[22]

Bond did speak out again on railway matters, however, and repeated his use of the pseudonym "A Student of Law and Politics." His lengthy commentary appeared in the *Evening Telegram* in April 1922, framed as a response to a report written by R.C. Morgan, the CPR import, which had appeared in late January.[23] In summary, Morgan argued that the rail and coastal steam services should be reorganized and rationalized, and that it had to be accepted that the railway was not, and never would, be "a commercial venture"—an accurate observation. Traffic was too light, freight and passenger rates too low, costs too high, and the branch lines were a burden. He recommended that the government maintain the railway, but that a lessee should operate the rail and coastal steam services. The implication was that a new contract with the Reid company or a successor should be negotiated. The CPR brass was not in favour of government management and Morgan was following this line.

Bond found the report to be little more than a case for the Reids, who were apparently to be absolved "from crimes of omission and commission." He used the opportunity to review both the colony's political history since the late 1890s and his own role in it. He particularly objected to what he saw as special pleading—that the Reids had not fully understood what they were taking on in 1898 and that the branch lines had been imposed on the company. He also disputed that there had been improper competition in the coastal steamer service. R.G. Reid and his sons had always known exactly what they were doing, and the current problems resulted from the company failing to fulfill its contractual obligations by developing its land holdings. Moreover, the company had become a "political machine" that had intervened in, and manipulated, local politics in its own interest. Successive governments had failed to enforce the contracts—and as for the branch lines, he agreed with Morgan that they were a disaster. They had been a payback to the Reids for supporting Morris through two elections, with a third on the horizon. Bond wanted a showdown with the company and justice for the colony before any new agreement was made. These were stirring words (if impractical), and Bond's authorship must have been widely suspected, if not known. He wrote "The Aftermath" over a collection of newspaper cuttings relating to yet another attempt to bring him back into active politics that year.[24]

In late April, the lawyer and former Tory politician William Howley was approached by a citizens' committee concerned about allegedly excessive government expenditures. Howley advised against going through the estimates and suggesting cuts, and it was decided to invite Bond to address a meeting. Both the group's chairman—George Parsons—and Howley were assured by Alexander Parsons, an old Bond associate, that Bond would come if invited by a public meeting.[25] The gathering took place on April 28 and drew a large crowd. Howley reported that hundreds had to be turned away, and that it was a "thoroughly representative" turnout, though merchants and professionals were thin on the ground (and no "professional politicians" were present). Resolutions were passed to the effect that the financial condition of the country was so desperate that meetings should be held all over the island, and that such a meeting in St. John's should be addressed by Bond—"the one man to whom we can look with confidence to help and guide us at the present time."[26] The chairman then went out to Whitbourne. Bond was not only recovering from a lengthy bout of pneumonia, but was in any case reluctant to speak in public. He agreed to put his views in writing, having been assured that "party politics was in no way mixed up with the movement and that no active politicians had any connection therewith." The document could be read at a meeting that Parsons said (mistakenly) would be held on May 8, and published simultaneously.[27] Bond speedily wrote his piece but there followed a muddle over publication, which did not occur until May 18.

The financial condition of the country, he said, was the result of "the incapacity, neglect or wilful design" of recent governments, but the electors should remember that it was they who voted them in and everyone was liable for repaying the debt. "It seems to have been forgotten that all public money comes out of private pockets." If voters wanted some tax relief and a pledge that taxes would not increase, the answer lay with the ballot box: "Return the clearest, brainiest, and most independent men you can induce to represent you . . . that will prove your guarantee." In addition, governments had to recognize that they were trustees, and that "all excess in the public expenditure beyond the legitimate, actual wants of the country, is not only a pecuniary waste, but a great political, and, above all, a great moral evil." The colony certainly faced severe problems in the all-important fish trade, but "we have been living for some time now riotously and recklessly on borrowed money," and there had been improper government expenditures: "Unnecessary departments, hosts of unnecessary officials, excessive departmental allocations. . . . Let it be understood by all . . . there can be no reduction in taxation until a reduction is first made in Civil Government." The citizens of St. John's and the Board of Trade clearly wanted this, and the government should listen. There was "something radically wrong with the body politic," and the only cure was to remove the cancer of "debt, waste, [and] plunder."[28]

These interventions seem to have been well-received, but their impact on government decision-making was slight. Governor Harris did not mention them in his reports. It is possible that Bond's letter concerning the Humber proposition was a factor in the government's decision in March to reject a guarantee on the full amount needed, which infuriated Coaker.[29] But this action did not mean that the scheme was dead. The Reids and Armstrongs began to explore ways to raise the money that would reduce the colony's financial responsibility, and they succeeded. The definite prospect of a Humber development meant, in turn, that an agreement with the Reid Company had to be negotiated. The end result was a government takeover of the railway and its allied operations, which took effect in 1923. Badly needed work began at Corner Brook and in the Humber Valley, and Squires had a sure-fire issue—"Put the Hum on the Humber"—for the election he sprang in May 1923. As long as Squires was prime minister, there would be no sign of the severe financial cutbacks that Bond thought necessary.

The dissolution prompted another round of speculation about the possibility of Bond's return to politics, which he firmly quashed on February 23.* Squires, he thought, had called the election "to hide his political crimes from the House of Assembly. He has pledged this Country to back the Reid Humber deal to the amount of Ten Million Dollars. If only I had the strength how the feathers would fly. My poor Country! 'The last phase.'"[30] Nevertheless, Bond's name was used by both sides, and the *Evening Telegram* revived his previous statements to bolster its attacks on Coaker.

It did not much matter—Squires won the election with a ten-seat majority. But the political situation soon spun out of control. A cabinet revolt forced Squires to resign on July 23. William Warren took over, backed by Coaker, and an independent inquiry was launched into serious allegations of graft involving Squires and Dr. Alexander Campbell, the former Minister of Agriculture. It was carried out by an English lawyer,

---

* *Evening Telegram*, February 19, 23, and 24, 1923; Bond to George Bond, March 3, 1923 (RBP 1.02.033). Bond later wrote to his niece, "It's too late in the day . . . too late I am sorry to say for me to try and clean up the mess that has been made of our public life" (Bond to Roberta Bond, December 25, 1923, RBP 1.02.031). For some comments on "that creature Squires," see Bond to Fraser Bond, December 18, 1922 (RBP 1.02.029).

Thomas Hollis Walker. Although the charges were largely upheld, Squires and his allies were able to defeat the government on April 23, 1924. A second Warren government lasted only four days, mainly because of hostility to the FPU from Roman Catholic politicians and Water Street interests, now represented by an emerging political figure, Walter Monroe.[31] Warren advised the new governor, Sir William Allardyce,* to send for Coaker, who declined the invitation to form a ministry. Eventually Albert Hickman did so, and held on until the June 2 election (Warren having earlier been granted a dissolution†).

Even before Warren's defeat in the Assembly, the published evidence from the Hollis Walker inquiry prompted wringing of hands and more pleas for Bond to act like a true Cincinnatus and return to save his country. For example, a newspaper article in mid-March called for a new Liberal Party to be led by Bond, a "statesman of unsullied reputation. . . . Newfoundland has never seen his like before; will it ever see his like as Prime Minister again?"[32] Walter Monroe confirmed that there was talk of a new party that, if led by Bond, could sweep the country and "get the old land on its feet"—but could Bond see himself allying with Cashin, Crosbie, or Morine?[33] Four petitions with more than three hundred signatures arrived from Bay Roberts and area, asking Bond to return—"[We] have entirely lost confidence in the ability and integrity of the Professional Politicians now before the country"[34]—and more letters followed. Newfoundland must be saved, wrote Charles Steer, a prominent businessman: "All along the Street, your splendid manhood and conduct of the affairs of this Colony, are continually spoken of."[35] Even Monroe tried again. But the appeals ceased once it was clear, on May 11, that it was Monroe himself who would lead a "Liberal-Conservative Party" against Hickman's "Liberal-Progressive Party." Monroe won a comfortable majority.

Bond, of course, had refused all requests to re-enter politics. He told

---

* Allardyce was governor from September 1922 until October 1928.

† These events are covered in Noel, *Politics*, 158–76. Noel (and *ENL* 1:713) states that Allardyce invited Bond to form an administration before asking Coaker, but there is no mention of this in the governor's report on the crisis (Allardyce to Thomas, conf., May 10, 1924, CO 532/275, 171–75).

Steer that if his health had been better "my services would have been tendered to the public." He informed Monroe that, since his resignation, he had "not given five minutes serious thought to the idea of again contesting the Constituencies at a General Election." There was no point in offering himself "as a willing sacrifice on the altar of political expediency."[36] He added in a letter to Charles Jeffrey, the *Evening Telegram*'s editor, that what was happening was "politics of a character that I have never been accustomed to, that I have no sympathy with, and that I cannot countenance."[37] He privately told George Bond that "the call is absurd, and compliance therewith would be an exhibition of madness."[38]

By the time the next election took place, in 1928, Bond had died. Before his death, there do not seem to have been further calls for him to "save the country," though there was a short-lived movement in 1926 to have him appointed governor. Bond thought that, too, was "a mad idea": "I would much prefer to snare rabbits for a livelihood than to entertain the Aristocracy that now finds its way into Government House."[39] He was spared witnessing the suspension of responsible government in 1934 and the imposition of Commission Government, but he would not have been surprised at those outcomes. He would have ascribed it to extravagance, a decline in the standards of public life, and the breakdown of the two-party system after the FPU entered politics.

Bond's last years have been well described elsewhere.[40] His health steadily deteriorated and he was alone in The Grange after April 1924, apart from a housekeeper and domestic employees.* His few friends in St. John's were disappearing. His niece Roberta, who had qualified as a medical doctor, stayed with him for some months in 1925–26, but this only temporarily alleviated the gloom—and Bond did not think that women should be physicians. Indeed, Roberta's independent attitudes and her marriage in 1926 to an older man troubled him a great deal.†

* The 1921 *Nominal Census for Trinity Bay* listed (421-22) a household consisting of Bond, Sarah Roberts, and two female servants from Bonavista, both Methodist. Three people were employed on the farm (PANL, GN 2/39/A).

† Roberta (b. 1901) died in 1966; an obituary ("Dr. Roberta Bond Nichols") is in the *Canadian Anaesthesists' Society Journal* (14:12, 1967, 152).

By early 1927, Bond was failing, and there was little that his friend and doctor, the elderly J. Sinclair Tait, could do for him.* His birthday, February 25, was "the saddest and most trying I have ever experienced," he wrote to his brother, and a stroke had left him without the use of his left arm and hand.[41] George Bond—who was in uncertain health himself†—travelled to The Grange from Halifax and found a very difficult patient:

> I immediately suggested that he go to bed and lie down. . . . He would have preferred remaining in the Library on the couch but . . . he started to walk upstairs with my help very slowly. But he was grievously exhausted when he got to his room and could not do more than pant for breath for some time. . . . But he got to bed finally and either slept or became semi-conscious. . . . But he would not, could not rest in bed. . . . So it went on day after day night after night. . . . And then his moaning, and crying out "Oh my Oh" as the paroxysms took him and wondering sometimes what he had done to be so punished, were most distressing to hear. . . . [He] pitched into me heartily and loudly. . . . Oh those dreadful days.[42]

Robert Bond died on March 16, 1927. He was 70 years old. Following his wishes, there was no state funeral. Instead, there was a simple ceremony at Whitbourne on March 21, attended by local people as well as dignitaries and friends who came by special train from St. John's. Among the visitors was William J. Browne, at that time an MHA for St. John's West. On entering The Grange, he recalled that:

> We found a wide hall with rich tapestries and caribou heads adorning the walls. The body lay in the drawing room. There was a distinguished air about the face; he had a strong, al-

---

* Bond told Tait in January that he was very unwell and asked him to send twelve bottles of whisky (Bond to Tait, January 21, 1927, RBP 2.02.011).

† George Bond to Cluny Macpherson, January 24, 1927 (MUN, ASC, Coll. 236, 5.09.00). George Bond had collapsed on a Halifax sidewalk early in January 1927.

> most aquiline nose, deep set eyes and a graceful sweep of a moustache. But there was weariness about the expression. . . . The principal mourner was his brother, Reverend Dr. Bond, who walked behind the hearse holding onto the coffin for assistance along the route. It was a reverent funeral. . . . Rarely has a person who once walked the earth so proudly, been buried so simply. . . . A small boy pumped the organ, first with one hand and then with the other, and the Village Choir was in attendance. The church was filled.[43]

Bond was buried in the Whitbourne Anglican cemetery.[44] It was "a sunny but very windy and bitterly cold day."[*]

NOTES

1 Bond to Robinson, February 13, 1922 (RBP 3.39.005).
2 Sir J. J. Goodhart to [unknown], March 24, 1913 (RBP 2.02.002).
3 For instance, Bond to Fraser Bond, November 1921, and to George Bond, November 29, 1924 (RBP 1.02.024, 1.02.034).
4 Bond to Reid Newfoundland Co., August 30, 1904; Bond to J.M. Kent, November 21, 1907 (PANL, GN 2/5/84D; RBP 2.07.003).
5 Bond to Colonial Secretary, July 29, 1920 (PANL, GN 2/5/84D).
6 P.J. Summers to A. Mews, June 25, 1921 (PANL, GN 2/5/84D).
7 Bond to Colonial Secretary, September 6, 1924 (PANL, GN 2/5/84D).
8 Summers to H.J. Russell, September 14, 1925, and Bennett to Bond, October 27, 1925 (PANL, GN 2/5/84D).
9 Bond to George Bond, November 29, 1924 (RPB 1.02.034).
10 Bond to George Bond, June 22, 1923 (RBP 1.02.033).

---

* George Bond to Fraser Bond, March 25, 1927 (RBP 2.10.011). Bond's will (1914) stipulated that he was to be buried in the family plot in the General Protestant Cemetery in St. John's, which was then to be "permanently closed." Why the location was changed is not known. George Bond thought that his brother probably changed his mind after the death of his cousin, Sarah Roberts, who was buried at Whitbourne (George Bond to Fraser Bond, April 7, 1927, RBP 2.10.016). The will is in RBP 2.10.001, and can be viewed online at http://nl.canadagenweb.org/as_wills_robertbond.htm.

11 Bond to J.A. Robinson, February 13, 1922 (RBP 3.39.005).
12 Father S.J. Whelan to Bond, January 5 and 11, 1921 (RBP 2.02.011).
13 Kent to Bond, September 30, 1920 (RBP 3.39.001).
14 Crowe to Bond, private, December 17, 1921 (RBP 2.03.016).
15 Morine, *Railway Contract*, 47–48; Hiller, *The Newfoundland Railway, 1881–1949*, 22–23.
16 Hiller, "The Politics of Newsprint," 3–39.
17 *Evening Telegram*, February 7, 8, and 11, 1922.
18 W.J. Walsh to Bond, February 8, 1922 (RBP 3.39.005); *ENL* 5:503.
19 Robinson to Bond, February 8, 1922 (RBP 3.39.005).
20 Bond to Robinson, February 13, 1922 (RBP 3.39.005).
21 Robinson to Bond, February 16, 1922 (RBP 3.39.005).
22 Bond to Robinson, February 20, 1922 (RBP 3.39.005).
23 *Evening Telegram*, April 12 through April 28, 1922 (copies in RBP 10.01.080); "Report of R.C. Morgan, Esq., on Railway Operation in Newfoundland, 1922" (*JHA*, 1922, appendix, 112).
24 RBP 10.01.080.
25 Howley to Bond, May 25, 1922 (RBP 3.39.005).
26 Howley to Bond, April 29, 1922, and G.R. Parsons to Bond, April 29, 1922 (RBP 3.39.005).
27 Bond to Howley, May 15, 1922 (RBP 3.39.005).
28 *Daily News*, May 18, 1922 (RBP 3.39.004).
29 Harris to Churchill, secret, March 30, 1922 (CO 194/303, 117).
30 Annotation on a press clipping, February 1923 (RBP 1.02.033).
31 *ENL* 3:599–601.
32 Scrutator, "About Men and Things," *Evening Telegram*, March 15, 1924.
33 Monroe to Bond, April 21, 1924 (RBP 3.39.007).
34 The petitions (late April 1924) are in RBP 3.39.007.
35 Steer to Bond, May 8, 1924 (RBP 3.39.007).
36 Bond to Steer, May 12, 1924, and Bond to Monroe, April 29, 1924 (RBP 3.39.007).
37 Bond to Jeffrey, May 6, 1924 (RBP 3.39.007). For Jeffrey, see *ENL* 3:103–104.
38 Bond to George Bond, April 14, 1924 (RBP 1.02.034).
39 Bond to George Bond, April 22, 1926 (RBP 1.02.044).
40 Baker and Neary, "Sir Robert Bond," 33–43.
41 Bond to George Bond, February 28, 1927 (RBP 1.02.046).
42 George Bond to Fraser Bond, March 25, 1927 (RBP 2.10.011).
43 Browne, *Eighty-Four Years a Newfoundlander*, 1:150–51.
44 *Evening Telegram* and *Daily News*, March 22, 1927.

Conclusion

Bond's death was marked by fulsome obituaries in the local press. A moving letter from Dr. Tait, who had known him for many years, predicted that "the name of Robert Bond will live on in ever increasing volume by all those who love and appreciate worth and native ability."[1] His old adversary, Lord Morris, published a generous tribute:

> He was a fearless advocate and an attractive and convincing speaker. No personal or party allegiance could win his adherence to any measure he did not believe in. Industrious and painstaking, he was ever ready to consider any policy or measure that aimed at the advancement of Newfoundland and the amelioration of her people. . . . Looking down through that long vista of years, I am glad to know that our differences were on questions of public policy, not private or personal. . . . There were few if any who did not recognize that in his support and advocacy there was always a genuine ring of honesty of view and conviction, and those he most differed from never questioned the underlying patriotic spirit actuating him in his public life.[2]

When the House of Assembly opened in May, Monroe described Bond as "a man of rare gifts," and mentioned "his engaging personality, his gift of oratory and his pleasing manner." He also referred to Bond's bequest to the colony, which was controversial.[3]

George Bond was the sole executor of his brother's will, made in 1914. It directed that the Whitbourne estate (including The Grange) should be transferred to the governor and the Executive Council, "to be held in trust

Fraser Bond, son of the Reverend George Bond, probably at The Grange, undated. (ASC, RBP 12.02.015)

by them for the people of Newfoundland as a Model Farm forever." All other "real and personal property" was to be sold and the proceeds invested in government bonds. The interest would be paid to Robert Bond's nephew Fraser, whom Bond saw as his heir.* There were other details and instructions, which included a bequest for Roberta—jewellery and $1,000 per annum, "so long as she shall remain a spinster."† Fraser was to receive most of his uncle's other property, including his KCMG paraphernalia and his papers. The Museum would be given various ceremonial caskets and illuminated addresses, "and all the natural history specimens in my residence, shot and mounted by me."‡ There was a formal ceremony at the Museum later in 1927 (October 7).§

George Bond, bequeathed books but nothing else, was an unhappy executor. Fraser Bond was, at first, disappointed and angry that The Grange was bequeathed to the colony, and he directed some harsh criticism at his father and uncle.¶ George pointed out to him that, despite what the will said, the future of the Whitbourne estate was uncertain, since the government was ambivalent about accepting it. Monroe first suggested that The Grange might be converted into a summer tourist hotel, its lakes offering an additional boating attraction. That might, in turn, generate enough revenue to support a

* George Bond's oldest son, Herbert, had drowned off Vancouver Island in 1910, aged 27 (RBP 1.01.018).

† Both George and Fraser Bond thought the will was unfair to Roberta—"but she hurt him terribly and [he] blamed her for his illness which was not altogether fair" (George Bond to Fraser Bond, April 14, 1927, RBP 2.10.004).

‡ Robert Bond's estate was valued at $92,750 (about $1.3 million in 2019 dollars).

§ George Bond complained that only one member of the Executive attended, besides Monroe (letter to Fraser Bond, October 7, 1927, RBP 2.10.004).

¶ Roberta Bond's views are not known.

model farm. George Bond agreed to think over the proposition. At Monroe's suggestion, he wrote to the governor explaining what he thought were his brother's intentions. The woodlands within the estate were untouched, he said; the town had been built in the area and The Grange and its gardens had been made into a park, "like a bit of England." Robert had constructed other buildings and had run a well-conducted dairy farm. That was his gift. But, George added, the estate would have to be looked after by an "expert farmer obtained from outside the Colony" and overseen by an independent and completely non-political commission. It should never be alienated for any other purpose, or privatized.[4] He also mentioned a possible link with the recently founded Memorial University College; its President, J.L. Paton, asked for advice from the Ontario Agricultural College at Guelph. The response was not encouraging.[5] A further complication was that the governor decided that he could not be a trustee, since that would involve him (and his successors) in politics.[6]

The government eventually decided to consult the legislature.[7] The bequest was discussed in Committee of the Whole on three occasions. Monroe did not hide his skepticism—the farm would entail an annual charge on the colony and there would have to be an endowment fund of at least $200,000. Bond had made a small profit by selling milk, but a subsidized public institution could not do the same and compete with local farmers. Moreover, Whitbourne was not a suitable place for a model farm—it was isolated and the soil was "nothing extra." Opinion in the Assembly was divided. Farmers were consulted—both in the St. John's area and on the west coast—and there was no vote.[8] In the end, Monroe's view prevailed and a formal letter was sent to George Bond in October. A model farm could not be operated without political control, since it would have to be funded by the government, and its produce could unfairly compete with that produced by "private farmers." Training students there would be expensive and Whitbourne was not a suitable location.[9]

George Bond was upset. He told Monroe "how keenly we had felt some of the things said in the House and that I thought the thing had been made a political football. I told him Dear Bob never dreamed that his offer would be refused, and that if he had known how it would have been treated, the offer would never have been made."[10] Earlier in the year he had written to Fraser that "his benefaction to the country ought to arouse deep respect and gratitude. In giving the Grange Estate he gave the country his only and beloved child. And all this done in 1914."[11]

The will had not provided for a refusal of the bequest, so George Bond submitted a series of questions to the Supreme Court.[12] The case was heard by Robert Bond's old political allies, Chief Justice William Horwood and Judge James Kent. They held (in January 1928) that the government could legally refuse the bequest and that, under Newfoundland property law, the Whitbourne estate should pass to George's son.[13] So Fraser Bond (1891–1965), who taught journalism at Columbia University, became a summertime visitor to Newfoundland. His sister, Roberta Bond Nichols (1901–66), is known to have returned to The Grange at least once, in 1930. George Bond died in Halifax in 1933 and was buried in the General Protestant Cemetery in St. John's.[14]

In 1945, the Boys' Reform School at Whitbourne was destroyed by fire. Discussions began about a replacement, possibly on the Bond estate. Fraser Bond was willing to sell some or all of the property; he was a bachelor with no children, and the upkeep and management of the estate probably took more time and money than he could afford. Moreover, his eyesight was failing. The Commission Government formally approved the purchase in 1946; it also decided to demolish The Grange, which it judged to be a fire hazard and not worth restoring. Discussions dragged on until 1949, when the provincial government of Newfoundland—for by now the "country" was part of Canada—took possession. A new Reform School would be built on the property, and it would have a "Sir Robert Bond Memorial Room." Fraser Bond packed up the historical material in the house, which he said, according to a newspaper report, should become

Roberta Bond, daughter of the Reverend George Bond, probably at The Grange, undated. (ASC, RBP 12.02.013)

"the property of Newfoundland, but when that time will be he is as yet uncertain. As he pointed out, the bequests left by his uncle to the Museum have fared badly."* He sold some of the furniture for placement in the Memorial Room, and loaned the official photographs.

The new provincial government decided against restoring The Grange in 1951; it was demolished the following year.† The remaining contents were dispersed and the Memorial Room never materialized. Though the premier of the day, Joseph Smallwood, professed to be a great admirer of Robert Bond, the way the liquidation of the Bond estate was handled showed a distinct lack of imagination and sensitivity.

Today, the site of The Grange has a commemorative plaque installed by the Canadian Historic Sites and Monuments Board—an irony in and of itself, given Robert Bond's anti-confederate proclivities. There is information about Whitbourne's famous resident in the town's small museum, which is housed in the former railway station. The Anglican Church—rebuilt since Bond's time—has a stained glass window donated in his memory by Fraser Bond and Roberta Bond Nichols. Robert Bond's grave is just outside the door, near that of Sarah Roberts. This a more definite, if more distant, memorial than other Newfoundland pre-confederation first ministers have received. They are interred in the various denominational cemeteries in St. John's or elsewhere, their plots are given no particular attention. Their houses, those that survive, do not bear plaques. Few of them are remembered today, other than by specialists. Bond's memorial is unusual. He was not buried in the family tomb in the General Protestant Cemetery, but reinforced his commitment to Whitbourne and what it represented for him. And though The Grange is gone, Bond is still remembered.

In the current cultural environment, the house and estate might have survived, but it was different in the early 1950s. Joseph Smallwood was selling a "new Newfoundland" that had broken with what had gone before

* *Evening Telegram*, August 8, 1949. The Commission Government was remarkably insensitive to the historical legacy of both the Museum and the Colonial Building. There was little (if any) local outcry.

† I am grateful to Edwina Suley for access to a chronology of The Grange compiled by the late John Gosse.

Sir Robert Bond's grave at Whitbourne, undated. (ASC, Coll. 236, Box 15)

and was taking a different direction. The conventional thinking of the time did not see "heritage" (in today's terms) as an industry that could produce substantial economic benefit. For all Smallwood's apparent admiration of Bond—he claimed to be in the same "great Liberal tradition"—he did not want to be haunted by Liberal ghosts. Nevertheless, he copied Bond by building a house and creating a farm outside St. John's and out of sight of the sea.*

Smallwood will not be forgotten because of his central, if controversial, role in bringing about confederation in 1949. The events of 1945–49 will continue to reverberate, since they mark the end of Newfoundland as a separate and, in some respects, sovereign political entity—a result that, after 1909, Bond feared was inevitable. Bond is seen as the leader who might have steered the country in another direction, and might conceivably have preserved the country's political independence. By the 1920s,

* The property was on Roache's Line, near Clarke's Beach. Smallwood edited the first two volumes of the *Encyclopedia of Newfoundland and Labrador*, which were published in 1981 and 1984.

though, significant financial damage had been done by the railway and the Great War. Bond was not in good health and he recoiled from the expedient but unpalatable compromises that would have had to be made with other politicians. He had had enough. And there was, in fact, little that he could have done. To a certain extent, Bond remained the country's political conscience. But given the circumstances, he could do no more.

In retrospect, Robert Bond can be criticized for failing to make his withdrawal from public life in 1914 absolute and final. He half-heartedly tried to move elsewhere, but did not. The Great War, his attachment to Sarah Roberts, his disputes with later governments, and the location of the estate were all relevant factors in this. But there was also his genuine affection for Newfoundland and for Whitbourne. It was where he felt he belonged. His commitment to his country helps explain why he remains prominent in local historical memory. A mystique grew up around his name in the 1920s when, though a distant recluse, he became identified (by some at least) as a potential national saviour. This perception was reinforced by the report of the Newfoundland Royal Commission in 1933:

> He [Bond] left behind him a reputation of far-sighted devotion to the interests of the Island and is generally regarded as the most statesmanlike figure in the line of Newfoundland Prime Ministers. To-day, a disillusioned people . . . single out the years of his Premiership as a period of orthodox finance and sane government when the fortunes of the Island were at their zenith; there was almost unanimous agreement among witnesses that the present period of misfortune might be regarded as having originated with his fall from power in 1908.[15]

Not surprisingly, Bond's long-time political rival, Alfred Morine, disagreed; he thought these comments exaggerated and unfair to other premiers who had "served the colony as well as Bond, and in some respects were more useful to it." In his draft history of Newfoundland—essentially his recollections and justifications—Morine argued that Bond's reputation was inflated: "He was a recluse in disposition, and, strangely enough, this distance . . . gave him a sort of halo with many." But what had he actually achieved and accomplished? "I can think of nothing particularly constructive to place to the special credit of Sir Robert Bond."*

It was, and remains, a fair question. Every society has its historical myths and stories—memory is highly selective—and one of these still presents Robert Bond as the unparalleled Newfoundland statesman and patriot. The witnesses who spoke to the Royal Commission were comparing Bond to those who followed him in office, and they were seeking explanations for the crisis that engulfed the country in the Great Depression. The causes of that crisis were complex; though questions of political leadership are relevant, they are not sufficient to explain what had happened. All the same, it is accurate to say that Bond was financially careful as prime minister, and that he had been fortunate to be in power as the late-nineteenth-century recession lifted and the colony became, temporarily, moderately prosperous. He was quite prepared to support borrowing large sums to build the trans-island railway (including some branch lines) and improve communications in general. His feud with the Reid family, too, was expensive. But the attempt to force reciprocity by retaliation after 1904 was a costly misjudgment. And one has to wonder how he would have acted had he been in power in August 1914—would there have been a Newfoundland Regiment, for instance?

Bond would probably have argued that the expansion and diversification of the economy justified the railway expenditures. He had great faith in the resources of the colony and in its future—at least until the 1920s. But there was only one important development that can be directly attributed to him: the establishment of the pulp and paper industry at Grand Falls and Bishop's Falls. Without the railway, that would never have happened. Beyond the forest industry, however, there was little in the way of economic development that came from opening the interior. Coal mines were never established at Grand Lake, there was no smelter on Bell Island, and the North Atlantic Short Line scheme was an illusion. Bond

* Morine, draft history, n.d., PANL, MG 271.2, folder 11. Morine died in 1944 at the age of 87.

overestimated the value of the country's natural resources—certainly its agricultural potential—and failed (like so many others, including William Coaker) to come to grips with the endemic structural problems of the fishing industry.

Where Bond scores highly is on his consistent assertion that Newfoundland possessed an equality of status with other British colonies of settlement. A colonial nationalist, he saw confederation with Canada as an unwelcome last resort and resisted pressure to become politically closer to Britain, a stance that some (including Morine) criticized as insular. Though he played a key role in settling the French Shore problem, in defining American fishing rights, and in sending the Labrador boundary issue on its way to an arbitrated resolution,* he found it difficult to accept two important factors of political life. The first was that diplomacy involves give and take; the second that, in the end, British interests would always prevail over those of Newfoundland. Bond was not a natural compromiser and he was not afraid of confrontation, as the American dispute demonstrated. That dispute, however, also showed that the colony was part of a larger geopolitical environment and because of its relative size it was bound to be subordinate to others.

Bond was not helped by his naturally reserved and private character or his short temper, nor by his inflexible opinions about public men and public policy. He was not an easy person. He was respected for his probity, his capacity for hard work, and his undoubted ability—and his dedication to his country was never questioned. But he was in some respects an impractical visionary. Over time, he became increasingly distant, both in person and geographically, as he grew older and spent more time at Whitbourne. A complicated man, Robert Bond was possibly the most able and committed of Newfoundland's pre-confederation prime ministers. His contribution should be respected and remembered—but it should certainly not not be exaggerated.

---

* The decision on the boundary was delivered on March 2, 1927. It was favourable to Newfoundland; whether Bond knew of it before he died on March 16 is not known.

NOTES

1 *Daily News*, April 22, 1927.

2 *Evening Telegram*, April 22, 1927.

3 Monroe, *PHA*, May 11, 1927, 5.

4 George Bond to Governor Allardyce, April 11, 1927 (RPB 2.10.011).

5 J.B. Reynolds to J.L. Paton, May 5, 1927 (RBP 2.10.013).

6 Allardyce to George Bond, April 17, 1927 (PANL, GN 8/211).

7 Monroe to George Bond, April 30, 1927 (PANL, GN 8/211).

8 *PHA*, May 18, June 9, and June 21, 1927, 55–78, 332–46, and 494–98.

9 W.S. Monroe to George Bond, October 8, 1927 (RBP 2.10.017).

10 George Bond to Fraser Bond, October 7, 1927 (RBP 2.10.004)).

11 George Bond to Fraser Bond, March 21, 1927 (RBP 2.10.015).

12 "Petition of George J. Bond . . . October 29, 1927" (RBP 2.10.001).

13 "In re Bond; Bond vs Bond et al," *Decisions of the Supreme Court of Newfoundland, 1927–1931* (St. John's, 1948), 109–128.

14 *Newfoundland Quarterly* 33, no. 1 (1933): 24.

15 *Newfoundland Royal Commission 1933 Report* (London: HMSO, 1933), 37. Also known as "the Amulree Report."

APPENDIX

Newfoundland and Responsible Government

During the period covered by this book, Newfoundland possessed responsible government, which evolved into dominion status after 1907.* However, the country never changed its name, and continued to be known until 1949 as the "Colony of Newfoundland."

Responsible government meant that the colony was in control of its internal affairs. The British, or imperial, government was responsible for external affairs which, in Newfoundland's case, included fisheries treaties that Britain had signed with France and the United States before responsible government was instituted in 1855.

The colony was governed by a legislature with two houses—the elected House of Assembly and the appointed Legislative Council—both of which met in the Colonial Building. The Assembly originally consisted of thirty members, increasing later to thirty-six; Labrador was not included. It was presided over by the Speaker. The Legislative Council, chaired by the president, consisted of fifteen members appointed by the governor on the recommendation of the premier/prime minister. The number could only be increased (as it was on occasion) with the permission of the imperial government. It was an approximation to the British House of Lords, just as the Assembly was an approximation to the British House of Commons. All legislation had to be approved by both houses and signed by the governor, with final consent being given in London. Any legislation could be "reserved," which meant that Royal

---

* The fundamental text is A.B. Keith, *Responsible Government in the Dominions* (Oxford: Clarendon Press, 1912 [three volumes] and 1928 [two volumes]).

assent was denied or postponed by either the governor or the imperial government; matters thought to be of local concern were not generally interfered with. Suspending clauses* were often used.

Elections took place every four years, except in unusual circumstances, when the governor would have to agree to dissolve the House of Assembly. Districts elected one to three MHAs, depending on their population; parties often ran slates of candidates. Candidates and voters had to be male, and there was a property qualification for electors until 1890; such qualifications for candidates lasted into the 1920s. There was universal male suffrage after 1890. The governor asked the leader of the victorious party to form a government.

The colonial "government" consisted of the premier or prime minister—the latter term came to be used increasingly after 1900—and a number of ministers, some without portfolio, which formed the Executive Council (the "Executive" or "cabinet"). There were ministers who were not part of the Executive, but it always included the attorney general/minister of justice, the colonial secretary and the receiver general/minister of finance and customs. The surveyor general/minister of agriculture and mines was also usually a member.† Other important departments were Marine and Fisheries (after 1898), and the Board of Works/Department of Public Works. When meeting on its own, this council was officially known as the "Committee of Council"; the presence of the governor was required for a full and formal meeting of the Executive Council.

The Executive had to be supported by a majority in the House of Assembly, but the governor could ask a minority party to form a government if there was a possibility of its gaining a majority. This was unusual, but an opposition party could move a vote of non-confidence when it suspected that the government had lost majority support.

The governor was an important figure. He had influence, his powers

---

* A suspending clause meant that the legislation (or a section of it) would not come into force unless the governor-in-council or the imperial government agreed.

† There was a reorganization of the civil service in 1898, which changed some departmental names.

were considerable, and Government House was the preeminent social location in St. John's. There were times when the governor had to act as an umpire and he was supposed to remain neutral and uninvolved directly in colonial politics. This was not always easy, especially as most governors had no experience of colonies with responsible government. The governor's fundamental task was to ensure that the colonial government functioned smoothly. He was expected to report on all local matters to the Colonial Office in London; it was headed by the colonial secretary, who was always a politician. The governor's reports were often routine but frequently he would write "confidential" or "secret" dispatches giving his opinion about local men and affairs, the classification depending on how widely the dispatch would be circulated. The governor would sometimes write privately to Colonial Office officials, as well. His dispatches and other communications would be placed in folders, on which officials, and sometimes the colonial secretary, would write their comments (or "Minutes"), sometimes with a draft reply. The governor also sent and received encoded telegrams, particularly on urgent matters, and made recommendations about the granting of honours, which were highly valued.

NOTES ON THE LEGISLATURE

An important aspect of legislative proceedings was the use of committees. These were sometimes "select committees," struck to work on a particular problem or piece of legislation. "Joint Select Committees" included members of both houses of the legislature, for the same purpose. A "Committee of the Whole House" could also be established by either branch of the legislature; this was more usually done by the Assembly. The Speaker would leave the chair, to be replaced by a chairman of committees, of which there were usually several. Rules of debate were less formal in committee, and its report would be voted on by the house when it returned to official session and the Speaker (or President) was in the chair.

At the beginning of each new parliamentary session, the governor (or his representative) read the Speech from the Throne in the Legislative

Council chamber, and he prorogued the legislature there. For such events, members of the Assembly were summoned to that chamber by "the Gentleman Usher of the Black Rod," the Council's senior officer.

BIBLIOGRAPHY

PRIMARY SOURCES / ARCHIVES AND LIBRARIES IN CANADA

Ottawa

Library and Archives Canada (LAC)

- 9th Earl of Elgin fonds, MG24-A16
- Earl Grey fonds, MG27-IIB2
- Lord Stanley (Earl of Derby) fonds, MG27-IB7
- R.G. Dun and Co. fonds, MG28-III106 (Microfilm of collection at the Harvard Business School)
- Sir John Abbott fonds, MG 26-C
- Sir John Thompson fonds, MG28-D
- Sir Mackenzie Bowell fonds, MG26-E
- Sir Wilfrid Laurier fonds, MG26-G

St. John's, Newfoundland and Labrador

Archives and Special Collections Division (ASC), QEII Library, Memorial University of Newfoundland

- Rev. George John Bond Collection, Coll. 236
- Sir Robert Bond Collection (RBP), Coll. 237
- Sir William Coaker Collection, Coll. 009
- Sir William Whiteway Collection, Coll. 026

Registry of Deeds

Roman Catholic Church Archives (RCA)

- Edward P. Roche fonds, collection 107
- Michael F. Howley fonds, collection 106

The Rooms Provincial Archives (PANL)

- Alfred B. Morine fonds, MG 271
- Government fonds, i.e., Newfoundland government departmental files, which include Executive Council records and correspondence of the

governor with the colonial government, including:
GN 1, Office of the Governor
GN 2, Office of the Colonial Secretary
GN 3, Registry of Applications, Grants, Leases, etc.
GN 8, Office of the Prime Minister
Reid Newfoundland Company fonds (RNCP), MG 17
Sir James S. Winter fonds, MG 836
Sir Walter E. Davidson fonds, MG 136
Sir William V. Whiteway fonds, MG 213

PRIMARY SOURCES / ARCHIVES AND LIBRARIES IN THE UK

Birmingham University Library

Joseph Chamberlain papers

British Library, London

1st Marquis of Ripon papers, Add. Mss. 43556-43558

Hatfield House

3rd Marquis of Salisbury papers (consulted when the collection was located at Christchurch College Library, Oxford)

National Archives, London

Cabinet Office, 37, volume 28
Colonial Office (CO), series 42, 194, 447, 532, 537, 880, 885
Foreign Office (FO), series 371800/91 (Sir Edward Grey fonds); 880/331 (Sir James Bryce fonds)

Queen's College, Taunton

College Registers 1843–87

PRIMARY SOURCES / NEWSPAPERS

Dates indicate the publication years consulted. Unless otherwise indicated, newspapers were published in St. John's, Newfoundland.

Canadian Gazette (London), select years, 1890s
Daily News, 1894–1914 and select years thereafter

Daily Tribune, 1892–93

Evening Chronicle, 1908–12

Evening Herald, 1890–1914, select years thereafter

Evening Mercury, 1882–89

Evening Telegram, 1879–1914 and select years thereafter

Free Press, select years, 1903–14

Harbor Grace Standard (Harbour Grace), select years only.

Newfoundland Colonist, select years to 1892

Newfoundland Trade Review, select years from first publication (1892)

Newfoundlander, select years to 1884

Patriot and Terra Nova Herald, select years to 1890

Public Ledger, select years to 1882

Terra Nova Advocate, select years to 1890

The Times (London), 1894, 1898

Times and General Commercial Gazette, select years to 1895

PRIMARY SOURCES / PRINT PUBLICATIONS

Abstract Census and Return of the Population &c. of Newfoundland, 1857. St. John's: Queen's Printer, 1858.

Abstract Census and Returns of the Population of Newfoundland and Labrador, 1884. St. John's: Queens Printer, 1886.

Decisions of the Supreme Court of Newfoundland: The Reports, 1904–1911. St. John's: King's Printer, 1912.

Decisions of the Supreme Court of Newfoundland: The Reports, 1927–1931. St. John's: King's Printer, 1948.

Further Correspondence Relative to the Newfoundland Fishery Question. London: HMSO, 1908 (Cd. 3765).

Journal of the House of Assembly (JHA). St. John's: various publishers, 1882–1914.

MacGregor, Sir William. *Report on the Trade and Commerce of Newfoundland, for the Four Years Ending with the 30th June, 1906.* St. John's, n.d.

Minutes of Proceedings of the Colonial Conference, 1907. London: HMSO, 1907 (Cd. 3523).

Nominal Census for Trinity Bay, manuscript in PANL, GN 2/39/A.

Proceedings of the House of Assembly and Legislative Council. St. John's: various publishers, 1909–1914.

SECONDARY SOURCES / MULTI-VOLUME WORKS

Dictionary of Canadian Biography (DCB)

All *DCB* volumes are published by the University of Toronto Press and Les Presses de l'Université Laval. Dates of publications consulted are: Vol. 1, 1966; Vol. 8, 1985; Vol. 11, 1982; Vol. 12, 1990; Vol. 13, 1994; Vol. 14, 1998; Vol. 15, 2005; Vol. 16, online (publication pending). Entries are also available on line: www.biographi.ca.

Aldrich, F.A. "Harvey, Moses." Vol. 13:445–56.

Baker, Melvin. "Baird, James." Vol. 14:31–32.

———. "Cashin, Sir Michael Patrick." Vol. 15:193–195.

———. "Coaker, Sir William Ford." Vol. 16: available online.

———. "Crowe, Harry Judson." Vol. 15:245–46.

———. "Harvey, Augustus William." Vol. 13:450–54.

———. "Mackay, Alexander McLellan." Vol. 13:651–53.

———. "McGrath, Sir Patrick Thomas." Vol. 15:643–44.

———. "Monroe, Moses." Vol. 13:451–54.

Baker, Melvin, and Peter Neary. "Bond, Sir Robert." Vol. 15:122–30.

Beck, Boyde. "Howlan, George William." Vol. 13:481–83.

Cell, Gillian T. "Whitbourne, Sir Richard." Vol. 1:668–69.

Crosbie, Barbara A. "Howley, Michael Francis." Vol. 14:512–14.

Cuff, Robert. "Reid, Sir Robert Gillespie." Vol. 13:859–62.

Handcock, W. Gordon. "Codner, Samuel." Vol. 8:164–67.

Hiller, James K. "Boyle, Sir Charles Cavendish." Vol. 14:130.

———. "Carter, Sir Frederic Bowker Terrington." Vol. 12:161–65.

———. "Des Voeux, Sir George William." Vol. 13:269–70.

———. "Kent, Robert John." Vol. 12:482–83.

———. "Morris, Edward Patrick, 1st Baron Morris." Vol. 16: available online.

——— . Murray, Sir Herbert Harley." Vol. 13:749–71.

———. "O'Brien, Sir John Terence Nicholls." Vol. 13:774–76.

———. "Shea, Sir Ambrose." Vol. 13:942–47

———. "Squires, Sir Richard Anderson." Vol. 16: available online.

———. "Thorburn, Sir Robert." Vol. 13:1031–33.

———. "Whiteway, Sir William Vallance." Vol. 13:1089–95.

———. "Winter, Sir James Spearman." Vol. 14:1073–76.

Hodgins, Bruce W. "Todd, Alpheus." Vol. 11:883–85.

Hughes, Richard. "Murray, Alexander." Vol. 11:630–33.

Jones, Frederick. "Hoyles, Sir Hugh William." Vol. 11:431–34.

McCann, W.P. "Pilot, William." Vol. 14:841–42.

Miller, Carman. "Clouston, Sir Edward Seaborne." Vol 14:219–22.

———. "Grey, Albert Henry George, 4th Earl Grey." Vol. 14:439–41.

Regehr, Theodore D. "Shaughnessy, Thomas George, 1st Baron Shaughnessy." Vol. 15:923–27.

Rompkey, Ronald. "Reid, Sir William Duff." Vol. 15:866–67.

Story, G.M. "McNeily, Alexander James Whiteford." Vol. 14:730.

———. "Prowse, Daniel Woodley." Vol. 14:850–854.

———. "Rogerson, James Johnstone." Vol. 13:895–896.

Encyclopedia of Newfoundland and Labrador (ENL)

Volumes 1 and 2. J.R. Smallwood (ed.). St. John's: Newfoundland Book Publishers (1967), 1981, 1984.

Volumes 3–5. C.F. Poole (ed.). St. John's: Harry Cuff Publications, 1991, 1993, 1994.

SECONDARY SOURCES / BIOGRAPHY

Berger, Carl. *The Writing of Canadian History: Aspects of English-Canadian Historical Writing since 1900*. 2nd ed. Toronto: University of Toronto Press, 1986.

Lee, Hermione. *Biography: A Very Short Introduction*. Oxford: Oxford University Press, 2009.

Morgan, Kenneth O. "Writing Political Biography." In *The Troubled Face of Biography*, edited by Eric Homberger and John Charmley, 33–48. New York: St. Martin's Press, 1988.

O'Brien, Patick K. "Political Biography: A Polemical Review of the Genre." *Biography* 21, no. 1 (1998): 50–57.

Pimlott, Ben. "The Future of Political Biography." *The Political Quarterly* 61, no. 2 (1990): 214–223.

Possing, Birgitte. "Biography: Historical." In *International Encyclopedia of the Social and Behavioural Sciences*, 2nd ed., edited by James Wright. Amsterdam: Elsevier, 2015.

Riall, Lucy. "The Shallow End of History? The Substance and Future of Political Biography." *Journal of Interdisciplinary History* 40, no. 3 (2010): 375–397.

Snowman, Daniel. "Historical Biography." *History Today* 64, no. 11 (2014). www.historytoday.com.

Tosh, John. *The Pursuit of History.* Harlow: Longman, 1999.

Whitaker, Reg. "Writing About Politics." In *Writing About Canada. A Handbook for Modern Canadian History*, edited by John Schultz. Scarborough: Prentice Hall Canada, 1990

SECONDARY SOURCES / MAIN TEXT

Alexander, David G. "Development and Dependence in Newfoundland, 1880–1970." *Acadiensis* 4, no. 1 (1974), 3–31.

———. "Literacy and Economic Development in Nineteenth-Century Newfoundland." *Acadiensis* 10, no. 1 (1980), 3–34.

———. "Newfoundland's Traditional Economy and Development to 1934." In *Newfoundland in the Nineteenth and Twentieth Centuries: Essays in Interpretation*, edited by James Hiller and Peter Neary, 17–39. Toronto: University of Toronto Press, 1980.

Armour, James E. "'Castles in the Air': The Life, Times and Influence of the Reverend Moses Harvey (1820–1901)." MA thesis, Memorial University, 2016.

Baker, Melvin. "Absentee Landlordism and Municipal Government in 19th-Century St. John's." *Newfoundland Quarterly* 79, no. 4 (1984): 164–71.

———. "'Challenging the 'Merchants Domain': William Coaker and the Price of Fish, 1908–1919." *Newfoundland and Labrador Studies* 29, no. 2 (2014): 189–226.

———. "'Coaker Week,' May 1912: The clash between Patrick McGrath and William Coaker." *Newfoundland Quarterly* 107, no. 1 (2014), 53–57.

———. "A History of St. John's City Council, 1888 to 1981." 1984. www.ucs.mun.ca/~melbaker/citycouncil.htm.

———. "The St. John's Fire of July 8, 1892: The Politics of Rebuilding, 1892–1895." Unpublished paper, Memorial University, 1982.

———. "William Ford Coaker: The Formative Years, 1871–1908." *Newfoundland and Labrador Studies* 27, no. 2 (2012): 223–66.

Baker, Melvin, Christopher Curran, John Joy, and Robin McGrath, eds. *Ireland's Eye in Newfoundland and Labrador: Thomas Talbot's Letter to a Friend in Ireland (1882).* St. John's: Law Society of Newfoundland and Labrador, 2009.

Baker, Melvin, and Peter Neary. "Sir Robert Bond (1857–1927): A Biographical Sketch." *Newfoundland Studies* 15, no. 1 (1999): 1–54.

Bannister, Jerry. *The Rule of the Admirals: Law, Custom and Naval Government in Newfoundland, 1689–1832*. Toronto: University of Toronto Press, 2003.

———. "'The Sport of Historic Misfortune': Judge Prowse and the Story of Newfoundland." In *Discourse and Discovery: Sir Richard Whitbourne Quartercentennial Symposium, 1615–2015 and Beyond*, edited by Melvin Baker, Christopher Curran, and J. Derek Green, 263–314. St. John's: Law Society of Newfoundland and Labrador, 2017.

Brown, R.C. *Canada's National Policy, 1883–1900: A Study in Canadian-American Relations*. Princeton: Princeton University Press, 1964.

Browne, W.J. *Eighty-Four Years a Newfoundlander: Memoirs of William J. Browne*. Vol. 1. St. John's: privately published, 1981.

Busch, Briton Cooper. "The Newfoundland Sealers' Strike of 1902." *Labour/Le Travail* 14 (Fall 1984): 73–101.

Cadigan, Sean T. *Death on Two Fronts: National Tragedies and the Fate of Democracy in Newfoundland, 1914–1934*. Toronto: Allen Lane, 2013.

———. *Newfoundland and Labrador: A History*. Toronto: University of Toronto Press, 2009.

Callahan, James M. *American Foreign Policy in Canadian Relations*. New York: MacMillan, 1937.

Campbell, Charles S. *Anglo-American Understanding, 1898–1903*. Baltimore: John Hopkins Press, 1957.

Candow, James E. *The Lookout: A History of Signal Hill*. St. John's: Creative Publishers, 2011.

———. *Of Men and Seals: A History of the Newfoundland Seal Hunt*. Ottawa: Canadian Parks Service, 1989.

Cashin, Peter J. *My Life and Times, 1890–1919*. St. John's: Breakwater Books, 1976.

Chadwick, St. John. *Newfoundland: Island into Province*. Cambridge: Cambridge University Press, 1967.

Chu, Kam Hon. "Too Big to Fail? The Newfoundland Bank Crash of 1894." *Kredit und Kapital* 41, no. 2 (2008): 161–195.

Clarke, Jason. "Railway Branch Line Construction in Newfoundland, 1909–1914." Honours BA diss., Memorial University, 1997.

Coaker, W.F. , ed. *The History of the Fishermen's Protective Union of Newfoundland*. St. John's: Union Publishing Co., 1920.

———. *Past, Present and Future.* Port Union: Advocate Publishing, 1932.

———, ed. *Twenty Years of the Fishermen's Protective Union of Newfoundland from 1909–1929.* St. John's: Advocate Publishing, 1930.

Colton, Glenn. "Imagining Nation: Music and Identity in Pre-Confederation Newfoundland." *Newfoundland and Labrador Studies* 22, no. 1 (2007): 27–38.

Dennett, Tyler. *John Hay:From Poetry to Politics.* New York: Dodd, Mead, 1933.

Des Voeux, G.W. *My Colonial Service in British Guiana, St. Lucia, Trinidad, Fiji, Australia, Newfoundland, and Hong Kong, with Interludes.* London: James Murray, 1903.

Devine, P.K. *Ye Olde St. John's.* St. John's: Newfoundland Directories, 1936.

Eddy, John, and Deryck Schreuder, eds. *The Rise of Colonial Nationalism: Australia, New Zealand, Canada, and South Africa First Assert their Nationalities, 1880–1914.* Sydney: Allen and Unwin, 1988.

English, Christopher, ed. *Barrels to Benches: The Foundations of Law on Newfoundland's West Coast.* St. John's: Law Society, 2010.

Fitzpatrick, Ronald J. "Archbishop M.F. Howley, the Roman Catholic Church, and the Fishermen's Protective Union of Newfoundland." History 3120 paper, Memorial University, 1997.

———. "Render Unto Caesar? The Roman Catholic Church and the Denominational Equipoise in the Newfoundland Civil Service." History Honours paper, Memorial University, 1999.

Foran, Edward B. "Battle of the Giants: Bond and Morris." In *The Book of Newfoundland,* vol. 3, edited by J.R. Smallwood, 153–70. St. John's: Newfoundland Book Publishers, 1967.

Forsey, Eugene A. *The Royal Power of Dissolution of Parliament in the British Commonwealth.* Toronto: Oxford University Press, 1943.

Fraser, A.M. "The Hague Arbitration." In *Newfoundland: Economic, Diplomtic, and Strategic Studies,* edited by R. A. MacKay, 400–410. Toronto: Oxford University Press, 1946.

Gluek, Alvin C., Jr. "Programmed Diplomacy: The Settlement of the North Atlantic Fisheries Question, 1907–12." *Acadiensis* 6, no. 1 (1976): 43–70.

Graham, Frank W. *"We love thee Newfoundland": Biography of Sir Cavendish Boyle KCMG, Governor of Newfoundland, 1901–1904.* St. John's: Valhalla Press, 1979.

Hallett, M.E. "The 4th Earl Grey as Governor-General of Canada, 1904–1911." PhD thesis, London University, 1970.

Hansard, House of Commons, online. https://api.parliament.uk/historic-hansard/sittings/1907/may/index.html

Hansard, House of Lords, 3rd series, vol. 350 (February 5 to March 2, 1891).

Harris, Michael. *Rare Ambition: The Crosbies of Newfoundland.* Toronto: Penguin Books, 1993.

Hatton, Joseph, and Moses Harvey. *Newfoundland, the Oldest British Colony: Its History, Its Present Condition, and Its Prospects in the Future.* London: Chapman and Hall, 1883.

Hewitt, Keith W. "Exploring Uncharted Waters: Government's Role in the Development of Newfoundland's Cod, Lobster and Herring Fisheries, 1888–1913." MA thesis, Memorial University, 1992.

Hiller, James, and Peter Neary, eds. *Newfoundland in the Nineteenth and Twentieth Centuries: Essays in Interpretation.* Toronto: University of Toronto Press, 1980.

Hiller, J.K. "The Constitutional Crisis of 1908–09: A sub-plot." Unpublished lecture to the Newfoundland Historical Society, 1974.

———. "A History of Newfoundland, 1874–1901." PhD thesis, University of Cambridge, 1971.

———. "The Politics of Newsprint: The Newfoundland Pulp and Paper Industry, 1915–1939." *Acadiensis* 19, no. 2 (1990): 3–39.

Hiller, James. "Confederation Defeated: The Newfoundland Election of 1869." In *Newfoundland in the Nineteenth and Twentieth Centuries,* edited by James Hiller and Peter Neary, 67–94. Toronto: University of Toronto Press, 1980.

———. "The Origins of the Pulp and Paper Industry in Newfoundland," *Acadiensis* 11, no. 2 (1982): 42–57.

———. "The Political Career of Robert Bond." In *Twentieth-Century Newfoundland,* edited by James Hiller and Peter Neary, 11–45. St. John's: Breakwater, 1994.

———. "The Railway and Local Politics in Newfoundland, 1870–1901." In *Newfoundland in the Nineteenth and Twentieth Centuries,* edited by James Hiller and Peter Neary, 123–147. Toronto: University of Toronto Press, 1980.

———. "Robert Bond and the Pink, White and Green: Newfoundland Nationalism in Perspective." *Acadiensis* 36, no. 2 (2007): 113–33.

Hiller, James, and C.J.B. English, eds. "Newfoundland and the Entente Cordiale, 1904–2004." *An occasional publication of Newfoundland and Labrador Studies* 1. St. John's: Memorial University, 2007.

Hiller, James K. "The 1895 Newfoundland-Canada Confederation Negotiations: A Reconsideration." *Acadiensis* 40, no. 2 (2011): 94–111.

———. "The 1904 Anglo-French Newfoundland Fisheries Convention: Another Look." *Acadiensis* 25, no. 1 (1995): 82–98.

———. "Appointing Magistrates on the French Treaty Shore: The Diplomacy of Caution," 19–58. In *Barrels to Benches: The Foundations of Law on Newfoundland's West Coast*, edited by Christopher English. St. John's: Law Society of Newfoundland and Labrador/Project Daisy, 2010.

———. "Bond, Bait and Bounties: The Newfoundland Government and the Negotiation of the Entente Cordiale," 77–94. In "Newfoundland and the Entente Cordiale, 1904–2004," edited by James Hiller and C.J.B. English, *An occasional publication of Newfoundland and Labrador Studies* 1. St. John's: Memorial University, 2007.

———. "Corruption and Collapse, or Did Squires Do It?," 83–90. In *Amulree's Legacy: Truth, Lies and Consequences*, edited by Garfield Fizzard. St. John's: Newfoundland Historical Society, 2001.

———. "Is Atlantic Canadian History Possible?" *Acadiensis* 30, no. 1 (2000): 16–22.

———. *The Newfoundland Railway, 1881–1949*. St. John's: Newfoundland Historical Society, 1981.

———. "The Trinity Bay Election Trial, 1894: Electioneering and Local Government." *Newfoundland and Labrador Studies* 26, no. 2 (2011): 215–29.

Hong, Robert G. "'An Agency for the Common Weal': The Newfoundland Board of Trade, 1909–1915." MA thesis, Memorial University, 1998.

———. "Newfoundland's 1906 Chinese Head Tax." *Newfoundland and Labrador Heritage Website*. 2006. www.heritage.nf.ca/articles/society/chinese-head-tax.php.

Howley, James Patrick. *Reminiscences of Forty-Two Years of Exploration in and about Newfoundland*. Edited by W.J. Kirwin, Patrick A. O'Flaherty, and Robert Hollett. St. John's: Memorial University English Language Research Centre, 2009. http://research.library.mun.ca/id/eprint/1895

Hunter, Mark C. *To Employ and Uplift Them: The Newfoundland Naval Reserve, 1899–1926*. St. John's: ISER Books, 2009.

Hyam, Ronald. "The British Empire in the Edwardian Era." In *The Twentieth Century*, edited by Judith M. Brown and William R. Louis,

64–87. Vol. 4 of *The Oxford History of the British Empire.* Oxford: Oxford University Press, 1999.

———. "The Colonial Office Mind 1900–1914." In *The First British Commonwealth. Essays in Honour of Nicholas Mansergh*, edited by Norman Hillmer and Philip Wigley. London: Frank Cass, 1980.

———. *Elgin and Churchill at the Colonial Office, 1905–1908: The Watershed of the Empire-Commonwealth.* London: Macmillan, 1968.

Innis, Harold A. *The Cod Fisheries: The History of an International Economy.* Toronto: University of Toronto Press, 1954.

Jessup, Philip C. *Elihu Root.* Hamden, CT: Archon Books, 1964.

Joyce, R.B. "MacGregor, Sir William (1846–1919)." In vol. 5 of *Australian Dictionary of Biography*. Melbourne: Melbourne University Press, 1974.

———. *Sir William MacGregor*. Melbourne: Oxford University Press, 1971.

Keith, A.B. *Responsible Government in the Dominions*. Oxford: Oxford University Press, 1912.

———, ed. *Selected Speeches and Documents on British Colonial Policy, 1763–1917.* Oxford: Oxford University Press, 1961.

Kendle, John E. *The British Empire-Commonwealth, 1897–1931*. Melbourne: Cheshire, 1972.

———. *The Colonial and Imperial Conferences, 1887–1911: A Study in Imperial Organization.* London: Longmans, 1967.

Kennedy, Dale. *Britain and Empire, 1880–1945*. London: Longman, 2002.

Kennedy, John C. *Encounters: An Anthropological History of Southern Labrador.* Montreal and Kingston: McGill-Queen's University Press, 2015.

Keough, Willeen G. "Contested Terrains: Ethnic and Gendered Spaces in the Harbour Grace Affray." *Canadian Historical Review* 90, no. 1 (2009): 29–70.

Kerr, Kenneth J. "A Social Analysis of the Members of the Newfoundland House of Assembly, Executive Council, and Legislative Council for the Period 1855–1914." MA thesis, Memorial University, 1973.

Knowling, William R. "'Ignorant, Dirty and Poor.' The Perception of Tuberculosis in Newfoundland, 1902–1912." MA thesis, Memorial University, 1996.

Korneski, Kurt. *Conflicted Colony: Critical Episodes in Nineteenth-Century Newfoundland and Labrador.* Montreal and Kingston: McGill-Queen's University Press, 2016.

———. "Development and Degradation: The Emergence and Collapse of the Lobster Fishery on Newfoundland's West Coast, 1856–1924." *Acadiensis* 61, no.1 (2012): 21–48.

———. "Development and Diplomacy: The Lobster Controversy on Newfoundland's French Shore, 1890–1904." *International History Review* 36, no. 1 (2014): 45–69.

La Morandière, Charles de. *Histoire de la Pêche Française de la Morue dans l'Amérique Septentrionale.* 3 vols. Paris: Maisonneuve et Larose, 1964.

Lambert, Carolyn. "Far from the Homes of their Fathers: Irish Catholics in St. John's, Newfoundland, 1840–1886." PhD thesis, Memorial University, 2010.

———. "This Sacred Feeling: Patriotism, Nation-Building, and the Catholic Church in Newfoundland, 1850–1914." In *Religion and Greater Ireland. Christianity and Irish Global Networks, 1750–1950*, edited by Colin Barr and Hilary M. Carey. Montreal and Kingston: McGill-Queen's University Press, 2015.

Leith-Ross, F.W., and Marc Brodie. "Goode, Sir William Athelstane Meredith," *Oxford Dictionary of National Biography* . www.oxforddnb.com.

Letto, Douglas. *Newfoundland's Last Prime Minister: Frederick Alderdice and the Death of a Nation*. Portugal Cove-St. Philip's: Boulder Publications, 2014.

Loture, Robert de. *History of the Great Fishery of Newfoundland.* Translated by C.C. Taylor. Washington: US Fish & Wildlife Service No. 213, 1957.

MacKay, R.A., ed. *Newfoundland. Economic, Diplomatic, and Strategic Studies.* Toronto: Oxford University Press, 1946.

Madden, A.F. "Changing Attitudes and Widening Responsibilities, 1895–1914." In vol. 3 of *The Cambridge History of the British Empire*, edited by E.A. Benions et al, 344–53. Cambridge: Cambridge University Press, 1959.

Mannion, Patrick. *A Land of Dreams: Ethnicity, Nationalism, and the Irish in Newfoundland, Nova Scotia, and Maine, 1880–1923.* Montreal and Kingston: McGill-Queens University Press, 2018.

Mansergh, Nicholas. *The Commonwealth Experience.* London: Weidenfeld and Nicolson, 1969.

Martin, Wendy. *Once Upon a Mine: Story of Pre-Confederation Mines on the Island of Newfoundland.* Montreal: Canadian Institute of Mining and Metallurgy, 1983.

Maunder, John E. "The Newfoundland Museum: Origins and Development." 1991. www.therooms.ca/the-newfoundland-museum-origin-and-development.

May, Sir Thomas Erskine. *A Treatise on the Law, Privileges, Proceedings, and Usage of Parliament.* 12th ed. London: Butterworth, 1917.

McCann, Phillip. "The Politics of Denominational Education in Nineteenth-Century Newfoundland" and "Denominational Education in the Twentieth Century in Newfoundland." In *The Vexed Question: Denominational Education in a Secular Age*, edited by William A. McKim. St. John's: Breakwater Books, 1988.

———. *Schooling in a Fishing Society: Education and Economic Conditions in Newfoundland and Labrador, 1836–1986.* 2 vols. St. John's: ISER Books, 1994.

McCarthy, Michael, Frank Galgay, and Jack O'Keefe, *The Voice of Generations: A History of Communications in Newfoundland.* St. John's: Robinson-Blackmore, 1994.

McDonald, Ian D.H. *"To Each His Own": William Coaker and the Fishermen's Protective Union in Newfoundland Politics, 1908–1925.* St. John's: ISER Books, 1987.

Mitchell, Harvey. "Canada's Negotiations with Newfoundland, 1887–1895." *Canadian Historical Review* 40 (1959): 277–93.

———. "The Constitutional Crisis of 1889 in Newfoundland," *Canadian Journal of Economics and Political Science* 24, no. 3 (1958): 323–31.

Morine, Alfred B. *The Railway Contract, 1898, and Afterwards.* St. John's: Robinson, 1933.

Neary, Peter. "Grey, Bryce, and the Settlement of Canadian-American Differences, 1905–1911." *Canadian Historical Review* 49, no. 4 (1968): 357–80.

———. *Newfoundland in the North Atlantic World, 1929–1949.* Montreal and Kingston: McGill-Queen's University Press, 1996.

Noel, S.J.R. "Politics and the Crown: The Case of the 1908 Tie Election in Newfoundland." *Canadian Journal of Economics and Political Science* 33, no. 2 (1967): 285–91.

———. *Politics in Newfoundland.* Toronto: University of Toronto Press, 1971.

O'Brien, Mike. "Producers versus Profiteers: The Politics of Class in Newfoundland During the First World War." *Acadiensis* 40, no. 1 (2011): 45–69.

O'Brien, Patricia R. "The Newfoundland Patriotic Association: The Administration of the War Effort, 1914–1918." MA thesis, Memorial University, 1982.

O'Flaherty, Patrick. Introduction to *Reminiscences* by James P. Howley. Edited by W.J. Kirwin, Patrick A. O'Flaherty, and Robert Hollett. St. John's: Memorial University English Language Research Centre, 2009.

———. *Lost Country. The Rise and Fall of Newfoundland, 1843–1933*. St. John's: Long Beach Press, 2005.

O'Neill, Paul. *The Oldest City: The Story of St. John's, Newfoundland.* Erin, ON: Press Porcepic, 1975.

Ommer, Rosemary, ed. *Merchant Credit and Labour Strategies in Historical Perspective*. Fredericton: Acadiensis Press, 1990.

Oliver, Elizabeth D. "The Rebuilding of the City of St. John's After the Great Fire of 1892: A Study in Urban Morphogenesis." MA thesis, Memorial University, 1983.

Orde, Anne. *The Eclipse of Great Britain: The United States and British Imperial Decline, 1895–1956*. London: St. Martin's Press, 1996.

Overton, James. "Economic Crisis and the End of Democracy: Politics in Newfoundland During the Great Depression," *Labour/Le Travail* 26 (1990): 85–124.

Payne, Brian J. *Fishing a Borderless Sea: Environmental Territorialism in the North Atlantic, 1818–1910*. East Lansing: Michigan State University Press, 2010.

Pope, Peter E. *Fish into Wine: The Newfoundland Plantation in the 17th Century.* Chapel Hill: University of North Carolina Press, 2004.

Prowse, D.W. *A History of Newfoundland from the English, Colonial, and Foreign Records.* London: Macmillan, 1895.

Reeves, W.G. "Alexander's Conundrum Reconsidered: The American Dimension in Newfoundland Resource Development, 1898–1910." *Newfoundland Studies* 5, no. 1 (1989): 2–37.

———. "Aping the 'American Type': The Politics of Development in Newfoundland, 1900–1908." *Newfoundland Studies* 10, no. 1 (1984): 44–72.

———. "The Fortune Bay Dispute: Newfoundland's Place in Imperial Treaty Relations Under the Treaty of Washington, 1871–1885." MA thesis, Memorial University, 1971.

———. "'Our Yankee Cousins': Modernization and the Newfoundland-American Relationship, 1898–1910." PhD thesis, University of Maine, 1987.

Reynolds, David. *Britannia Overruled: British Policy and World Power in the Twentieth Century.* Harlow: Longman, 2000.

Rompkey, Ronald, ed. *Garrison Town to Commercial City: St. John's, Newfoundland, 1800 to 1900.* St. John's: DRC Publishing, 2012.

———. *Grenfell of Labrador: A Biography.* Toronto: University of Toronto Press, 1991.

Rose, George A. *Cod: The Ecological History of the North Atlantic Fisheries.* St. John's: Breakwater Books, 2007.

Rowe, F.W. *The Development of Education in Newfoundland.* Toronto: Ryerson Press, 1964.

Rowe, Ted. *Robert Bond: The Greatest Newfoundlander.* St. John's: Creative Publishers, 2017.

Saywell, J.T., ed. *The Canadian Journal of Lady Aberdeen.* Toronto: Champlain Society, 1960.

Senior, Eleanor. "The Origin and Political Activities of the Orange Order in Newfoundland, 1863–1890." MA thesis, Memorial University, 1960.

Sexty, Suzanne. "The Brehms: Newfoundland's First Family of Margarine." *Newfoundland Quarterly* 101, no. 2 (2008): 30–33, 45–49.

Smallwood, Joseph R. *I Chose Canada: The Memoirs of the Honourable Joseph R. "Joey" Smallwood.* Toronto: Macmillan of Canada, 1973.

Smrz, Jiri. "Cabot 400: The 1897 St. John's Celebrations." *Newfoundland Studies* 12, no. 1 (1996): 16–31.

Stanley, G.F.G. "Further Documents Relating to the Union of Newfoundland and Canada, 1886–1895." *Canadian Historical Review* 29, no. 4 (1948): 370–86.

Stevens, Paul, and John T. Saywell, eds. *Lord Minto's Canadian Papers* Vol. 2. Toronto: The Champlain Society, 1983.

Sykes, Philip. *Albert E. Reed and the Creation of a Paper Business, 1860–1960.* London: Reed International, 1980.

Tansill, C.C. *Canadian-American Relations, 1875–1911.* Gloucester, MA: Peter Smith, 1964.

———. *The Foreign Policy of Thomas F. Bayard.* New York: Fordham University Press, 1940.

Tarrant, D.R. *Marconi's Miracle: The Wireless Bridging of the Atlantic.* St. John's: Flanker Press, 2001.

"The Transfer of the *Evening Herald.*" *Newfoundland Quarterly* 12, no. 4 (1913): 20.

Thistle, James. "The Bank Crash of 1894." History 6201 paper, Memorial University, n.d.

Thompson, Frederic F. *The French Shore Problem in Newfoundland: An Imperial Study*. Toronto: University of Toronto Press, 1961.

Todd, Alphaeus. *Parliamentary Government in the British Colonies*. London: Longmans, Green, 1880.

Waite, P.B. *The Man from Halifax: Sir John Thompson, Prime Minister*. Toronto: University of Toronto Press, 1985.

Whiteway, William V. *Duty's Call: Sir W.V. Whiteway States His Position*. St. John's, 1904.

Wilkshire, Michael, ed. and trans. *A Gentleman in the Outports: Gobineau and Newfoundland*. Ottawa: Carleton University Press, 1993.

Williams, Ralph C. *How I Became a Governor*. London: Murray, 1913.

Willson, Beckles. *The Truth About Newfoundland, The Tenth Island: Being an Account of Our Senior Colony, Its People, Its Politics, Its Problems, and Its Peculiarities*. London: Grant Richards, 1901.

Wishart, I.S. "The General Protestant Academy." *Newfoundland Quarterly* 87, no. 4 (1994): 27–32.

SECONDARY SOURCES / WEBSITES

Dictionary of Canadian Biography: www.biographi.ca

Dr. Melvin Baker's website: www.ucs.mun.ca/~melbaker

Newfoundland and Labrador Heritage: www.heritage.nl.ca

INDEX

This index does not include references to the endnotes or the Bibliography.